LET THE PEOPLE SING:
HYMN TUNES IN PERSPECTIVE

LET THE PEOPLE SING:
HYMN TUNES IN PERSPECTIVE

PAUL WESTERMEYER

GIA Publications, Inc.
Chicago

To

Robert Batastini
who conceived this project and trusted me with it,

Kristin Rongstad
whose assistance made it possible,

those
who "found out musical tunes,"

those
who learned about them, and

those
who sang the faith with them but
"have no memorial as if they had never been"

G-6476
Copyright © 2005, GIA Publications, Inc.
7404 S. Mason Ave., Chicago, IL 60638

www.giamusic.com

ISBN: 1-57999-353-2

Book layout: Philip Roberts
Cover design: Martha Chlipala

TABLE OF CONTENTS

Richard Storrs Willis
Adapted from Robert Schumann
Louis Henry Redner
John Zundel
William Fiske Sherwin
James R. Murray
Arthur Henry Messiter
William H. Walter
George William Warren

Argentine
Brazilian
Chinese
Dutch
English
Finnish
French
Ghanaian
Icelandic
Irish
Japanese
Native American
Polish
Scottish
Sicilian
Silesian
South African
Swedish
Taiwanese

1. The First Half of the Twentieth Century
Ralph Vaughan Williams
Charles V. Stanford
Sydney Nicholson
John Ireland
Cyril Taylor
Martin and Geoffrey Shaw
Walter Greatorex

2. The Second Half of the Twentieth Century
Jan Bender
Jacques Berthier and Taizé

Lee Hastings Bristol
V. Earle Copes
Peter Cutts
Richard Dirksen
Hugo Distler
Harold Friedell
Marty Haugen
Hal Hopson
David Johnson
Jane Marshall
Richard Proulx
Erik Routley
Carl Schalk
Natalie Sleeth
Alfred M. Smith
Heinz Werner Zimmermann

ABBREVIATIONS

Bap ....*The Baptist Hymnal*

Chal ....*Chalice Hymnal*

Cong Song..*Congregational Song*

CW ....*Christian Worship: A Lutheran Hymnal*

CWH..*Christian Worship: Handbook* (Aufdemberge)

CUMH..............................*Companion to the United Methodist Hymnal* (Young)

Cov ....*The Covenant Hymnal: A Worshipbook*

EH ....*The English Hymnal with Tunes*

HWB ....*Hymnal: A Worship Book Prepared by Churches in the Believers Church Tradition*

HCHWB ....*Hymnal Companion* [to *Hymnal: A Worship Book*] (Fyock)

HCLBW..............*Hymnal Companion to the Lutheran Book of Worship* (Stulken)

H82 ....*The Hymnal 1982 according to the Use of The Episcopal Church*

H82C ....*The Hymnal 1982 Companion* (Glover)

HTI..*The Hymn Tune Index* (Temperley)

KDK ....*Das katholische deutsche Kirchenlied* (Bäumker)

LBW ....*Lutheran Book of Worship*

MCH ....*The Music of Christian Hymns* (Routley)

MDEK ....*Die Melodien der deutschen evangelischen Kirchenlieder* (Zahn)

Mor ....*Moravian Book of Worship*

NC..*The New Century Hymnal*

NGDMM ....*New Grove Dictionary of Music and Musicians*

Pres ....*The Presbyterian Hymnal*

PsH ....*Psalter Hymnal*

PsHH ....*Psalter Hymnal Handbook* (Brink/Polman)

R ....*Renewing Worship Songbook*

Meth ....*The United Methodist Hymnal: Book of United Methodist Worship*

VU..*Voices United: The Hymn and Worship Book of The United Church of Canada*

Wor3 ....*Worship Third Edition: A Hymnal and Service Book for Roman Catholics*

PREFACE

An author depends upon many people. My dependence for this book is overwhelming.

1) When I completed a first draft, I realized how many people and places I had been recalling and relying on as I wrote. I could not have written this without what they provided. Though I wrote the dedication first, only gradually did I come to realize its meaning and the towering significance of the people who sang the faith with "no memorial as if they had never been."[1] Before beginning the body of the text, I was thinking of that quotation as connected primarily to past generations. Afterwards I realized I had not only been trying to "hear" unknown assemblies of believers who sang for millennia before I was born, but also I was hearing in my memory the actual singing of the congregations I have served, been a part of, and visited. They have joined the singing cloud of witnesses who have no memorial, and they taught me what this topic is about.

It is impossible to detail all these communities of faith. They include the ones I served for periods of years in the Reformed and Evangelical portions of the United Church of Christ and in the Episcopal and Lutheran traditions; Congregational, Methodist, Presbyterian, and Roman Catholic ones where I substituted or served for brief stints; and ones from all the traditions and more that are represented in the hymnals surveyed here (see the first chapter for these) that I have visited on my own or where my students were serving in Canada, England, and Europe.

It is common to focus on the church's problems, both petty and serious. I could easily detail many of them. However, most of the congregations in my experience have transcended their squabbles and are more honestly described as healthy communities of song around Word, font, and table; they have taken their musical vocation seriously. (Their health is not unrelated to their singing, a largely unexplored topic for another time.) The congregations I have known have been seas of sanity, grace, prayer, proclamation, moral deliberation, and song in a world too often characterized by lust for power and greed.

They taught me about this topic. They taught me that congregations sing much more than they are usually given credit for. They taught me to seek out the essence and the best of the church's heritage for them and to lead it well on their behalf. Their choirs taught me to trust their instincts and judgment. They and their choirs taught me the hymnic lore and the faith. That does not mean they knew everything or were always right. The ones I served clearly expected me to bring to them my judgments and what my musical vocation in the church gave me access to from the wider church on their behalf—which they were willing to discuss and then use or reject as seemed wise. But they understood the faith, knew a lot more, were interested in learning a lot more, and could sing a lot more than I had been culturally primed to expect. They challenged me and kept my feet to the fire.

Another thing they taught me is the unusually cross-generational character of hymn singing. There are few cross-generational groups and activities in our society. The church, with its worship and hymn singing, stands out as a healthy and notable exception when it refuses to be controlled by the culture's generational ghettos. Children are a part of this uncommon configuration. I am very grateful to the children for what they have taught me about learning and singing hymns with the rest of the church in its worship. That has not only been instructive. It has been delightful beyond measure. Old people who are losing their hearing, sight, and other capacities are another part of this uncommon configuration. They taught me about the importance of memory in singing hymns with the rest of the church at worship. The people in between the youngest and the oldest also belong to this uncommon configuration. They have taught me about hymn singing "in the midst of earthly life," with all the joys and sorrows of human contingency in the vast expanse and embrace of God's grace.

Congregations have taught me about their resilience and capacity to sing quite independently of pastoral leadership. They are able to withstand some awful assaults, intentional and unintentional, from those who are called to lead them. However, there are also pastors who do superb things in their churches and communities, who love the people and are faithful stewards of Word and sacraments, and who have the ego strength to get out of the way in support of singing congregations. I have been privileged to know and work with some of these pastors in their local churches. Knowingly and unknowingly, they have taught me many things about the topic of this book. They include my uncle, John Westermeyer, as well as John Tietjen, Jack Naegele, Robert Hunsicker, William Fleener, George Stapleton, Paul Landahl, and Robert Hausman. Were I to add campus pastors, David McCurdy, John Helt, Robert Brusic, and Gary F. Anderson would be included.

2) Without those "who found out musical tunes," this book could not exist. The church owes them a deep debt of gratitude. This book expresses my tribute better than anything I could say here.

3) I owe a less obvious, though equally important, debt of gratitude to those who learned about the tunes, the tune writers, and their times and places. I could never have written this without the research many scholars and writers have provided. Though it fights all my instincts, I had to stop myself from going down every detailed path of primary research, learning instead to trust what others could tell me about it. Otherwise, I would still be writing the first chapters.

I am deeply grateful to all these writers and researchers. Many of them are cited in the footnotes. I hope I have treated them fairly and accurately, without being overly profuse, but with enough detail for those who wish to chase down sources or pursue related paths. I apologize for unconscious omissions or mistakes. Those who are not cited in the footnotes include my teachers, colleagues, and students from whom I have learned both detail and context, but the sources of which I can no longer sort out. All of these people are part of the cloud of witnesses, usually with a bit more—though still mostly unknown—memorial than the singing congregations.

My music teachers and church music colleagues need a particular word of gratitude. There are too many of them to name, though my college teacher and colleague T. Howard Krueger deserves to be singled out for continually encouraging me to keep after topics like this one. In addition, my colleagues at St. Olaf College—Anton Armstrong, John Ferguson, and Robert Scholz—have provided unusually strong insight and support.

Musicians are often criticized for a lack of interest in congregational singing. Sometimes the criticism is accurate, and sometimes musicians have done awful things, intentional and unintentional, to congregations. Bad choices of music, bad tempos, and the stifling of the congregation's breath are among the musical sins of organists and other musicians. It is also true, however, that the musical discernment of my teachers, colleagues, and students has been immensely helpful in understanding hymn singing. A goodly number of them have been deeply concerned about it and have carried it out quite well. They have taught me where hymn tunes come from and how best to help congregations sing them. Organists I have worked with most recently—David Cherwien, John Ferguson, and Mark Sedio—are uniquely gifted exemplars.

I am grateful to numerous groups and individuals related specifically to this book. They include Luther Seminary for the sabbatical time to do this work and for the foresight to support it; Thrivent Financial for Lutherans for a Sabbatical Fellowship; Bruce Eldevik, Sally Sawyer, Annie Janzen, and the rest of the Luther Seminary Library staff who, in librarians' typically "salt of the earth" way, chased down all my requests; Keith Havergo, Don Sandborg, Jana Ratkovich, David Ottoson, and the rest of the computer staff at Luther Seminary for their support; Master of Sacred Music Teaching Assistant Zebulon Highben, who carefully proofed each chapter as I wrote and made perceptive corrections and suggestions; Sara Birkeland, Emily Brink, Arland Hultgren, Doris Moye, Howard Moye, Carl Schalk, and Mark Sedio for responses to specific points as I was writing; and David Music for giving me a copy of the *Handbook to The Baptist Hymnal*, which appears to be impossible to purchase. Sara Birkeland, one of the Master of Sacred Music graduates, set my mind at rest in the fine teaching and conducting she did for me while I was on sabbatical writing this book.

Many readers graciously read parts or the whole of the first draft and supplied deeply valuable criticisms and corrections. It is impossible to indicate how important they have been. What you have in front of you is substantially altered from what I provided them, partially because I immediately began making changes myself, but just as often because of their comments. They should not be held responsible for what I have said—that is my responsibility; but they provided a scholarly and ecumenical community that helped me think out this topic in ways I could never have done on my own. Some of them proofed in detail for punctuation, word choice, and syntax; they also went after substance and organization, providing perspective that helped me beyond my narrower vision. They agreed and disagreed with me and with one another, proposed additions and subtractions, pushed here and pulled there—all with delightfully honest candor, and with a careful yet passionate zest that is rare and highly to be prized. The stack of comments they sent, sometimes on many single-spaced pages, is over six inches high. That does not include their telephone calls. I cannot thank them enough. They include Emily Brink, Robert Brusic, Carl Daw, John Ferguson, Robert Hausman, David Music, Mary Oyer, Paul Richardson, Carl Schalk, Robert Scholz, Morgan Simmons, Marilyn Stulken, Scott Weidler, Tim Westermeyer, and Carlton Young. After I worked in the comments of these readers, I sent the revised manuscript to several other seasoned readers who gave me another set of helpful comments. I cannot thank them enough either. They include Harry Eskew, Hugh McElrath, and Austin Lovelace.

Two classes I taught as the Routley Lecturer at the 2004 Montreat Conferences on Worship and Music, one from June 20–26 and the other from June 27–July 3, served as valuable sounding boards for the Appendix and worked through parts of it with a Presbyterian filter. Then, in January 2005, I used the entire book for an interim class at St. Olaf College. That class found typographical mistakes and made further valuable suggestions.

These classes instructed me as well. They and the individual readers represent the deliberative community of the baptized, using hymn tunes as the grist for a constructive dialogue about the faith of the church and its worship in relation to the world, with clarity of purpose and common central concerns, but with multivalent points of view, which include strong agreements and disagreements. A book like this is a small part of a wonderfully nuanced and ongoing conversation in the life of the church.

I owe a large debt to my family and its associations—my home church where my earliest memories are of hymn singing; my father, mother, and extended family who sang hymns there; my father who, though an electrical engineer by profession, was an autodidact in hymnody and taught a Sunday school class about it; my wife's home church and family who sang hymns not only in their church's worship services, but also at our wedding; and my children and their children from whom I have learned as they learned to sing hymns with congregations. I need to pay particular thanks to my wife, Sally, not only for her vigorous hymn singing, but for her support once again in this project—as in many other ones before and after my doctoral dissertation, which was dedicated to her—even when it became a single-minded and all-consuming passion.

4) Finally, there are two people who have made this book possible. Without them it would never have been written. Kristin Rongstad, my Master of Sacred Music administrative assistant at Luther Seminary, helped me think out the project, charted the tunes and allied details in fourteen hymnals; got the necessary help to put them into a database; took care of the Master of Sacred Music program while I was on sabbatical; coordinated readers; chased down my continual requests, made copies of things I needed, and typed in and made a file of all the musical examples; got the first drafts printed for readers, mailed them out, and kept in touch with GIA as needed; and from beginning to end gave me thoughtful criticisms as a continual sounding board. She did all this delightfully, accurately, quickly, and with a contagious joy. I was freed to study and write, knowing I could contact her for wise counsel and that she was taking care of whatever needed care whenever and wherever it was needed.

5) I did not choose to write this book. Robert Batastini asked me to do it. I was somewhat ambivalent when he asked. Since I had learned to trust his judgment and vision, however, I agreed. The topic gradually seized my imagination and then became a daily obsession as I increasingly saw its value, need, and importance well beyond its usual narrow definitions. I am grateful not only for the invitation, but even more grateful for the confidence he placed in me. He made the assignment and its dimensions clear, then trusted me to figure them out. He was always present with advice whenever I needed it, but he never intruded with hassling or silly legalisms. He has been a joy to work with. Without his clear invitation and gentle but unwavering support, I would never have attempted a project like this. I am very glad, thanks to him, that I made the attempt.

Paul Westermeyer
Advent 2004

---

1   This quotation and the one before it in the dedication come from Ecclesiasticus, or the Wisdom of Jesus Son of Sirach, the first from 44:5 and the second from 44:9. They are skillfully set to music by Ralph Vaughan Williams, though the text by contemporary norms is unfortunately sexist as it stands ("Let us now praise famous men"), which has recently precluded its use.

I. General Considerations

1. The Topic

As I indicated in the Preface, I wrote this book on a sabbatical. Many schools like Luther Seminary wisely provide sabbatical time for their professors to read, study, and write; so people know what sabbaticals are. If they asked what I was doing, and I told them I was on sabbatical writing a book, they understood. The next question, however, was the tough one. "What are you writing about?" "Hymn tunes," I answered. Silence, a blank stare, or a puzzled expression usually greeted that answer. Then I would explain that I was indeed writing a *New York Times'* best seller about, yes, hymn tunes, and that they had heard rightly.

The topic of this book is not likely to be on the *New York Times'* best seller list. It may not even engage the attention of people in the church who sing hymns regularly. They are likely, quite legitimately, to want to sing hymns without thinking about or studying the melodies they are using. I have to admit, even though I had long realized how important hymn tunes are, that I was not overly enthusiastic about this project when Robert Batastini first asked me to undertake it, largely because it is so complicated. Once I set to work, however, a renewed sense of its importance began to dawn on me; and the complications took a backseat to the drive to try to figure out how to make the topic comprehensible.

As I will say in the concluding Perspective, hymn tunes are little things that are not regarded as having very much value. They symbolize and relate deeply, however, to big things, well beyond the obvious musical ones, like the priesthood of all believers, participatory congregations, the vocation of

Christians, how people in the church are treated by their leaders, and how texts and even the Christian faith as a whole are interpreted. They are part of a rich and interesting history that tells us about these and other matters. I invite you to the journey. It is a journey worth taking by those who have a "professional" interest, like church musicians, pastors, and teachers, but also by those who have a more "amateur" interest, like members of congregations who sing hymns and whose singing may be enhanced by it. Finally, it is for anybody who may want to know about hymn tunes and whose understanding will be increased by it.

We need to begin with some resources and relatively weighty considerations. If that is not necessary for your purposes, and you want to get to the tunes themselves right away, you can easily skip or skim the rest of this chapter and turn directly to Chapter II (or any of the other chapters that may relate to your interests). If you want sources, the larger context, and background, read on from here; or skim less quickly. Whatever you do, even if you skip or skim the rest of this chapter, it would be good to read the next paragraph to know how two critical words will be used.

2. "Hymns" and "Tunes"

As used in this study, the word "hymn" means a text (and generically includes metrical psalms). The word "tune" or "melody" means music. "Hymn" is often understood in common parlance to denote both text and music, because unconsciously the two so easily fuse together as one. That is not a bad thing and points to a profound perception of unity, not unlike Augustine's definition.[1] In a study like this one, however, the two have to be distinguished. Our concern here is essentially about the tunes that carry the hymns, not the hymns themselves—that is, not the texts.

3. This Book

This book began with a request from Robert Batastini to update Erik Routley's *The Music of Christian Hymns*[2] as part of a set of Routley's books that GIA Publications is editing. After numerous conversations with a number of people, that idea was abandoned. We decided that this is one of Routley's texts that should be appreciated for what it is and allowed to remain as it is. It was Routley's third go at the topic, the second[3] of which he called a "40 percent" abridgment of the first,[4] the first being his doctoral dissertation at Oxford.[5] Routley referred to the dissertation as "so long that . . . it must have defeated" his examiners,[6] but *The Music of Christian Hymns* is no small matter either. Its 184 double-columned pages of small print, 605 examples, bibliography, and indices combine to make for an encyclopedic volume reflecting Routley's mental capacity to soak up a huge mass of detail and shape it into a narrative.

To try to edit and update his book would require knowing as much as Routley knew about hymn tunes and being able to lay it out coherently, tampering with Routley's inimitable style, and arguing with him as he always seems to invite. Whatever edited book might be produced would be either the current text with a limp commentary or a massive and turgid reworking. Neither would elucidate matters very much. Better to leave Routley's work as it is, with gratitude.

The idea of a new book about hymn tunes, however, was not thereby negated. We need such a book, but not an encyclopedia that explores the detailed metamorphosis of every hymn tune. In addition to Routley's work, we have plenty of encyclopedic and dictionary resources for hymn tunes and related matters: Nicholas Temperley's massive four-volume index of over 108,000 English-language tunes (over 19,000 different ones) from 1535 to 1820;[7] Diehl's[8] and Perry's[9] indices; D. DeWitt Wasson's index of 33,000 tunes;[10] Johannes Zahn's classic index of over 8,800 German evangelical melodies;[11] an unpublished index by Peter Cutts organized by meter, somewhat like Zahn's; Bäumker's[12] and Higginson's[13] work for Roman Catholic hymnody; *The New Oxford Book of Carols* for carols;[14] the worship music dictionary Edward Foley recently edited, with entries related to hymnody;[15] numerous hymnal companions with both topical articles and briefer detailed entries on individual hymn tunes and their composers;[16] Robert McCutchan's book which, though dated, still helpfully explains hymn tune names;[17] articles on all manner of topics related to hymn tunes in journals, especially in *The Hymn*, the journal of The Hymn Society in the United States and Canada;[18] CD-ROM resources like *The Electronic Encyclopedia of Hymnology*[19] or the one about the Lutheran musical heritage;[20] and online resources that can be accessed by pushing a few keys.[21] (This list does not include all the sources that are fundamentally concerned with texts that inevitably relate in various ways to tunes as well, like Julian's still valuable encyclopedic volumes,[22] the best current briefer "survey"[23] and "introduction,"[24] and J. R. Watson's splendid study of the English hymn.[25])

What we need is an overview of the tunes that bear the church's hymns, with comments about hymn singing as we go. This book attempts to supply that need. The intent is to provide a snapshot of the forest rather than portraits of individual trees.[26] Individual trees do have to come into view, however, or a study like this is meaningless; so examples of tunes from different periods and of various types with issues they raise need to be given. But there is no attempt to cite every tune or the complete development and variations of individual tunes. This means major genres, points of creativity, earliest sources, and pitfalls are the concern, but not every twist and turn—nor the author's or anybody else's favorite tunes or specific versions of those tunes, which may or may not be mentioned. We can all piece those into the narrative on our own.

Though the topic does not make this as possible as I would like, I have tried to avoid overly complicated notes, source materials, and minute details to keep the book concise and accessible. The topic is huge, however. It demands notes that give important subsidiary comments and at least secondary source materials for those who want them. (Those who do not can avoid them.) Without their presence readers can easily be lost in a forest, or, to change the metaphor, in a city with no map of the streets. The problem is that the details can entice us into tiny side streets. Those side streets are quite interesting and worthy of investigation, but they can quickly obscure the highways. I have tried to discipline myself to give only enough details to make understanding possible. They are accessible elsewhere or can be investigated in other kinds of studies. One of our current problems is that the mass of detail itself makes us lose our way. Some studies ought to attempt perspective. That is what is sought here.

This book gratefully takes into account what Routley did, depends on it, cites it, and responds to it, but it is a different book altogether. Since it was stimulated by his work, however, it is like his in four respects. First, it is about what the congregation sings. Choirs may sing what is described here in simple or complex settings; they may well assume a hymnic congregational undergirding as many composers like J. S. Bach did, and what they sing is to be joyfully celebrated for what it is and contributes—but choral music is not the topic here. The central concern of this study is congregational, what non-trained members of the Christian church can sing in their worshiping assemblies without rehearsal.

Second, as just implied, this study is primarily about what is sung in the church's public worshiping assemblies. There is a legitimate place for the private singing of individuals in small groups, or for large groups who assemble to hear hymns used non-congregationally. The concern here is for neither of those occasions. It is instead for what the church sings when it gathers in public to worship God, where private interests and individual agendas are sacrificed for the common good.

Third, it is fundamentally about hymn tunes defined as relatively short musical structures that fit regular "stanzaic" poetic textual structures called hymns, which stanza by stanza repeat the musical structures.[27] It is not about all the non-metrical music a congregation sings—as in psalm tones, canticles, antiphons, refrains, prayer responses, the Ordinary of the Mass, the *Sursum corda*, and similar dialogues between presider and people.

Fourth, its major concern is hymn tunes in the English-speaking Anglo-European heritage as experienced primarily in the United Sates of America. We are legitimately concerned in our time about what we have come to call global hymnody. Michael Hawn has pulled together some of the components of this rich and vast resource.[28] What we who are English-speaking Anglo-European Americans have not yet come to see, partly because of our xenophobia and partly because we simply need more time to gain perspective, is that our resources are one part of this large global repertoire.[29] Our temptation is either to investigate everything else to the exclusion of our heritage (often on the premise that our own traditions are bad), or to investigate our heritage to the exclusion of everything else (often on the premise that everybody else's traditions are bad). Either of those choices is wrong and leads to a dead end. We need to see the whole and how we are part of it. We need to examine, therefore, both what we sing and have sung as well as what others sing and have sung. We need to sing the song of others, as Michael Hawn has explained, but that does not mean neglecting our song, as he has also explained.[30]

However we proceed, we can only work at small parts of the whole at any one time, and we have to realize that no community can escape its skin. We have to do the work in our own heritage if we are to sing at all; but, if we do it to the exclusion of the rest of the world, we isolate ourselves at our peril. Creativity and new musical life come from cross-fertilization and from seeing the cross-fertilization that is already present in our own stream, which is itself many streams. The only way to get at that is to study it. What we do here is unapologetically about one piece (with many parts) of the whole, the English-speaking, American, Anglo-European piece, always viewed as part of the larger picture even when the larger picture is not explicitly mentioned.

4. TUNES FROM FOURTEEN HYMNALS

As I indicated, this is a huge topic. In order to bring it under some control, I began by trying to get a sense of what hymn tunes are in use in English-speaking Anglo-European churches in the United States and to some extent in Canada, and through them to impose some limits. To that end, Kristin Rongstad, my assistant in the Master of Sacred Music program at Luther Seminary, graciously and with amazingly speedy accuracy, generated a list of the hymn tunes and their allied details in fourteen hymnals. She then worked with Keith Havergo, database administrator at Luther Seminary, to make a database of this material. From it I started counting and discovered that the 8,386 entries from these 14 hymnals comprise 2,787 different hymn tunes. About 400 of those tunes are repeated 5 to 9 times in the 14 hymnals, about 200 are repeated ten to fourteen times, about 100 are repeated 15 to 19 times, and just over 50 are repeated 20 times or more. The information gleaned from the database may not be especially scientific, or precisely accurate; but it does give a sense of the central pool from which this portion of the church has been drawing its tunes.

The hymnals Kristin Rongstad and I chose to include[31] are from the last round of hymnal production that began with the *Lutheran Book of Worship* in 1978 and ran to close to the end of the twentieth century. We made no particular attempt to be up to date with supplements, the many published and unpublished new tunes that continue to appear singly or in clusters, or the new round of hymnal editing that is now under way. Since hymn tunes transcend generations, the older ones that have survived repeated use are the ones we need to study. Relatively few tunes last from any given period, so attempts to be up to date with what is new are doomed to be out of date very quickly. Several generations from now, it will be time to study the tunes that may have survived from our period.

5. Ecclesiological Presuppositions

The ecclesiological presupposition at work here is that the nature of the church presumes continuity from age to age. This presupposition may well be labeled conservative, but it is really radically liberating. It frees us from the idolatry of fads, locates new life in God rather than in human ingenuity no matter how momentarily intriguing, and highlights the finest of human crafting for the glory of God over very long periods so that we are not stuck in the mistakes and constraints of any one time and place including ours.[32] It presumes that we and our generation, like all its past generations, did not invent the church, but that we are baptized into its stream, which precedes and follows us. It presumes the Holy Spirit has been and will, as promised, continue to be active in that stream.

A related presupposition in the choice of hymnals is that this is a book for and about the church. Those outside the church are warmly welcomed to the conversation, but it is not a book about hymn tunes in the culture more generally. That is a legitimate book, but it is not this one. Since this one is about the church, it faces the deadly dilemma of the church's divisions. These fractures mean that the bones and ligaments of the church's life together have been broken and torn, contrary to Christ's intention.[33] With the rest of its life, the church has ripped apart its common song and has no common discipline to help put it together. Rather than stand in relationship, figure things out with each other, and sing together, the church has split itself into pieces and denied itself the wisdom of its differences—musical and otherwise.

If a common discipline is lacking, we are left with the individual disciplines of our divisions. Each hymnal chosen, therefore, is from pieces of the broken body of the baptized, and each has its own checks and balances. Books assembled by individuals or independent groups, though valuable, were not chosen because they are not disciplined by the checks and balances of some portion of the body of the baptized.

I am aware that not all the groups represented in these fourteen hymnals agree with my presuppositions. The Baptists and Anabaptists may be least likely to agree, and the Reformed may be a bit ambivalent; yet those in Baptist, Anabaptist, and Reformed traditions account for a large portion of the hymnals we surveyed. That is the lay of the land, and my ecclesiological presuppositions mean I welcome their disagreement.

Representation itself is a problem. Roman Catholics, Episcopalians, and Methodists—who include the Evangelical United Brethren in the United Methodist merger, are each represented by only one hymnal. There is only one hymnal specifically from Canada. One each may not be enough for these groups, especially in the case of Roman Catholics, since they have no single official hymnal; but to add more hymnals makes it impossible to know where to stop. For Lutherans we have not included *Lutheran Worship* of the Missouri Synod, since it is so close to the *Lutheran Book of Worship*, which the Missouri Synod helped to assemble. To provide some balance in this instance, however, we did include the recent *Christian Worship* of the Wisconsin Evangelical Lutheran Synod.

The sampling raises concerns, not only because some hymnals were or were not included, but because congregations vary in how they use their hymnals. Some churches use them almost exclusively, some little or not at all. I do not intend to be bound by the sampling, in any case. My responsibility to make judgments precludes that, as does the necessity to glean historical perspective. What the sampling does provide is a template, a set of proportions, and a center of gravity to which, given my presuppositions, I must attend and from which I shall primarily draw examples—with all the inconsistencies of each hymnal's forms for citations and meters left to stand as they are given.[34] By checking which tunes are most used, I can at least get some sense of what is in use and cite it.[35] That is obviously not enough of a criterion. Classic tunes that have long usage over the church's history, whether we all use them or not at the moment, need to be weighted more heavily than those with less tenacity across generations. But I am not free to choose favorites or to make my own proportions.

As will be apparent, to provide another check on my biases and those of our generation, I plan to proceed in a fundamentally historical fashion, though this is not strictly speaking a history. That means some tunes that may receive little or no usage among us will be cited to clarify or amplify as necessary. Since the intent here is to be brief (which did not turn out to be as possible as I had hoped) not everything that could be covered is covered.

6. A Common Song

A profoundly constructive and positive note emerges from the counting Kristin Rongstad made possible for us. It trumps our divisiveness and indicates that we have not been able to pull our song apart as much as a superficial glance suggests. The tunes we use cross our confessional divisions, and their number is small enough to form a common core. In spite of our fractures, we still tend to sing a common song. From the fourteen hymnals we surveyed,[36] thirty-two tunes are common to nine (about two-thirds) of the hymnals, twenty-seven common to ten of them, thirty-seven common to eleven, twenty-two common to twelve, twenty-eight common to thirteen, and forty-four common to all fourteen hymnals.[37] That makes a total of 190 tunes. If you analyze those 190, you discover that they come from the twelfth century or earlier through the twentieth century and from a wide variety of styles. If you analyze the texts associated with them, you discover many more texts than tunes—over 800 of them. That number quickly diminishes if you ask which texts are used with the same tunes (of the 190) in the various hymnals: seventeen are common to nine hymnals, twenty-five to ten, twenty-three to eleven, sixteen to twelve, thirteen to thirteen, and twenty-nine to all fourteen. That totals 123 texts to which you can add 24 more if the same texts with different tunes (still from the 190) are included. Those 147 texts are from the fourth to the twentieth centuries and from across the whole gamut of the church's liturgical year, occasions, and themes.

This is a remarkable circumstance. During the period when these hymnals were produced, a "culturally friendly" civil religious and commercial crusade that took the sting and mercy out of the faith dismantled the church's historic patterns of worship; omitted, modified, or truncated biblical readings and ecumenical creeds; and abandoned hymns. In spite of this, a common catholic heritage of hymnody nevertheless remains in the church's hymnals. Visits to congregations reveal that, wherever the people are singing participants rather than spectators at worship, that hymnic heritage is in fact being used. It may be weak or vigorous or somewhere on a spectrum between those two extremes, but it is present.

Though this circumstance is remarkable, it should not surprise us. It points to the church that by its nature loves the culture around it but will not be embraced by its death and keeps on singing the various themes of its song in season and out of season no matter who or what tries to stop it. That song, from Baptists to Roman Catholics, relies on a common core that has not been co-opted by cultural fads, but sings out the subversive message of liberation in Christ in spite of all the forces—no matter how large—arrayed against it.

7. TROUBLE AND A CHALLENGE

While all that I have just said is true, the analysis also reveals a troubling and countervailing motif, namely that over 40% of the common texts and over 48% of the common tunes come from the nineteenth century. If a nineteenth-century *style* is used as the criterion, the percentages are even higher.[38] This is in part because the nineteenth century was a productive historical turning point when many authors, composers, and editors bequeathed to us a large and rich array of hymnic materials. It would be wrong for us to avoid this vein in our history and the people to whom we owe grateful tribute. It would also be wrong to avoid acknowledging nineteenth-century mistakes, as in Victorian romanticizing of, or "patent lies" about, Christmas.[39] Both the good and the bad have been bequeathed to us. The problem in either case is that the nineteenth century is gone and has left its shell. What has put some leaders of the church into such a frenzy of fear is their realization that the shell is a dead casket. Their analysis is correct, but their frantic solution to substitute a new "contemporary" shell is disastrous. It allies the church's message to an even thinner skin that will atrophy more quickly than the one from the nineteenth century, which, in at least some of its manifestations, included depth from the church's earlier life that undercut its mistakes. The error of allying the church with any period points to the truth of William Inge's observation: "The church that marries the spirit of an age becomes a widow in the next generation."[40] It also traps the church in the culture's allegiance to Caesar, or the Caesar of commerce, and not to Christ.

This study challenges the church to resist a narrow hymnic practice from any single period and to embrace the fullness of its resources, which help protect it from idolatry. As I indicated earlier, it gets at that challenge primarily from within the resources of the Anglo-European portion of the church from which it comes. As I also indicated, it resonates with Michael Hawn's message in his study of global hymnody. The relationship between the two is not the topic of this book, but readers can make their own connections.

8. WORDS AND TUNES

Hymn tunes carry the words of the hymns, and words are central to the church's song. Much of what is involved in this study, therefore, is of necessity a matter of words, so we will not avoid texts either in the discussion or in the examples. If a tune is primarily attached to a specific text or has a long association with a text, the first stanza of that text in a version from one of the fourteen hymnals (or occasionally an update) is given in the example. If there is no such association, or there are many associations, one possibility has been chosen. It may be from another period and bear no relationship at all to the tune's genesis. While I have tried to be sensitive to the textual issues we struggle with, like inclusiveness or poetic quality, I have allowed tunes and their associations rather than concerns about texts to determine choices. Since this book is not fundamentally about the hymns (texts), its primary concern is the music bearing the texts. To that we attend in the following pages.

Since the topic is tunes, musical details have to be considered. This is not meant to be a technical treatise solely for those with a great deal of musical understanding, but to avoid music and the technical details it brings with it would be to avoid the topic. Every musical term and detail cannot be defined and explored. Syntactic musical definitions and explorations are the stuff of a music theory text, not a book like this. Those with musical expertise or interest can dwell on the musical details as much as they choose. Generalists can scan or avoid them and still understand the rest of the descriptions, overviews, and perspectives.

9. HYMNS AND WORSHIP

None of what I have just said should discourage those who simply want to see what tunes are out there and where they have come from. Those who choose to use the book like that are more than welcome, but there is yet one more item of business for those who wish to see the value and relation of this study to the church and its worship.

Hymns relate to the worship of the church in numerous ways. Sometimes they are intrinsic to it, sometimes less so. For example, hymns of personal devotion, which at first bear no relation to public worship, can be embraced by the church for its communal gatherings. At the devotional level, they may not have tunes at all. They take tunes to themselves as they become communal. The reverse is also possible: hymns written for public worship can prove to be more suitable for private devotion. In this case, they may shed their tunes. Sometimes, if the church forgets the faith and the structures and patterns that embody it but continues to sing hymns anyway, the hymns may well carry the fullness of the faith in spite of the church's amnesia. They may even call the church back to its faith.

This study is concerned about hymnody in relation to the church's public gatherings when its patterns and structures are healthy. That reminds us again of our period's denominational divisions and a curious paradox. I suggested before that denominational groups provide checks, balances, and discipline for their members. With the checks and balances go postures and perspectives that grow out of important denominational roots. These get at central themes we avoid at our peril. However, there are even deeper roots and relationships under the denominational ones that push toward common flowerings. In our period the investigation of separate confessional roots itself has led to reevaluations and reconfigurations that reveal these deeper and more common ecumenical roots.

These have, possibly paradoxically but probably not surprisingly, accentuated internal divisions. Some divisions *within* denominational groups are sharper than divisions *between* denominational groups. A mix of Episcopalians, Presbyterians, and Roman Catholics, for example, may well agree with one another on any number of issues more than they agree with some members of their own confessional bodies.

This reconfiguring is apparent at worship. It once was possible to distinguish between a Presbyterian and a Lutheran practice. (At least we thought it was possible; often we minimized or neglected significant differences that were actually present within what was presumed to be a single common confessional allegiance). Such distinguishing has become increasingly difficult—though it is still present and is not likely to disappear because of a tradition's healthy inertia. What has emerged through the inertia, however, is a quite remarkable consensus about worship across the ecumenical spectrum. Common liturgical research and grassroots cross-denominational practice from the nineteenth century onward has brought Roman Catholic, Anglican, Lutheran, Reformed, English Baptist, continental Anabaptist, and Wesleyan communities into a new dialogue and has whetted their appetites for contact with Eastern Orthodoxy. Common agreements and concerns for many groups have emerged about baptism. Common ecumenical shapes for the Eucharist and prayer offices have become clear. A common (or at least a largely common) three-year lectionary has brought congregations together across denominational divisions. Resources have been widely shared in hymnals and other publications related to worship. Though some have resisted this ecumenical consensus, it has also been widely affirmed in quiet ways that do not garner press coverage. Perhaps that is how the church always moves, like silent yeast, not destructively visible tornados.

I refer to that consensus in the following remarks, no matter what denominational grouping a church may officially relate to. I will avoid denominational labels because in this context they have become confusing, contradictory, and meaningless. I do not mean thereby to minimize their importance. Unless we deal with what they stand for—in a constructive ecumenical conversation, if we are wise—we will be in trouble down the road. I simply mean here to describe relationships that transcend our divisions and hold promise for our life together as the whole body of Christ, no matter where or among whom they occur.

Sundays and Festivals around Word and Table

Gathering. Hymns relate to the church's Sunday and festival worship around Word and table at various points. At the beginning of the gathering rite a hymn or hymns may well be employed, but the *Kyrie* ("Lord, have mercy") or the *Gloria in excelsis* ("Glory be to God on High") or both may also follow. What we have at the beginning, then, is a hymn, or hymns, on the edge of worship. In some ways they duplicate the "hymns" (the *Kyrie* is technically a litany, not a "hymn," and the *Gloria* is a "hymn" of praise that in its classic form is not stanzaic like most of what we refer to as hymns) that will follow. They move from the time and space of daily life into the time and space of worship. They are hospitable hinge points that, for some communities, are more important than for others. Though important, the hymns in the gathering rite are not central. The church's worship can proceed without them and sometimes has done that.

The Word. During the service of the Word, the psalmody between the Old Testament reading and the Epistle is the central musical event. It may but is not likely to employ "hymn" tunes. If *metrical* psalms are used, "hymn" or "psalm" tunes will be present, but psalm *tones*—and the intervenient refrains or antiphons that may go with them—best fit the psalms when left in their natural state as poetic prose. The verse (or whatever the intervenient choral piece may be called) between the Epistle and the Gospel is equally unlikely to employ a hymn tune. It is generally related to the choir's specific responsibility, not the congregation's, though congregations can sing an "alleluia" or a hymn or a canticle here; and choirs, in order to make a connection of some sort, may usefully employ hymn tunes or musical themes from them.

It is during the Hymn of the Day after the Sermon, possibly before it, that hymns are most profoundly connected to worship on Sundays and festivals for those communities who sing a hymn at this point. Here a hefty hymn works best to relate to the readings and themes, with enough breadth so that it is not geared to a narrow association with the texts, but over time bears the weight of the chunk of meaning the church has assigned a particular day. I am aware that some communities are committed to silence after the preaching of the Word and would not have a Hymn of the Day. They hold an honorable position. They remind us that silence can allow the Word to resonate deeply and that it is a much-needed respite from our perpetual racket, which, without some reprieve, dulls our senses and drains life of meaning. It is equally true, however, that a pregnant silence after preaching can break into song, and that our song can give the Word equally as much if not more space to resonate deeply. A response with that sort of resonance is what the Hymn of the Day is about.

Though they did not yet have a large repertoire of hymns to draw from, I suspect that the "hymn" singing of early Christians, to which Pliny referred in his letter to the emperor Trajan around the year 112, may reflect the primal beginnings of the Hymn of the Day.[41] It may also reflect the beginnings of the *Gloria in excelsis* in the entrance rite, or may signal the fecund ground for both. In any event, Pliny's comments place this musical event in connection with the service of the Word, not the meal around the table. In the service of the Word, the Hymn of the Day has developed in relation to the theme of the particular day and its readings, so that across the year the church has sung its story in a series of central hymns that recount the core of the faith. This dynamic generated cycles of hymns in relation to Daily Prayer, annual festivals, and saints; Graduals and sequences; and the Hymn of the Day as Lutherans developed it,[42] which in turn was part of the stimulus for the cantatas of J. S. Bach.

The Appendix gives a list of possibilities from which congregations could construct for themselves a Tune of the Day sequence for the church year, with what I hope are enduring tunes and texts. It has been prepared on the premise that such a sequence is one of our pressing needs. We have a wonderful plethora of hymns and tunes to choose from. It includes not only the church's historic resources, but the Anglo-European "hymnic explosion" of the last part of the twentieth century and all the global materials that have joined those resources. While this embarrassment of riches is cause for celebration, it poses a dilemma for finite creatures: no single community can possibly sing it all, much less know anything but a very small portion of its existence. The problem finite communities of faith face is deciding what they ought to learn; what is of enduring value; what will, taken together, tell the whole story; and what is worth the time and effort to include in their memory banks. A Tune of the Day for each Sunday and festival of the church year tries to get at these issues. It does not preclude other tunes and their hymns. It welcomes them throughout the service in various roles and from various styles. A Hymn of the Day (and that is the underlying issue—a hymn of the day, approached here from the standpoint of tunes, because that is what this book is about) sequence simply suggests what hymns and tunes over the course of a Church Year might be sung in response to the balance of the whole story, what hymns and tunes might bear repetition year after year, what hymns and tunes from the church's past make valuable ongoing contributions to the community of faith, and what hymns and tunes might be worth committing to the memory bank.

The Meal. At the offertory, when the bread and wine are brought forward (and when an offering of money may also be received), a hymn, anthem, and the offertory verse may be sung. (Instrumental music is also possible.) A hymn here may employ a congregational hymn tune, but the anthem and offertory verse are the choir's responsibility and are less apt to use such tunes.

The central musical component in the Eucharistic part of the service, parallel to psalmody in the Word service, is the greeting and invitation that flows between the presider and the assembly in the *Sursum corda* ("Lift up your hearts") and leads through the Preface to the *Sanctus* ("Holy, Holy, Holy"). Like psalmody, "hymn" tunes may be employed for metrical versions of the *Sanctus*, but the more natural state of the *Sanctus* is a single, through-composed melody that does not repeat in a stanzaic way but bears weekly repetition. The *Sanctus* and the rest of the Ordinary of the Mass strongly suggest the importance of chant.[43] This study in no way minimizes that importance, though in general the topic falls outside its borders.

The *Agnus Dei* ("Lamb of God") is the characteristic first hymn at communion during the "fraction" (breaking of the bread). Like the *Kyrie*, it is a litany, not what might be called a hymn—unless cast into a metrical version—and not therefore likely to employ hymn tunes. During communion hymns may follow the *Agnus Dei*. They can range from meditative to festive and utilize many styles and forms, just like the banquet during which they are being sung. A variety of tunes and styles is part of this banquet. While the Hymn of the Day relates to the Word of God, the mind, and the narrative structures that are central to many of the tunes in this study, the "hymnody" around the meal is related to sacrament, body, fiesta, meditation, and more cyclic structures that can be repeated with constant variation and layers of density. This latter type is more characteristic of what today might be called global or world hymnody. It is a major component of any full-orbed congregational song, but it is not the center of this study.

After communion, some communities use a hymn of praise or a canticle. It may be a stanzaic hymn with its particular hymn tune. If it happens to be a metrical setting of the *Nunc dimittis*, such a tune is likely. When the canticle is in its original state of poetic prose, however, a psalm tone or melody not used in a stanzaic way is more natural.

Sending. Some communities add another hymn before or after the Benediction. This dismissal music has the reverse hinge character of the entrance rite. Different communities or parts thereof regard it with various degrees of importance. The dismissal rite itself has the dynamic of a quick and decisive end: *Ite misse est*, "The Mass is ended," or, as some communities translate that, "Go in peace. Serve the Lord," to which the people respond, "Thanks be to God." The point is, "Go quickly now to the world to be the body of Christ you have just received." Parts of the church want to "stay and sing" yet a bit more either before or after this dismissal, before they move back into the time and space of daily life to take up their proclamatory and ethical responsibilities. Again, as at the beginning, hymnody here, though important, is at the edge of worship, not one of its central components. It may be cast in any number of styles.

Daily Prayer

While hymns are employed in all sorts of important ways throughout the Sunday or festival service of Word and table, as I have just indicated, except for the Hymn of the Day they are not really intrinsic to it. They *are* intrinsic to Daily Prayer. There, with canticles, readings, and prayer, they form a daily round of life at worship before God. Characteristically, they are morning and evening hymns bordering the day's rhythm; but prayer offices may occur throughout the day, and the hymns may include all the themes of the Christian faith.

Morning and Evening Prayer, the central daily prayer offices, are used and modified in a wide variety of ways among us. Though their essential character consists of quite brief morning and evening gatherings at the beginning and the end of the day, few communities other than monastic or educational ones live in close enough proximity to one another to pray together daily. So we have a whole range of more isolated uses in brief or lengthy forms: individuals or families who pray in the morning, at night, or at meals; small groups from a local church that on one or more days of the week assemble for prayer, usually in the morning; small ecumenical groups who assemble for fifteen minutes or so during their lunch hours one or more times during the week at a church in the Chicago Loop, for example; large assemblies who come together for occasional lengthy hymn festivals that elongate Evening Prayer and include many hymns arranged in the simplest and most complex ways with organs and other instruments. Hymns are natural components of all these services, even if they are omitted.

Perspective: Central Matters

In recent years, Christians have been arguing about what instruments and musical styles to use at worship. When you back up and look at the church's worship in the integrity of its ecumenical shape, these arguments become secondary and recede into the periphery. It becomes clear that, though they may raise important matters, they are not central and may even derail the church into dead ends. What is central is the church's song around font, Word, table, and daily prayer. Communities of faith will of necessity sing in the musical styles of which they are capable in their time and place. They are wise if they respect the wisdom and practice of the church from many times and places to avoid their own idolatrous tendencies, but they have to filter them through their idioms and capacities. Otherwise they are silenced.

What this finally means is a universal reality that the church of late has tended to forget, namely, that the heart of the church's song is vocal and congregational—it needs to be accessible for untrained singers who form congregations. That means its center of gravity is an unaccompanied unison line, and that means it has to be possible without instruments. Harmony and instruments are welcomed. The musical resources of the whole human race, with all its vocal and instrumental ingenuity, are not only welcomed, but are to be employed as creatively as possible. That is what has generated the wonder and joy of choirs. But all that is necessary for Christian worship—in addition to water, Word, prayer, bread, and wine, of course—are people with voices and unison lines they can sing. Where there is no harmony and where there are no instruments, the people still have the birthright of song. And where there is harmony with or without instruments, what the people have to sing still has to fit their capacities—that is, it has to be possible without harmony and not dependent on instruments.

I do not mean to say that harmony and instruments are bad. As will become especially obvious in the nineteenth-century hymns, some fine hymn tunes presume harmony. Parts of the church have sung and still sing with great beauty and vigor in harmony. I love to join their part-singing. So do many other people. Eastern Orthodox, Moravians, Mennonites and some other Anabaptists, some Lutherans, some Presbyterians, some Baptists, some Anglicans, some Methodists, some Roman Catholics, and those who have used Victorian tunes or African American spirituals are among these groups. Parts of the church have also used all sorts of instrumental resources in their hymn singing. I have joined their numbers with great relish. The point is that what most of the human race most of the time is able to do without rehearsal is to sing in unison. That is what congregations do. It is no accident that most of the church most of the time has sung in unaccompanied unison, and that chant, chorales, psalm tunes, and in some sense the early Methodist mindset all fit that performance practice.[44]

In the examples, insofar as possible, only the melody lines of most tunes are given. There are some instances where the harmony has to be present, and there are others where many people would say the harmony should be present. It is given when it has to be there, but it is avoided it if at all possible, more than some commentators would like.

The following pages privilege what belongs to the congregation. That is why streams like the chorale and psalm tune ones need careful attention: they are from communities of the church who have consciously worked hard at congregational song and have left us a goodly heritage that still has force. I make no apologies for the privileging. It does not in any sense rule out the most complex choral and instrumental possibilities one can imagine, broken to Word and sacraments,[45] of course. All of that is most warmly welcomed to the church's worship, but it is the topic of other books. In this book, the congregation's voice, also broken to Word and sacraments, is the central concern.

10. Terms

Most hymnals give four references with each hymn: the author or source of the text, the composer or source of the music, the name of the tune, and the meter. The first two are obvious. The last two require comment.

Names of Tunes

Hymn tunes have sometimes been closely associated with one text and then named for that text. Sometimes they have been named for a text with which they were once associated, though we now connect them to another text or to other texts. Sometimes they have been named for places or people, so that their names have no apparent textual associations at all.

Since in many cases a single tune can be used for more than one text, it becomes impossible to identify it by the name of a text unless the tune itself takes on the text's name. The name of the tune becomes important because different communities use the same tune for different texts. If you use a text rather than a tune name to identify a tune, its identity is in doubt. Occasionally tunes have more than one name, which obviously confuses matters and requires clarification, but most of the church has settled on common names for tunes. The usual convention for tune names is to employ all uppercase letters (NUN KOMM, DER HEIDEN HEILAND) and to give them above or below the hymn itself. To identify texts, the norm is to use quotation marks around the first line with upper and lower case letters as in a title ("Savior of the Nations, Come"). On a hymnal page, if the title of the text is given, it usually appears above the hymn in bold without quotation marks.

Meter

"Meter" in hymns has two meanings. One is the poetic meter, which refers to the way accented and unaccented syllables are arranged. The first line of "Our God, Our Help in Ages Past," for example, has eight syllables arranged in four sets of two. Each set is called a poetic foot. A foot has two or more syllables, one accented and the other one or ones unaccented. In this case the foot is called iambic, which means there are two syllables, the first unaccented and the second accented.[46] Meter in this sense is not generally listed with hymns. You have to scan the text to figure it out.

The other meaning of meter refers to numbers or abbreviations for them. These are given on the page of most hymns. They are related to the poetic meter, but need to be distinguished from it. The number of digits denotes the number of lines in a stanza, and each individual digit gives the number of syllables in the given line. In "Our God, Our Help in Ages Past" the numbers we call meter in this sense are 8686. That is, the four digits mean there are four lines. The first and third lines have eight syllables, the second and fourth have six. This scheme, since it is so common in English hymnody, is called Common Meter, abbreviated as CM. Short Meter is 6686, and Long Meter is 8888. If you double these, a "D" goes with the abbreviations (CMD, SMD, and LMD). Other meters do not have such abbreviations, though a D may be used to indicate the repeat of doubled ones, as in 5554 D or 6464 D.

The discussion of meter introduces some critical, though not superficially obvious, components of our study. First, it indicates tunes have to be matched to texts. Accents of tunes have to fall in the right places, and the number of notes in the tune has to accommodate the number of syllables in the text. Beyond the matter of matching tunes to text in an arbitrarily correct way, there is also the matter of what might be called "tone." A tune that has the right metrical scheme may not fit every text with that scheme. Further, different traditions have different opinions about this and make different choices, as the Appendix amply demonstrates.

Mary Oyer, one of the most perceptive hymnists and leaders of hymns in our generation, suggests that there is more here than meets the eye or ear.[47] Though "fraught with problems of consistency," she writes, "[meter opens up] aesthetic questions related to text." Dots in some hymnals "show groupings within rhyme patterns, as in 'I to the Hills' [in 86.86][48] or 88.88 for 'Jesus Shall Reign.'"[49] Austin Lovelace thinks dots should be used in just this way "to indicate something of the rhyme scheme."[50] This requires careful attention to the text. The first example Oyer gives (86.86) is in the rhyme scheme *ab.cb*, and the second (88.88) *aa.bb*. As Routley has shown in an insightful discussion of meter, there are implications here for matching text and tune that even someone as skilled as Vaughan Williams missed.[51]

Second, the aesthetic implications go well beyond the matter of matching text and tune. "Why," asks Oyer, "are 8s and 6s so prominent in English, but not in French and German?" She recalled a Japanese student who "could not think in 8s and 6s when [she] assigned [her students] to write a metrical psalm in CM," and she noted that 7s and 5s are more common for Japanese and Chinese cultures, closer to Haiku. Then she added, "I believe that the proportions in hymn tune phrase lengths—symmetrical or asymmetrical—have much to do with the notion of the hymn."[52]

Third, a severe discipline is immediately apparent. This is not an arbitrary matter, imposed by some external authority or circumstance. It grows out of the nature of hymn singing itself. Hymns are congregational. They are for people who are primarily not musicians, and they are generally sung without practice. They have to be organized, therefore, into some scheme that can be readily apprehended. The church, like all communities that sing folk song, has gravitated to what works, the stanzaic structure of hymns with disciplined metrical requirements that make them possible.

Fourth, such a severe discipline is a bane and a blessing. It is a bane in that the seeming simplicity of the scheme can tempt one to think the writing of hymns and tunes is a simple matter. It is a blessing in that the severest discipline has the capacity to make the finest art. In the first instance, one can construct a hymn or tune that will seem to follow all the "rules" and may even appear immediately attractive, but it will wear thin after repeated usage. In the second instance, in the hands of skillful writers and composers (who may well be anonymous and not the most famous composers), remarkably durable creations can be crafted. Congregations sort this out over time and repeat what is worth repeating. They too can be snared, even for a generation or more, but what is not worth keeping disappears unless leaders force it. Even then it disappears when the leaders die. Leaders who force their will usually pay the price (or their communities do) and cause future turmoil. Our task here is to listen to the wisdom of the church over long stretches of time and to sort out what is worth singing.

---

1   Augustine said a hymn has to have "these three things: not only praise, but of God, and singing." Quoted in David W. Music, ed., *Hymnology: A Collection of Source Readings* (Lanham: The Scarecrow Press, Inc., 1996), 19.

2   Erik Routley, *The Music of Christian Hymns* (Chicago: GIA Publications, 1981), hereafter MCH.

3   Erik Routley, *The Music of Christian Hymnody: A Study of the development of the Hymn Tune since the Reformation, with Special Reference to English Protestantism* (London: Independent Press Limited, 1957).

4   Routley, MCH, Preface, second paragraph.

5   Erik Routley, "A Historical Study of Christian Hymnody: Its Development and Discipline" (Ph.D. dissertation, Oxford University, 1952), 769 pages.

6   Ibid.

7   Nicholas Temperley, ed., *The Hymn Tune Index: A Census of English-Language Hymn Tunes in Printed Sources from 1535 to 1820*, 4 vols. (New York: Oxford University Press, 1998), hereafter HTI.

8   Katharine Smith Diehl, *Hymns and Tunes – An Index* (New York: Scarecrow, 1966).

9   David W. Perry, *Hymns and Tunes Indexed* (Croydon: Hymn Society of Great Britain and Ireland, 1980).

10   D. DeWitt Wasson, comp., *Hymntune Index and Related Hymn Materials*, 3 vols. (Lanham: The Scarecrow Press, Inc., 1998).

11   Johannes Zahn, *Die Melodien der deutschen evangelischen Kirchenlieder aus den Quellen geschöpft und mitgeteilt*, 6 vols. (Gütersloh: C. Bertelsmann, 1889–1893, repr. Hildesheim, 1963), hereafter MDEK.

12   Wilhelm Bäumker, *Das katholische deutsche Kirchenlied in seinen Singweisen von den frühesten Zeiten bis gegen Ende des siebzehnten Jahrhunderts*, 4 vols. (Hildesheim: Georg Olms Verlagsbuchhandlung, 1962; first published Freiburg im Breisgau: Herder, 1883–1911), hereafter KDK.

13 J. Vincent Higginson, *Handbook for American Catholic Hymnals* (Boston: Hymn Society of America, 1976).

14 Hugh Keyte and Andrew Parrot, eds., *The New Oxford Book of Carols* (Oxford: Oxford University Press, 1992).

15 Edward Foley, ed., *Worship Music: A Concise Dictionary* (Collegeville: The Liturgical Press, 2000).

16 For example, Emily R. Brink and Bert Polman, eds., *Psalter Hymnal Companion* (Grand Rapids: CRC Publications, 1998), hereafter PsHH; Raymond F. Glover, ed., *The Hymnal 1982 Companion*, 4 vols. (New York: The Church Hymnal Corporation, 1990, 1994), hereafter H82C; Marilyn Kay Stulken, *Hymnal Companion to the Lutheran Book of Worship* (Philadelphia: Fortress Press, 1981), hereafter HCLBW; Carlton R. Young, *Companion to the United Methodist Hymnal* (Nashville: Abingdon Press, 1993), hereafter CUMH.

17 Robert Guy McCutchan, *Hymn Tune Names: Their Sources and Significance* (New York: Abingdon Press, 1957).

18 The Hymn Society, Boston University School of Theology, 745 Commonwealth Avenue, Boston, MA 02215-1401, 1-800-THE HYMN, hymnsoc@bu.ecu, www.hymnsociety.org.

19 W. Daniel Landes and Mark G. Putnam, *The Electronic Encyclopedia of Hymnology* (Nashville: Putnam Graphics and Media Design, 2000).

20 Carlos Messerli and Carl Schalk, et al., eds., *Celebrating the Musical Heritage of the Lutheran Church* (Thrivent Financial for Lutherans, n.d.)

21 Temperley's index, for example, is continually being updated and can be accessed at http://hymntune.music.uiuc.edu/hti1/default.asp.

22 John Julian, *A Dictionary of Hymnology* (New York: Dover Publications, 1957, reprint of 2nd ed., 1907), or other reprints.

23 William Reynolds, Milburn Price, and David Music, *A Survey of Christian Hymnody*, 4th ed. (Carol Stream: Hope Publishing Company, 1999, 1st ed., 1963).

24 Harry Eskew and Hugh T. McElrath, *Sing with Understanding: An Introduction to Christian Hymnology*, 2nd ed. (Nashville: Church Street Press, 1995, 1st ed., 1980).

25 J. R. Watson, *The English Hymn: A Critical and Historical Study* (Oxford: Clarendon Press, 1997).

26 Erik Routley did this sort of thing with an English cast in *English Hymns and Their Tunes: A Survey* (London: Hymn Society of Great Britain & Ireland, 1981), a pamphlet of 23 pages first written in 1964 and updated in 1981. I have in mind something less aphoristic than this.

27 J. R. Watson has a wonderful discussion about the linear character of the text and the circular character of the tune. See Watson, *The English Hymn*, 26. The rest of Watson's second chapter, called "The Singing of Hymns, and the Experience of Metre," gives perceptive insights into this matter. For the relation to memory, see Rebecca Wagner Oettinger, *Music as Propaganda in the German Reformation* (Aldershot: Ashgate, 2001), 25–26, 34, and 49.

28 C. Michael Hawn, *Gather into One: Praying and Singing Globally* (Grand Rapids: William B. Eerdmans, 2003).

29 See Dale T. Irvin, "Global Faith: Not Made in the USA," *The Christian Century* 121, no. 15 (July 17, 2004): 28–31 and the books by Lamin Sanneh and Wilbert R. Shenk that are cited there.

30 See, for example, his seven assertions in Hawn, *Gather into One*, 14–17.

31 These are the following, with the abbreviations to be used hereafter:
The Baptist Hymnal (Nashville: Convention Press, 1991), Bap
Chalice Hymnal (St. Louis: Chalice Press, 1995), Chal
Christian Worship: A Lutheran Hymnal (Milwaukee: Northwestern Publishing House, 1993), CW
The Covenant Hymnal: A Worshipbook (Chicago: Covenant Publications, 1996), Cov

Hymnal: A Worship Book Prepared by Churches in the Believers Church Tradition (Elgin: Brethren Press; Newton: Faith and Life Press; Scottdale: Mennonite Publishing House, 1992), HWB

The Hymnal 1982 according to the use of The Episcopal Church (New York: The Church Hymnal Corporation, 1985), H82

Lutheran Book of Worship (Minneapolis: Augsburg Publishing House, 1978), LBW

Moravian Book of Worship (Bethlehem: Moravian Church in America, 1995), Mor

The New Century Hymnal (Cleveland: The Pilgrim Press, 1995), NC

The Presbyterian Hymnal (Louisville: Westminster/John Knox Press, 1990), Pres

Psalter Hymnal (Grand Rapids: CRC Publications, 1987), PsH

The United Methodist Hymnal: Book of United Methodist Worship (Nashville: The United Methodist Publishing House, 1989), Meth

Voices United: The Hymn and Worship Book of The United Church of Canada (Etobicoke: The United Church Publishing House, 1996), VU

Worship Third Edition: A Hymnal and Service Book for Roman Catholics (Chicago: GIA Publications, 1986), Wor3.

32 Another way to say a similar thing is to ask with Kenneth A. Myers whether music in the church is commodity or legacy, and whether one consideration for choosing music in church ought to be whether it has lasting value over five generations. (From the question-and-answer period of the lecture "Media, Music, and the Meaning of Life: Miscellaneous Notes about Notes and Their Habits," Stadium Village Church, Minneapolis, Minnesota, April 21, 2004. *Myers is the author of All God's Children and Blue Suede Shoes* [Wheaton: Crossway Books, 1989].

33 See John 17:11.

34 I have in a few cases drawn examples from publications that grow out of one of these books and give updated versions. Without changing the substance of tune or text—or of credit or copyright information—notation has been edited for style throughout for the sake of visual uniformity. Consult the Acknowledgment index for current copyright information.

35 I began by listing every occurrence of every tune cited from the 14 hymnals we tabulated. After several chapters, it became clear this was of no use and cluttered up pages with lengthy footnotes and an overwhelmingly oppressive alphabet and number soup. I deleted it in favor of listing only what is necessary to understand a specific point. Readers can easily consult the alphabetical index of tunes that most hymnals supply.

36 There are surely mistakes in the counting that follows, but the figures are accurate enough to allow a sense of the landscape to emerge, which is what I was trying to discover.

37 Tunes common to 9 to 13 hymnals are marked in the Tune Index with a single asterisk (*), those common to all fourteen with a double asterisk (**).

38 Carl Daw, hymn writer and executive director of the Hymn Society in the United States and Canada, refers to this movement as prodigal sons who have squandered their inheritance.

39 Hawn, *Gather into One*, 218–219, quotes John Bell, who acknowledges that many Christmas carols "are good," but then says, "There is no biblical evidence to support the theory that 'snow had fallen, snow on snow,' but there is substantial evidence to suggest that Jesus did not 'honor and obey' throughout his childhood. What about running away from his family when he was in Jerusalem? . . . The Victorians dumped on us a legacy of forced piety, sentimentalism and deceptive images of God in their hymns."

40 See Paul Westermeyer, "Liturgical Music: *Soli Deo Gloria*" in *Liturgy and the Moral Self: Humanity at Full Stretch Before God, Essays in Honor of Don E. Saliers*, ed. E. Byron Anderson and Bruce T. Morrill (Collegeville: The Liturgical Press, 1998), 207.

41 See the correspondence of Pliny to Trajan in David W. Music, ed., *Hymnology: A Collection of Source Readings* (Lanham: The Scarecrow Press, Inc., 1966), 4.

42 For a quick overview see Stulken, *Hymnal Companion to the Lutheran Book of Worship*, xiii–xiv.

[43] See Eugene L. Brand, "Singing the Church's Song," *Cross Accent* 11, no. 3 (Fall 2003): 24–26.

[44] The Methodist one is mixed. John Wesley had in mind a monophonic ideal that gravitated to harmony, and early Methodists preferred unaccompanied singing though they gravitated to the use of organs. See Paul Westermeyer, *Te Deum: The Church and Music* (Minneapolis: Fortress Press, 1998), 214–215, and Temperley, HTI, I, 53 and 55.

[45] By "broken to" I mean set next to, contextualized by, made new by, transformed by Word and sacraments. All art and music, like everything from the culture, is in the economy of grace renewed and transformed by the Gospel. This works itself out not in flights of fancy, but in being set next to and thereby transformed by the means by which God in Christ through the Holy Spirit chooses to address us, namely, Word and sacraments.

[46] For a more complete discussion of these matters, which gets to the heart of things quickly, see Austin Lovelace, *The Anatomy of Hymnody* (Chicago: GIA Publications, 1965).

[47] Correspondence, June 27, 2004. In this book, since the various hymnals from which the examples are taken do not agree on this matter, there is no consistency.

[48] HWB, #563.

[49] HWB, #319.

[50] Correspondence, August 28, 2004.

[51] Erik Routley, *An English-Speaking Hymnal Guide* (Collegeville: The Liturgical Press, 1979), v, where he suggests that Vaughan Williams (in the 1933 edition of *The English Hymnal*, #539) matched a tune in 888.888 with a text in 8.8.8.8.88 (rhyme scheme a.b.a.b.cc). Though one might argue that his example could be ambiguous, Routley is probably right.

[52] Correspondence, June 27, 2004.

II. The Oldest Tunes and Congregational Song

1. Chant Tunes

The music the people of Israel and the early church used for their texts is obscure and unknown to us. The following texts were sung: the psalms, canticles like Moses' and Miriam's song in Exodus 15 or Hannah's song in 1 Samuel 2, New Testament canticles like Mary's song in Luke 1, and other New Testament "hymns" like Ephesians 5:14. All of these biblical texts come to us, however, without their musical settings.[1] Nobody can be sure how the *Phos Hilaron*[2] or psalms, hymns, and canticles used in daily prayer sounded in their earliest musical dress. The Ordinary of the Mass, as Luther implies,[3]—at least the *Kyrie, Gloria in excelsis, Sanctus, Agnus Dei*, and perhaps the *Credo* (Nicene Creed)—was originally sung by the people. What melodies were used for these and other texts or how they may have been sung we do not know with any certainty, except that for the first centuries of the church's history they were not metrical or stanzaic.

We do know that for the first millennium musical instruments were not used in the church[4]—and still are not used in the Orthodox Church. We also know that a single unison line called monophony was employed. The multi-voiced polyphony that began to develop in the ninth and tenth centuries in the West and the instruments that entered later were for trained musicians.[5] These developments tended to silence the people, though there have probably always been assemblies of the baptized who sang at worship throughout the church's history.[6] Just as today, some congregations sing, some do not, some sing a little, some a lot, some sing poorly, some very well. Until the seventeenth and eighteenth centuries, and in some cases even in the nineteenth, congregations who sang did so essentially in unison and without instrumental accompaniment. After the sixteenth century the music may have become more "rhythmic" in some communities, though an ongoing rhythmic diversity has probably characterized the congregation's singing across the church's history.[7]

It is usually assumed that the stanzaic hymn as we know it today, which stands behind the tunes we are considering, entered the Latin church in the fourth century.[8] Ambrose (340–397) is the most important figure in this development. He wrote hymns, but probably not the tunes for them.[9] "We know nothing about either the manner of performance of these works or the music employed."[10] Though "nothing certain is known about hymn melodies before the eleventh century, when they were first written down in decipherable forms,"[11] the chant tunes pre-date written sources and some would say may be "as early as the fifth and sixth centuries."[12] Whenever they first were composed and however they may have sounded through generations of use, chant tunes represent a very old stratum of the church's music. Here are some examples.

VENI, REDEMPTOR GENTIUM, associated with Ambrose's text of the same name, comes as we know it from a twelfth- or thirteenth-century source. Its stepwise motion, judicious use of thirds, and gentle curves up to the fifth at the end of the second phrase and then back down make it quite singable. It is a good example of chant tunes and spawned several chorale melodies, as will become evident in the next chapter.

VENI REDEMPTOR GENTIUM
LM

Re-deem-er of the na-tions, come; Re-veal your-self in vir-gin birth,

The birth which a - ges all a - dore, A won-drous birth, be-fit-ting God.

Text: Att. Ambrose of Milan, 340-397; tr. Charles P. Price, b.1920, © 1982
Tune: Plainsong, Mode 1

H82 #55

SPLENDOR PATERNAE is another tune from a thirteenth-century source, also named for an Ambrosian text, in this case a morning hymn. The tune is thoroughly stepwise, except for the leap of a fourth to and from the fifth scale degree. This leap is prepared by and flows easily out of the upward melodic motion to the fourth scale degree in the first phrase.

SPLENDOR PATERNAE
LM

O Splen-dor of God's glo-ry bright, From light e-ter-nal bring-ing light,

Thou Light of lights, light's liv-ing spring, True Day, all days il-lu-min-ing.

Text: Ambrose of Milan, *Splendor paternae gloriae*, 4th c.; tr. composite   HWB #646
Tune: Sarum plainsong, *Sarum Antiphonal*

JAM LUCIS is a simpler, almost totally stepwise tune that uses only four pitches. Its first and last lines aid the memory by duplicating one another. The two inner lines are balanced by first pushing up to the third scale degree and then back down to the final. Associated with a sixth-century Compline hymn ("Te lucis ante terminum," "To You before the Close of Day"),[13] the tune is hardy enough to bear repetition, but is the essence of congregational simplicity.[14]

JAM LUCIS
LM

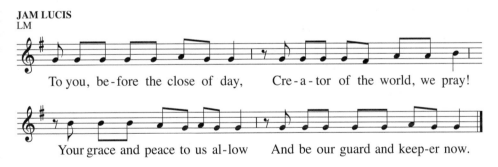

To you, be-fore the close of day,   Cre-a-tor of the world, we pray!

Your grace and peace to us al-low   And be our guard and keep-er now.

Text: Compline office hymn, c. 8th c.; tr. John M. Neale, 1818-1866, adapt.   LBW #277
Tune: Benedictine plainsong, mode VI

CONDITOR ALME SIDERUM, "using wider melodic intervals and gaining a touch of elegance,"[15] is named for the ninth-century evening Advent hymn with which it is associated, "Creator of the Stars of Night" (or other translations like "O Lord of Light, Who Made the Stars").[16] It is also sometimes used as the melody for the third-century *Phos Hilaron*[17] and other texts.[18]

CONDITOR ALME SIDERUM
LM

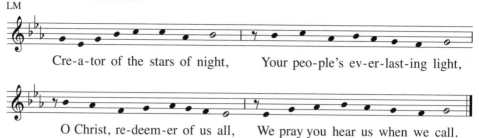

Cre-a-tor of the stars of night,   Your peo-ple's ev-er-last-ing light,

O Christ, re-deem-er of us all,   We pray you hear us when we call.

Text: Latin, 9th cent.; vers. *Hymnal 1940*, alt., © 1940, The Church Pension Fund
Tune: Plainsong mode IV

R #104

Not all chant tunes are as simple as the ones just cited. VEXILLA REGIS is within a congregation's grasp, but its longer phrases and melismas pose more challenges.[19]

VEXILLA REGIS
LM

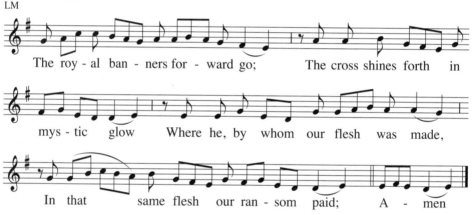

The roy - al ban - ners for - ward go;   The cross shines forth   in

mys - tic   glow   Where he, by   whom   our flesh   was   made,

In   that   same flesh   our ran - som   paid;   A -   men

Text: Venantius Honorius Fortunatus, 530-609, tr. composite
Tune: Sarum plainsong, mode I

LBW #125

This tune may be as old as the sixth-century text by Fortunatus (ca. 530–ca. 609) for which it is named. Fortunatus prepared his hymn for use in 569 as part of a procession of a relic of the "True Cross" which Queen Radegund of Clothaire had secured for a monastery she founded in Poitiers. The text transcended its original intent, and, as a profound meditation on the cross, became associated with Holy Week.

VEXILLA REGIS may have been sung in a regular rhythmic way as in the following modal rhythmic realization.[20]

VEXILLA REGIS
LM

Text: Venantius Fortunatus, c.530-609; tr. John M. Neale, 1818-1866, alt.
Tune: Mode I: Realization in modal rhythm by Schola Antiqua, 1983, ©

Wor3 #435

One may assume this version posed fewer challenges than the less regular mix of twos and threes, though it is perfectly possible that some worshiping assemblies practiced an irregular speech rhythm of some sort. (Provided a tune is congregational, assemblies of Christians can sing far more than they are usually given credit for.)

A similar text by Fortunatus, "Pange, lingua, gloriosi proelium," gives the tune PANGE LINGUA its name. This text may have been used at the end of Radegund's procession. Both text and tune have been embraced by the church for use during Holy Week.[21] The single fifth (at the end of the fourth phrase) is prepared by the fourth note in the first phrase (D) and the centrality of the fourth scale degree (A). Otherwise the tune proceeds by conjunct motion, thirds, and one fourth, all within an octave from one degree below the final. A slightly different version is a touch more melismatic and perhaps a bit more accessible.[22]

PANGE LINGUA
878787

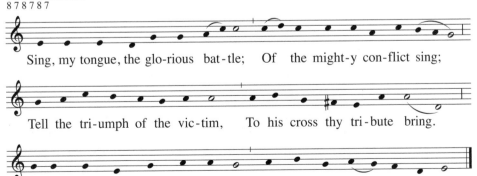

Text: Venantius Honorius Fortunatus, 540?-600?; ver. *Hymnal 1982*, after John Mason Neale, 1818-1866
Tune: Plainsong, Mode 3, *Zisterzienser Hymnar*, 14th c.

H82 #166

VENI CREATOR SPIRITUS is yet again named for a text, this one used at ordinations for the last ten centuries and usually attributed to Rhabanus Maurus (776–856). The tune is profoundly congregational, organized in four phrases that balance one other in the shape of one question with its answer followed by another question with its answer. The rhythm, like VEXILLA REGIS, has been interpreted by hymnal editors either as a series of twos and threes in various combinations or as a series of continuous threes until the brief exception at the beginning of the doxology after the last stanza.[23]

VENI CREATOR SPRITUS
LM

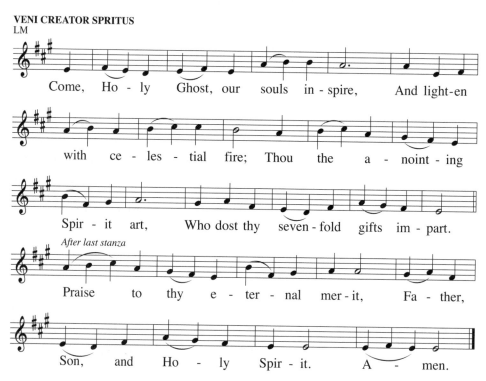

Text: Attr. Rhabanus Maurus, 8th-9th c.; tr. John Cosin, 1627
Tune: *Vesperale Romanum*, Mechlin, 1848; adapt. from *Hymns for Church and School*, 1964

Meth #651

So far, all the tunes cited are Long Meter, except PANGE LINGUA, which is 87.87.87. We come now to a tune with an "irregular" meter, VICTIMAE PASCHALI LAUDES. It is a "sequence," which requires some explanation. Sequences may have begun as tropes—that is, interpolations of text or music or both into a preexisting piece—which then developed independently. David Hiley, an expert on chant, "suggests that there are so many opinions" concerning the origins of sequences "that he chooses not to give one."[24] "In general," says J. Michael Thompson, director of the Schola Cantorum of St. Peter the Apostle in Chicago, "these were poetic texts, most with parallel verse structure, providing an extended reflection on a feast or season."[25] Whatever their origins may have been, they began in the ninth century and were set between the biblical readings from the Epistle and Gospel in the Word service of the Mass. They are one way the church has sought to break open texts with music, not unlike Bach cantatas that came centuries later.

The success of sequences proved to be their undoing. They multiplied to such an extent that by the sixteenth century there may have been as many as 5,000 of these "hymns," one or more for almost every day of the church year.[26] In such numbers they obscured rather than interpreted, cluttering up the Mass to such an extent that the Council of Trent (1545–1563) suppressed all but four of them: "Victimae paschali laudes"[27] for Easter, "Veni sancte Spiritus"[28] for Pentecost, "Lauda Sion"[29] for Corpus Christi, and the "Dies Irae"[30] for the Requiem. Lutherans pared them down somewhat less extensively.

VICTIMAE PASCHALI LAUDES is named for an eleventh-century sequence, usually attributed to Wipo of Burgundy (d. ca. 1050), which was well known during the Middle Ages and is the oldest of the sequences retained by the Council of Trent. The tune, though it was quite popular, is not congregational in the sense of the previous ones. It narrates the Easter story in a continuous line, not in a repeated musical way as for a regular stanzaic structure. It is important not only in its own right, but also because it spawned two more tunes we shall encounter later, CHRIST IST ERSTANDEN and CHRIST LAG IN TODESBANDEN, and may stand behind GENEVAN 80.[31] An interesting aspect of this tune is the avoidance of the sixth degree. Though listed as Mode 1, Dorian, the characteristic sharped sixth degree of that mode (B-natural in the following example) is precisely what is missing. Maybe it was once there and disappeared, but as we have it there is always a leap over that pitch. (For some comments about modes, see below.) It is instructive to observe the similarity between this tune and the common one for the "Dies Irae," especially at the phrase "Speak, Mary, declaring," as compared with the phrase on "Teste David" in the "Dies Irae."[32]

VICTIMAE PASCHALI
PM

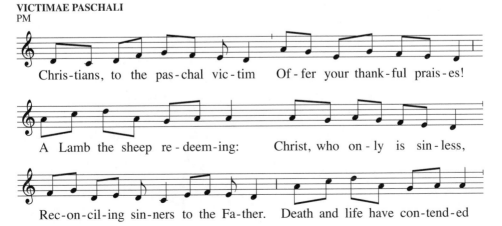

29

In that com-bat stu-pen-dous; The prince of life, who died, Reigns im-mor-tal.

Speak, Mar-y, de-clar-ing   What you saw when way-far-ing.

"The tomb of Christ, who is liv-ing, The glo-ry of Je-sus' res-ur-rec-tion;

Bright an-gels at-test-ing,   The shroud and nap-kin rest-ing.

My Lord, my hope, is a-ris-en; To Gal-i-lee he goes be-fore you."

Christ in-deed from death is ris-en,   Our new life ob-tain-ing.

Have mer-cy, vic-tor King,   ev-er reign-ing! A - men

Text: Attr. Wipo of Burgundy, 11th c.; tr. The English Hynmal, 1906
Tune: Mode I; attr. Wipo of Burgundy, 11th c.

LBW #137

Another tune linked to a trope is DIVINUM MYSTERIUM. It probably comes from the thirteenth century and is named for a trope on the *Sanctus*.[33] Since the nineteenth century it has been attached to an English version of a text by Prudentius (348–ca. 413), "Corde natus ex Parentis," usually in John Mason Neale's translation, "Of the Father's Love Begotten," but more recently in a version closer to the first line of the Latin, "Of the Parent's Heart Begotten."[34]

This tune is another example of alternate rhythmic possibilities. It seems originally to have been in a triple meter, which is the way it comes to us through *Piae Cantiones* (1582), as follows.

DIVINUM MYSTERIUM
8 7 8 7 8 7 7

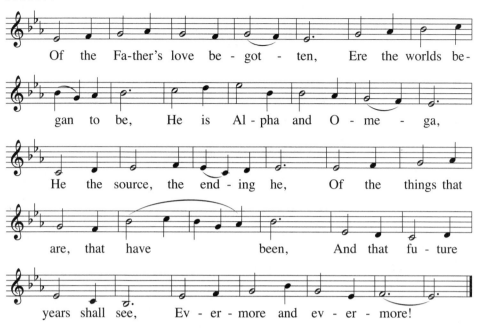

Of the Fa-ther's love be - got - ten, Ere the worlds began to be, He is Al - pha and O - me - ga,
He the source, the end - ing he, Of the things that
are, that have been, And that fu - ture
years shall see, Ev - er - more and ev - er - more!

Text: Marcus Aurelius Clemens Prudentius, 348-410?; tr. John Mason Neale, 1818-1866 and Henry W. Baker, 1821-1877, alt.   H82 #82
Tune: Sanctus trope, 11th c.; adapt. *Piae Cantiones,* 1582

In the twentieth century, Winfred Douglas equalized its note values in the Episcopal Hymnal of 1916.[35] The following is the way most American hymnals have printed it.[36]

DIVINUM MYSTERIUM
8 7 8 7 8 7 7

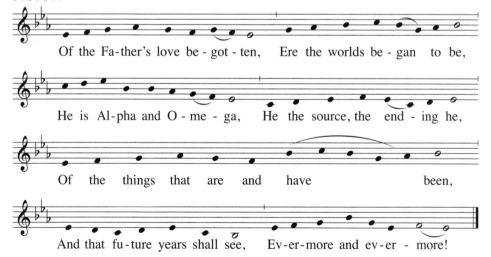

Of the Fa-ther's love be - got - ten, Ere the worlds be - gan to be,
He is Al-pha and O - me - ga, He the source, the end - ing he,
Of the things that are and have been,
And that fu -ture years shall see, Ev-er-more and ev-er - more!

Text: Aurelius Clemens Prudentius, *Corde natus ex Parentis;* tr. John M. Neale and Henry W. Baker, 1851, 1861   HWB #104
Tune: Plainsong, 13th c., *Piae Cantiones,* 1582

VENI, EMMANUEL comes from a fifteenth-century processional used by French Franciscan nuns, filtered through *The Hymnal Noted* (London, 1854), where it appeared with John Mason Neale's translation now known as "Oh, Come, Oh, Come, Emmanuel."[37] Routley called this the "most popular of Advent hymns" and "first-rate hymnody," though he added that the rhythmic form of the melody we use stands outside the plainsong tradition.[38] The tune was given in the fifteenth-century processional as a trope for a funeral responsory, "Libera me, Domine," with the text "Bone Jesu." A second melody, note-against-note, went with it. Keyte and Parrot are not sure whether "Veni, veni, Emmanuel" or the funeral responsory trope was the original text.[39] They give the Franciscan note against note version with "Veni, veni, Emmanuel" and point out the "neat fit" of the text and tune. Here is the melody with "Bone Jesu" as Routley gives it (corrected[40]), followed by a modern rendering with "Veni, veni, Emmanuel" in Neale's translation.

BONE JESU

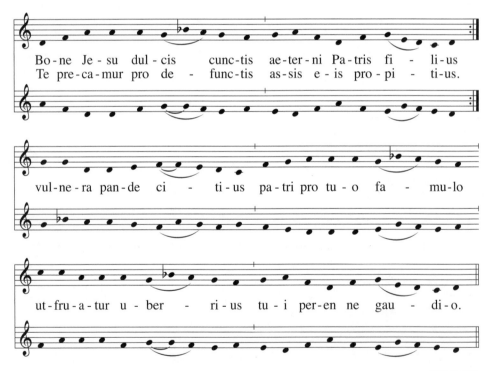

Bo - ne Je - su dul - cis   cunc-tis ae - ter - ni Pa - tris fi - li - us
Te pre - ca - mur pro de   -   func-tis as - sis e - is pro - pi - ti - us.

vul - ne - ra pan - de ci - ti - us pa - tri pro tu - o fa - mu - lo

ut - fru - a - tur u - ber - ri - us tu - i per - en ne gau - di - o.

MCH, Ex 307A

VENI EMMANUEL
LM with refrain

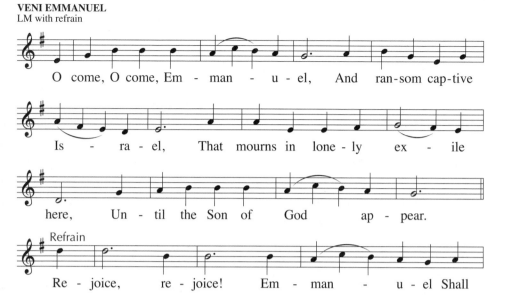

Text: Latin hymn, 12th c.; tr. John Mason Neale, 1851   Chal #119
Tune: French melody, 15th c.

2. ASSOCIATIONS OF THE EARLIEST TUNES AND THE CHURCH'S SINGING

This brief survey immediately raises general matters related both to the church's earliest tunes and to its singing more generally. *First*, chant tunes are associated with daily prayer at the beginning and end of the day, with the church year, and with the Word service of the Mass. That is, they grew out of the church's worship in its daily, yearly, and weekly (Sunday) rhythms.

Second, they are closely attached to texts and to their use in worship, which suggests that they stem from the inner essence of the church's message, meaning, and being. They are intrinsic, not extrinsic, to the church. They are generated from the inside out, not from the outside in. They point to the integrity of the church's song and its distinct sound, not to a derivative external sound superimposed on the church's being from without. That does not mean musical elements of the culture were absent or unused, an obvious impossibility, though the early church's rejection of instruments points to a turning away from the culture's music. Nor does it mean chants are fundamentally about word painting, though word painting is not absent from them. It means the church created a synthesis of sound that expressed its integrity, with musical elements constructed to articulate the flow of worship. (This last point can best be appreciated when the chant repertoire is viewed as a whole, its strophic pieces seen in conjunction with non-strophic ones, and its various settings of the same non-strophic text for use at different points in the Mass compared with one another.)

Third, several elements make most of these tunes congregational, meant not for professional musicians, but for normal people to sing without training. One element, closely related to their connection to texts, is that they are vocal. They are conceived for human voices and stand on their own without any need of instrumental assistance. A second element is their central stepwise motion. Leaps are rare and never exceed a fourth or fifth. Leaps that do occur are carefully prepared so that untrained singers can accommodate them. Third, the range of the tunes is narrow, usually a sixth or less, possibly a seventh. Fourth, a regular structure means that the tune, once learned, can be repeated easily to different words that fit the structure.

The sequence and the trope are exceptions. VICTIMAE PASCHALI has more difficult leaps, stretches itself over a range of an octave and a fourth, and is irregular. Not surprisingly, it is the least congregational of these tunes and points to the choral stratum of chant. DIVINUM MYSTERIUM also has a range of an octave and a fourth, but is regular and contains less difficult leaps. Not surprisingly, it is more congregational than VICTIMAE PASCHALI.

Fourth, these tunes have their grounding in a "modal" framework, that is, an ordering of pitches in melodic lines that came before our system of major and minor keys. That is why a mode and its number are often given on the hymnal page with them. The relationships of the notes in these modal melodies can be understood by arbitrarily constructing scales on the white keys of the piano,[41] from D to D (1, called dorian), E to E (3, called phrygian), F to F (5, called lydian), and G to G (7, called mixolydian). (Modes 2, 4, 6, and 8 use the same scales with adjustments in range and reciting notes and are prefixed by "hypo"—hypo dorian, hypo phrygian, etc.) I purposely said "grounding," because some chant tunes are clearly modal, while others, at least in the form we have them, are major or minor. PANGE LINGUA, for example, is obviously Mode 3 (phrygian). DIVINUM MYSTERIUM, however, though often listed as Mode 5 (lydian), is just as obviously what we call major. VICTIMAE PASCHALI LAUDES, as I indicated above, is presumably dorian but avoids the dorian characteristic. What is the point here? Some chant tunes, while profoundly vocal and congregational, may nonetheless feel ancient to us because of their modal character. Others may feel less so. Some may have gravitated toward our major and minor keys in spite of what the listed mode seems to suggest.[42]

Fifth, we employ keyboard instruments for almost all of our music, including our hymn tunes, and our keyboard instruments are almost always equally tempered. These early tunes would have been sung without that equal temperament. It is worth observing that choirs or congregations who sing for extensive periods without keyboard help naturally gravitate to unequal temperaments. Though this may seem like an arcane matter, it has to do with the actual sound of a group and is quite practical.

Sixth, Routley thought that "congregational singing was unknown" in the church until the late Middle Ages and that chant tunes were professional chamber music sung by monks alone.[43] I think he was wrong. The New Testament references,[44] the Pliny-Trajan correspondence cited in Chapter I, the testimony of Clement of Rome and Ignatius of Antioch,[45] the hymns Ambrose wrote for the people,[46] and the hardy congregational character of the tunes we have (even if they bear only the remotest relation to the earliest models) all suggest otherwise. It is surely true that this matter is fraught with great difficulty, as McKinnon has shown.[47] It is very hard if not impossible to nail down with precision who sang what and how it was sung. Nicholas Temperley may be right that the conscious integration of the vernacular hymn into Christian worship "began only with the Reformation,"[48] though disagreement about that is possible. But those are all different matters from suggesting that congregational singing was unknown. It may have been different from what we know, and there surely was no large body of hymns or hymnbooks comparable to ours. But people without written documents in "oral cultures" have well-developed memories. Long before chant was written down, it was carried by the church in its oral memory. Formulas like what we call psalm tones are ancient and essentially congregational in nature. When monks as choirs came into the picture, they could have helped as well as hindered congregational singing. People can sing refrains or other hymnic fragments in alternation with choirs or cantors. Singing may not have been as "together" as our artistic post-nineteenth-century choral practice tends to make us assume. And the practice may have varied as widely as ours does.

Seventh, Routley is onto something important in his discussion of rhythm and its tie to the human body.[49] Whether the usual distinction he makes between "non-bodily" music in and "bodily" music out of the church can be maintained quite as tightly as he suggests may be questioned, however, because a congregational group that sings a melody will bend it to a rhythm that invariably has bodily characteristics.[50] If it is true that only monks sang as professional choirs in the worship of the church until the late Middle Ages, it may be that a "beat" and the body could be counteracted, though even that may be a stretch. If wider assemblies of the church sang, as I think likely, it would seem impossible to avoid bodily pulsations of some sort. The question, finally, is whether the "non-material" nineteenth-century understanding of chant taken by Solesmes, which invariably colors our analysis, accurately reflects historical practice prior to the nineteenth century,[51] or whether a variety of practices has prevailed before and since then. My hunch is that a wide variety of practices has prevailed in response to various cultural and ethnic settings. I suspect Walter Buszin was right when he noted that "in the great [hymn tunes] of the Church" rhythm is "always basic and present" in such a way so as not to dominate and "becloud" the living voice of the Gospel "in order to extol itself."[52] The rhythm, however—as in chant, chorales, Genevan psalm tunes, and twentieth-century tunes—pushes toward the irregular rather than the regular because regularity symbolized by the tyranny of the bar line is too "earthbound."[53] Music at worship tends to suspend the regularity of earthly metrical pulsation with a transcendent vision. When tunes move toward equal notes and motor rhythms become a cultural musical control as in the eighteenth century, the irregular tendencies seek expression outside the congregation's orbit as in the harmonizations and cross rhythms of J. S. Bach's music. We shall return to this topic in connection with the dance at the end of this chapter and in Chapter V.

Eighth, the only way to get at questions about who sang when, and how it sounded, is to do detailed research in very specific and narrowly defined times and places among a variety of Christian assemblies—rural and urban, large and small, cathedral and parish,[54] rich and poor, of various classes and ethnicities, and in various mixes.[55] Even then little conclusive evidence is likely to be found. The singing of Christians assembled for worship has seldom gotten into the record.[56] Even when it has left a trace, it has at best been only imperfectly described in words since its character and context come and go just like music itself at worship. Preachers, their written sermons; musicians, their written pieces; and accounts of worship or choirs, legal documents, and historical evidence of one sort or another that we keep seldom tell us about a congregation's singing. When it is mentioned, we often get tantalizing incompleteness or secondary importance. Consider this account that John Adams (1735–1826), as a member of the Continental Congress, wrote to his wife Abigail about St. Mary's Catholic Church in Philadelphia.

> The music, consisting of an organ and a choir of singers, went all the afternoon except sermon time, and the assembly chanted most sweetly and exquisitely.[57]

Or, consider Plymouth Congregational Church in Brooklyn in the middle of the nineteenth century where the record of the people's singing has been left to us because of the high profile of the preacher and the musician, Henry Ward Beecher (1813–1887) and John Zundel (1815–1882). (See Chapter XII for more about this.) The small, low profile congregation—especially among the poor and the dispossessed—where the singing may be the strongest, seldom gets into the historical record.[58] How many of these assemblies there have been in the course of the church's history we will never know.

3. *LEISEN*

As noted earlier, one of the congregational tunes spawned by VICTIMAE PASCHALI LAUDES is CHRIST IST ERSTANDEN.[59] It represents a genre of German vernacular folk hymns called *Leisen* because of the repetition of some form, often shortened, of "Kyrie eleison" (sometimes modified to "Alleluia") at the end of each stanza. Still found in a number of our hymnals with characteristic variations, CHRIST IST ERSTANDEN with its text dates from the twelfth century or earlier and was sung by the people at festivals and at the Mass—sometimes as a vernacular trope that alternated with a choir or a cantor singing the Latin sequence "Victimae paschali laudes" on which it is based. It originally had a single stanza, but it stimulated additional ones by writers like Michael Weisse (1480–1534) of the Bohemian Brethren. Martin Luther (1483–1546) especially liked this hymn and made an adaptation of it, which we will encounter later.

CHRIST IST ERSTANDEN
PM

Christ is a - ris - en From the grave's dark pris - on. So let our joy
rise full and free; Christ our com - fort true will be. Al - le - lu - ia!
Were Christ not a - ris - en, Then death were still our pris - on.
Now, with him to life re - stored, We praise the Fa - ther of our Lord.
Al - le - lu - ia! Al - le - lu - ia, al - le - lu - ia,
al - le - lu - ia! Now let our joy rise full and free;
Christ our com - fort true will be. Al - le - lu - ia!

Text: German hymn, c. 1100; tr. Martin L. Seltz, 1909-1967, alt., © Concordia Publishing House
Tune: J. Klug, *Geistliche Lieder*, 1533

LBW #136

Several features of this tune are noteworthy. First, it balances stepwise motion with carefully structured leaps of thirds and fourths. Second, it has a rhythmic kick that allows singers to express the jubilation of the Easter message. The eighth note pickup at the beginning of the third, seventh, ninth, and fourteenth phrases employs a common German musical hiccup. (Some hymnals remove this delight.) The syncopation on the "Alleluia" at phrases 5, 10, and 16 are outbursts of joy. Third, the more melismatic "Alleluias" at phrases 11–13 give the voice a chance to glide along in the pleasure of a delightful vocalise. Fourth, the tune ranges just over an octave, but prepares the extremities in such a way that the whole piece becomes an engagement in vocal pleasure and not a snare.

There are a number of other *Leisen*. They generally appear today only in hymnals with a Germanic Lutheran heritage since Luther added stanzas and, with his right-hand musical man Johann Walter (1496–1570), adapted the tunes. Examples include GELOBET SEIST DU,[60] MITTEN WIR IN LEBEN SIND,[61] and NUN BITTEN WIR.[62]

4. *CANTIOS* AND CAROLS

CHRIST IST ERSTANDEN is associated with the liturgy. There are also medieval tunes not originally tied to the liturgy called *Cantios*, which Konrad Ameln distinguishes from chant tunes because of their "songlike character."[63] QUEM PASTORES and NUNC ANGELORUM, with similar beginning lines, are among these and are still in use. They originally had Latin texts and took on German (and then English) ones.

QUEM PASTORES
8 8 8 7

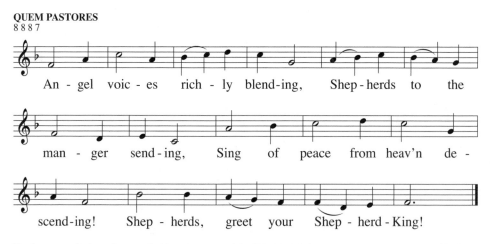

Text: *Quem pastores laudavere;* German carol, 15th c.; adapt. by James Quinn, SJ, b.1919, © 1969   Wor3 #395
Tune: German Carol, 15th c.

NUNC ANGELORUM
Irregular

The glo-rious an - gels came to - day, A - glow with light in-
To shep-herds who by moon's bright ray Did in the field o'er

to the night of dark - ness deep, "Joy, great joy and
sheep their si - lent vig - il keep,

tid - ings glad We bring from heav'n re - sound - ing, For

you, for you and all the world a - bound - ing."

Text: German carol, 14th c.; tr. composite, © 1969, Concordia Publishing House
Tune: German carol, 14th c.

LBW #68

Ameln saw mixed language carols as forming "a connecting link" between chant tunes and *Cantios*. IN DULCI JUBILO is the tune for one of these "macaronic" carols, which joyously and unself-consciously mixes Latin with the vernacular—in this case the German in a dialect from the area of Mainz and Worms. Text and tune probably come from the fourteenth century and are still in wide use today. Though dance has been suggested to some, the hymn and its tune may or may not have been linked with dance in their origins. However that may be, the catchy melody bounces along in a triple rhythm that is easily sung and danced. The fundamentally stepwise motion is at first broken only by a rising third and a downward fifth, which prepare the delightful swing of the upward fifth in the second last phrase. The melody outlines the tonic chord, if one can use that terminology in this early music, with a hint at the relative minor as the phrase with the upward leap begins.

IN DULCI JUBILO
6 6 7 7 7 8 5 5

Good Chris-tian friends, re - joice With heart and soul and voice;

Give ye heed to what we say: Je - sus Christ is born to-day.

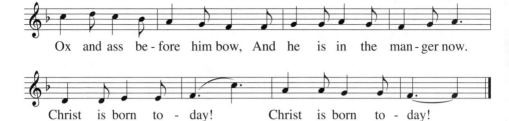

Ox and ass be-fore him bow, And he is in the man-ger now.

Christ is born to - day! Christ is born to - day!

Text: German/Latin, medieval; tr. John M. Neale, 1853, alt.   PsH #355
Tune: German, 14th c.

GREENSLEEVES is often called an English "carol," though "the word 'carol' admits of so many definitions that any anthologist needs to establish a set of criteria that will govern selection."[64] The layout of *The New Oxford Book of Carols* by texts suggests that they, not their tunes, are definitive. Carols have not been much used in church services until recently. What is called "carol-singing" dates from the late nineteenth century and relates to a broad array of Christmas music, which inevitably includes GREENSLEEVES. This tune first comes into view in 1580 in England, but the assumption is usually made that it was well known before that.[65] It is a haunting minor melody whose ambivalent sixth degree, when sharped, implies dorian and whose naturally flatted seventh degree, while strongly emphasized at the beginning of the refrain, also ambivalently moves to its sharpened position. The placement of these alterations varies and gives the tune different casts. Here is one version.

GREENSLEEVES
8 7 8 7 with refrain

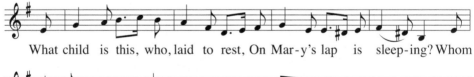

What child is this, who, laid to rest, On Mar-y's lap is sleep-ing? Whom

an - gels greet with an-thems sweet, While shep-herds watch are keep-ing?

This, this is Christ the King, Whom shep-herds guard and an-gels sing;

Haste, haste to bring him laud, The babe, the son of Mar - y.

Text: William C. Dix, 1837-1898   H82 #115
Tune: English melody; harm. *Christmas Carols New and Old*, 1871

Perspective: Congregational Song, Dance, and the Body

It may be that carols have been on the periphery of the church's song at worship partially because their texts provide ambiance as much as theological content and because of their more regular metric character, but also because congregational song has been divided from dance in the West. This brings us back to the human body.

If a tradition assumes that the body is to be denied at worship, the embodied nature of sound will in some way also be denied, and a disembodied sound of some sort will be sought. If a tradition assumes, on the other hand, that dance is central to worship, there will be a rhythmic character to the sound that works out of the nature of dance, but not necessarily an embodiment that relates to the essential dynamic of the congregation's voice—unless the two have been held together as in some non-Western cultures by sensitively subtle drumming. This leads to the following thoughts.

There is no doubt that one or the other of the two perspectives just enunciated has been a theological force with a musical influence. In the West probably more denial than embrace of the body has been present, and, for good or ill, dance has been separated from worship. The theological force and its musical influence cannot be minimized, but two other forces should not be overlooked or minimized either. One is the essential dynamic of the congregation's voice. The other is the nature of Christian worship where a transcendent vision tends to suspend earthbound metrical regularity. The congregation's voice has its own character and integrity, which, though influenced by the narrower theological themes and musical practices of a given tradition, nonetheless paradoxically trumps them by its very being and by the overriding character of Christian worship itself.

The incarnational nature of the Christian faith receives embodiment not only in Word, sacraments, and vocations, but in the bodily voice of the people at worship. That voice, unless it is squelched, takes on a rhythmic shape. It is not the rhythmic shape that denies the body, nor is it the rhythmic shape that looks outside itself to dance or other regular metrical shapes. It proceeds from its own inner dynamic where pulsation is present in all sorts of patterns, but dance-like regularity is not a central feature. That is why hymnals often print hymn tunes without meter signatures, which are more allied to eighteenth- and nineteenth-century instrumental forms and the "tyranny of the bar line" than they are to the character of hymn singing and its freer "tactus" at worship.

If you observe people who lead congregational song well either from the organ or by voice and gesture, you notice a rhythmic quality that is not on the printed page. All music performed well has this quality, of course, which is why good music teachers always talk about getting music "off the printed page." Congregational singing has its own unique feature in this regard. Sensitive dance band instrumentalists who play for congregational singing soon realize they have to adjust to it, or they will sap the assembly's singing. Organists and other congregational song leaders who try to articulate thoughts about this invariably speak of the rhythm of hymn singing as something that cannot be put into words, is not exactly metronomic, and cannot be measured precisely. It has to do with the nature of communal breathing and can perhaps be defined, for lack of a better term, as congregational drag transformed by Christian vision. It is the ordinary musical capacity of humanity made new. I do not mean the term "drag" negatively. I mean it as a uniquely positive and distinctively wonderful quality. It is something that pulls across the time and space of a singing assembly, a big sonic envelope whose individual pulsations come together in unexpected and surprisingly unified ways. It can spin into a powerful rhythmic drive, but even then its vocal center is not exactly metronomic or the same as dance.

Some cultures have held dance and song together by drumming. In that circumstance, the voice of the people is still protected, usually with surprisingly complex irregularity. The church in the West has pulled them apart, and each has assumed its own dynamic. In that circumstance it is no accident that vocal rather than dance-like associations have been paramount for the congregation's song.

5. THROUGH *PIAE CANTIONES*

DIVINUM MYSTERIUM, discussed above, comes to us through *Piae Cantiones*, printed in 1582. Theodoric Petri (or Theodoric Peter), from the Swedish-speaking province in southern Finland called Nyland (now Uusimaa), pulled together what he called "Sacred Songs of Church and Cloister of the clergy of past ages, in common use in the Renowned Realm of Sweden, newly and accurately revised and corrected."[66] This book fell into the hands of John Mason Neale (1818–1866)—English linguist, liturgical scholar, and remarkable translator of Greek and Latin hymnody—who wrote "Good King Wenceslas" for one of its tunes, TEMPUS ADEST FLORIDUM. The tune may come from the fourteenth century and sometimes is paired with "Gentle Mary Laid Her Child." It is a jolly melody in a major key. Like NUNC ANGELORUM, it repeats the first phrase in "bar form," which will be described in more detail in the next chapter. After the repeat, the tune reaches up to the fifth, comes down the scale by step, and then repeats that figure in the last phrase.

TEMPUS ADEST FLORIDUM
7 6 7 6 D

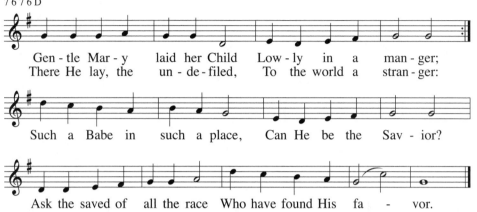

Gen - tle Mar - y   laid her Child   Low - ly   in   a   man - ger;
There He lay, the   un - de - filed,   To   the world a   stran - ger:

Such   a   Babe   in   such   a   place,   Can   He   be   the   Sav - ior?

Ask   the   saved   of   all   the   race   Who   have   found   His   fa - vor.

Text: Joseph Simpson Cook, 1859-1933
Tune: *A Spring Carol*, c. 14th c.

Bap #101

Several other tunes still in common use come to us through this same collection. PERSONENT HODIE has its origins in the fourteenth century.

PERSONENT HODIE
6 6 6 6 6 with refrain

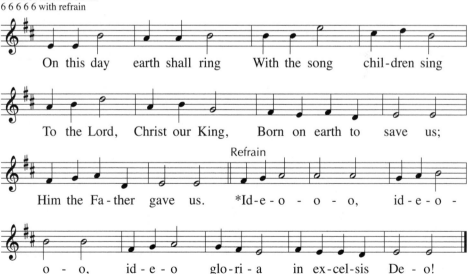

On   this   day   earth   shall   ring   With   the   song   chil-dren   sing

To   the   Lord,   Christ   our   King,   Born   on   earth   to   save   us;

Refrain

Him   the   Fa - ther   gave   us.   *Id-e - o - o - o,   id - e - o -

o - o,   id - e - o   glo - ri - a   in   ex-cel-sis   De - o!

*therefore

Text: *Piae Cantiones*, 1582; tr. Jane M. Joseph
Tune: *Piae Cantiones*, 1582

Meth #248

PUER NOBIS, which we join to many texts, comes from the fifteenth century.

PUER NOBIS
LM

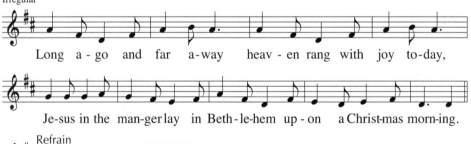

Text: Latin, 5th c.   H82 #193
Tune: Trier MS., 15th c.; adapt. Michael Praetorius, 1571-1621

RESONET IN LAUDIBUS comes from a sixteenth-century source, the *Geistliche Lieder* of 1543 by the Wittenberg printer Joseph Klug, but it may have fourteenth-century origins. It has relationships with IN DULCI JUBILO and QUEM PASTORES and takes various forms.[67] Ameln applies *Cantios* to both PUER NOBIS and RESONET IN LAUDIBUS.[68]

RESONET IN LAUDIBUS
Irregular

Text: Edward Traill Horn III, 1909-1994; © 1958, Service Book & Hymnal. Ref.; tr. Percy Dearmer, 1867-1935,   Cov #185
      © 1928, Oxford University Press. Words admin. Augsburg Fortress
Tune: German melody, 14th c.

PUER NOBIS and TEMPUS ADEST FLORIDUM glide along mostly by step. RESONET IN LAUDIBUS is triadic like IN DULCI JUBILO, but goes down rather than up. PERSONENT HODIE strides immediately up a fifth and then to the upper octave, but the leaps are balanced in the refrain by stepwise motion and repeated notes. The repeated rhythm drives the tune forward. It is balanced by two sets of delightful rhythmic extensions that pull rather than push (one repeated at the end of the stanzas and the end of the refrain in measures 7–8, 9–10, and 17–18, and the other repeated at the beginning of the refrain at measures 11–12 and 13–14). All of these tunes have a muscular and disciplined folk energy, which, while attractive and engaging, does not call attention to itself so as to hamper the text and the singers. These tunes ride text and singers along in secure yet gleeful abandon.

---

1   Various attempts have been made to reconstruct some of this music, one of the most recent by a group called SAVAE (San Antonio Vocal Arts Ensemble). See their CD called *Ancient Echoes*, available through World Library Publications, Schiller Park, Illinois, ISBN-1-58549-164-1.

2   For settings of the *Phos Hilaron*, see H82 #s 25, 26, and 36; LBW, page 143 and #279; PsH #s 548 and 549; Meth #686; and Wor3 #679.

3   Martin Luther, "An Order of Mass and Communion," *Luther's Works*, vol. 53, trans. Joseph A. Jungmann, ed. Julian Fernandes (Philadelphia: Fortress Press, 1965), 36. Mary Ellen Evans, *The Mass: An Historical, Theological, and Pastoral Survey* (Collegeville: The Liturgical Press, 1976), 224–226 sketches a similar initial congregational orientation, which developed into magnificent sixteenth-century choral polyphonic settings, valuable for occasional feast-days in cathedrals but regrettably attempted Sunday after Sunday in city and country in a "grand façade," which could only "in some measure" compensate "for the personal experience of the mystery that was denied many people and for entry into the sanctum to which they no longer had access."

4   There are those, Marilyn Stulken among them (correspondence, June 17, 2004), who wager that at some point or points in this period instruments were used by some people in church. This is possible, but the evidence is hard to find. See David W. Music, *Instruments in Church: A Collection of Source Documents* (Lanham: The Scarecrow Press, Inc., 1998); Johannes Quasten, *Music and Worship in Pagan & Christian Antiquity* (Washington: National Association of Pastoral Musicians, 1973), 98–99 and 126–127 (and the rest of the book); James McKinnon, *Music in Early Christian Literature* (Cambridge: Cambridge University Press, 1987); and Quentin Faulkner, *Wiser Than Despair: The Evolution of Ideas in the Relationship of Music and the Christian Church* (Westport: Greenwood Press, 1996), Chapter 4.

5   There is no attempt here to cover the Eastern tradition. For some insights into it, see the first chapter of Vladimir Morosan, *Choral Performance in Pre-Revolutionary Russia* (Madison: Musica Russica, 1994, rev. of 1984).

6   See, for example, Richard J. Schuler, "The Congregation: Its Possibilities and Limitations in Singing," *Cum Angelis Canere*, ed. Robert A. Skeris (St. Paul: Catholic Church Music Associates, 1990), 321.

7   For rhythmic issues see S. John Blackley, "Rhythmic Interpretation of Chant," ed. Glover, *The Hymnal 1982 Companion*, hereafter H82C, I, 238–252.

8   That we are dealing with stanzaic hymns immediately indicates a Western linguistic context. The repetition of different texts to the same tune does not work so well in Asian and African "tonal" languages. See Hawn, *Gather into One*, 84 and 108.

9   See James W. McKinnon, "Ambrose," *The New Grove Dictionary of Music and Musicians*, I, ed. Stanley Sadie (London: Macmillan Publishers Limited, 1980), 313–314, hereafter NGDMM.

10   Tom R. Ward, "The Office Hymn," Glover, H82C, I, 269.

11   Ibid., 272.

12   Joan A. Fyock, comp., *Hymnal Companion Prepared by Churches in the Believers Tradition* (Elgin: Brethren Press, 1996), 79, hereafter HCHWB.

13   Text and tune are given together in LBW #277 and CW #595. H82 #217 gives another more complex version of the tune—or a different tune with the same name. Routley, MCH, Ex. 3, gives the tune as in LBW and CW with one alteration.

14   For other translations with more florid tunes, see H82 #s 44 and 45.

15   Routley, MCH, 11B.

16   Chal #127, H82 #60; HWB #177; LBW #323; Meth #692, Pres #4, Wor3 #368.

17   As in H82 #26 and Pres #548. The *Phos Hilaron* is one of the most ancient hymns of the church, which the East has revered more than the West. (See Keith A. Falconer, "The Development of Plainchant to the Counter Reformation," Glover, H82C, I, 161. A description of the lamp-lighting ceremony in the early church that this hymn accompanied can be found in Gregory Dix, *The Shape of the Liturgy* [London: Dacre Press, 1960, 1st ed., 1945], 87.) For a survey of the many English translations, see M. Eleanor Irwin, "PHOS HILARON: The Metamorphoses of a Greek Christian Hymn," *The Hymn* 40:2 (April 1989): 7–12.

18   Chal #378, NC #111, Pres #168, VU 743.

19   As indicated in the first chapter, examples are taken from the fourteen hymnals and left to stand, from here on without comment, as they are given in those books. This tune is listed as Mode 1, that is, dorian (see below for a discussion of modes), but it is minor.

20   Another possibility can be found at H82 #61.

21   The text is at LBW #118, the tune at LBW #120 with the text of the same name by Thomas Aquinas (1227–1274). The text and tune (varied from the LBW version) are together in H82 #166 and HWB #256. A different tune with the same name is used at H82 #165. The tune with Aquinas's text is given at Wor3 #813.

22   LBW #120.

23   For the tune with its Latin text, see Wor3 #479. For English and French versions, see VU #200. For various settings with English, see Chal #269 (paraphrased text), Cov #281, H82 #502, LBW #472, Meth #651 (the source of the example given here), and Pres #125,

24   J. Michael Thompson, "Sequence," *Worship Music: A Concise Dictionary*, 278.

25   Ibid.

26   See Michael Edgar Krentz, "The Use of Sequences in German Lutheran Churches during the Sixteenth Century," DM Research Project (Evanston: Northwestern University, 1981), 3.

27   H82 #183, LBW #137.

28   H82 #226 and Wor3 #857, the tune of which should not be confused with the tunes of the same name by Jacques Berthier and Samuel Webbe.

29   H82 #320.

30   CW #209. For the tune more commonly associated with this text, see *The Liber Usualis* (New York: Desclee Company, 1959), 1810, or Kyriale (New York: J Fischer & Bro., 1927), 96.

31   See John D. Witvliet, *Worship Seeking Understanding: Windows into Christian Practice* (Grand Rapids: Baker Academic, 2003), p. 219.

32   The "Dies Irae" melody can be found in the *Liber Usualis*, 1810–1813, and in modern notation in Robert Chase, *Dies Irae: A Guide to Requiem Music* (Lanham: The Scarecrow Press, Inc., 2003), 645.

33   See Louis Weil, "Of the Father's Love Begotten," Glover, H82C, 3A, 155–156, for the Latin text. The Latin with an English translation that does not shy away from male pronouns is given in Hugh Keyte and Andrew Parrott, *The New Oxford Book of Carols* (Oxford: Oxford University Press, 1992), 53–57.

34   NC, #118. Unfortunately this version removes the five-note melisma three phrases from the end.

35   *The Hymnal As Authorized and Approved for Use by the General Convention of the Episcopal Church . . . MCMXVI* (New York: The Church Pension Fund, 1933), #74.

36   For more detail, see David Music, "Of the Father's Love Begotten," Glover, H82C, 3A, 82, and Keyte and Parrott, 58.

37   Originally "Draw Nigh, Draw Nigh, Emmanuel."

38   Routley, 89B–90A.

39   Keyte and Parrot, 45.

40   The clef and text in the example from Routley, MCH, Ex 307A, are corrected here and a flat added at "ne" of "vulnera," as in Keyte and Parrot, *The New Oxford Book of Carols*, 43 (though one could wonder if the whole tune was originally dorian). For a copy of the beginning of the original, see Manuel Erviti, "O come, O come, Emmanuel," Glover, H82C, 3A, 106.

41   They can begin on any pitch and have sharps or flats to keep the relationships between whole steps and half steps the same, just like major and minor keys. Using the white keys is a convenient way to see the pitch relationships easily, just as using the white keys from C to C shows the relationships for a major key and A to A the relationships for a minor one.

42   A few years ago some students asked me for a list of representative tunes for modal, major, minor, and pentatonic (five pitch) tunes. Finding examples was not difficult for everything but lydian. (Some examples are: NOEL NOUVELET [VU #186] for dorian, AUS TIEFER NOT [HWB #133] for phrygian, VENI CREATOR [Pres #125] for mixolydian, VENI, EMMANUEL [Cov #120] for minor, ein feste burg [H82 #687-8] for major, NEW BRITAIN [Chal #546] for pentatonic). The only lydian tune I could find (or that my students have been able to find—they have joined the search) is a recent one, KIT SMART by Alec Wyton at H82 #491. There may be older tunes that were lydian (ADORO TE DEVOTE – LBW #199, and DIVINUM MYSTERIUM – LBW #42, are marked that way, but they are major as they stand; and ES IST GENUG – CW #158, begins as lydian, but does not stay there), but they are not evident today.

43   Routley, MCH, p. 9.

44   See Paul Westermeyer, *Te Deum: The Church and Music* (Minneapolis: Fortress, 1998), 39–61.

45   Ibid., 62.

46   See Augustine, *Confessions*, IX, vii.

47   See James McKinnon, *Music in Early Christian Literature* (Cambridge: Cambridge University Press, 1987), 7–11.

48   Nicholas Temperley, "Hymn IV. Protestant," NGDMM, 8, p. 846. "Vernacular" and "integral" are at issue here. If one simultaneously thinks, as Temperley suggests, that Calvin founded his "reformed worship on the practice of the primitive church" or that Luther thought that was what he was doing, those terms may be applicable long before the Reformation.

49   Routley, MCH, 12.

50   R. John Blackley, "Rhythmic Interpretation of Chant," Glover, H82C, 1, 242, suggests tunes were not organized in regularly recurring patterns of longs and shorts, but matched the regular syllabic rhythm of the texts, which he distinguishes from free syllabic rhythm. Whatever these three forms might be, and whether or not in practice they interacted with one another to form a fourth possibility, a bodily rhythmic pulsation of some sort is unavoidable.

51   For Solesmes, rhythm is "an act of the mind" and not "something material." See Dom Joseph Gajard, *The Solesmes Method*, trans. R. Cecile Gabain (Collegeville: The Liturgical Press, 1960). Gustave Reese's analysis of this issue still is worth pondering: Gustave Reese, *Music in the Middle Ages* (New York: W. W. Norton & Company, 1940), 140–148.

52   Quoted in Daniel Zager, "Popular Music and Music for the Church," *Lutheran Forum* 36:3 (Fall 2002): 24.

53   I am grateful to William Mahrt for articulating this insight at the Gregorian Chant Workshop, Cathedral Basilica of Saint Mary, Minneapolis, Minnesota, September 11, 2004.

54   For a study of parish music in a later period, see Nicholas Temperley, *The Music of the English Parish Church* (Cambridge: Cambridge University Press, 1979). Temperley's "Historical Introduction" in HTI, I, also gets at these matters.

55   These questions may be regarded as subsets of what we now call inculturation. Peter Jeffery, "A Chant Historian Reads *Liturgiam Authenticam*," *Worship* 78:3 (May 2004): 240, says "that much of this history is still little known and barely researched," and our faulty tendency to pit "tradition" against "inculturation" makes it difficult for us to formulate the research questions that have to be asked.

56   There are notable exceptions in our period when we have been more concerned to study and document what worshiping congregations have sung, and when we have recording techniques to freeze it. *The Hymn: A Journal of Congregational Song* of The Hymn Society in the United States and Canada has numerous articles about actual congregational singing. An unofficial tape of the Old Regular Baptists from Blackey, Kentucky, singing at the Hymn Society meeting in Princeton, New Jersey, on June 10, 1982, gives a good illustration of their singing without being filtered through carefully controlled recording grids. But it still, of necessity, leaves out their worshiping context. Jeff Todd Titon and Kenneth M. George, *Powerhouse for God* (Chapel Hill: The University of North Carolina Press, 1982), 0-8078-4084-X, is a recording with a booklet that documents actual worship services at Fellowship Independent Baptist Church in Stanley, Virginia in 1977 and 1978. Here one gets a better recording than the unofficial Old Regular Baptist one, and the recording provides as much context as possible without actually being there. A similar recording and booklet in the same American Folklore Series is Bret Sutton and Pete Hartman, *Primitive Baptist Hymns of the Blue Ridge* (Chapel Hill: The University of North Carolina Press), 0-8078-4083-1. Remarkable attempts to reconstruct actual historical services with all their music (including the congregation's singing) have been made by Paul McCreesh with the Gabrieli Consort and Players: *Bach Epiphany Mass c. 1740* (Hamburg: Deutsche Grammophon, 1988), Archiv 457 631-2; *Praetorius Christmette, Lutheran Mass for Christmas Morning as It Might Have Been Celebrated around 1620* (Hamburg: Deutsche Grammophon, 1994), Archiv 439 931-2; and *Schütz Christmas Vespers as It Might Have Been Celebrated at the Court of Dresden c. 1664* (Hamburg: Deutsche Grammophon, 1999), Archiv 289 463 046-2. The actual contexts are, of course, absent, and a congregational "choir" functions as the congregation.

57   Quoted from http://www.ushistory.org/tour/tour_stmary.htm.

58   Temperley, HTI, I, 12, for example, says "[m]any small town [eighteenth-century English] churches undoubtedly went on singing the old psalm tunes with little or no professional assis-tance, because of their relative poverty and their isolation from the fashions of the metropolis."

59   Another version of this tune is called SURGIT IN HAEC DIES (Wor3 #452).

60   CW #33, LBW #48.

61   CW #534, LBW #350.

62   CW #190, LBW #317.

63   Konrad Ameln, *The Roots of German Hymnody of the Reformation Era* (St. Louis: Concordia Publishing House, 1964), 12.

64 Keyte and Parrot, *The New Oxford Book of Carols*, xii. In Westermeyer, Te Deum, 134–137, I have attempted to summarize some of the obscure complexity carols pose, and Alan Luff does it in "The Carol," Glover, H82C, 282–287.

65 In Keyte and Parrot, *The New Oxford Book of Carols*, it is first given in the nineteenth century with Dix's text, "What Child Is This."

66 Routley, MCH, 18, gives the complete title and details.

67 Zahn, MDEK, 5, #s 8573–8575, gives some of these.

68 Ameln, 13.

III. Chorale Tunes

1. Chorales

It is often presumed to be self-evident that Martin Luther was a popular panderer who asked why the devil should have all the good tunes and raided the bars for his music. Apart from assuming sacred and secular distinctions that "did not exist"[1] at the time, if you look for sources to support assertions like these you quickly discover, as Routley says, that there is no truth in what he called such "slanders."[2] (Bars do not deserve such slanders either.) "The very last thing Luther was, or could have been, was what we now call an adapter of popular styles."[3] The word "popular" itself is hard to apply since it meant something more inclusive and deep-seated than our meaning.[4] Luther made some pointed comments that set God's "noble, wholesome, and cheerful creation" of music against the "perverted minds who prostitute this lovely gift of nature and art with their erotic rantings." He advised that "special care" be taken to shun the latter.[5] For worship[6] he and those around and after him deepened the congregational character of tunes in existence from chant and *Leisen*; drew on German folk songs, art songs, and *contrafacta* (pieces where one text is substituted for another while keeping the same tune); and wrote new tunes. In these ways they extended the church's congregational music into "chorales."

"Chorales" are vernacular German congregational hymns that stem from the sixteenth-century Reformation. Derived from the German word *Choral*, meaning Gregorian chant (plainsong)—or sometimes seen as derived from *choraliter*, that is, in the manner of chant, namely, unison and unaccompanied— the term is a bit imprecise because it can refer to both text and tune or tune alone.

Chorales represent a continuation of the Germanic heritage of hymn singing among the people, stimulated by the reforming activity of Martin Luther and his conscious effort on behalf of the people's song. His work influenced the course of hymnody in the Western church, remains in use, and continues to stimulate new tunes.

Since chorale tunes are named for, and associated with, particular texts that build on the church's historic liturgical practice, especially in relation to Word and table on Sunday, they developed naturally in three categories: the Ordinary of the Mass, the Proper of the Mass, and the Church Year.

2. THE ORDINARY OF THE MASS

The parts of the Ordinary of the Mass were among the first pieces cast into the vernacular for the congregation. Choirs still sang choral settings of the Ordinary in Latin while the congregation had vernacular settings it could sing, and the mix made possible all sorts of combinations: 1) a service completely in Latin, 2) a service completely in German, 3) the substitution of a German chorale for any portion of a Latin text, 3) the substitution of a German chorale for any Latin or German prose text, 4) the addition of a German chorale to any Latin or German prose text, 5) additions of German chorales to the Mass, either before or after the sermon, or during communion.[7] The congregation's tunes for the vernacular texts were conceived in unison without accompaniment like their chant predecessors, and the ones for the Ordinary were adapted from the church's heritage. The following are among those in use today.

Kyrie eleison

KYRIE GOTT VATER was adapted, possibly by the pastor Johann Spangenberg (1484–1550), from the ninth-century trope, "Kyrie, fons bonitatis."[8] This piece remains a through-composed trope cast into the vernacular, not a metrical hymn.

KYRIE, GOTT VATER
PM

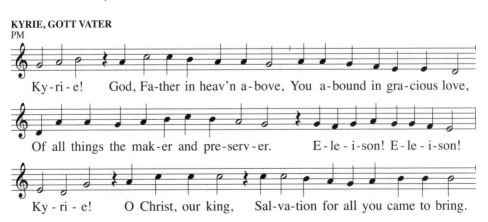

Ky-ri-e!   God, Fa-ther in heav'n a-bove, You a-bound in gra-cious love,

Of all things the mak-er and pre-serv-er.   E-le-i-son! E-le-i-son!

Ky-ri-e!   O Christ, our king,   Sal-va-tion for all you came to bring.

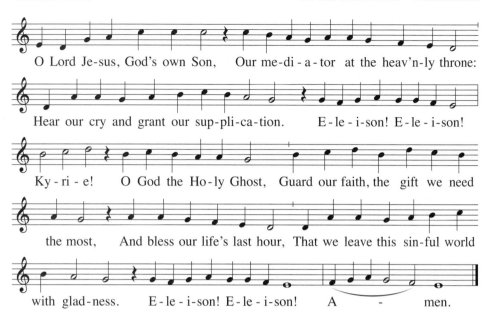

O Lord Je-sus, God's own Son,   Our me-di-a-tor at the heav'n-ly throne:

Hear our cry and grant our sup-pli-ca-tion.   E-le-i-son! E-le-i-son!

Ky-ri-e!   O God the Ho-ly Ghost,   Guard our faith, the   gift   we   need

the most,   And bless our life's last hour, That we leave this sin-ful world

with glad-ness.   E-le-i-son! E-le-i-son!   A - men.

Text: Latin, c.1100; tr. W. Gustave Polack, 1890-1950, alt., © Concordia Publishing House   LBW #168
Tune: *Kyrie fons bonitatis*, c.800, adapt.

Gloria in excelsis

ALLEIN GOTT IN DER HÖH is the tune for a metrical version of the *Gloria in Excelsis*. Tune and text are the work of the cantor, pastor, and teacher Nikolaus Decius (ca.1485–ca.1546).[9] His source for the tune was a chant setting of the *Gloria* used at Easter,[10] now given the flavor of cantios and carols and cast into bar form (see below). ALLEIN GOTT IN DER HÖH was apparently "sung for the first time on Easter Sunday, April 5, 1523, in Braunschweig."[11]

ALLEIN GOTT IN DER HÖH
8 7 8 7 8 8 7

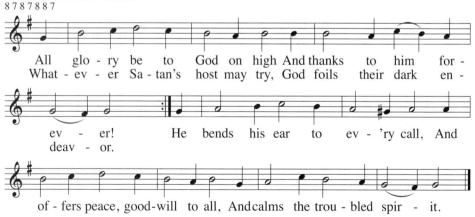

All   glo-ry be   to   God on high And thanks   to   him   for-
What-ev-er Sa-tan's host may try, God foils   their dark   en-

ev - er!   He bends his ear   to   ev-'ry call, And
deav - or.

of-fers peace, good-will to all, And calms the trou-bled spir-it.

Text: Nicolaus Decius, *Allein Gott in der Höh*, 1522, Gesang Buch, 1525; tr. Gilbert Doan, © 1978, *Lutheran Book of Worship*   HWB #122
Tune: Nicolaus Decius, 1522, *Deutsche Evangelische Messe*, 1524

Credo *(Nicene Creed)*

Luther or Johann Walter fashioned WIR GLAUBEN ALL from a fourteenth-century melody used for the Nicene Creed. (Luther expanded the single-stanza text to a three-stanza metrical version of the Creed).

The version given here comes from the first printings of the *Lutheran Book of Worship*. Later printings changed the C-natural at the end of the fourth phrase on "given" to a C-sharp, which makes it consistent with the other comparable places in the tune and friendlier to congregations. (For more about this matter, see below under *Perspective: Sacred/Secular and Modal/Tonal*.)

WIR GLAUBEN ALL
88888D

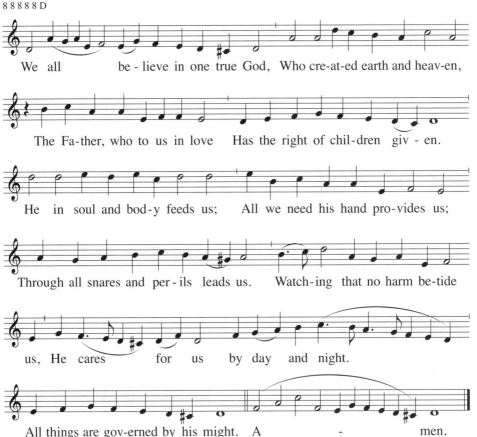

We all   be - lieve in one true God, Who cre-at-ed earth and heav-en,

The Fa-ther, who to us in love   Has the right of chil-dren giv - en.

He   in soul and bod-y feeds us;   All we need his hand pro-vides us;

Through all snares and per - ils leads us.   Watch-ing that no harm be-tide

us, He cares   for   us   by day and night.

All things are gov-erned by his might.   A   -   men.

Text: Martin Luther, 1483-1546; tr. *The Lutheran Hymnal*, alt., © 1941, Concordia Publishing House   LBW #374
Tune: Latin credo, c. 1300

Sanctus

Luther adapted JESAIA, DEM PROPHETEN from an eleventh-century chant setting of the *Sanctus.*[12] Like the *Kyrie*, this is again through-composed.

JESAIA, DEM PROPHETEN
PM

I - sa-iah in a vi-sion did of old The Lord of hosts en-

throned on high be-hold: His splen-did train was wide out-spread un-til

Its stream-ing glo-ry did the tem-ple fill. A-bove his throne the

shin-ing ser-a-phim With six-fold wings did rev-'rence un-to him:

With two each ser-aph hid his glo-rious face, And two a-bout his

feet did in-ter-lace, And with the oth-er two he soared on high;

And one un-to an-oth-er thus did cry: "Ho - ly,

Ho - ly, Ho - ly is the Lord of hosts!

His glo - ry fill-eth all the earth!" The beams and lin-tels at

their cry-ing shook, And all the house was filled with bil-lowing smoke.

Text: Martin Luther, 1483-1546; tr. Martin H. Franzmann, 1907-1976, © 1978, *Lutheran Book of Worship,* admin. by Augsburg Fortress LBW #528
Tune: Martin Luther, 1483-1546

Agnus Dei

CHRISTE DU LAMM GOTTES bears a relation to KYRIE GOTT VATER, the first Gregorian psalm tone, and therefore to the *Kyrie* Luther mentions in his "German Mass."[13]

CHRISTE, DU LAMM GOTTES
6 10 6 6 10 6 6 6 10 4

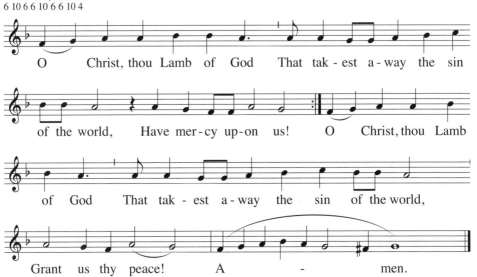

Text: German, 1528; tr. unknown
Tune: Kirchenordnung, Braunschweig, 1528

LBW #103

Another version of the *Agnus Dei* was made by Decius, O LAMM GOTTES, UNSCHULDIG. It is derived from a thirteenth-century chant setting.[14]

O LAMM GOTTES, UNSCHULDIG
7 7 7 7 7 7 8

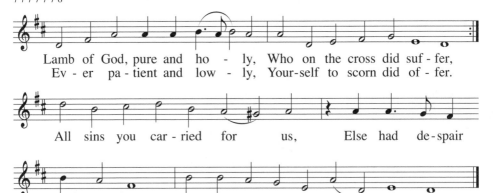

Text: Nikolaus Decius, c. 1485-after 1546; tr. composite
Tune: Nikolaus Decius, c. 1486-after 1546

CW #268

These are both typically litanic structures with the feel of metrical hymns.

The lengthy versions of the Creed and *Sanctus* give an indication of the deep respect and high expectation Luther had for congregations. Normal people can sing them with considerable gusto, but they are not "popular" in the superficial passing sense of the "slanders" mistakenly attributed to Luther. They are popular in the abiding sense of the deep vein of folk song—the song of the folk: hardy and potent stuff like rock smoothed by water, but not momentary as in what is "sweet, soft, clinging. . . "[15] All the chorales have this rugged and durable quality, though—as the settings of the *Kyrie*, *Gloria in excelsis*, and *Agnus Dei* indicate—they are not all as challenging as the vernacular versions of the Creed and the *Sanctus*.

3. THE PROPER OF THE MASS, DAILY PRAYER, AND PSALMS

Introit, Sermon, Post-Communion

Hymns with their tunes were substituted for the Proper and were often used enough to feel like the "ordinary." NUN BITTEN WIR, mentioned in the last chapter and discussed below with KOMM, HEILIGER GEIST under Pentecost, was used for the Introit.

The seventeenth-century tune LIEBSTER JESU, still widely used, is associated with Tobias Clausnitzer's (1619–1684) sermon hymn, "Dearest (or "Blessed") Jesus, at Your Word."[16] Its composer, Johann Rudolph Ahle (1625–1673), was a church musician and mayor. His tune, originally reflecting the soloistic influence of Italian opera, was "reconstructed" for congregational use to something like one of our versions when it was joined to Clausnitzer's text, which named it.[17]

LIEBSTER JESU, WIR SIND HIER
7 8 7 8 8 8

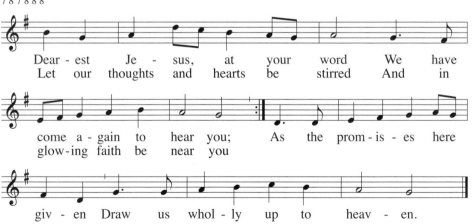

Text: Tobias Clausnitzer, 1619-1684, tr. Catherine Winkworth, 1829-1878, adapt.   LBW #248
Tune: Johann R. Ahle, 1625-1673

GOTT SEI GELOBET UND GEBENEDEIET, a fifteenth-century congregational *Leise*,[18] continued to be used in one of its pre-Reformation ways as a post-communion hymn. Luther added two stanzas to its single-stanza text. As we have it, the tune suggests major, but its background may well be mixolydian (Mode 7, without a sharped seventh degree).[19]

GOTT SEI GELOBET UND GEBENEDEIET
PM

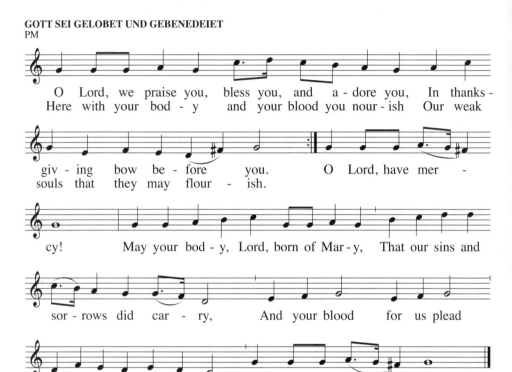

Text: German folk hymn, 15th c.; tr. *The Lutheran Hymnal*, 1941, alt., © 1941, Concordia Publishing House   LBW #215
Tune: J. Walther, *Geistliche Gesangbüchlein*, 1524

Psalms

The most far-reaching development was Luther's substitution of a hymn for the Gradual,[20] making way for "what was to become the distinctive *Graduallied*."[21] The Gradual and most of the changeable portions of the service from week to week, with the exception of the biblical readings, are from the psalms. The psalms are also central to daily prayer services, and there, too, Luther intended to simplify them "for congregational use."[22] Luther set out therefore in the early 1520s to "make German Psalms for the people" with clear meaning for each one "as close as possible to the Psalm" but without worrying about "exact wording."[23] He called for others more able than he to do this work, but composed several examples himself, working out versions of Psalms 12, 14, 46, 67, 124, 128, and 130. Psalm 46, "A Mighty Fortress," with its tune EIN FESTE BURG, is the best known of these. Simultaneously, with these new free metrical versions, the psalms in their original poetic prose continued to be sung in Lutheran practice to psalm tones.[24]

For Psalm 46, Luther moved freely into a hymn of comfort in which Christ holds the field against whatever assaults may come, much like "Christ Jesus Lay in Death's Strong Bands." (See below under "Easter" for this text and its tune.) The rounded bar form tune (see below for comments about bar form) Luther wrote for the text, EIN FESTE BURG,[25] is, in its original rhythmic form, a secure and jubilant textual dance[26] that trips up the foe.[27] Only in its later isometric form did it become a partisan battle cry that mistakenly turned Luther's energetic paradox (a fortress moves and fights for us) into immobile stasis.[28]

EIN FESTE BURG
878755567

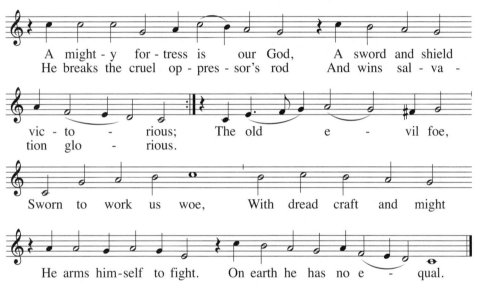

Text: Martin Luther, 1483-1546; tr. hymnal version, 1978, © 1978 *Lutheran Book of Worship*, admin. by Augsburg Fortress   LBW #228
Tune: Martin Luther, 1483-1546

Luther's tune has been viewed as based on any number of sources, some more plausible than others: chant, a French chanson, a Psalter psalm tune, and Hans Sachs' "Silberweise."[29] Friedrich Blume sketched a broader scope by seeing Luther's tunes like EIN FESTE BURG and VOM HIMMEL HOCH (see below for a discussion of this tune) as part of a very old melody type that reaches "back to the early period of Eurasian population migrations."[30] Its characteristics include "a descending melodic idea within the span of an octave," a strongly major orientation, the importance of the dominant, and "an emphatic rhythm at the beginning."[31] The elusive though sometimes plausible character of particular sources, along with the broader scope Blume defines, combine to point to this conclusion: Luther had a unique gift to harness the musical milieu he inhabited not for soloistic or individual purposes, but for "congregational participation."[32] He is not the only one who has done this, but his skill at it was unsurpassed and continues to suggest constructive directions.[33]

AUS TIEFER NOT (also known as DE PROFUNDIS), another tune Luther wrote for a psalm, was intended for his versification of Psalm 130. As a haunting phrygian melody in bar form that begins with the drop of a fifth adapted well to its text, the wide use it has received is not surprising.

AUS TIEFER NOT
8 7 8 7 8 8 7

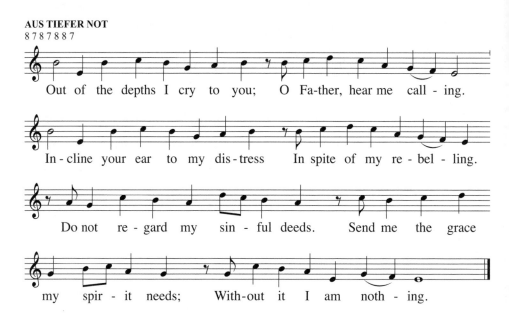

Text: Martin Luther, 1483-1546; tr. Gracia Grindal, b.1943, © 1978, *Lutheran Book of Worship*, admin. Augsburg Fortress   LBW #295
Tune: Martin Luther, 1483-1546

4. THE CHURCH YEAR

Lutheran theory and practice supported "liberty in the ceremonies," but this did not suggest the private opinion or "anything goes" mentality that our period tends to assume. At issue was a disciplined catholicity adapted to local needs which adhered to "the *de tempore* principle: . . . the basic character of the day [was preserved] as well as the content of individual portions of the service."[34] This perspective and practice—linked to the Gradual psalm, the *Leisen*, and their relation to the sequence[35]—led to the development of a repertoire of tunes for texts that covered the entire church year.[36] Some of them are still in use today and include the following, organized here by seasons of the Church Year.

Advent

Ambrose's Advent hymn "Veni redemptor gentium," discussed in Chapter II, was well known in Germany. Luther translated it into German. Then he, or possibly Walter, simplified its chant tune, VENI REDEMPTOR GENTIUM, into the chorale tune that takes its German name from Luther's translation, NUN KOMM, DER HEIDEN HEILAND.[37]

NUN KOMM, DER HEIDEN HEILAND
7 7 7 7

Text: Ambrose of Milan, ca. 374; tr. composite
Tune: Johann Walter, 1496-1570   R #109

In the chorale tune the rhythm is secured by removing most of the melismas; an insistent rhythmic pulse is set in motion, the melody is modified, the judicious third is expanded to an equally judicious fourth, and the last line is repeated exactly as the first. A quite remarkable congregational melody results, one of the most remarkable and durable melodies we will encounter. Konrad Ameln[38] gives four other tunes that were spun off from VENI, REDEMPTOR GENTIUM, among them the sturdy ERHALT UNS, HERR (not associated with Advent).

ERHALT UNS, HERR
LM

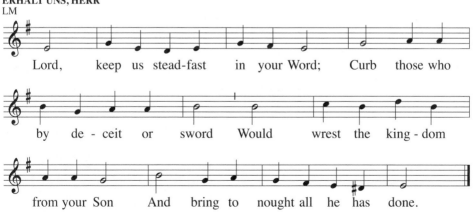

Text: Martin Luther, 1483-1546; tr. Catherine Winkworth, 1829-1878, alt.
Tune: J. Klug, *Geistliche Lieder*, 1543   LBW #230

At the end of the sixteenth century, another Advent hymn, "Wake, Awake," was written, known today as the "King of the Chorales." Both the text and its tune, WACHET AUF, were by Philipp Nicolai (1556–1608), given in his *Frewden-Spiegel dess ewigen Lebens* (Frankfurt, 1599). Nicolai was one of numerous Lutheran hymn writers and pastors who ministered in the midst of plague and controversy.

WACHET AUF
898898664448

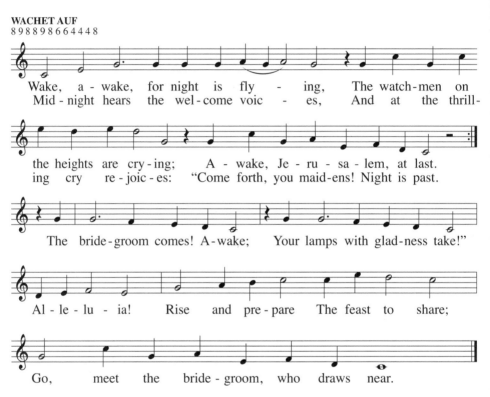

Wake, a-wake, for night is fly - ing, The watch-men on
Mid - night hears the wel - come voic - es, And at the thrill-

the heights are cry-ing; A - wake, Je - ru - sa - lem, at last.
ing cry re - joic - es: "Come forth, you maid-ens! Night is past.

The bride-groom comes! A-wake; Your lamps with glad-ness take!"

Al - le - lu - ia! Rise and pre - pare The feast to share;

Go, meet the bride - groom, who draws near.

Text: Philipp Nicolai, 1556-1608; tr. Catherine Winkworth, 1829-1878, and Martin A. Seltz, b.1951, © 1999, Augsburg Fortress   R #103
Tune: Philipp Nicolai, 1556-1608

Perspective: Bar Form, Rhythmic and Isorhythmic,
Common Musical Coinage

Nicolai's tune raises a number of issues that we need to parse out. First, like ALLEIN GOTT IN DER HÖH and numerous other tunes before it, WACHET AUF is an example of a commonly used structure called "bar form," which means a three-part form that can be diagramed as AAB (two *Stollen* [AA] forming the *Aufgesang*, followed by a concluding *Abgesang* [B]). WACHET AUF, and to a lesser extent ALLEIN GOTT IN DER HÖH, are more precisely "rounded bar form," because the end of B repeats the end of A. This form has nothing to do with bars as in taverns. Its name probably comes from *Barat*, which in fencing means "a skillful thrust." *Meistersingers*, medieval guilds of cultivated singers from whom chorale writers derived bar form, apparently used the shortened form "*Bar*" to distinguish their artistry "from the artless songs" of those they deemed not as artistic as they.[39]

Second, the original form of this tune, like many chorales, was "rhythmic" (as in the version given above). By the time these tunes got to eighteenth-century congregations, such as the ones J. S. Bach (1685–1750) served in Leipzig, their "rhythmic" character had been smoothed out and slowed down to an "isometric" form where notes and measures had become equal in length and fermatas were added at the ends of phrases.[40] Bach made up for the lack of rhythmic interest with remarkably skillful harmonizations. These were choral settings, however, not congregational ones. The congregation knew the tunes and could hear them and their texts with new insights as a choir sang them to Bach's harmonizations. The congregation might even have joined the choir on the melody line, though that is a disputed point and less rather than more likely, but Bach's harmonizations were not conceived for a congregation in its native musical language. Since Bach's settings are so skillful, however, and since we have tended in recent periods to print all hymns in four-part harmony in isometric versions, tunes like WACHET AUF have often been transmitted in our hymnals with Bach's harmonizations.[41] (One is given below with HERZLICH TUT MICH VERLANGEN, under "Lent.") To use the same Bach harmonization over and over for each stanza of a hymn, however, denies Bach's intent (he used one stanza or at most an occasional two with one of his harmonizations) and is fundamentally an anti-congregational move. The rich harmonic syntax does not bear that kind of repetition, and such repetition blocks its power.

Third, though Nicolai wrote the tune, a common musical coinage is in play here where individual authorship is not so important as communal ownership and memory.[42] The triadic opening phrase of WACHET AUF is like the fifth Gregorian psalm tone, and Nicolai's tune may have been stimulated by the "Silberweise" of Hans Sachs (1494–1576) of Nuremberg.[43]

Another tune associated with Advent, BEREDEN VÄG FÖR HERRAN, came a century later in the Swedish tradition. It was part of *Den Swenska Psalmboken* (Stockholm, 1697), where it appeared with figured bass for a table grace, though the Advent text "Prepare the Royal Highway" now allied to it was written by Frans Mikael Franzén and comes from much later, 1812. The tune might bear a relation to IN DULCI JUBILO, but its roots probably lie in another sixteenth-century German folk tune.[44] It works well with the Advent text, striding along nicely in bar form on the "royal highway," then spinning off in jubilation at "Hosanna to the Lord."

BEREDEN VÄG FÖR HERRAN
76767766

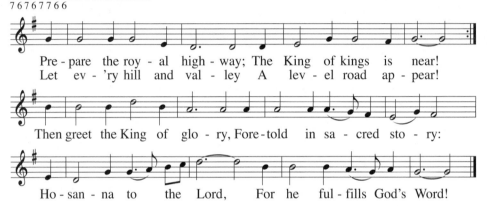

Text: Frans Mikael Franzen, 1772-1847; tr. hymnal version, 1978, © 1978, *Lutheran Book of Worship,* admin. Augsburg Fortress   LBW #26
Tune: Swedish folk tune, 17th c.

Christmas

Luther's Christmas hymn, "From Heaven Above," is a *contrafactum.* Probably in 1534 (the earliest known appearance in print was in 1535) Luther modified a text and tune used for a children's ring dance and added to it in order to tell the Christmas story. Soon, however, he decided a new melody was needed for his text, so he composed one. (It first appeared in 1539.) We use that melody, called VOM HIMMEL HOCH.[45] Though a bit gentler, like EIN FESTE BURG it employs a descending melody within an octave, is major, emphasizes the dominant, and begins with a strong rhythm.

VOM HIMMEL HOCH
LM

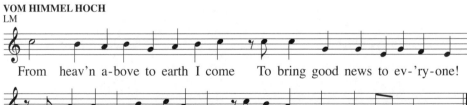

Text: Martin Luther, 1483-1546; hymnal translation, © 1978, *Lutheran Book of Worship,* admin. Augsburg Fortress   LBW #51
Tune: V. Schumann, *Geistliche Lieder,* 1539

Daniel Zager thinks Luther's decision to write a new tune was made because he drew a distinction between a style that might be used at home and a style appropriate for use in church.[46] Luther himself gave an indication of his concerns about what fits where in another of his Christmas hymns ("From Heaven the Angel Troop Came Near"), which has the same rhythmic structure as "From Heaven Above." In church he called for either the tune A SOLIS ORTUS or his tune VOM HIMMEL HOCH. For the boys (in school), he suggested the more difficult tune PUER NATUS IN BETHLEHEM.[47] The ring dance tune is not mentioned at all and drops from sight.[48]

While considering Luther's instructions here, we should not miss his sense of the community's ownership and the occasion. Regarding "From Heaven the Angel Troop Came Near"—a text he wrote—he said, "But let it be published without my name. And let it be named, 'A Hymn for Christmas.'"[49]

LOBT GOTT, IHR CHRISTEN,[50] another tune associated with Christmas, boldly strides along on the frame of a fifth, pushes beyond it to the sixth, but avoids the leading tone. This tune goes with the "great exchange" text—God in Christ takes on our frame, and we in exchange get God's realm and glory—in stanza 4 of the hymn given below. Though originally independent of one another, text and tune were both written by Nikolaus Herman (1480–1561) for children, as was Luther's VOM HIMMEL HOCH. Herman was a teacher, organist, and choirmaster in Bohemia with Pastor Johann Mathesius, a student and friend of Luther's.

LOBT GOTT, IHR CHRISTEN
86866

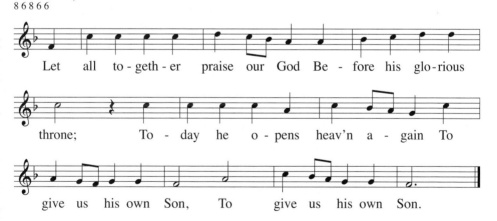

Let all to-geth-er praise our God Be-fore his glo-rious throne; To-day he o-pens heav'n a-gain To give us his own Son, To give us his own Son.

Text: Nikolaus Herman, c. 1480-1561; tr. F. Samuel Janzow, b.1913, © 1969, Concordia Publishing House   LBW #47
Tune: Nikolaus Herman, c. 1480-1561

Epiphany

The Epiphany hymn, "O Morning Star," came to be known as the "Queen of Chorales." As for its kingly partner (WACHET AUF), Philipp Nicolai wrote both the text and the tune. (Both chorales also come from the same source, *Frewden-Spiegel dess ewigen Lebens*). WIE SCHÖN LEUCHTET is once more in rounded bar form. Again, the dancing rhythmic original version (given here) turned into the later plodding, isometric one, which often appears today with a harmonization by J. S. Bach.[51] A common musical coinage is again at work also, in that the tune may have been adapted by Nicolai from the one for Psalm 100 in Wolff Köphel's *Psalter* (Strasburg, 1538).[52]

WIE SCHÖN LEUCHTET
PM

Text: Philipp Nicolai, 1556-1608; tr. hymnal version, © 1978, *Lutheran Book of Worship*, admin. Augsburg Fortress   LBW #76
Tune: Philipp Nicolai, 1556-1608

Perspective: Tune Names, Hymnals, Learning Hymns, and Organs

WIE SCHÖN LEUCHTET illustrates how chorale tunes came to be named, which raises issues about how they were introduced and used. They were named for the texts for which they were written or with which they were originally associated, but then other texts were used with them. So, for example, WIE SCHÖN LEUCHTET is still used for numerous texts other than "O Morning Star."[53] Prior to our large hymnals in pew racks, pocket-sized service books and hymnals—which congregants used at home and carried with them to and from church services—were published as text-only editions. In them, the name of the proper tune was given, but not the tune itself (which was carried in people's memories). "Eigene Melodie" meant the text had its "own" melody, named for and therefore identified by the given text. A text with a tune named for another hymn would have the other tune listed. Above the metrical version of Psalm 23, "Der Herr ist mein getreuer Hirt," for instance, the reader could find: "Mel. ["melody"] Allein Gott in der Höh sei Her,"[54] the tune named for "All Glory Be to God on High." (Sometimes "Weise" ["melody"] was used instead of "Mel." followed by the tune name.[55]) In hymnals where tunes were given, the melody without harmonization was printed in small notes with the hymn, untitled if named for the hymn, and titled if taken from another hymn.

Though hymn books developed quickly, according to Blume they originally may not have been intended for the people.[56] Hymns, along with other songs, were widely distributed on broadsheets, however, sometimes with visual woodcuts.[57] The expense of hymnals, the oral culture in which most people could not read but were primed to remember more texts (with tunes) than we,[58] and Luther's apparent expectation that the people would memorize their parts of the liturgy (the reverse of the tendency in our period always to do something "new," which precludes memory) meant that the first hymnals were for the pastor, cantor, and choirs.[59] Though we today are given to think that singing congregations sprang out of nowhere, Luther's concern for the people and their song took work.[60] It would have been naïve then as now to expect people who had at best sung minimally at worship to learn to sing a growing repertoire of hymns without help and loving concern. The problem was solved in several ways: hymns were learned by the children in school, the boys of the choir were placed among the congregation, a cantor stood before the people in the middle of the nave to lead the singing,[61] youth met on Sunday afternoons to practice the hymns, and choirs not only learned polyphonic settings of chorales but also led the congregation in their unison and unaccompanied singing of them.[62] The result of this hymn singing led to a clamor for the printing of hymnals. "The enormous popular response to the hymns of Luther and his friends resulted in countless reprints of his hymns and hymnals; almost a hundred Lutheran hymnals were published in Luther's lifetime."[63]

It needs to be remembered that this unison singing took place without organ accompaniment, which was not present until the seventeenth century. The use of the organ with the congregation's singing "spread only slowly and was by no means universal even in the nineteenth century."[64] Luther did not mention the organ much, and its development in builders like the Silbermanns and Schnitgers was yet to come. Luther was content with the organ, as with paintings, sculptures, and other external adornments, so long as it served the Gospel and was not reduced to meritorious or mindless "going through the motions." The Wittenberg faculty in 1597 said the use of the organ was "unobjectionable."[65]

Some Lutheran church orders forbade the organ, and secular organ music was not allowed because it had no texts and could not be broken to the Word like a *contrafactum*. The organ nonetheless was given many opportunities for use and development, the same as Latin Mass compositions and Latin and German motets. In alternating stanzas with the congregation, it functioned in the same way as polyphonic choral settings. Alternation, a time-honored practice in the church, was required because congregations had long hymns of many stanzas to sing and needed physical and mental respites. (In the Reformation period, chorales were always sung as total unities of thought, not "torn apart"[66] with stanzas omitted.) This practical necessity made possible artistic interpretive and proclamatory possibilities that were not lost on composers and choirs. The same was true for introductions. The organ could be used to introduce a chorale. The practical necessity of setting the pitch for the congregation at first took shape as the organist objectively introduced the tune. Gradually exegetical and interpretive— that is, in some sense preaching—roles developed for the organist.[67] It becomes clear why this tradition spawned and continues to spawn so many organ and choral pieces (with and without instruments) based on chorales, and how both the strongest congregational folk song and the strongest musical artistry have been so happily partnered.

Lent

HERZLICH TUT MICH VERLANGEN or PASSION CHORALE is associated with the well-known Lenten text, "O Sacred Head, Now Wounded." Another tune in bar form, it again has both rhythmic and isometric versions. Here is the earlier rhythmic one.

HERZLICH TUT MICH VERLANGEN
7 6 7 6 D

O   sa - cred head, now wound-ed, With grief   and shame weighed down,
Now scorn - ful - ly   sur - round - ed With thorns, thine on - ly   crown;

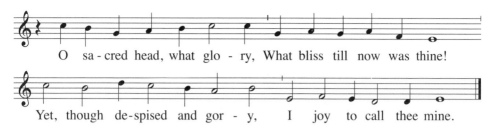

O sa-cred head, what glo-ry, What bliss till now was thine!

Yet, though de-spised and gor-y, I joy to call thee mine.

Text: attr. Bernard of Clairvaux, 1091-1153; Paul Gerhardt, 1607-1676; tr. composite, alt.   LBW #116
Tune: Hans L. Hassler, 1564-1612

Later isometric versions of chorales usually lose something. In this exceptional case, the isometric version has more to commend it because of the weight of the text. The rhythmic interest still is gone, however. As indicated above, J. S. Bach's harmonizations substitute harmonic interest for the rhythmic absence. People without musical training often find harmonizations non-congregational, though they can still sing the melody. Others have learned to love and long for Bach's harmonizations, such as the following, which employs the isometric form of the tune.

PASSION CHORALE
7 6 7 6 D

O sa-cred Head, now wound-ed, With grief and shame weighed down,
Now scorn-ful-ly sur-round-ed With thorns, thine on - ly crown:

How pale thou art with an - guish, With sore a-buse and scorn!

How does that vis-age lan - guish Which once was bright as morn!

Text: Anon. Latin; tr. Paul Gerhardt, 1656, and James W. Alexander, 1830   Meth #286
Tune: Hans L. Hassler, 1601; harm. by J.S. Bach, 1729, alt.

Perspective: Sacred/Secular and Modal/Tonal

Two points need to be noted about this tune. First, as one of the most interesting *contrafacta*, it points to what we have seen all along, a friendly movement between, for lack of better terms, "sacred" and "serious secular." It was written by the Lutheran church musician Hans Leo Hassler (1564–1612).[68] He published it in his *Lustgarten neuer teutscher Gesäng, Balletti* (Nuremberg, 1601), a collection of secular German songs and instrumental pieces. Hassler gave it in a five-part setting[69] for an artistic love song to "Maria" whose name was spelled out in an acrostic by the first letter of each stanza of the text. In 1613, after Hassler's death, the funeral hymn "Herzlich tut mich verlangen"[70] joined the melody and named it. Then, in 1625 it was matched to "Ach, Herr, mich armen Sünder," another deeply serious text, this one based on a penitential psalm, Psalm 6.[71] Finally it joined Paul Gerhardt's (1607–1676) "O Sacred Head" in the 1656 edition of Johann Crüger's (1598–1662) *Praxis Pietatis Melica* (Berlin).[72] That final marriage stuck and gave the tune its second name, PASSION CHORALE, though it has continued to be used for other texts and to have a life of its own beyond congregational song. For example, Paul Simon employed it for his "American Tune" after Art Garfunkel introduced it to him via one of Bach's harmonizations.[73]

Second, the modality or tonality of this melody provides insights into it and the nature of chorale tunes more generally. If you look at the melody by itself without harmony you might say it is Mode 3 or "phrygian," that is, its first and last notes are its "final," and the scale it implies is like our natural minor except that the second degree is flatted. The opening leap of a fourth and the cadence at the end of the second phrase may suggest simple minor, however, which turns the first and last notes into the fifth of the scale. The endings of the first, fifth (counting the repeat), and final phrases with lowered second and lowered seventh degrees, point toward phrygian. Indeed, if you harmonize the piece according to its tonal logic, you get phrygian half cadences at those points, suggesting minor. Hassler, however, and Bach in the version given above, harmonized them as major so that the "final" becomes not the fifth, but the third of the tonic chord. J. S. Bach worked with a version of the tune that moved the penultimate note up a fourth, thereby undercutting some of the phrygian character and making the major harmonization more intrinsic.

The point is that we are dealing in this music with a modal underlay, which is pushing toward our major and minor keys and especially toward the sharped seventh degree of the major. The sharped seventh degree gets into HERZLICH TUT MICH VERLANGEN in the harmony of the first of the two cadential chords of the first and last phrases when harmonized in major, but it can also get into melodies themselves. In WIR GLAUBEN ALL, for example, though the melody is Mode 1 or dorian, at the cadential points on the final or fifth the penultimate notes of the phrases tend to be sharped. Originally, these sharps were not in the printed version, but were sung and then entered printed versions.[74]

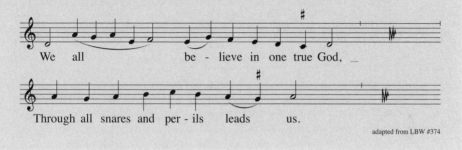

We all be - lieve in one true God, ...

Through all snares and per - ils leads us.

adapted from LBW #374

INNSBRUCK or O WELT, ICH MUSS DICH LASSEN is another remarkable melody and *contrafactum*, which took on Lenten and many other associations. The tune originates at least a century before HERZLICH TUT MICH VERLANGEN, found in a four-voice choral art song by Heinrich Isaac (1450–1517) published in 1539 for the secular text "Innsbruck, ich muss dich lassen" ("Innsbruck, I Must Now Leave You"). This melody may be much older than Isaac's piece. It was altered and joined to a reworking of the text for the church, "O Welt, ich muss dich lassen"[75] ("O World, I Must Now Leave You"). This move named the tune. By the time of the 1647 edition of Crüger's *Praxis Pietatis Melica* (Berlin), it had morphed into an isometric version[76] and joined Paul Gerhardt's "Nun ruhen alle Wälder" ("Now All the Woods Are Sleeping,"[77] also translated "The Duteous Day Now Closeth"[78] and "Now Rest Beneath Night's Shadow"[79]). Among its many texts are Gerhardt's Lenten hymn "O Welt, sieh hier dein Leben" ("O World, See Here Your Life," in John Kelly's translation from the second line, "Upon the Cross Extended"[80]), "O Food to Pilgrims Given,"[81] and "O Bread of Life from Heaven."[82]

Here it is with Gerhardt's evening hymn in its rhythmic version. Its compass is an octave from fifth to fifth. Within that span it moves in two three-phrase groups. The second group begins by spinning out of the first, but then immediately move into a repeat of the first and the second before coming to rest in an arc around the tonic. The result is a deeply satisfying melodic journey.

O WELT, ICH MUSS DICH LASSEN
7 7 6 7 7 8

Now rest be-neath night's shad-ow   The wood-land, field, and mead-ow

The world in slum-ber lies.   But you, my heart, a - wak - ing

And prayer and mu - sic mak-ing: Let praise to your cre - a - tor rise.

Text: Paul Gerhardt, 1607-1676; tr. *The Lutheran Hynmnal*, 1941, alt., © 1941, Concordia Publishing House   LBW #282
Tune: Heinrich Isaac, c. 1450-1517

HERZLIEBSTER JESU, a tune associated more closely with Lent only, usually goes with Johann Heermann's (1585–1647) hymn, "Ah, Holy Jesus." It first appeared in 1640 with a harmonization[83] in the predecessor of *Praxis Pietatis*, Johann Crüger's *Newes vollkömliches Gesangbuch Augsburgischer Confession* (Berlin). The tune seems to have its roots in a melody from the Genevan Psalter for Psalm 23[84] and another melody by Johann Hermann Schein (1586–1630), who was one of the cantors in Leipzig at the St. Thomas Church prior to J. S. Bach.[85] In a minor key (and not in bar form), it gradually makes its way up to a climax at the sixth and then back down an octave plus a second, only to explode in the last two measures up an octave, after which it recedes by step down to the tonic. While still potent, HERZLIEBSTER JESU points to a seventeenth-century smoothing out of the rugged sixteenth-century edges, parallel to the more introspective texts of authors like Gerhardt and Heermann in this same period.

HERZLIEBSTER JESU
11 11 11 5

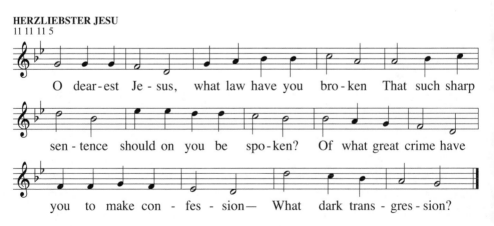

O dear-est Je - sus, what law have you bro-ken That such sharp

sen - tence should on you be spo-ken? Of what great crime have

you to make con - fes - sion— What dark trans - gres - sion?

Text: Johann Heermann, 1585-1647, abr.; tr. Catherine Winkworth, 1827-1878   CW #117
Tune: Johann Crüger, 1598-1662

Easter

CHRIST LAG IN TODESBANDEN gets us back to bar form and the sixteenth century's ruggedness. As noted earlier, VICTIMAE PASCHALI LAUDES spawned the *Leise* CHRIST IST ERSTANDEN. These two, in turn, stimulated Luther's classic hymn "Christ Jesus Lay in Death's Strong Bands" and its tune, which first appeared in 1524 in Walter's *Geystliche gesangk Buchleyn* (Wittenberg). Here is the dorian mode[86] with vigorous prophetic punch to celebrate the death of death.

CHRIST LAG IN TODESBANDEN
87877874

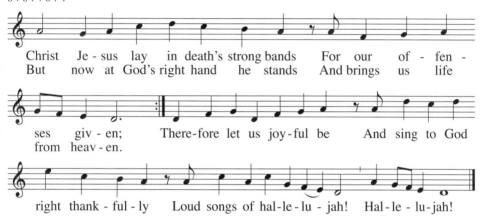

Christ Je - sus lay in death's strong bands For our of - fen -
But now at God's right hand he stands And brings us life

ses giv - en; There-fore let us joy - ful be And sing to God
from heav - en.

right thank - ful - ly Loud songs of hal-le-lu - jah! Hal-le-lu-jah!

Text: Martin Luther, 1483-1546; tr. Richard Massie, 1800-1887, alt.   LBW #134
Tune: J. Walther, *Geistliche Gesangbüchlein*, 1524

Pentecost

Many hymns to the Holy Spirit, with their tunes, come from the chorale heritage.[87] Those still in use are found mostly only among Lutherans. KOMM, HEILIGER GEIST, HERRE GOTT[88] is one of them. The hymn itself comes from an eleventh-century Latin text, which was translated into German in the fifteenth century or earlier and was well known in Germany as a single stanza. Luther added two more stanzas, all three of which were published in 1524 in the Erfurt *Eyn Enchiridion* with the melody that went with the single German stanza, an adaptation of the chant tune. (The tune is given here as in the *Lutheran Book of Worship*, but with what apparently was an "acknowledged error."[89] The last note of the second, third, fifth, sixth, and seventh phrases should be a quarter note, like the rhythm given in Zahn.[90])

KOMM, HEILIGER GEIST, HERRE GOTT
7 8 8 8 8 8 8 10 8

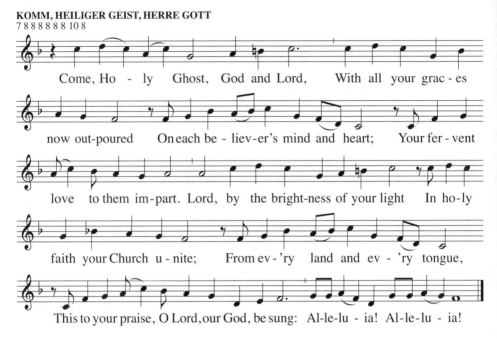

Come, Ho - ly Ghost, God and Lord, With all your grac - es

now out-poured On each be - liev-er's mind and heart; Your fer - vent

love to them im-part. Lord, by the bright-ness of your light In ho-ly

faith your Church u - nite; From ev - 'ry land and ev - 'ry tongue,

This to your praise, O Lord, our God, be sung: Al-le-lu - ia! Al-le-lu - ia!

Text: Martin Luther, 1483-1546, tr. *The Lutheran Hymnal*, 1941, alt., © 1941, Concordia Publishing House   LBW #163
Tune: *Enchiridion*, Erfurt, 1524

KOMM, HEILIGER GEIST, HERRE GOTT is a *Leise* with a pentatonic frame on the first, second, third, fifth, and sixth degrees of the scale. The fourth degree comes as a color point that gets pulled up or down depending on the direction of the tune, and the seventh degree of the scale occurs once as a passing tone at the end just before the "Alleluia." A similar but more pentatonic Leise, also probably as old as its thirteenth-century first stanza, is NUN BITTEN WIR.[91] Here there is no fourth degree and a similar single occurrence of the passing tone seventh in the "Lord, have mercy" at the end. (Luther added three stanzas to this text, too.)

NUN BITTEN WIR
10 9 11 9 4

To God the Ho - ly Spir - it let us pray Most of all for faith

up - on our way, That he may de-fend us when life is end-ing

And from ex - ile home we are wend - ing. Lord, have mer-cy!

Text: source unknown   LBW #317
Tune: J. Walther, *Geistliche Gesangbüchlein*, 1524

Two other tunes associated with the Holy Spirit, Pentecost, and the church need to be mentioned here. From the nineteenth century, they represent later developments in this tradition. One is DEN SIGNEDE DAG for a fifteenth-century Scandinavian text and its reworking by the Danish hymn writer Nikolai F. S. Grundtvig (1783–1872).

DEN SIGNEDE DAG
989898

O day full of grace that now we see Ap - pear - ing on earth's ho - ri - zon, Bring light from our God that we may be Re - plete in his joy this sea - son. God, shine for us now in this dark place; Your name on our hearts em - bla - zon.

Text: Nikolai F.S. Grundtvig, 1782-1872; tr. Gerald Thorson, b.1921, © 1978, *Lutheran Book of Worship*, admin. by Augsburg Fortress   LBW #161
Tune: Christoph E. F. Weyse, 1774-1842

The other is KIRKEN DEN ER ET GAMMELT HUS, also tied to a text by Grundtvig.

KIRKEN DEN ER ET GAMMELT HUS
8888888

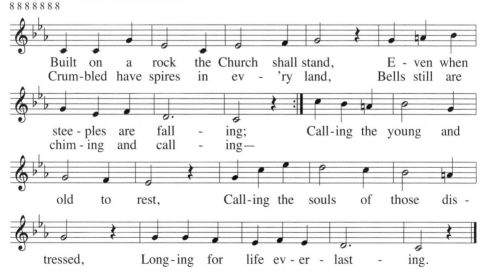

Built on a rock the Church shall stand, E - ven when stee - ples are fall - ing;
Crum-bled have spires in ev - 'ry land, Bells still are chim - ing and call - ing—
old to rest, Call-ing the souls of those dis - tressed, Long-ing for life ev - er - last - ing.

Text: Nikolai F. S. Grundtvig, 1783-1872; tr. Carl Doving, 1867-1937, adapt., © 1958, *Service Book & Hymnal*,   LBW #365
   admin. by Augsburg Fortress
Tune: Ludvig M. Lindeman, 1812-1887

DEN SIGNEDE DAG is by Christoph E. F. Weyse (1774–1842), a Danish church musician, composer, organist, and improviser. KIRKEN DEN ER ET GAMMELT HUS is by Ludvig M. Lindeman (1812–1887), a Norwegian church musician, teacher, organist, improviser, composer, and collector of folk melodies. Both of these tunes, as nineteenth-century creations, have left the rugged waters of the sixteenth century for smoother isometric conditions and the influence of the organ. What they lack rhythmically they make up for harmonically, but the tunes still have sufficient melodic interest to stand alone. Though one may choose not to call them chorales in a strict sense, they nonetheless clearly fit into this stream. The opening intervals of DEN SIGNEDE DAG are reminiscent of WACHET AUF, and KIRKEN DEN ER ET GAMMELT HUS is in bar form.

5. STANDING FOR THE REST

This chapter has been organized into the chorale's natural categories. It has clustered around the sixteenth century and the beginnings of the development of the chorale, but moved beyond them. If it were a systematic historical survey, the list would have been restricted to the period of and immediately after the Reformation and filled out more completely with tunes that may be less familiar to us, ones found in the "Liturgical and Topical Index" given in *Luther's Works*.[92] Chorale tunes related to Luther's Catechism and other ones used by Lutherans, but less well known in the wider ecumenical church,[93] would need to be added, such as DIES SIND DIE HEILGEN ZEHN GEBOT (also known as IN GOTTES NAMEN FAHREN WIR[94]) and CHRIST, UNSER HERR.[95] Let three more tunes stand for what is left out. They also symbolize how these tunes spread beyond their original uses, pointed forward, and had ecumenical ties.

1) As with the Psalms, Luther wanted to treat canticles in free metrical settings, still keeping their original forms. He constructed such a text from the *Nunc Dimittis* (Simeon's Song from Luke 2:29–32) for the festival of the Presentation of the Lord. Either he or Johann Walter wrote the dorian tune MIT FRIED UND FREUD to go with it. They were published in Walter's *Geistliche gesangk Buchleyn* in 1524. Today when this chorale is used, it usually functions as a post-communion canticle.

MIT FRIED UND FREUD
8 5 8 4 7 7

In peace and joy I now de-part   As   my Lord wills   it;

Se-rene and qui-et is my heart;   Glad-ness fills   it.

This the Lord has prom-ised me,   That death is but a slum-ber.

Text: Martin Luther, 1483-1546; tr. composite
Tune: *Geystliche gesangk Buchleyn*, Wittenberg, 1524, alt.

CW #269

2) VATER UNSER goes with Luther's metrical version of the Lord's Prayer. It will come up among the Methodists in the eighteenth century.[96]

VATER UNSER IM HIMMELREICH, DER DU
8 8 8 8 8 8

Our Fa-ther, who from heav'n a-bove   Bids all of us to live in love

As mem-bers of one fam-i-ly   And pray to you in un-i-ty,

Teach us no thought-less words to say,   But from our in-most hearts to pray.

Text: Martin Luther, 1483-1546; tr. composite
Tune: Attr. Martin Luther, 1483-1546

CW #410

3) HERZLICH LIEB, from Strasbourg in 1577, is a remarkable melody with an equally remarkable text by Martin Schalling used by J. S. Bach at the end of his St. John Passion. It links Luther and Nicolai as well as chorales and Genevan psalm tunes.

HERZLICH LIEB
PM

Lord, thee I love with all my heart; I   pray thee, ne'er from me de-part;
Earth has no pleas-ure   I would share, Yea, heav'n it - self were void and bare

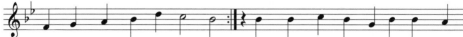

With ten - der mer-cy cheer me.   And should my heart for sor-row break,
If thou, Lord, wert not near me.

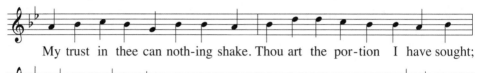

My trust in thee can noth-ing shake. Thou art the por-tion I have sought;

Thy pre-cious blood my soul has bought. Lord Je - sus Christ, My God

and Lord, my God and Lord,   For-sake me not! I trust thy Word.

Text: Martin Schalling, 1532-1608; tr. Catherine Winkworth, 1829-1878, alt.   LBW #325
Tune: B. Schmid, *Orgeltabulatur-Buch*, 1577

The Germanic, Slavic, and Scandinavian streams developed beyond the tunes given in this chapter. Two chapters from now, we will turn to those developments. In the next chapter, we move to another stream with sixteenth-century roots, metrical psalm tunes.

---

1   See Rebecca Wagner Oettinger, *Music as Propaganda in the German Reformation* (Aldershot: Ashgate, 2001), 2. For a *Perspective* on sacred and secular, see Chapter VII.

2   Erik Routley, *Christian Hymns Observed: When in Our Music God Is Glorified* (Princeton: Prestige Publications, Inc., 1982), 18. For more detail about this see Paul Westermeyer, *The Church Musician*, rev. ed. (Minneapolis: Augsburg Fortress, 1997), 130–132 and Daniel Zager, "Popular Music and Music for the Church," *Lutheran Forum* 36:3 (Fall 2002): 21–23.

3   Routley, MCH, 21B.

4   See Rebecca Wagner Oettinger, *Music as Propaganda in the German Reformation*, 17–35.

5   Martin Luther, "Preface to Georg Rhau's *Symphoniae iucundae*," Luther's Works, Vol. 53, *Liturgy and Hymns*, ed. Ulrich S. Leupold (Philadelphia: Fortress Press, 1965), 324.

6   Rebecca Wagner Oettinger, *Music as Propaganda in the German Reformation*, has begun to unpack the largely unexplored topic that titles her book. Music used as propaganda lives in a complex symbiosis with hymn tunes and the music of worship. It is an important matter that deserves continued study, but it is not our topic here. Much of the twentieth and twenty-first centuries' malaise is the attempt to make music solely propagandistic and worship its ally. Other periods—the Reformation among them—have experienced this temptation, though probably not to the extent of our fiercely competitive economic

exploitation of the other. The doxology and grace of the Christian message in all periods expose and break this bondage.

7   These are from Friedrich Blume, rev. Ludwig Finscher, trans. F. Ellsworth Peterson, "The Period of the Reformation," *Protestant Church Music: A History* (New York: W. W. Norton & Company, 1974), 63. Robin Leaver, *Goostly Psalmes and Spirituall Songes*, (Oxford: Clarendon Press, 1991), 16, gives a more detailed list of how chorales were sung in the liturgy.

8   *Liber Usualis*, 19. The trope is given in Stulken, HCLBW, 258.

9   For a discussion of Decius' dates, see Markus Jenny, "The Dates of Nikolaus Decius and 'All Glory Be to God on High,'" *The Hymn* 42:3 (July 1991): 39.

10 *Liber Usualis*, 16 (beginning with the music at "et in terra pax. . .").

11 Jenny, "The Dates of Nikolaus Decius. . .," 39.

12 *Liber Usualis*, 61.

13 Martin Luther, "German Mass and Order of Service," *Luther's Works*, Vol. 53, 58. This relationship was not lost on J. S. Bach who in the *Kyrie* of his F Major Mass, BWV 233, gives the melody of CHRISTE DU LAMM GOTTES, the *Agnus Dei*, to the oboe and horn.

14 *Liber Usualis*, 42.

15 Eva Mary Grew, "Martin Luther and Music," *Music and Letters* XIX (1938): 76.

16 LBW #248, Pres #454. The German title of the tune is *"Liebster Jesu, wir sind hier,"* the same words Benjamin Schmolck (1672–1737) used to begin his baptismal hymn (LBW #187, Pres #493).

17 See Stulken, HCLBW, 272 and Carl Schalk, "Blessed Jesus, at thy Word," Glover, H82C, 3B, 832.

18 See Bäumker, KDK, 1, 716–719 for various forms and sources.

19 Ibid., 716, #384.

20 Martin Luther, "German Mass and Order of Service," *Luther's Works*, vol. 53, 74. For a broader discussion see Edward Klammer, "De Tempore Hymn," *Key Words in Church Music*, ed. Carl Schalk (St. Louis: Concordia Publishing House, 1978), 163.

21 Leaver, *Goostly Psalmes and Spirituall Songes*, 3.

22 Robin Leaver, "English Metrical Psalmody," Glover, H82C, 1, 321. See also Leaver, *Goostly Psalmes and Spirituall Songes*, 26.

23 Leupold and MacDonald, "The Hymns," *Luther's Works*, vol. 53, 221.

24 Luther himself, for example, apparently pointed Psalm 111 in the Klug Wittenberg hymnal of 1533 with the first psalm tone. See *Luther's Works*, Vol. 53, 181–183.

25 Both rhythmic and isometric versions are given in CW #s 200 and 201, H82 #s 687 and 688, HWB #s 165 and 329, LBW #s 228 and 229, NC #s 439 and 440, Pres #s 259 and 260, PsH #s 468 and 469, and Wor3 #s 575 and 576.

26 Robert Scholz (correspondence, June 8, 2004) objects to the word "dance." He says (correspondence, June 4, 2002) EIN FESTE BURG "is a vocal piece in the style of a Minnelied...The alternation of triple (usually 6/4) and duple is generally based on word stress and not on dance rhythms. It is a much more supple and elegant rendering when sung in this manner, and people, who were used to hearing secular songs with this sort of 'changing meter' based on the text, would not have much trouble singing it that way... The tripping dance, I believe, is something that has happened since organists have accompanied, and metrically grounded, singers have sung this as a piece in duple with all the triple portions done as syncopations against the basic continuing duple meter. This is further enhanced by a fast tempo that probably is part of our culture and driven by organists who want to get some excitement going." Scholz's analysis is accurate, though choral settings of EIN FESTE BURG by composers like Praetorius have a rhythmic kick about them that surely bore some relation to congregational singing. Scholz is also correct about "dance," if you construe its definition as he implies. I mean it much more broadly, to include a piece based on word stress that "dances" like the text.

27   This is true whether Luther wrote it this way or Walter worked it over and gave it its "rhythmic pattern." Blume, "The Period of the Reformation," *Protestant Church Music*, 66.

28   Tim Westermeyer (correspondence, June 18, 2004) is not convinced I have the textual imagery right with the interpretive framework of either form of the tune, which, as in the comments of Robert Scholz at FN 26, suggests how fecund this text and tune have been and still are. Like all the worthy creations of the Christian church, they suggest the thick and multivalent texture of their congregational use and the ongoing conversations they propel. These conversations themselves are thickly textured. They seldom, if ever, have clear or simple conclusions, though they proceed from a general scope and meaning that are perfectly lucid.

29   For a good summary, see Robin Leaver, "A Mighty Fortress Is Our God," Glover, H82C, 3A, 1282–1286.

30   Blume, "The Period of the Reformation," *Protestant Church Music*, 38.

31   Ibid.

32   Leaver, "A Mighty Fortress," Glover, H82C, 3A, 1285.

33   For comparisons, see Blume, "The Period of the Reformation," *Protestant Church Music*, 37, and Robin Leaver, "Savior of the Nations, Come!" Glover, H82C, 3A, 99–100.

34   Blume, "The Period of the Reformation," *Protestant Church Music*, 64.

35   See Krentz, "The Use of Sequences," 12–13. Krentz argues for the *Leisen* rather than the Gradual hymn in this connection, but it may be that both are undergirding factors.

36   This has been an ongoing concern among Lutherans as in Denmark in 1683 when Thomas Hansen Kingo (1634–1703) was commissioned to prepare a hymnal with two hymns for every pericope of the church year. (See Edward A. Hansen, "Scandinavian Hymnody, Denmark," Stulken, HCLBW, 35.)

37   For other versions see Bäumker, KDK, I, 244.

38   Ameln, *The Roots of German Hymnody of the Reformation Era*, 18–21. (Routley, unlike most other sources—for example, Zahn, MDEK, 1, #1174 and Robin Leaver, "Savior of the nations, come!" Glover, H82C, 3, 99—traces NUNN KOMM, DER HEIDEN HEILAND to JESU DULCEDO CORDIUM. See Routley, MCH, 23, Exs. 28 and 22.)

39   Horst Brunner, "Bar form," NGDMM, 2, 156.

40   Ulrich S. Leupold, trans. George MacDonald, "The Hymns," *Luther's Works*, vol. 53, 205, says the beat was fairly rapid and "not until the eighteenth century did the isometric form of the melody in equal quarter or half notes supplant the polyrhythmical version." Just how the "rhythmic" treatment of the chorales took shape originally is "still largely unclear," but "it is certain that the real performance was not just the simple isometric presentation of the melody that has been generally customary since the middle of the seventeenth century" (Blume, "The Period of the Reformation," *Protestant Church Music*, 65–66). The sources agree about the practice in the period of the Reformation, but disagree about how long it extended, probably because developments differed from place to place.

41   As in H82 #61, NC #112, Pres #17, Meth #720, and VU #711.

42   As Temperley, HTI, I, 30, points out, "most of the earliest, and many of the greatest, hymn tunes in English-speaking [not only English-speaking] usage are anonymous."

43   See Carl Schalk, "'Sleepers, Wake!' A voice astounds us," Glover, H82C, 3A, 118.

44   Harald Göransson, "Prepare the Way, O Zion," Glover, H82C, 3A, 122–123.

45   For these details, see *Luther's Works*, vol. 53, 289–290, and Robin Leaver, "From heaven above to earth I come," Glover, H82C, 3A, 150–154. Our hymnals have this tune more often in its rhythmic rather than its isometric version. Rhythmic examples are CW #s 21 and 38, HWB #205, H82 #80, LBW #51, Pres #54, PsH #339, Wor3 #388, and NC #130. Isometric examples are Chal #146, Cov #161, Mor #386, Pres #496, and VU #72.

46   Zager, "Popular Music and Music for the Church," 22. (See also Rebecca Wagner Oettinger, *Music as Propaganda in the German Reformation*, 26, where the usual tunes used for news and ballads in ale houses and inns appear as a whole distinct from the ones used at worship,

though much in Oettinger's book suggests ones used in worship could be put to propagandistic use outside worship. For the reverse, see page 47, where tunes learned in schools were intended for worship and not the streets. In all cases, an understandable, though unfortunate and sad anti-Roman polemic was present.)

47 *Luther's Works*, vol. 53, 306. For puer natus see Zahn, MDEK, 1, #192a.

48 It is given in *Luther's Works*, vol. 53, 307, with "From Heaven the Angel Troop Came Near."

49 *Luther's Works*, vol. 53, 306.

50 CW #s 41 and 90, HWB #s 213 and 331, LBW #s 47, 300, and 35, Mor #374, PsH #192, and VU #545.

51 As in Chal #105 (a hybrid), Cov #191, Meth #247, NC #158, Pres #69, PsH #357, and Mor #278. Sometimes both the rhythmic and the isometric versions are given, as in H82 #s 496 and 497 as well as LBW #s 76, 138, and 459 versus #s 43 and 73, and Wor3 #s 389 and 390.

52 See Stulken, HCLBW, 77, for the Psalter tune.

53 As in LBW #s 43, 73, 138, and 459, or CW #s 162, 184, 241, and 622.

54 As in *Kirchenbuch für Evangelisch-Lutherische Gemeinden* (Philadelphia: General Council Publication Board, 1906), #373.

55 As in *Evangelisches Gesangbuch für Rheinland und Westfalen* (Dortmund: W. Crüwell, 1901).

56 Blume, "The Period of the Reformation," Protestant Church Music, 65.

57 Leaver, *Goostly Psalmes and Spirituall Songes*, 6. For the extent of this distribution and more detail, see Rebecca Wagner Oettinger, *Music as Propaganda in the German Reformation*, 9 and 26.

58 See Rebecca Wagner Oettinger, *Music as Propaganda in the German Reformation*, 23–26.

59 The early books were of two sorts. One was a congregational book, the *Etlich Christliche Lyeder Lobgesang und Psalm*—known as the "Achtliederbuch" of 1524, which was compiled from broadsheets with a Wittenberg imprint, but published in Nuremberg. (See Leaver, *Goostly Psalmes and Spirituall Songes*, 6.) The other, another 1524 publication, was Walter's *Geystlicher gesangk Buchleyn* (*Geistliche Gesangbüchlein*), a collection of polyphonic motets based on chorales to be used in alternation with the congregation's unison stanzas. This was published in a congregational edition, "fur die leyden," in the next year, 1525. (See Leaver, *Goostly Psalmes and Spirituall Songes*, 9.)

60 Temperley, HTI, 1, 6, thinks Luther failed at this, whereas the Reformed branches of the church succeeded. I think both succeeded, though in different ways—the Lutheran with the help of choirs and in alternation with them, the Reformed without choirs or alternation. (Compare Leaver, *Goostly Psalmes and Spirituall Songes*, 81 and 102, FN5. See also Albert Schweitzer, J. S. Bach, [Boston: Bruce Humphries Publishers, 1962, first published in French in 1905], I, 24–40, who, though he recounts a mixed history, can be understood as supporting Temperley until Rationalism and Pietism. While instructive, Schweitzer fails to see the connection in Luther between artistic and theological insights and then misses part of the landscape, including Bach's tacit assumption of the presence and importance of the chorale in the voice and being of the congregation.)

61 See Leaver, *Goostly Psalmes and Spirituall Songes*, 103–104.

62 Much detail in this paragraph is from Blume, "The Period of the Reformation," *Protestant Church Music*, 65. See also Leaver, *Goostly Psalmes and Spirituall Songes*, 8, and Rebecca Wagner Oettinger, *Music as Propaganda in the German Reformation*, 49–50.

63 *Luther's Works*, 53, 317.

64 Hugh Keyte and Andrew Parrot, eds., *The New Oxford Book of Carols* (Oxford: Oxford University Press, 1992), 660.

65 Keyte and Parrot, *The New Oxford Book of Carols*, 660.

66 Blume, "The Period of the Reformation," *Protestant Church Music*, 105.

67 I am dependent for much of the detail in this paragraph on Blume, "The Period of the Reformation," *Protestant Church Music*, 64 and 105–113.

68   For his story and that of other such early Lutheran musicians, see Carl Schalk, *Music in Early Lutheranism: Shaping the Tradition* (St. Louis: Concordia, 2001).

69   This setting is in the Accompaniment Edition, Volume 2 of H82 at #169.

70   By Christoph Knoll (1563–1630). The text with source material and a literal translation can be found in Mark S. Bighley, *The Lutheran Chorales in the Organ Works of J. S. Bach* (St. Louis: Concordia Publishing House, 1986), 127–131.

71   By Cyriacus Schneegass (1546–1597). See Bighley, *The Lutheran Chorales*, 264–266.

72   This book was first published by Crüger in 1644. The most important hymn collection of the seventeenth century, it was reedited and expanded even after Crüger's death well into the next century.

73   Paul Simon, "American Tune," *There Goes Rhymin' Simon* (Warner Bros. Records Inc., 1973), 9 25589-2.

74   Stulken, HCLBW, 420 says "the original form does not include the four C-sharps or the G-sharp used here [in the LBW]," and indeed in the first printings of the LBW at #374 the second C-sharp was (probably inadvertently) omitted, as in the version given above under the *Credo*. Zahn, MDEK, 4, #7971, gives both the 1524 form of the melody and the form from 1545 that was commonly used into the seventeenth century, with sharps above the notes in question (as in the two phrases given in the example here). That points to the complexity of what is known as *musica ficta*, the introduction of non-diatonic pitches, which may well have been employed in actual singing. CW #271 gives WIR GLAUBEN ALL in its natural dorian state without any chromatic alterations to the tune, though the harmonization is minor.

75   Robin Leaver, "The Duteous Day Now Closeth," Glover, H82C, 3A, 83, says this happened in a broadsheet in 1555. Other sources (Aufdemberge, CWH, 595) say 1598 with the text by Johann Hesse, pastor of St. Mary Magdalene Church in Breslau.

76   All three versions are given in Leaver, "The Duteous Day Now Closeth," Glover, H82C, 3A, 84.

77   HWB #657, LBW #276.

78   H82 #46.

79   CW #587, LBW #282.

80   CW #113.

81   H82 #309, Meth #631.

82   LBW #222.

83   Given in H82 #158.

84   Routley, MCH, gives this tune at Ex. 81.

85   See Stulken, HCLBW, 223–224.

86   The dorian character is even more obvious in the awkward second phrase of the B section in an alternate (and less satisfactory) version of the tune, given in Zahn, MDEK, 4, # 7012b.

87   Zahn, MDEK, 5, 531, lists twelve beginning with "Komm, Heiliger [or heilger] Geist."

88   CW #176 and LBW # 163.

89   Scott Weidler, correspondence, August 16, 2004.

90   Zahn, MDEK, 4, 421–422, #7445a.

91   CW #190 and LBW #317.

92   Ulrich S. Leupold, trans. George MacDonald, "The Hymns," *Luther's Works*, vol. 53, 209–210.

93   Ibid., 210.

94   CW #285. See Zahn, MDEK, 1, #1951.

95   LBW #79.

96   Luther's complete metrical version of the Lord's Prayer, for which the tune is named, is given in CW #410. A version by Marie Post based on Dewey Westra and the Heidelberg Catechism is given in PsH #562. For shortened versions, see CW #407, LBW #442, and PsH #208; and for other texts H82 #575, Meth #410, and various other hymns in CW and LBW.

IV. METRICAL PSALM TUNES

1. GENEVAN

Background

John Calvin (1509–1564) kept the Word and table sequence of the Mass as the norm for weekly worship on the Lord's Day (Sunday), but he abolished the Mass itself along with all the inherited music associated with the church. In its place he substituted metrical psalms—that is, psalms translated into the vernacular in rhyme and meter—and a few other texts sung by the congregation to newly composed psalm tunes. As James Hastings Nichols notes, the liturgy of the Calvinists was the sung psalmody of the people.[1] Metrical versions of the Ten Commandments replaced the Gradual and followed the Confession according to Calvin's "third and principal use" of the law,[2] a metrical version of the Apostles' Creed was sung after the prayers while the bread and wine were prepared,[3] and a metrical version of the *Nunc dimittis* was sung at the end of the service.[4] Otherwise only metrical psalms were sung. The elements of the Ordinary of the Mass that Luther adapted for the people "dropped out of use" among the Calvinists.[5]

Some hymn singing did seep into Calvinist practice, and after several centuries displaced metrical psalms; but in the sixteenth and seventeenth centuries in the French Reformed Church psalmody was the norm. It spread even more strongly to the Netherlands and Hungary, where it is still retained today.[6] People brought their Psalters to church,[7] and—as in Wittenberg with chorales—sang complete psalms,[8] not several selected stanzas.

Also as in Luther's Wittenberg,[9] worship was not restricted to the Sunday communion (or ideal of communion) service.[10] "The twentieth-century Protestant Church [which is] locked six days a week has no precedents in the Reformation. All the Reformed churches of the sixteenth century conducted weekday services before and after working hours"—morning and evening prayer with sermon,[11] as did Lutherans. That is, besides the services on Sundays, there were many organized opportunities to sing psalms. "Tables" of psalms were posted,[12] and time was given for psalm singing. Mid-seventeenth century New England psalm singing "in the Genevan manner" could "last as long as one half hour" (and the sermon two to three hours with a "stretch in the middle").[13]

Organization

It is obvious that psalm tunes organize themselves differently from what we have seen so far in either the chant or chorale traditions. They begin with and cluster around the metrical psalms in the Genevan Psalter, which is why they can be named "Genevan" followed by the number of the psalm.[14] The Genevan Psalter is a collection of all 150 biblical psalms in French metrical versions by Clement Marot (ca. 1496–1544) and Theodore Beza (1519–1605). The tunes, at least for the pivotal 1551 version, were shaped, edited, and written by Louis Bourgeois (ca.1510–1560), a music teacher in Geneva. After numerous partial versions, beginning in Strasbourg in 1539, to which more and more psalms and tunes were gradually added, the complete Genevan Psalter (*Les pseaumes mis en rime françoise, par Clement Marot et Théodore Bèze*) was published in Geneva in 1562. The "creator of the new melodies [the ones that were composed for the remainder of the psalms that had not yet been included in earlier editions] was a certain 'Maitre Pierre' [whose] identity . . . remains a mystery." As Emily Brink explains, the tunes were consciously attached to specific texts.[15]

> Calvin's intention was to provide a distinct tune for every psalm, so that each psalm would have its own identity. Every tune would then bring to mind a particular psalm. The psalter didn't quite reach this goal: it contains 125[16] melodies for 152 texts (the 150 psalms and two canticles). Fifteen tunes were used twice, four tunes were used three times, and one tune is used four times...[17]

Characteristics

Besides their organization, there are other differences between the Lutheran and Reformed melodies. Before we try to understand those, let us delineate their similarities. There are a number of significant ones. Both 1) are profoundly congregational, 2) are conceived to be unaccompanied, 3) are to be sung in unison – or, more precisely, in octaves, men an octave lower than women and children,[18] 4) employ a wide variety of meters, 5) often use bar form, 6) utilize a modal vocabulary as well as a continuing gravitation toward major and minor keys, 7) originally moved at faster than stodgy paces—Genevan tunes were sometimes derided as "Geneva jigs," and 8) were originally rhythmic but over time got smoothed out (and slowed down) into isorhythmic contours.[19] In both traditions, a cantor or precentor taught the children who in turn joined the cantor in teaching the melodies by singing them with the congregation.[20]

The differences are equally significant. 1) While many new hymns and hymnals were spawned among the Lutherans in a kind of free-for-all around the historic liturgy and church year, the Calvinists fashioned a highly concentrated and restricted body of metrical psalms and tunes around a reconceived liturgical practice. 2) Calvin expected texts to be set syllabically, not with melismas, which were rare exceptions.[21] Lutherans did not rule out melismas as long as they were congregational. 3) The unaccompanied and unison character of Calvinist singing was the result of a theological conviction about the "weight" and "majesty" of psalm singing in church, versus what could be sung at home[22] in "light" and "frivolous" harmonized note against note or polyphonic settings.[23] For Lutherans, unison singing was a practical congregational reality without theological presuppositions that drove it.

4) This point is related to the last one. Calvin regarded chant and instruments as a foreign tongue,[24] yet wanted a unique performance practice that was related to but distinct from the world.[25] Luther welcomed chant, instruments, and the best of the culture's musical resources as part of God's good creation, its crafting, and a gracious and accessible "continuity with the practice of the whole church."[26] There is an important distinction between the two reformers here, but, contrary to another current "slander," Calvin did not hire secular songwriters to rob pubs of their tunes any more than Luther did.[27] As John Witvliet has shown, Genevan psalm tunes were probably more dependent on Gregorian chant than on secular chansons,[28] yet were "both alike and unlike [these] two vastly different musical repertories."[29] They, like Lutheran chorales, were sung at home and elsewhere outside the liturgy, but at the liturgy this music of "weight and majesty" was set apart, "free of secular overtones."[30] Geneva's discipline did not mistake it as coming from worldly pleasure, nor was playing loose with it countenanced. "One incident of notoriety featured a number of youths who were arrested for singing psalms derisively in the Geneva streets."[31]

The final difference is the most difficult to explain, but the most profound and important. If you have been part of a congregation that sings Lutheran rhythmic chorales and Genevan psalm tunes, at times in their original unaccompanied unison, you can more easily understand what is difficult to put into words. Both are deeply congregational, communal, and powerful, but the Lutheran chorale has a responsive and explosive freedom about it whereas the psalm tune, in what Witvliet calls a "common refrain" of Calvin, incites "the people to prayer and to praise God."[32] The former is proclamatory and prophetic with rugged and loose edges, the latter supplicatory and priestly with a binding quality that smoothes off the rough edges. The former fits a community that is not sure there is a third use of the law, while the latter expresses the third "and principal"[33] use of the law in sonic form. The following melodic and rhythmic differences of musical syntax embody these issues. 1) Though there are leaps, the Reformed melodies nonetheless proceed from a more stepwise melodic conception than the Lutheran ones. 2) Whereas the Lutheran chorale is apt to begin with a bounce off a strong beat, the Genevan psalm tune tends to glide into the beat with a longer but less forceful gathering note and then encloses shorter notes in an embrace of succeeding longer ones, often in patterns that are repeated from line to line. (The Bohemian Brethren tunes, in contrast to both Lutheran and Calvinist ones, tend to begin with an emphatic initial push on the beat. See Chapter V.) These characteristics will become clear as we proceed with examples.

Examples in the Order of the Psalter

If you sing through Genevan psalm tunes on your own, you may find them bland. If you live with them a while and experience them in unison in community, you will understand their power, though, of course, they are not all of equal value. As usual, time has separated the wheat from the chaff. Here are some of the more long-lived examples in the numerical order of the Psalter. Unless otherwise indicated, all of these come from the 1551 edition of the Genevan Psalter and were composed or adapted by Louis Bourgeois.

GENEVAN 12,[34] also known as DONNE SECOURS for Clement Marot's version of Psalm 12, is better known today for its connection with Georgia Harkness's text, "Hope of the World." This is a dorian tune where the rhythm of the first line is duplicated in the third and the rhythm of the second line in the fourth. The embrace of quarter notes between half notes is obvious throughout.[35]

GENEVAN 12
11 10 11 10

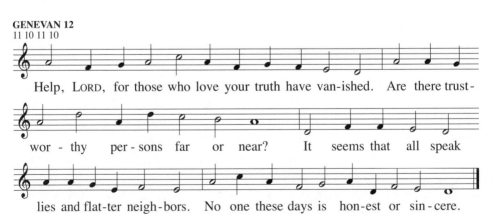

Text: Psalm12; vs. Marie J. Post, 1983, © 1987, CRC Publications   PsH #12
Tune: Louis Bourgeois, 1551

GENEVAN 25 spins itself out in a major key with an attractive syncopated bump at the fifth note. Later, in the sixth measure (counting the repeat of the first two measures), a delightful series of threes and twos are reminiscent of the last part of the A section of WIE SCHÖN LEUCHTET (discussed in Chapter III). Quarters are nestled between half notes in an even more conjunct flow than GENEVAN 12.

GENEVAN 25
87877878

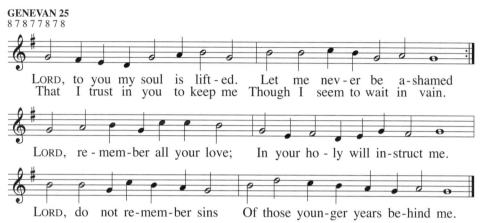

Text: Psalm 25; vs. Stanley Wiersma, 1980, © 1987, CRC Publications
Tune: Louis Bourgeois, 1551
PsH #25

GENEVAN 42 or PSALM 42 is characterized again by alternating threes and twos in conjunct motion. It is also known as FREU DICH SEHR, because in 1613 it was published in the Lutheran stream in Görlitz in *Harmoniae sacrae* with a funeral hymn that began with those words. Marilyn Stulken suggests this melody originally went in 1505 with a French folk song.[36] Like GENEVAN 25, it is in bar form and a major key, but unlike GENEVAN 25 it is much better known and has been used with a number of texts.

GENEVAN 42
87877788

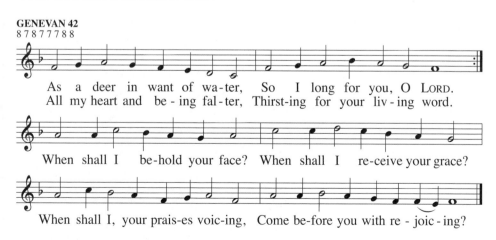

Text: Psalm 42-43, vs. *Psalter Hymnal*, 1987, © 1987, CRC Publications
Tune: Louis Bourgeois, 1551
PsH #42

GENEVAN 42 shed its 87 87 77 88 meter and took on Long Meter Double in the Anglo-Genevan Psalter of 1560 for a setting of Psalm 27. Robin Leaver sees it as "refashioned" by Heinrich Albert into another fine tune called GOTT DES HIMMELS.[37]

GENEVAN 47 is jubilant, syncopated music for clapping hands and singing to God with shouts of joy, in a major key with alternating twos and threes like the last two. It is not in bar form, however, but strings together six melodic lines with the same rhythm, the last of which begins as an inversion of the first and concludes by repeating the end of the third.

GENEVAN 47
5 5 5 5 5 5 D

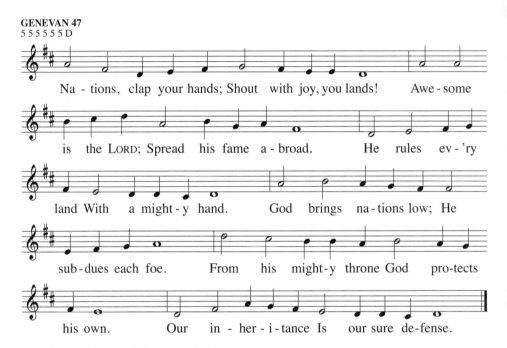

Text: Psalm 47; vs. *Psalter Hymnal*, 1987, © 1987, CRC Publications   PsH #47
Tune: Louis Bourgeois, 1551

GENEVAN 65 originally went with Psalm 72 in the 1551 version of the Genevan Psalter.[38] In bar form and a minor key, it may not have anything especially distinguishing about it, but it represents the characteristics of this tradition well as it carries this psalm of praise in an earthy way by an opening downward fifth and a reiterated stepwise cadence downward to the tonic.

GENEVAN 65
9 6 9 6 D

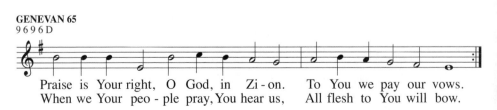

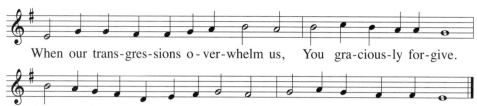

When our trans-gres-sions o-ver-whelm us,   You gra-cious-ly for-give.

How sat-is-fied Your cho-sen ser-vants;   With-in Your courts they live.

Text: Stanley Wiersma, 1980
Tune & Text: © 1987, CRC Publications

Pres #201

(For the sake of comparison, it is instructive to note how differently Giuseppe Verdi treated this text—"Te decet hymnus in Sion." As part of the first movement of his Requiem, the stepwise upward movement of the hymnic line he stretched out in fugal entries to span a two-octave stretch from bass to soprano points to a very different worldview in a nineteenth-century choral and Italian operatic context.)

GENEVAN 68 or O MENSCH BEWEIN is not by Bourgeois, but probably by Matthäus Greiter (1490–1550), a Catholic monk and cantor at the Minster in Strasbourg who became a Lutheran, married, may have edited Calvin's first Psalter in Strasbourg in 1539, and at the Catholic Interim in 1549 rejoined the Catholic Church. (This kind of ecumenical life is not uncommon for church musicians.)

GENEVAN 68
887887D

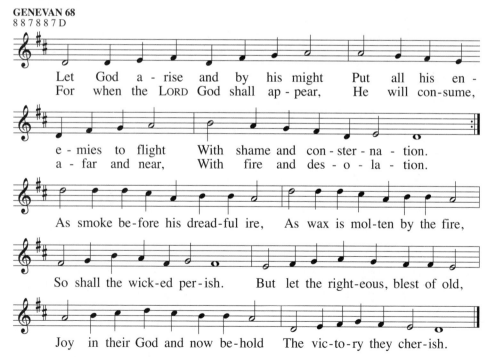

Let God a-rise and by his might   Put all his en-
For when the LORD God shall ap-pear,   He will con-sume,

e-mies to flight   With shame and con-ster-na-tion.
a-far and near,   With fire and des-o-la-tion.

As smoke be-fore his dread-ful ire,   As wax is mol-ten by the fire,

So shall the wick-ed per-ish.   But let the right-eous, blest of old,

Joy in their God and now be-hold   The vic-to-ry they cher-ish.

Text: Psalm 68; vers. Psalter Hymnal, Copyright © 1987, CRC Publications
Tune: Genevan Psalter, 1539

PsH #68

This tune has been put to an amazing variety of uses. Greiter first composed it for Psalm 119 in 1525 or 1526,[39] it joined Psalm 36[40] in the 1539 Psalter, and in the 1562 Psalter it was used for Psalm 68 ("Let God arise, let his enemies be scattered"), which became the Calvinist national anthem, the "Huguenot Marseillaise." A long tune in bar form with affinities to chorales, Lutherans joined it to a deeply penitential text by Sebald Heyden, "O Mensch, bewein dein Sünde gross" ("O man, bewail your great sin"). J. S. Bach wrote a remarkable meditation on this text and tune in his *Orgelbüchlein* (BWV 622). It probably was the stimulus for Catholics in Cologne to create another tune, the one we know as LASST UNS ERFREUEN. It stimulated Watts to write his version of Psalm 146, "I'll Praise My Maker with My Breath," and it was a favorite of John Wesley's. It assumed an English dress in a shortened form known as OLD 113TH, now used for Wesley's revision of Watts' text, "I'll Praise My Maker While I've Breath."[41]

This is a hardy tune in a major key that nestles quarter notes between half notes and spans an octave with no asymmetrical or syncopated surprises. It starts from the lower tonic, works partway up the scale and back down, at midpoint explodes on the top octave, and then gradually falls back down to the lower tonic. It is a grand tune with an arch-like shape, but what has given it the capacity to serve such varied uses over such a long period is difficult to say.[42]

GENEVAN 77 was used for Psalm 86 in 1551,[43] but it migrated to Psalm 77 in 1562. It fits the cry of both. Its stepwise movement in a minor key is organized so that the first phrase is fashioned from four pitches around the tonal center of the first and then repeated in the second phrase as an unrelenting plea. At midpoint the first two phrases are modified and repeated a third higher as if to emphasize the pleading even more strongly. The final two phrases directly repeat the third and fourth. A sustained congregational entreaty has been crafted from a short and sorrowful musical motif.

GENEVAN 77
8 8 7 7 D

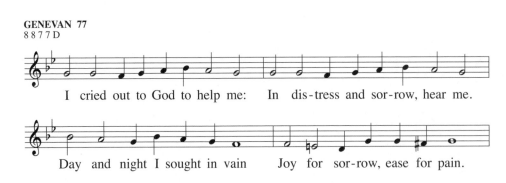

I cried out to God to help me: In dis-tress and sor-row, hear me.

Day and night I sought in vain   Joy for sor-row, ease for pain.

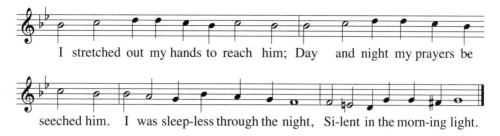

I stretched out my hands to reach him; Day and night my prayers be-
seeched him. I was sleep-less through the night, Si-lent in the morn-ing light.

Text: Psalm 77; vs. Helen Otte, 1985, © 1987, CRC Publications   PsH #77
Tune: Genevan Psalter, 1551

GENEVAN 98/118 or RENDEZ À DIEU is quite different. It was the setting for Psalm 118's song of thanksgiving in 1551[44] from which it took the name RENDEZ À DIEU, and it doubled up for Psalm 98's "new song" to God in 1562. It is often sung today to Erik Routley's metrical version of Psalm 98, "New Songs of Celebration Render," though it is used for a number of other texts as well, like Bland Tucker's metrical version of prayers from the *Didache*, "Father, We Thank Thee."[45] It is one of the grand, sweeping Genevan Psalter tunes.

GENEVAN 98
9 8 9 8 D

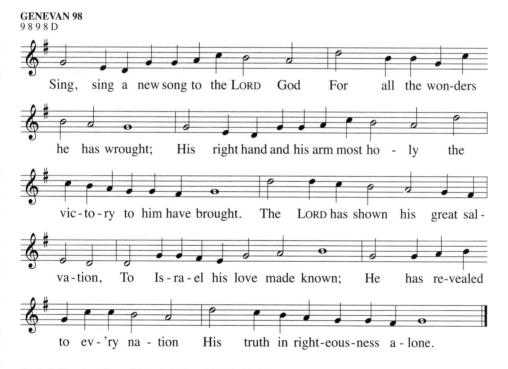

Sing, sing a new song to the LORD God For all the won-ders he has wrought; His right hand and his arm most ho-ly the vic-to-ry to him have brought. The LORD has shown his great sal-va-tion, To Is-ra-el his love made known; He has re-vealed to ev-'ry na-tion His truth in right-eous-ness a-lone.

Text: Psalm 98; vs. Dewey Westra, 1931, rev. Psalter Hymnal, 1987. © 1987, CRC Publications   PsH #98
Tune: Genevan Psalter, 1551

GENEVAN 100 is not well known in the ecumenical church and is not OLD HUNDREDTH, the tune often associated with Psalm 100. This tune, not GENEVAN 134 (see below), was used for Psalm 100 in the 1562 Psalter, though in 1551 it went with Psalm 131.[46] It begins as if it will be minor or major, but settles finally into phrygian.

GENEVAN 100
L M

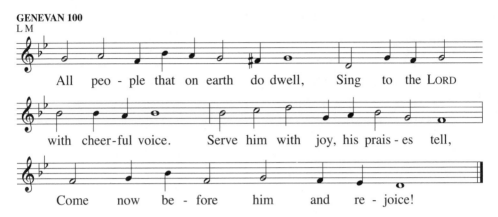

Text: Psalm 100; vs. William Kethe, 1561, alt.   PsH #100
Tune: Louis Bourgeois, 1551

For a longer and more obviously phrygian tune, see GENEVAN 51.[47]

GENEVAN 101 provides an instructive study in the metamorphosis of a melody. Here is its Genevan Psalter form with quarter notes characteristically nestled between half notes and the meter 11 11 10 4.

GENEVAN 101
11 11 10 4

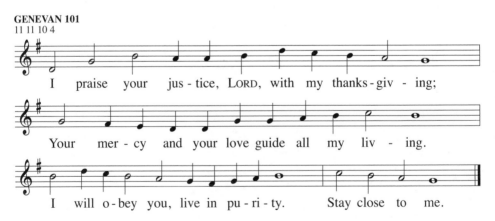

Text: Psalm 101; vs. Bert Witvoet, 1985, © 1987, CRC Publications   PsH #101
Tune: Louis Bourgeois, 1551

A hymn (not psalm) text, "Je te salue, mon certain Redempteur," which "appears to be a Protestant version of the Roman Catholic hymn "Salve Regina,"[48] was published in Strasbourg in 1545 in Clement Marot's *Psalms*. It was printed in an

1868 edition of Calvin's works, probably wrongly attributed to Calvin, and the English translation by Elizabeth Smith found its way into Philip Schaff's *Christ in Song* (New York, 1869). Smith's text is now in an altered version at #248 in the *Psalter Hymnal* with a 10 10 10 10 tune called JE TU SALUE, named for the French hymn, and modified from GENEVAN 101 like this.

JE TU SALUE
10 10 10 10

Text: French, 1545; tr. Elizabeth L. Smith, 1868, alt.   PsH #248
Tune: Louis Bourgeois, 1551, adapt. from his melody for Psalm 101

(This text is more commonly sung to TOULON as "I Greet Thee Who My Sure Redeemer Art." For TOULON, see below at GENEVAN 124.) JE TU SALUE is an adaptation of GENEVAN 101, modified with an addition to accommodate the 10 10 10 10 meter, but still essentially in the original rhythmic shape. In the English trajectory, GENEVAN 101 morphed into a Short Meter tune called ST. MICHAEL (not to be confused with MICHAEL by Herbert Howells[49]) where it runs along in a series of quarters with dotted halves at the ends of three of the four phrases.[50] Here it is in that form. Note the stop at the end of short phrases. This matter will receive a significant comment from Paul Richardson when we get to Short Meter.

ST. MICHAEL
SM

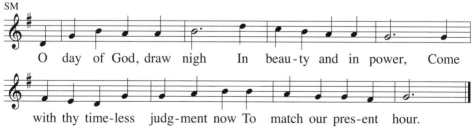

Text: Robert Balgarnie Young Scott, 1899-1987, © Emmanuel College, Toronto   H82 #601
Tune: Louis Bourgeois, 1510?-1561?

GENEVAN 103 is a six-line mixolydian tune, with shorter notes typically surrounded by longer ones. It sets Psalm 103's blessing of God. From the 1539 Strasbourg Psalter, it is not widely known but has been well received among the Dutch Reformed.

GENEVAN 103
11 11 10 D

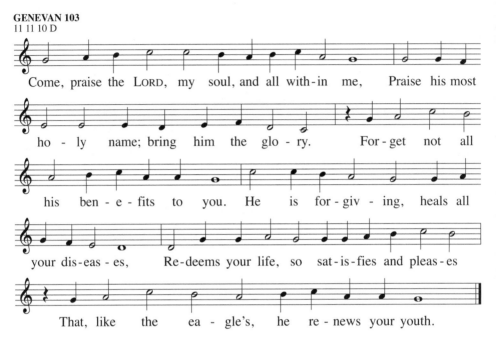

Come, praise the LORD, my soul, and all with-in me, Praise his most
ho - ly name; bring him the glo - ry. For - get not all
his ben - e - fits to you. He is for - giv - ing, heals all
your dis-eas - es, Re-deems your life, so sat-is-fies and pleas - es
That, like the ea - gle's, he re - news your youth.

Text: Psalm 103; vs. Helen Otte, 1986, © 1987, CRC Publications   PsH #103
Tune: Genevan Psalter, 1539

GENEVAN 107 is a dorian melody whose large leaps at the beginning remind one of SONNE DER GERECHTIGKEIT,[51] but in place of the forward verve there is a more anchored stability that sets this understanding of the Psalm's thanksgiving. The tune underwent minor changes when it took on William Kethe's English version of Psalm 107 in the Scottish Psalter of 1564. In that form as OLD 107TH it now appears with John Milton's "The Lord Will Come and Not Be Slow"[52] and Edward Plumptre's "Your Hand, O Lord, in Days of Old."[53]

GENEVAN 107
7 6 7 6 6 7 6 7

"Thanks be to God our Sav - ior," Let his re-deemed ones say.
"He shows us bound-less fa - vor; His love is sure each day."

From earth's re-mot-est lands   A cho-sen folk he rais-es,

Ran-somed from ty-rants' hands;   Join now to sound his prais-es.

Text: Psalm 107; vs. David J. Diephouse, 1985, © 1987, CRC Publications
Tune: Genevan Psalter, 1551

PsH #107

GENEVAN 124 or TOULON (where the third phrase of GENEVAN 124 is omitted—which Routley regarded as a "disreputable abridgement. . . leaving it like a ship without a keel"[54]) or OLD 124TH (where the third phrase of GENEVAN 124 is sometimes omitted[55]) is widely-known throughout much of the church and has been used for many texts, most commonly "God of the Prophets"[56] and "I Greet Thee Who My Sure Redeemer Art."[57] Though it began with a bit more rhythmic fire,[58] in its current version the first four lines repeat the same rhythm, and the last line alters it slightly near the end. Even without its earlier syncopation in the third line, it moves along boldly to set the text's affirmation that God is on our side against the foe.

GENEVAN 124
10 10 10 10 10

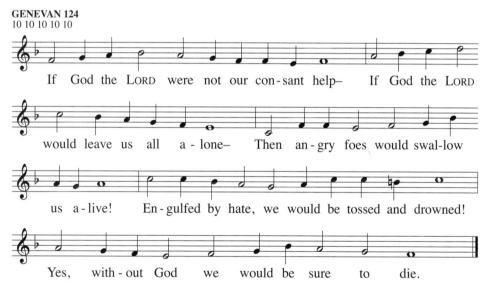

If God the LORD were not our con-sant help–   If God the LORD

would leave us all a-lone–   Then an-gry foes would swal-low

us a-live!   En-gulfed by hate, we would be tossed and drowned!

Yes, with-out God we would be sure to die.

Text: Psalm 124; vs. Calvin Seerveld, 1981, © 1987, CRC Publications
Tune: Genevan Psalter, 1551

PsH #124

GENEVAN 130, which comes from the 1539 Psalter, makes an instructive comparison with Luther's AUS TIEFER NOT[59] for the same psalm. (See Chapter III.) Both begin with a downward leap of a fifth, but after that the similarity ceases. Luther's tune immediately goes back up a fifth, and then—even though this is a cry from the depths—happily bounces off the beat at the second and succeeding phrases. It also takes twice as many leaps, sixteen versus eight for GENEVAN 130, which characteristically moves in more measured conjunct motion and embraces quarters between the halfs at the beginnings and ends of phrases.

GENEVAN 130
7 6 7 6 D

Out of the depths I cry, LORD. O Lord, please hear my call.

Let your ears be at-ten-tive; I beg for mer-cy, LORD.

If you marked our of-fens-es, O Lord, then who could stand?

But you grant us for-give-ness; There-fore we stand in awe.

Text: Psalm 130; vs. Robert D. Swets, 1981, © 1987, CRC Publications   PsH #130
Tune: Genevan Psalter, 1539

GENEVAN 134, used in the Genevan Psalter for Psalm 134, is the tune commonly known to much of the English-speaking church as OLD HUNDREDTH (OLD 100TH) because it was used in the Anglo-Genevan Psalter of 1561 for William Kethe's metrical version of Psalm 100. It is one of the best-known tunes in the church, marred only in congregational practice by the various rhythms to which it has been subjected. They cause vocal train wrecks when all the members of a congregation do not have the same rhythm in mind. Here the rhythm of all four phrases is the same. Melodically the second phrase repeats the first half of the first a third higher, then turns the second half of the first upside down to finish away from home on the supertonic. The third phrase slightly varies the contour of the first half of the first so it can conclude with the exact melodic contour of the end of the first, but a third lower. Then, leaps in the formerly conjunct quarter notes set up the last three notes from the second phrase, but now positioned to conclude on the tonic. The tightly woven structure suggests why this tune is so well known.

GENEVAN 134 (OLD HUNDREDTH)
LM

You ser-vants of the LORD our God Who work and pray both day and night, In God's own house lift up your hands And praise the LORD with all your might.

Text: Psalm 134; vs. Calvin Seerveld, 1981, © 1987, CRC Publications
Tune: Louis Bourgeois, 1551

PsH #134

GENEVAN 138, from the 1551 Psalter, bears a close resemblance to the widely-known Bohemian Brethren tune called MIT FREUDEN ZART, which went with the text that named it by George Vetter in his *Kirchengeseng* (Ivanãice, 1566). It has taken a couple of rhythmic shapes.[60] Marilyn Stulken says, "A French secular song, 'Une pastourelle gentille,' published by Pierre Attaingnant, 1529–1530, also bears some similarity," and she suggests the tune may come from "the late Middle Ages."[61] Like GENEVAN 68, it is a broad tune that spans an octave and gives congregations a wonderful ride over its arch.

GENEVAN 138
8 9 8 9 D

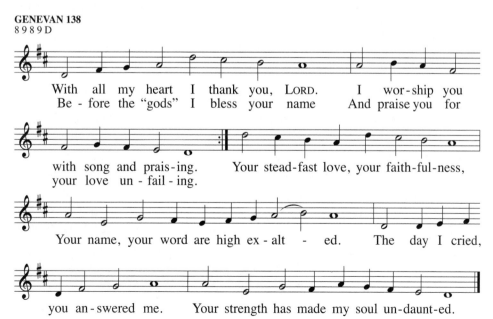

With all my heart I thank you, LORD. I wor-ship you
Be - fore the "gods" I bless your name And praise you for
with song and prais-ing. Your stead-fast love, your faith-ful-ness,
your love un - fail - ing.
Your name, your word are high ex - alt - ed. The day I cried,
you an - swered me. Your strength has made my soul un-daunt-ed.

Text: Psalm 138; vs. Stanley Wiersma, 1981, © 1987, CRC Publications
Tune: Genevan Psalter, 1551

PsH #138

Two Genevan tunes, originally paired with the rare texts that were not psalms, still are present among us and deserve to be mentioned before moving on. LES COMMANDEMENTS DE DIEU[62] is a tune by Bourgeois that was used for the metrical version of the Ten Commandments and passed through the chorale tradition as WENN WIR IN HÖCHSTEN NÖTEN SEIN.[63] NUNC DIMMITTIS or LE CANTIQUE DE SIMÉON,[64] often used today for "O Gladsome Light," was written by Bourgeois for Simeon's Song, the *Nunc dimittis* from Luke 2:29–32.

2. ENGLISH, SCOTTISH, AND WELSH

Meter

We have seen that GENEVAN 42 (FREU DICH SEHR) shed its 87 87 77 88 meter and took on Long Meter Double in the Anglo-Genevan Psalter of 1560 and that GENEVAN 101, which is 11 11 10 4, morphed into a Short Meter tune called ST. MICHAEL when it took on an English dress. These examples illustrate a central feature of English psalmody. Whereas Lutheran chorales and French psalm tunes employ many meters, English psalmody gravitates to a few: Short Meter (SM, 6686), Common Meter (CM, 8686), Long Meter (LM, 8888), and their use as repeats or "doubles"—Short Meter Double (SMD, 6686 6686), Common Meter Double (CMD, 8686 8686), and Long Meter Double (LMD, 8888 8888).[65] Routley explains the metric differences with a bit more precision. He says the "variety of meters" and "lyric freedom" of the Lutheran writers usually proceeded with rarely a ten-syllable line and usually eight syllables or fewer. The French "loved long lines but, normally, shortish stanzas, while the English showed an overpowering preference for the ballad, or Common, metre."[66] (The part about shortish French stanzas may not be accurate.[67]) The English also used fewer tunes, 66 tunes for 180 texts, according to Temperley.[68]

This means that, while chorales and Genevan psalm tunes have close ties to a central text for which they are often named (even though they may migrate to other texts as well), English metrical psalm tunes are more interchangeable and less associated with one specific text (even though the initial intention may have been, like the Genevan one, to have a tune for every text[69]). This gave rise to independent naming of tunes in the English practice, whereas for the Genevan and Lutheran streams the text was sufficient to identify the tune. It also gave rise to English and Scottish Psalters printed in what is sometimes called a "Dutch-door" format, with pages cut horizontally so that a tune is on one half of a page and a text on the other half.[70] The pages of the top half and bottom half can be turned independently of one another so that texts and tunes can be matched in various combinations, provided they have the same meter. This would be a hopeless endeavor for Genevan Psalters or for collections of Lutheran chorales, because the many meters of the tunes and texts in those genres provide little potential for such interchangeability.

Rhythm

"The rhythm of the earliest English psalm tunes is always irregular, as so often that of the Genevan was," says Routley.[71] He goes on to explain that "in successive printings" there are "inconsistencies. . . we constantly find rhythmic variations, and occasionally melodic variations too." Then he perceptively gets at the heart of the matter, not the details of a tune or its variations, but the underlying perspective.

> The principle that governed the composition of these primitive psalm tunes, inherited from Geneva, was the construction of a good melody which would, by its avoidance of the "beat" of either the march or the galliard, carry an external "sacred" quality. These people inherited a medieval conviction that the church was set apart from the world, and the one distinction they made between sacred and secular was to avoid a regular beat in the rhythm. This was assisted by their preference (also Genevan) for unaccompanied unison singing. A melody standing by itself and unimpeded by part writing could have a plainsong-like freedom of flow. . .[72]

One might add that the issue here is what common people who are not trained musicians can sing together. They can sing unaccompanied unison lines—even when some cultural contexts may make that seem strange. But what also needs to be noted is the concern for the church's distinctiveness, which has a musical embodiment in "freedom of flow" without instrumental or other external constraints. This may be seen as inherited from the medieval period for the English, as Routley suggests, and perhaps for Luther as well, since he is often regarded as still living in the medieval world. Calvin makes the idea of inheritance more difficult, however, since he is often regarded as living in or at least tilted toward the modern rather than the medieval world. I suspect the issue for the whole church—early, medieval, Reformation (Lutheran or Calvinist), counter-Reformation, modern, post-modern, or whatever—is that the distinctiveness is simply in the nature of the church, which makes any too cozy identification either with the culture or the museum untenable. That has musical implications. The implications are complex and never have simple solutions. Different traditions handle the relationships between Christ and culture[73] in different ways, and each generation contends with them anew; but they are avoided only by denying the church's being and message.

Worshiping Contexts

Congregational singing entered the English-speaking church "rather late in the Reformation period," says Nicholas Temperley, not until mid-sixteenth century,[74] although Miles Coverdale's (1488–1568) *Goostly Psalmes and Spirituall Songes*, which most likely came from around 1535 or 1536 and was "condemned to the flames in 1546,"[75] suggests an earlier but undocumented beginning in a complex web of associations with continental reforming activity.[76]

Congregational song took the form of psalm singing in two worshiping contexts. First, the Puritans who became Separatists and split from the Church of England as Presbyterians or Independents (Congregationalists) sang metrical psalms in ways derived from Calvin's liturgical practice.[77] Second, the Church of England (Anglicans) followed the *Book of Common Prayer*, which, parallel to Lutherans, cast the church's historic practice at worship into the vernacular. Anglicans, however, did not imbed hymnody in the Ordinary and Proper of the Mass or relate it to the Church Year as Lutherans did. Choirs sang the liturgy in choral settings, or congregations spoke it until the nineteenth century when John Merbecke's (ca. 1510–ca. 1585) congregational music for the Ordinary was retrieved[78] and hymns were related to the Church Year. In the sixteenth century, Anglican congregations sang metrical psalms

> before and after Morning and Evening Prayer, and also before and after
> Sermons; and moreover in private houses for their godly solace and comfort,
> laying apart all ungodly songs and ballads, which tend to nourishing vice, and
> corrupting of youth.[79]

Two Anglican traditions emerged, as Temperley has shown. In cathedrals and choral foundations, "choir-based liturgical singing" was the rule, though hymn singing "in later times" was not unknown there; and in parish churches "the congregational metrical psalm soon became the only musical aspect of worship."[80]

To summarize, both English Calvinists who broke from the Church of England and Anglicans sang metrical psalms. Like Lutherans and Calvinists, Anglicans—Calvinists or not—related the people's singing to the home, which is where it may have begun,[81] with its origins in the vernacular translations of Latin office hymns.[82] Anglicans related it to the liturgy as well, but more loosely than Luther or Calvin. The logical way to proceed with examples here, therefore, is in historical order.

Common Meter Double

"Virtually all the early English psalm tunes," says Routley, "were in Double Common Metre, the metrical psalms always being thought of in stanzas of four lines of fourteen syllables and indeed being printed so when they went into print."[83] They went into print in a progression similar to the Genevan Psalter, with the same completion date for England, 1562. For Scotland, the complete Psalter was published in 1564. It had more tunes and metrical variety than the English Psalter. The English one had 62 tunes. The Scottish one had 105 different tunes proper to specific psalms and 30 different meters.[84]

Routley saw two streams at work.[85] One was begun by Thomas Sternhold (d.1549) and the other by exiles from England in Geneva who, after 1556, produced several versions of an "Anglo-Genevan" Psalter to which we have already referred. Leaver charts a more complete picture of the sources.[86] The complete English Psalter in 1562 was called *The Whole Book of Psalmes, Collected into Englysh Meter by T. Starnhold, I. Hopkins & Others* (London) and is known as "Sternhold and Hopkins" or the "Old Version" or "Day's Psalter" because the printer John Day (1522–1584) published it. It went through a staggering number of editions[87] and was not challenged until 1696 in a "New Version," which we will encounter in Chapter VI.[88] The complete Scottish Psalter was attached to *The Forme of Prayers and Ministration of the Sacraments* (Edinburgh, 1564).

As in the Genevan psalm tunes and German chorales, the irregular rhythms of English psalm tunes were smoothed out over time into equal notes. ST. FLAVIAN is an example. It is a modification of the first half of a CMD tune that started out with an irregular rhythm of the Genevan type for Psalm 132 in Sternhold and Hopkins' "Old Version."

ST. FLAVIAN'S ancestor
CMD

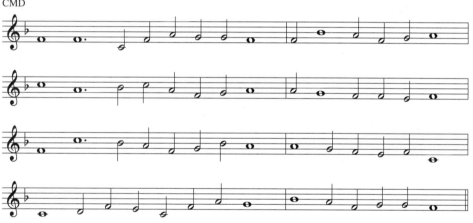

Tune: John Day, *English Psalter*, 1562   Stulken, HCLBW p.312

We have received ST. FLAVIAN through a mid-nineteenth century publication (Richard Redhead's *Church Hymn Tunes* [London, 1853]). In that form it has turned into Common Meter, and its longer gathering note at the beginning is gone along with the other longer notes, except for the dotted half notes that conclude the second and fourth phrases, similar to ST. MICHAEL. Maurice Frost says the tune was first used in this shortened form around 1599.[89] It has been attached to numerous texts.

ST. FLAVIAN
CM

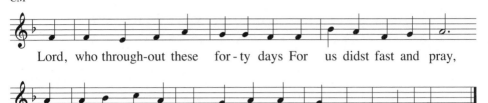

Lord, who through-out these for-ty days For us didst fast and pray,

Teach us with Thee to mourn our sins, And close by Thee to stay.

Text: Claudia F. I. Hernaman, 1873; alt.   Pres #81
Tune: Day's *Psalter*, 1562

Thomas Tallis

Around the time the Old Version was published, its printer, John Day, printed another complete metrical Psalter, this one by the Archbishop of Canterbury, Matthew Parker (*The Whole Psalter Translated into English Meter* [London, ca.1567]). Thomas Tallis (ca.1505–1585), probably the finest composer of his time and place, wrote nine tunes to go with it, the first eight in the church modes in numerical order. Three of them are still in common use.

1) THIRD MODE MELODY or THE THIRD TUNE is phrygian as its name suggests. Its original conception was angrier than we are apt to hear it. Parker's Psalter said, "The third doth rage: and roughly brayth."[90] It was used for Psalm 2, which in Parker's translation came out as,

> Why fum'th in sight: the Gentiles' spite
> in fury raging stout?[91]

We hear and sing this remarkable melody in a more mellow way, perhaps influenced by Ralph Vaughan Williams' equally remarkable *Fantasia on a Theme by Thomas Tallis*.

THIRD MODE MELODY
CMD

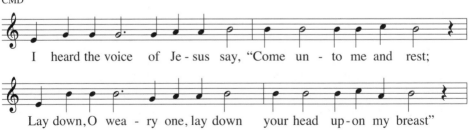

I heard the voice of Je-sus say, "Come un - to me and rest;

Lay down, O wea - ry one, lay down your head up-on my breast"

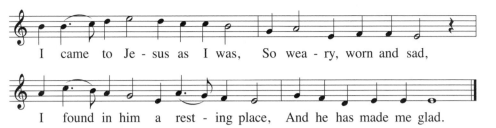

I came to Je - sus as I was, So wea - ry, worn and sad,

I found in him a rest - ing place, And he has made me glad.

Text: Horatius Bonar, 1846, alt.   Mor #606
Tune: Thomas Tallis, 1561

2) TALLIS' CANON (or THE EIGHTH TUNE because it was the eighth in Parker's Psalter—with mixolydian hints in the harmony, but not the tune) is best known, especially in its association with Thomas Ken's evening hymn, "All Praise to Thee, My God, This Night," from a century and a half later. Originally for Psalm 67 (which makes an interesting comparison with Luther's version of Psalm 67 set to ES WOLLE GOTT UNS GNÄDIG SEIN[92]), each phrase was repeated twice.[93] As we sing it, each phrase is sung once in a skillfully crafted tune that congregations can handle quite ably even in a four-voice canon.

TALLIS' CANON
LM

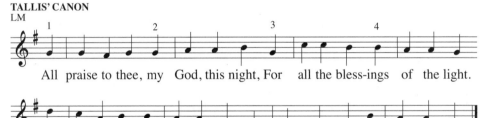

All praise to thee, my God, this night, For all the bless-ings of the light.

Keep me, O keep me, King of kings, Be - neath thine own al - might-y wings.

Text: Thomas Ken, 1694, appendix to *A Manual of Prayers*, 1695   HWB #658
Tune: Thomas Tallis, *The Whole Psalter Translated into English Metre*, 1561-1567

3) TALLIS' ORDINAL, the ninth and simplest tune in Parker's Psalter, has the melody in the soprano, not the tenor as was usual for tunes with harmonizations. It was not intended for a psalm, but for Parker's metrical version of "Veni Creator Spiritus," which was used in place of a similar text in the Ordinal (hence the name of the tune) of the Prayer Book for the ordination of priests. The third line repeats the first, and the second sets up the satisfaction of the last. "There is something ageless about this little tune,"[94] which is "the earliest-known hymn tune in common meter."[95]

TALLIS' ORDINAL
CM

The great Cre - a - tor of the worlds, The sov-er eign God of heaven,

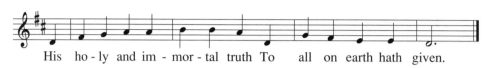

His ho - ly and im - mor - tal truth To all on earth hath given.

Text: *Epistle to Diognetus*, ca. 150; tr. F. Bland Tucker, 1895-1984, rev.   H82 #489
Tune: Thomas Tallis, 1505?-1585

Short Meter

SOUTHWELL, whose composer is unknown, is one of the earliest Short Meter tunes.[96] Its source is *The Psalmes of David in English Metre, with Notes of Foure Partes Set unto Them* (London, 1579) collected and harmonized by William Damon (also Daman, ca.1540–1591), where it is the setting for Psalm 45. This tune is unusual in that it is built by the repetition of a repeated note figure. Here it is in two rhythmic shapes and different keys. The first example in f minor with even note lengths comes through *Hymns Ancient and Modern* in the nineteenth century (where it went with Wesley's "Thou Judge of Quick and Dead"); the second example with dotted rhythms is as Damon gave it.[97]

SOUTHWELL
SM

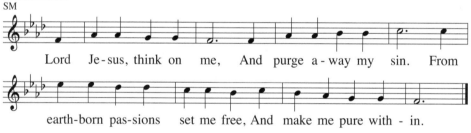

Lord Je-sus, think on me, And purge a-way my sin. From

earth-born pas-sions set me free, And make me pure with - in.

Text: Synesius of Cyrene, *Tenth Ode by Synesius*, ca. 375-414; tr. Allen W. Chatfield, *Songs and Hymns of the Earliest Greek*   HWB #527
    Christian Poets, 1876
Tune: W. Damon's *Psalmes of David*, 1579

SOUTHWELL
SM

Lord Je - sus, think on me, And purge a - way my sin;

From harm - ful pas-sions set me free, And make me pure with-in.

Text: Synesius of Cyrene, 375?-414?; tr. Allen William Chatfield, 1808-1896, alt.   H82 #641
Tune: *Daman's Psalter*, 1579; adapt. *Hymnal 1982*

In both of these versions short phrases are concluded with long notes. Paul Richardson perceptively points to a "critical turning point" here.

When we begin to have long notes between short phrases, we lose the momentum of the rhythmic breath and of the textual thought. This creates not merely a caesura, but a stop. I think this is a critical turning point in the history of the hymn tune. The breaths in chorales and psalter tunes come with the metric pulse of the longer notes, not after we have mentally "sat down."[98]

Common Meter and "Common" Tunes

WINCHESTER OLD is a well-known Common Meter tune, associated today with a paraphrase of Luke 2:8–15, which Tate and Brady included in the sixth edition of their *Supplement to the New Version of the Psalms* (London, 1708). A century earlier it originally went with a metrical version of Psalm 84 in the *Whole Book of Psalms* (London, 1592) published by the music printer Thomas East, also Este (d.1608). Nicholas Temperley regards it as "a member of a large family of tunes of which OLD 81ST" is the mother and OLD 120TH and Chapter 2 [or 8] of Christopher Tye's *Actes of the Apostles* (London, 1553) are members.[99]

WINCHESTER OLD

CM

While shep-herds watched their flocks by night, All seat-ed on the ground,

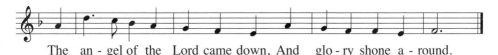

The an-gel of the Lord came down, And glo-ry shone a-round.

Text: Nahum Tate, 1625-1715   H82 #94
Tune: *The Whole Booke of Psalmes*, 1592

Perspective: The Bible in Meter, Common Vocabulary, Harmonizations
    1) In this period, a propensity to metricize the Bible and set the metrical versions to music moved beyond the psalms. Canticles as New Testament successors of the psalms were obvious candidates for this treatment, but casting a whole book of the Bible into meter suggests the extent of this interest at the time. The *Actes of the Apostles* is "a ballad-metre version" of the book of Acts, which Routley calls "delectable doggerel."[100] The anonymous poet managed to complete the first fourteen chapters. Christopher Tye (ca.1505–ca.1572), another fine

composer of the period, set each of the chapters to a harmonized and slightly contrapuntal CMD tune.

2) A common musical vocabulary is in play, parallel to the one in late seventeenth century Germany around tunes like MUNICH.[101] (See the next chapter.) Routley gives the setting from Chapter 8 of the *Actes of the Apostles*[102] and then says "exactly what the connection" is "between its second half and WINCHESTER OLD . . . is beyond speculation, or between its last phrase and that of OLD 81ST,[103] but it is clear that the typical Common tune in English psalmody owes a good deal to Tye's style."[104] Nicholas Temperley calls WINDSOR "one of the 'minimalist' tunes forged from the cells common to the music of the day, perhaps crafted by several hands, as anonymous as a table or woven cloth."[105] Some see it related to Chapter 3 of Tye's *Actes of the Apostles*, but Temperley points out that the "Tye piece is scarcely a 'tune'" and that what we have is more of "a general style and character."[106]

3) Collections of harmonized tunes became characteristic. WINDSOR first appeared in 1591 in two books of Damon's published after his death, *The Former* and *The Second Book of the Musicke of M. William Damon* (London), the first with the melody in the tenor as was normal for the period, and the second with the melody in the soprano as was unusual. Damon's *Psalms* from 1579 were also harmonized. So were Tallis' tunes in Parker's Psalter and the tunes in East's *Whole Book of Psalms*.

The harmonized music in these collections was fundamentally for recreational use at home, not for use in church. Damon's practice "of composing a new harmonization each time he visited a friend's house, for the friend's private enjoyment,"[107] tells the tale. So does the title of the 1591 publication—"Published for the recreation of such as delight in Musicke,"[108] and its part-book format—that is, set up in such a way that people could sit around a table and sing. We might add Routley's hint that the practice of unison singing in church was not regarded in Scotland or England with quite the legal force it had in Geneva.[109] In Scotland there was at least some harmonized singing in the assembled church at worship before the end of the sixteenth century. Gordon Munro says there is evidence that harmonized settings by composers like David Peebles (fl. 1530–1576, d. before 1592), Andrew Kemp (fl. 1560–1570), and Andrew Blackhall (1535/6–1609) were sung at worship services.[110]

WINDSOR is given by Damon in the same form in both of his 1591 books (despite their titles), with Psalm 116.[111] The melody is in the soprano, each phrase of which is prepared by very brief imitative entries in the lower three parts. In this form, the diminished fourth between the first two phrases of the melody (between the last two phrases a slightly different form of the melody from our version avoided the diminished fourth) is separated by rests and prepared by the harmony of the lower voices. When the tune proceeds as a unison line without a break as it would be sung in church, the two notes of the diminished fourth are set next to one another. Here it is in a Genevan-style version with quarter notes nestled between half notes and an interesting interplay of twos and threes.

WINDSOR
CM

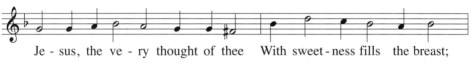

Je - sus, the ve - ry thought of thee   With sweet - ness fills   the breast;

But sweet - er far thy face to see,   And in   thy pres - ence rest.

Text: Latin, 12th c., tr. Edward Caswall, 1814-1878, alt.   H82 #642
Tune: William Damon, 1540?-1591?

Here it is with the rhythm more regularized, but still in a Genevan flavor of quarters between halves.

WINDSOR
CM

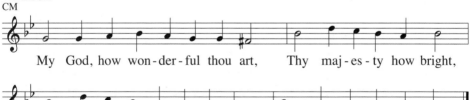

My   God, how won - der - ful thou art,   Thy   maj - es - ty how bright,

How   beau - ti - ful thy mer - cy seat,   In   depths of burn - ing light!

Text: Frederick William Faber, 1814-1863   H82 #643
Tune: William Damon, 1540?-1591?

And here it is in a more isometric version where successive quarter notes almost turn it into two phrases, each leading to a dotted half. Whereas WINCHESTER OLD moved to the dominant at the end of the second phrase, windsor moves to the relative major at that point. This version of the tune accentuates that movement by minimizing the cadences of the first and third phrases.

WINDSOR
CM

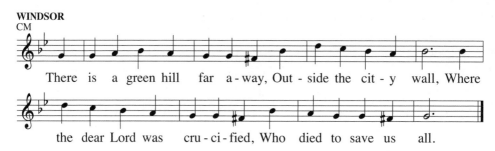

Text: Cecil F. Alexander, 1823-1895   LBW #114
Tune: Damon, *Booke of Musicke,* 1591

Temperley says that "although WINDSOR was new in 1591, there is no good reason to suppose that Damon was the author of the melody,"[112] which suggests it preceded Damon's little setting of it. That may be so, although a diminished fourth, even between phrases, might be expected to trip up a congregation, which is probably one reason (another is a continuing modal undertow) why it appeared in *The Book of Psalmes* by Henry Ainsworth (Amsterdam, 1612) with a F-natural throughout (no sharps even in the final cadence).[113] The tune apparently works with the F-sharp because the tonic is so strong that the first note of the second and fourth phrases can be easily found by congregations as they simultaneously delight in the darker ambiguity of the diminished fourth. (Congregations do not think this out. They simply experience it.) Whether or not the tunesmith (or tunesmiths) who uncovered this melody sensed this characteristic, the tune "vied in popularity with OLD HUNDREDTH itself, appearing in more than seven hundred publications between 1591 and 1820."[114] East's book of 1592 was one of those publications to which we must give some closer attention.

East "provided every psalm with a tune,"[115] a new wrinkle he introduced to English psalm books, though he repeated many tunes. The tunes were also harmonized, but the "landmark" character of his book, according to Temperley, was "its extensive use of a new kind of four-line tune for the great majority of the psalms." "Great majority" was an understatement, for in the second edition in 1594 East noted three Common Meter tunes and one Short Meter tune and said, "The Psalmes are song [sic] to these 4 tunes in most churches of this Realme." Temperley indicates East "set no less than 107 of the 176 psalm and hymn texts to one of these. Four other common-meter tunes were used only once each." (The "hymn texts" were like the ones in the Old Version, metrical versions of canticles, the Athanasian Creed, the Lord's Prayer, the Ten Commandments, prayers, and "The Creed.") Since these tunes were attached to so many texts but no specific one, they needed to be identified. East named them. He generally employed geographical references. That set in motion a practice still in force, of choosing names, often of a church or a location, without any textual reference.

What East did, says Temperley, "was not so much an innovation as a recognition of what already had taken place."[116] The Common Meter Double metrical psalm of four lines with fourteen syllables to a line had broken into two and came out as Common Meter, that is, four shorter lines that alternately employ eight and six syllables. A few such anonymous but commonly known tunes were used in England, with parallel developments in Scotland and Wales. *The CL. Psalms of David* printed in 1615 in Edinburgh grouped twelve monophonic "common tunes" together under this heading: "THE XII COMMON TUNES, TO the which all Psalmes of eight syllables in the first line, and six in the next may bee sung."[117] Temperley cites the Welsh collection, *Llyfr y Psalmau* (London, 1621) by the archdeacon and poet Edmwnd Prys (1544–1623), which had twelve comparable monophonic tunes, and notes that the three "national repertories overlap in complex ways," all preferring the four-line Common Meter tune. Then he says it was this sort of tune that is "the real rock on which English-language psalmody and hymnody have been founded" rather than the older longer psalm tunes.[118] In Scotland the "'12 common tunes' remained almost unchallenged for two centuries and more," and in England and America "twenty or more of the tunes never fell out of favor."[119] The Short Meter tunes SOUTHWELL, WINCHESTER OLD, and WINDSOR in the more usual Common Meter are among these "common" tunes. Here are several others still in use.

CHESHIRE is a haunting tune in minor that adroitly balances conjunct, disjunct, upward, and downward motion within a seventh. It appeared in East's 1592 *Whole Book of Psalmes* in a harmonization by the madrigalist John Farmer (fl.1591–1601) for Psalm 146 and in one by the lutenist and composer John Dowland (1563–1626) for "A Prayer for the Queenes [sic] Most Excellent Majesty."

CHESHIRE
CM

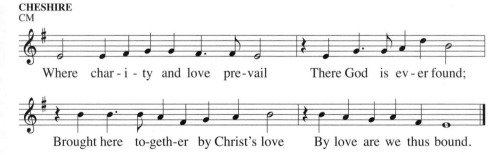

Text: Latin; tr. by Omer Westendorf, 1916-1998, © 1960, 1961, World Library Publications   H82 #581
Tune: *The Whole Booke of Psalmes*, 1592

DUNDEE is one of the twelve common tunes from the 1615 Scottish Psalter where it was called FRENCH TUNE. The editor and composer Thomas Ravenscroft (ca. 1582–ca. 1635) called it DUNDY TUNE in his *Whole Book of Psalmes* (London, 1621). Since WINDSOR was also sometimes called DUNDIE, the resultant jumble has introduced a certain perplexity. DUNDEE is a gracious little tune that spans an octave and a second, moves up to the fifth and back to the tonic in the first two phrases, then presses to the top octave in the third phrase before it repeats the second in the last. It propels itself forward by landing on the subdominant at the end of the first phrase and the dominant at the end of the third.

DUNDEE
CM

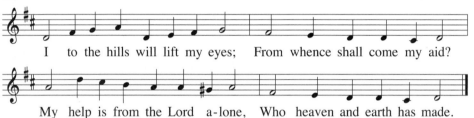

I to the hills will lift my eyes; From whence shall come my aid?
My help is from the Lord a-lone, Who heaven and earth has made.

Text: *The Psalter*, 1912; alt., 1988   Pres #234
Tune: *Scottish Psalter*, 1615

CAITHNESS is cut from the same cloth. It too spans an octave and a second and begins with the same intervals. Unlike DUNDEE, however, it then moves down and immediately up by step to the fifth at the end of the second phrase. In the third phrase, the stepwise movement continues upward before it leaps down a minor sixth and then proceeds by step before it comes to rest on the tonic at the end. In a reversal of the harmonic sequence of DUNDEE, the first and third phrases first imply the dominant and then the subdominant. This was one of the common tunes given in a harmonized version without a text in the 1635 Scottish Psalter, *The Psalmes of David in Prose and Meter* (Edinburgh). (Routley says there was a "complete absence before 1625 of any harmonized Psalters in general circulation" in Scotland.[120]) It was named for a county in the far northeast of Scotland and first called CAITHNESS TUNE.

CAITHNESS
CM

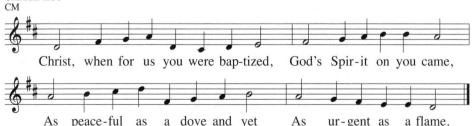

Christ, when for us you were bap-tized, God's Spir-it on you came,
As peace-ful as a dove and yet As ur-gent as a flame.

Text: F. Bland Tucker, 1895-1984, rev.   H82 #121
Tune: *The Psalmes of David in Prose and Meeter*, 1635

Perspective: The Precentor's Nightmare

To see two similar tunes like DUNDEE and CAITHNESS set side by side is to suffer the precentor's nightmare. Samuel Sewall (1652–1730), a New England chief justice and judge, served Old South Church in Boston as its precentor. Remember, he had to lead the congregation without any instrumental or choral help at all. In his diary for the Lord's Day on February 2, 1718, he wrote this: "In the Morning I set York Tune, and in the 2nd going over, the Gallery carried it irresistibly to St. David's, which discouraged me very much."[121] Here are the tunes in question.

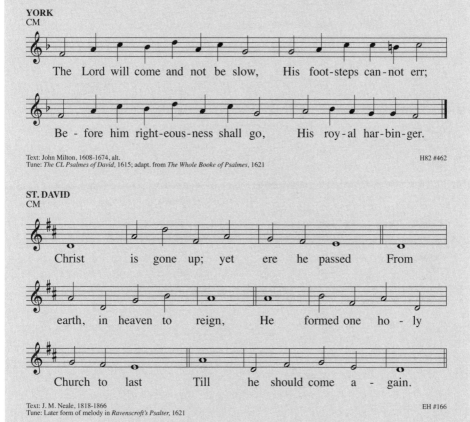

YORK
CM

The Lord will come and not be slow, His foot-steps can-not err;

Be - fore him right-eous-ness shall go, His roy-al har-bin-ger.

Text: John Milton, 1608-1674, alt.
Tune: *The CL Psalmes of David*, 1615; adapt. from *The Whole Booke of Psalmes*, 1621

H82 #462

ST. DAVID
CM

Christ is gone up; yet ere he passed From

earth, in heaven to reign, He formed one ho - ly

Church to last Till he should come a - gain.

Text: J. M. Neale, 1818-1866
Tune: Later form of melody in *Ravenscroft's Psalter*, 1621

EH #166

The leaps of these tunes—which may stand behind ST. ANNE, to be discussed in Chapter VI—could lead to pitfalls, even though they have fewer obvious similarities than DUNDEE and CAITHNESS. In either case, congregational confusion could easily stand at the precentor's doorstep.

DUNFERMLINE, one of the twelve common tunes in the 1615 Scottish Psalter, moves to the dominant at midstream like WINCHESTER OLD. It comes to us in three rhythmic versions, like WINDSOR. Here is a version with Psalm 1.

DUNFERMLINE
CM

How bless'd are they who, fear-ing God, From sin re-strain their feet,

Who will not with the wick-ed stand, Who shun the scorn-er's seat.

Text: based on Psalm 1, *Psalter*, 1912, alt.　　　　　　　　　　　　　　　　HWB #525
Tune: *The CL Psalmes of David*, 1615

Routley regarded BRISTOL as one of the "most brilliant" common tunes,[122] though it is little used today. It comes from Ravenscroft's *Whole Book of Psalmes* in 1621. Whereas DUNDEE, CAITHNESS, CHESHIRE, and DUNFERMLINE all work upwards from the tonic and span an octave or so, BRISTOL works down from the fifth and stays within a fifth, except for the leading tone at the end of the third phrase, which only increases the compass to a minor sixth. For three phrases, it gradually sinks lower as it moves through the dominant and then makes a summation in the last phrase.

BRISTOL
CM

Hark! the glad sound! the Sav - ior comes, The Sav-ior prom-ised long:

Let ev - 'ry heart pre-pare a throne, And ev - 'ry voice a song.

Text: Philip Doddridge, 1702-1751　　　　　　　　　　　　　　　　　　H82 #71
Tune: *The Whole Booke of Psalmes*, 1621

Orlando Gibbons
SONG 67 is one of the common tunes. It comes from the Welsh collection of 1621 by Edmwnd Prys where it was set to Psalm 1 and may have been written by Prys.[123] In 1623 it was used as the setting for a metrical version of Acts 1, the "67th Song" in George Wither's *Hymnes and Songs of the Church* (London, 1623), authorized for publication, but never published because it contained hymns.[124]

Orlando Gibbons (1583–1625) contributed all the tunes to this book except this one, for which he apparently supplied the bass line.[125] It is the most gradually arch-like of all the common tunes we have encountered.

SONG 67
CM

Text: Matthew Bridges, 1800-1894, alt.   H82 #697
Tune: *Llyfr y Psalmau*, 1621

Gibbons was one of the best organists and composers from this period. He is a transitional figure from the anonymous tunes to those stamped by individuals. Of the sixteen tunes Gibbons provided for Wither's book, seven are still in use. Most of them are in one or two of the fourteen hymnals we consulted (SONG 4,[126] SONG 22,[127] SONG 24,[128] and SONG 46[129]—the last actually the "47th" in Wither's publication, but mis-numbered and known as SONG 46), but SONG 34 is in three of the hymnals, SONG 1 is in four, and SONG 13 (also known as CANTERBURY) in eight. Taken together, that is a remarkable record, especially for a composer of Gibbons' stature. Usually first-rate composers have little interest in or capacity to write hymn tunes, an enormously difficult task. Routley thought Gibbons did not have congregations in mind and dashed his tunes off in a hurry.[130] Whether or not he is right, here are three of Gibbons' tunes that have served congregations well. (The second of these is given in two versions.)

SONG 1
10 10 10 10 10 10

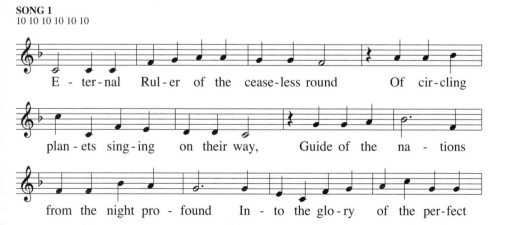

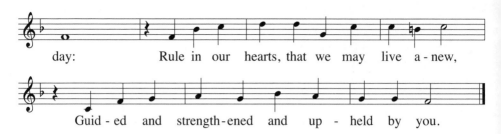

Text: John White Chadwick, 1864, alt.   VU #571
Tune: Orlando Gibbons, 1623, alt.

SONG 13
7777

Text: Samuel Longfellow, 1864, alt.   PsH #423
Tune: Orlando Gibbons, 1623

The version of SONG 13 just given is an altered one known as CANTERBURY. Here is a version closer to Gibbons' original.[131] This is one of those rare instances where the ornamented final phrase, which might appear to be anti-congregational, works because the sixteenths ride up so easily on pitches that were just sung. (Mary Oyer, whose Mennonite tradition is a cappella, says, "We have found this possible for singing."[132])

SONG 13
7777

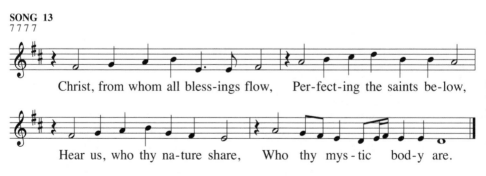

Text: Charles Wesley, *Hymns and Sacred Poems*, 1740, alt.   HWB #365
Tune: Orlando Gibbons, *Hymnes and Songs of the Church*, 1623

The next tune, song 34, is the same as SONG 9, except for the rhythm of the first line.[133] (In SONG 9 the fourth and fifth notes are twice as long.) The two rhythms have been interchanged in some publications.

SONG 34
LM

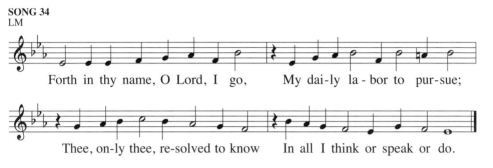

Forth in thy name, O Lord, I go,   My dai-ly la - bor to pur-sue;

Thee, on-ly thee, re-solved to know   In all I think or speak or do.

Text: Charles Wesley, 1707-1788
Tune: Orlando Gibbons, 1583-1625

LBW #505

The meters of these tunes immediately jump off the page after all the CM tunes we have encountered. They signal a new world that alters the way a congregation breathes and sings. There is also another sensibility about these tunes. They are not as "anonymous as a table or woven cloth," but bear the stamp of a single and skillful compositional hand. At issue is not better or worse, but "different." There are two worlds here—which, in Routley's words, will "crack" as we will see in Chapter VI—but for now live side by side, as the next two tunes illustrate. These two have some, but not much, use among us today.

Two More "Anonymous" Seventeenth-century Tunes
Let two anonymous tunes stand for all the ones not cited here. CULROSS (pronounced Kew-ross, Routley says[134]) comes from the 1635 Scottish Psalter, edited by Edward Millar, and may have been written by him.

CULROSS
CM

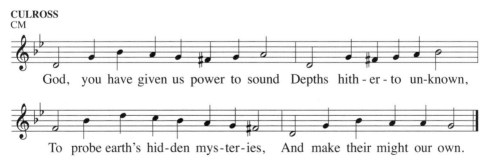

God, you have given us power to sound Depths hith - er - to un-known,

To probe earth's hid-den mys-ter-ies, And make their might our own.

Text: George Wallace Briggs, 1875-1959, alt., by permission of Oxford University Press
Tune: *The Psalmes of David in Prose and Meeter*, 1635

H82 #584

This tune has a curious feature. Its "first and third phrases harmonize each other in invertible counterpoint."[135]

COLERAINE in its current shape as given here is in bar form. It was originally a Long Meter tune without the repeat of the first two lines, one of the few LM tunes in this set. First published in 1681 in an Irish anthology called *La Scala Santa*, it did not enter English-speaking hymnody until the 1904 edition of *Hymns Ancient and Modern*.[136]

COLERAINE
888888

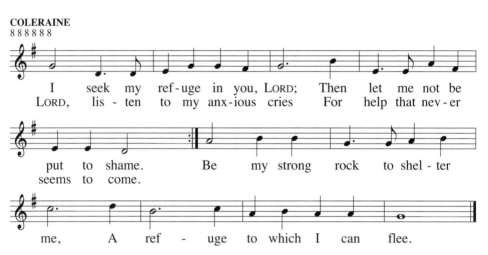

I seek my ref-uge in you, LORD; Then let me not be
LORD, lis-ten to my anx-ious cries For help that nev-er

put to shame. Be my strong rock to shel-ter
seems to come.

me, A ref - uge to which I can flee.

Text: Psalm 31; vers. Marie J. Post, 1985, © 1987, CRC Publications   PsH #31
Tune: *La Scala Santa*, Ireland, 1681

We now leave the Psalter tune stream and return to the one we left at the end of Chapter III. After following its course, we will return to this one at the beginning of the eighteenth century in Chapter VI.

---

1   James Hastings Nichols, *Corporate Worship in the Reformed Tradition* (Philadelphia: The Westminster Press, 1968), 34f.

2   See Bard Thompson, *Liturgies of the Western Church* (Cleveland: Meridian Books, 1961), 191 and 198.

3   Ibid., 204

4   Ibid., 208.

5   Nichols, 56.

6   The Reformed Church in Japan has "just completed the final installment of psalms set to Genevan Psalm tunes" [correspondence with Emily Brink, June 7, 2004].

7   Reformed Psalters, like Lutheran hymnals, were hot items in the sixteenth century. As indicated in the last chapter, "Almost a hundred Lutheran hymnals were published in Luther's lifetime" (*Luther's Works*, 53, 317). As to Psalters, Édith Weber says that "in 1562 alone more than 30,000 copies" of the Genevan Psalter were sold, "and more would have been, had not the civil and religious situation in France been so explosive" (Emily R. Brink, "The Genevan Psalter," Brink/Polman, PsHH, 28). John Witvliet says that within a few years of the complete Psalter's publication in 1562, "the number of the Genevan Psalter may well have reached one hundred thousand in over thirty editions, in addition to the thousands of copies printed in translation in nine languages" (John D. Witvliet, *Worship Seeking Understanding: Windows into Christian Practice* [Grand Rapids: Baker Academic, 2003], 205).

8   Nichols, 59.

9   See Luther, "Concerning the Order of Public Worship, *Luther's Works*, vol. 53, 12–14, and "The German Mass and Order of Service," *Luther's Works*, Vol. 53, 68–69.

10 Calvin did not get his wish of weekly communion in Geneva, and Reformed practice varied from weekly to monthly to quarterly, the last of these where Ulrich Zwingli's influence from Zurich was felt (and where there was no congregational singing or music of any kind).

11 Nichols, 59.

12 "Detailed tables . . ., which were framed and hung in the three Genevan churches, specified which psalms would be sung at each Sunday morning, Sunday afternoon, and Wednesday service. In 1549, the entire extant Psalter could be sung every seventeen weeks. By 1562, twenty-five weeks were required, the congregation singing upward of thirty stanzas per week" (Witvliet, *Worship Seeking Understanding*, 210).

13 Nichols, 95–96.

14 This naming and numbering can be seen in PsH where the first 150 "hymns" are metrical psalms in biblical order. About a fifth of the tunes for these are taken from the Genevan Psalter. Pres has fewer metrical psalms in its "Psalms" section, #s 158–258, and a few Genevan tunes.

15 Emily R. Brink, "The Genevan Psalter," Brink/Polman, PsHH, 31–32.

16 Temperley, HTI, I, 47, says 126. Leaver, *Goostly Psalmes and Spirituall Songes*, 52, says 128.

17 Emily R. Brink, "The Genevan Psalter," Brink/Polman, PsHH, 33. Brink gives a list of the specific tune repetitions in the Genevan Psalter. For more detail about the matching of tunes to texts see Witvliet, *Worship Seeking Understanding*, 216–217. For more complete detail and the tunes themselves, see Pierre Pidoux, *Le Psautier Huguenot, I, Les Mélodies; II, Documents et Bibliographie* (Kassel: Édition Baerenreiter Bâle, 1962), and a more dated book, Waldo Selden Pratt, *The Music of the French Psalter of 1562* (New York: Columbia University Press, 1939).

18 Unless only the "male portion" of the congregation sang, as Temperley, HTI, I, 6, hints. Temperley thinks "the strict Calvinist tradition had forbidden women to sing in church" (Nicholas Temperley, "The Lock Hospital Chapel and Its Music," *Journal of the Royal Musical Association* 118 [1993]: 64), but already in sixteenth century Strasbourg there are reports of women singing together with the men (Brink/Polman, PsHH, 29). At issue is whether the "strict Calvinist tradition" actually did shut out women and where it pertained (probably not in Strasbourg).

19 Emily R. Brink, "The Genevan Psalter," Brink/Polman, PsHH, 36–37.

20 See Leaver, *Goostly Psalmes and Spirituall Songes*, 41.

21 Psalm 6 was one of the exceptions. See PsH #6.

22 For a general discussion of "Hymn Singing at Home," see Temperley, HTI, I, 27–29.

23 See Westermeyer, *Te Deum*, 157.

24 See John Calvin, *Commentary on the Book of Psalms* (Grand Rapids: Wm. B. Eerdmans Publishing Company, 1949), Psalm XXXIII, vol. I, 539, and Psalm LXXI, vol. III, 98.

25 James McKinnon, "The Meaning of the Patristic Polemic Against Musical Instruments," *Current Musicology* I (1965): 70–71.

26 Carl Schalk, *Luther on Music: Paradigms of Praise* (Saint Louis: CPH, 1988), 45.

27 Though Richard Terry, *Calvin's First Psalter [1539]* (London: Ernest Benn Limited, 1932) has been superseded, Terry was not wrong when he quoted Prothero about Marot's psalms first being "sung to popular airs alike by Roman Catholics and Calvinists" (page iii) for "private use" (page v), nor was he wrong when he said this: "History is full of strange ironies, but none more strange than the chain of circumstances which led to Metrical Psalmody beginning as the favourite recreation of a gay Catholic court and ending as the exclusive 'hall-mark' of the severest form of Protestantism" (page iii). In any event, the music Calvin sought was something set apart with "weight and majesty."

28 For a list of plainsong sources of the melodies in Calvin's Psalters, see Leaver, *Goostly Psalmes and Spirituall Songes*, 49.

29 Witvliet, *Worship Seeking Understanding*, 219.

30 Leaver, *Goostly Psalmes and Spirituall Songes*, 49.

31 Ibid., 220, FN 73.

32 Ibid., 213–214.

33 John Calvin, *Institutes of the Christian Religion*, II, vii, 12 (Calvin, *The Institutes of the Christian Religion*, ed. John T. McNeill, *The Library of Christian Classics*, XX [Philadelphia: The Westminster Press, 1960], 360). The three uses of the law are laid out by Calvin in the *Institutes*, II, vii, 6–12. The first discloses sinfulness and propels to confession, the second restrains, and the third admonishes and urges on believers. Lutherans reverse the numbering of the first two and argue about whether the third exists or is present in the restraining use. I have tried to analyze these differences and their implications for the church's music in "Te Deum Laudamus: Church Music, the People's Office—Part 1: Past: Participation or Audience," *Cross Accent* 10:1 (Spring 2002): 30–36.

34 For the central naming here I am using the scheme of PsH where the first 150 "hymns" are metrical psalms in Biblical order. About a fifth of the tunes for these are taken from the Genevan Psalter, named "GENEVAN" followed by the number of the psalm.

35 Both Pratt, *The Music of the French Psalter of 1562*, 92, and Pidoux, *Le Psautier Huguenot*, I, 20, give more time at the cadences for this tune, and for some other ones.

36 Stulken, HCLBW, 128. Robin Leaver, "Comfort, Comfort Ye My People," Glover, H82C, 3A, 126–127, gives more detail about this.

37 LBW #266. See Leaver, "Comfort, Comfort Ye My People," Glover, H82C, 3A, 126.

38 Pidoux, *Le Psautier Huguenot*, I, 76, gives it with Psalm 72.

39 For the tune with this text, see Leaver, *Goostly Psalmes and Spirituall Songes*, 27.

40 Pidoux, *Le Psautier Huguenot*, I, 44, gives it with Psalm 36. So does Pratt, *The Music of the French Psalter of 1562*, 116.

41 See Robin Leaver, "I'll Praise My Maker While I've Breath," Glover, H82, 3B, 806–808, for more detail about this tune and its evolution. The shortened from appeared after Watts and Wesley. Watts had the earlier long one in mind, and Wesley printed the long version in his *Foundery Collection*.

42 Routley, MCH, 29B, gets at this in a long discussion of GENEVAN 68, which he regarded as foreshadowing the Genevan style and, unlike Lutheran tunes, immediately exportable.

43 Pidoux, *Le Psautier Huguenot*, I, 84, gives it with Psalm 86.

44 Ibid., 108, gives it with Psalm 118. Pratt, *The Music of the French Psalter of 1562*, 142, gives it with Psalm 66.

45 As in H82 #302, Meth #565, Wor3 #558,

46 Which is where Pidoux, *Le Psautier Huguenot*, I, 119, locates it.

47 PsH # 51.

48   Brink/Polman, PsHH, 387.

49   H82 #665.

50   Robin Leaver, "O Day of God, Draw Nigh," Glover, H82C, 3B, 1108–1109, details the metamorphosis.

51   LBW #210.

52   LBW, #318.

53   LBW, #431.

54   Routley, MCH, 32A.

55   As in CW #s 309 and 543.

56   Cov #621, CW #543, H82 #359, NC #358, and PsH #521.

57   Cov #66, NC #251, and Pres #457. (See above at GENEVAN 101.)

58   See Brink/Polman, PsHH, 260, for a description.

59   LBW #295.

60   Compare, for example, Wor3 #438 and LBW #421.

61   Stulken, HCLBW, 237.

62   PsH #153, HWB #469, and Pres #550.

63   CW #413, HWB #131, and LBW #303.

64   PsH #216, H82 #36, and Wor3 #679.

65   Routley, MCH, 38 and 46–47, gives the counts of meters for the English and Scottish Psalters.

66   Routley, MCH, 26B.

67   Emily Brink has done a partial count which calls into question Routley's analysis here (correspondence, June 7, 2004).

68   Temperley, HTI, I, 47.

69   Routley, MCH, 36A.

70   An example is *The Scottish Psalter 1929: Metrical Version and Scriptural Paraphrases, With Tunes* (London: Oxford University Press, 1930).

71   Routley, MCH, 36B.

72   Ibid.

73   The classic text is H. Richard Niebuhr, *Christ and Culture* (New York: Harper & Row, Publishers, 1951).

74   Nicholas Temperley, "The Tunes of Congregational Song in Britain from the Reformation to 1750," Glover, H82C, I, 349–350.

75   Leaver, *Goostly Psalmes and Spirituall Songes*, 80.

76   See Leaver, *Goostly Psalmes and Spirituall Songes*, especially 66, 81, and 82.

77   For an overview, see Westermeyer, *Te Deum*, 181–182.

78   Ibid., 168–170.

79   From the title page of *The Whole Book of Psalmes, Collected into Englysh Meter by T. Starnhold, I. Hopkins & Others* (1562).

80   Temperley, HTI, I, 7.

81   See Leaver, "English Metrical Psalmody," Glover H82 C, 1, 324.

82   Leaver, *Goostly Psalmes and Spirituall Songes*, 55.

83   Routley, MCH, 37A.

84   Gordon J. Munro, "Exploring 16-Century Scottish Psalm Tunes," a paper delivered at the annual conference of the Hymn Society in the United States and Canada, at St. John's University, Collegeville, Minnesota, July 14, 2004.

85   Routley, MCH, 37B and 45–46.

86   Leaver, *Goostly Psalmes and Spirituall Songes*, 253.

87   Temperley, HTI, I, 7, gives the statistics: "more than 800 editions, of which 452 had tunes." "Most editions contained from 46 to 65 monophonic tunes."

88   For an overview and sources see Westermeyer, *Te Deum*, 170–172.

89   Maurice Frost, *Historical Companion to Hymns Ancient and Modern* (London: William Clowes & Sons, Limited, 1962), 230.

90   Stulken, HCLBW, 346.

91   John Wilson, "To Mock Your Reign, O Dearest Lord," Glover, H82C, 3A, 344.

92   LBW #335.

93   See Frost, *Historical Companion*, 138, for this version. The tune begins in the tenor and follows in the soprano.

94   John Wilson, "Come Now, and Praise the Humble Saint," Glover, H82C, 3A, 511.

95   Brink/Polman, PsHH, 759.

96   Ibid., 536.

97   See Nicholas Temperley, "Lord Jesus, Think on Me," Glover, H82, 3C, 641.

98   Correspondence from Paul Richardson, June 2, 2004.

99   See CW #454, H82 #259 for OLD 120TH. For the *Actes of the Apostles*, see Nicholas Temperley, "While Shepherds Watched Their Flocks by Night," Glover, H82C, 3A, 182. Stulken, HCLBW, 337, like Routley, says Chapter 8 and gives the second half of that melody to which the end of WINCHESTER OLD relates. Leaver, *Goostly Psalmes and Spirituall Songes*, 305, says Chapter 8, and gives the whole melody.

100 Routley, MCH, 41A.

101 CW #279.

102 Ibid., Ex. 97. Maurice Frost, *English & Scottish Psalm & Hymn Tunes c.1543–1677* (London: S.P.C.K, 1953), 343–373, gives all fourteen tunes. (His version of the tune for Chapter 8, unlike Routley's, has an E-flat in the alto voice at measure 5.)

103 This tune can be found in *The English Hymnal* (1906) at #461.

104 Ibid., 41B. Nicholas Temperley, "While Shepherds Watched. . .,"Glover, H82C, 3A, 182, relying on Frost, says the ancestor is the tune for Chapter 2, not 8, which seems equally plausible.

105 Nicholas Temperley, "Jesus, the Very Thought of Thee," Glover, H82C, 3B, 1179.

106 Ibid.

107 Peter Le Huray, "Daman, William," NGDMM, 5, 169.

108 Routley, MCH, 41B.

109 Ibid., 39.

110 Munro, "Exploring 16-Century Scottish Psalm Tunes," and conversations with Munro on July 14, 2004.

111 Routley prints it out in MCH, Ex. 99.

112 Temperley, "Jesus, the Very Thought…,"Glover, H82C, 3B, 1179.

113 See W. Thomas Marrocco and Harold Gleason, *Music in America: An Anthology from the Landing of the Pilgrims to the Close of the Civil War, 1620–1865* (New York: W. W. Norton & Company, 1964), 26.

114 Temperley, "Jesus, the Very Thought…," Glover, H82C, 3B, 1178.

115 Nicholas Temperley, "The Tunes of Congregational Song," Glover, H82C, 1, 354.

116 Ibid.

117 Maurice Frost, *English and Scottish Psalm and Hymn Tunes* (London: S.P.C.K., 1953), 36. Frost lists the tunes: OLDE COMMON TUNE, KINGES TUNE, DUKES TUNE, ENGLISH TUNE, FRENCH TUNE, LONDON TUNE, THE STILT, DUMFERLING TUNE, DUNDIE TUNE, ABBAY TUNE, GLASGOW TUNE, MARTYRS TUNE.

118 Temperley, "The Tunes of Congregational Song," 355.

119 Ibid.

120 Routley, MCH, 39B.

121 Quoted in David W. Music, *Hymnology: A Collection of Source Readings* (London: The Scarecrow Press, Inc., 1996), 95.

122 Routley, MCH, 43B.

123 Ibid., 52A–B.

124 See Stulken, HCLBW, 288.

125 See Alan Luff, *Welsh Hymns and Their Tunes* (Carol Stream: Hope Publishing Company, 1990), 131–132.

126 H82 #346.

127 H82 #703.

128 PsH #s 167 and 308; VU #393.

129 H82 #328, Wor3 #s601 and 660.

130 Routley, MCH, 51B–52A.

131 The original is given in Frost, *English & Scottish Psalm & Hymn Tunes*, 425.

132 Correspondence, June 27, 2004.

133 See Frost, *English & Scottish Psalm & Hymn Tunes*, 424 and 429.

134 Routley, MCH, 43B.

135 Nicholas Temperley, "God, You Have Given Us Power to Sound," Glover, H82C, 3B, 1078.

136 Brink/Polman, PsHH, 158.

V. German, Slavic and Scandinavian Tunes

We look now at German, Slavic, and Scandinavian hymn tunes and their developments beyond the chorale. As already indicated the sixteenth century's public and rugged musical syntax moved toward a smoother and more introspective one. Here are some pieces of the trajectory in more detail.

1. Sixteenth Century

Bohemian Brethren

The Bohemian Brethren, ancestors of the Moravians with roots that go back to the Czech reformer Jan Hus (ca. 1369–1415), produced extensive hymnals in the sixteenth century, beginning in 1501 well before the Lutheran ones.[1] Jan Roh—also known as Johannes Horn (1490–1547)—and Michael Weisse (1480–1534) were among the important editors, poets, and tune writers. Though Luther and the Brethren did not see eye to eye theologically, and though Luther's tunes were more syllabic,[2] the tunes of the two traditions merged into a single Germanic heritage and influenced each other. Several of the Bohemian ones are still in ecumenical use.

SONNE DER GERECHTIGKEIT is a fifteenth-century folk song that comes through the Bohemian Brethren's *Kirchengeseng* (Ivancice, 1566). Like other melodies we have seen from this period, it is boldly built around tonic and fifth. It starts with a compelling stride that moves into a faster pace.

SONNE DER GERECHTIGKEIT
7 7 7 7 4

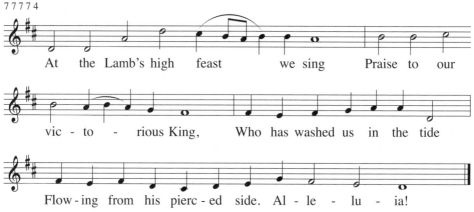

At the Lamb's high feast we sing Praise to our vic - to - rious King, Who has washed us in the tide Flow-ing from his pierc - ed side. Al - le - lu - ia!

Text: Latin hymn, 17th c., abr.; tr. Robert Campbell, 1814-1868, alt.
Tune: *Kirchengeseng,* Ivancice, 1566

CW #141

GOTTES SOHN IST KOMMEN, also known as AVE HIERARCHIA because of its association with a fifteenth-century Marian hymn of that name, was used with various texts by the Bohemian Brethren and finally named for "Gottes Sohn ist kommen" in 1544. It takes longer to move up an octave than SONNE DER GERECHTIGKEIT, does so more smoothly, and then moves even more smoothly to the lower fifth before it hints at the beginning and follows the smooth path to the final cadence.

AVE HIERARCHIA
6 6 6 6 6 6 Trochaic

Once he came in bless - ing All our sins re - dress - ing, Came in like-ness low - ly, Son of God most ho - ly; Bore the cross to save us, Hope and free-dom gave us.

Text: Jan Roh, 1544. Tr. Catherine Winkworth, 1863, alt., © 1978, *Lutheran Book of Worship*, admin. Augsburg Fortress
Tune: Medieval melody, adapt. Michael Weisse, 1531

Mor #270

GAUDEAMUS PARITER is in bar form. Like WIE SCHÖN LEUCHTET (see Chapter III) and with identical notes, except for a pickup in WIE SCHÖN LEUCHTET at the end of A, it momentarily and delightfully flips out of a simple background beat into a compound one at the eleventh and twelfth measures (counting the repeat of the first four measures). It comes from the hymnal that Roh (Horn) edited in 1544 (*Ein Gesangbuch der Brüder* [Nürnberg]), where it was paired with one of his texts.

GAUDEAMUS PARITER
7 6 7 6 D

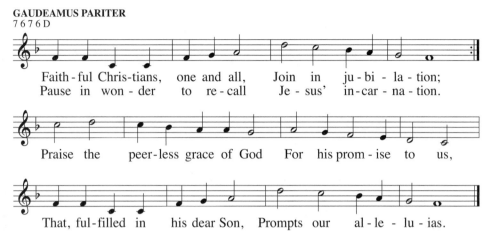

Faith-ful Chris-tians, one and all, Join in ju-bi-la-tion;
Pause in won-der to re-call Je-sus' in-car-na-tion.

Praise the peer-less grace of God For his prom-ise to us,

That, ful-filled in his dear Son, Prompts our al-le-lu-ias.

Text: Martin Michalec, 1541; tr. Jaroslav J. Vajda, 1989, tr. © 1989, Jaroslav J. Vajda   Mor #300
Tune: Jan Roh, 1544

FREUEN WIR UNS ALL IN EIN, unlike the tunes just mentioned, is minor. It comes from Michael Weisse's *Ein New Gesengbuchlen* (Jungbunzlau, 1531). Like all of these tunes, FREUEN WIR UNS ALL IN EIN is propelled by strong initial accents at the beginning of phrases. Strong initial accents also propel the Lutheran corpus, but those tunes are likely to bounce off rather than start on the strong beat (like EIN FESTE BURG), and Luther is more likely to start boldly at the top than the bottom of the scale. Here is FREUEN WIR UNS ALL IN EIN in its rhythmic form.

FREUEN WIR UNS ALL IN EIN
8 7 8 7

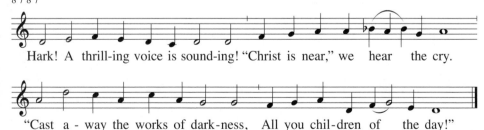

Hark! A thrill-ing voice is sound-ing! "Christ is near," we hear the cry.

"Cast a-way the works of dark-ness, All you chil-dren of the day!"

Text: Latin hymn, 1632; tr. Edward Caswall, 1814-1878, alt.   LBW #37
Tune: Michael Weisse, c. 1480-1534

Here it is in an isometric form.

FREUEN WIR UNS
LM

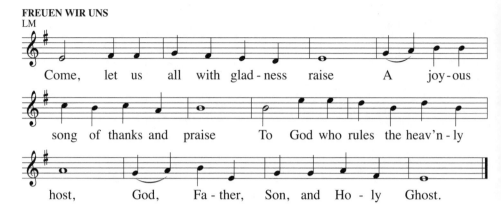

Text: Matthew of Kunwald, 1457 or Gabriel Komarovsky, 1467; tr. Michael Weisse, 1531; tr. Evelyn Renatus Hasse, 1911, alt.   Mor #519
Tune: Michael Weisse, 1531, alt.

Johan Steuerlein

WIE LIEBLICH IST DER MAIEN illustrates the smoother, less rugged, and more regular tendencies already present by the end of the sixteenth century. Johan Steuerlein—or Steurlein (1546–1613), a Lutheran church musician, poet, lawyer, and mayor—composed it in 1575 for "Mit Lieb bin ich umfangen" ("I'm enveloped by love"). In 1581 it was joined to a hymn by Martin Behm for which it is now named. (Its connection with "Sing to the Lord of Harvest" was made in the twentieth century.) Though in rounded bar form, it is more predictable than tunes from earlier in the century like EIN' FESTE BURG or ones from Steuerlein's period like WACHET AUF (see Chapter III). Robert Scholz wonders if it may be related to dance,[3] a relation that comes up in the next tune from one of Steuerlein's students.

WIE LIEBLICH IST DER MAIEN
7 6 7 6 D

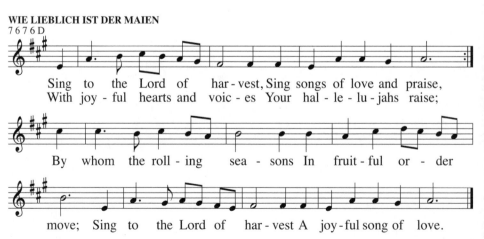

Text: John Samuel Bewley Monsell, 1866, alt.   VU #519
Tune: Johann Steurlein, 1575

2. Seventeenth Century

Melchior Vulpius

The tunes of Melchior Vulpius (ca. 1570–1615) in the early seventeenth century enliven Steuerlein's predictability by borrowing from dance. Vulpius was one of Steuerlein's students who became a Lutheran church musician and teacher. Walter Blankenburg regards him as the most important hymn tune composer of his period, the link between Martin Luther and Johann Crüger. Blankenburg says his originality lay in introducing to hymn tunes the rhythm of the *balletto*,[4] a sixteenth- and seventeenth-century lighthearted stylized Italian dance, which had a vocal component during Vulpius' lifetime. Hassler's *Lustgarten neuer teutscher Gesäng*, Balletti (Nuremberg, 1601) from which HERZLICH TUT MICH VERLANGEN (see Chapter III) was drawn, was a part of this context. The tunes we sing from Vulpius come from a hymnal he edited in 1609, *Ein schön geistlich Gesangbuch* (Leipzig). GELOBT SEI GOTT was used for a text by Michael Weisse, which named it. Here it is with one of the texts we use.

GELOBT SEI GOTT
8 8 8 with alleluias

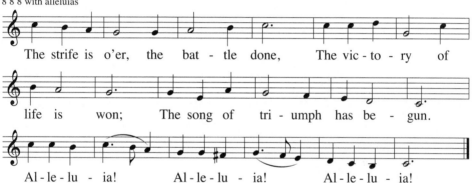

The strife is o'er, the bat - tle done, The vic - to - ry of
life is won; The song of tri - umph has be - gun.
Al - le - lu - ia! Al - le - lu - ia! Al - le - lu - ia!

Text: *Symphonia Sirenum*, Cologne, 1695; tr. Francis Pott, 1861
Tune: Melchior Vulpius, *Schönes Geistliches Gesangbuch*, 1609

Mor #361

CHRISTUS, DER IST MEIN LEBEN[5] was named for an anonymous text. The following text is one we use.

CHRISTUS, DER IST MEIN LEBEN
7 6 7 6

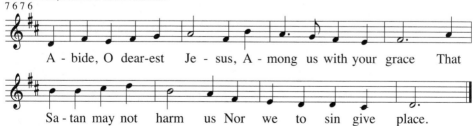

A - bide, O dear-est Je - sus, A - mong us with your grace That
Sa - tan may not harm us Nor we to sin give place.

Text: Josua Stegmann, 1588-1632; tr. August Crull, 1845-1923, alt.
Tune: Melchior Vulpius, c. 1570-1615, alt.

CW #333

Though GELOBT SEI GOTT includes syncopation, both it and CHRISTUS, DER IST MEIN LEBEN have Steuerlein's regularity about them. So do several other compelling melodies Vulpius wrote that are still in use, though not as extensively as these two. Here are three of them: DAS NEUGEBORNE KINDELEIN (a dance in minor originally for a Christmas hymn as its name implies, but used with various texts today),

DAS NEUGEBORNE KINDELEIN
8 8 8 8 8 8

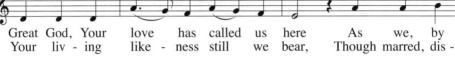

Great God, Your love has called us here As we, by
Your liv - ing like - ness still we bear, Though marred, dis -

love, for love were made. We come, with all our heart and
hon - ored, dis - o - beyed.

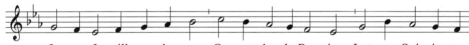

mind Your call to hear, Your love to find.

Text: Brian Wren, 1973, © 1977, Hope Publishing Co.   Pres #353
Tune: Melchior Vulpius, 1609

JESU, KREUZ, LEIDEN UND PEIN,

JESU KREUZ, LEIDEN UND PEIN
7 6 7 6 D

Je - sus, I will pon-der now On your ho - ly Pas-sion; Let your Spir - it now

en-dow Me for med - i - ta-tion. Grant that I in love and faith May the im-

age cher-ish Of your suf-f'ring, pain, and death, That I may not per-ish.

Text: Sigismund von Birken, 1626-1681; tr. August Crull, 1846-1923, alt.   LBW #115
Tune: Melchior Vulpius, c. 1560-1615

and LOBT GOTT DEN HERREN, IHR HEIDEN ALL.

LOBT GOTT DEN HERREN, IHR HEIDEN ALL
8 7 8 7 8 8 7

All praise to God who reigns a - bove, The God of
The God of won - ders, pow'r, and love, The God of

all cre - a - tion, With heal-ing balm my soul he fills,
our sal - va - tion!

The God who ev - 'ry sor - row stills To God all praise and glo - ry!

Text: Johann J. Schütz, 1640-90, abr.; tr. composite
Tune: Melchior Vulpius, c. 1570-1615

CW #236

Giacomo Gastoldi

IN DIR IST FREUDE by Giovanni Giacomo Gastoldi (ca.1550s–ca.1622) reflects the most obvious influence of the *balletto*. Gastoldi was an Italian Catholic priest and composer who wrote madrigals, masses, and psalm settings, but whose primary claim to fame is his *ballettos*. In his *Amorum filii Dei decades duae* (Erfurt, 1598) Johan Lindemann (ca.1550–ca.1634), a Lutheran cantor, put the text "In dir ist Freude" ("In Thee Is Gladness") to the tune Gastoldi had used for "A lieta vita," in his *Balletti a cinqve voce* (Venice, 1591).[6] The result of this contrafactum was the exuberant dance of joy we still sing today. Its two halves are each repeated. That is unusual for hymn tunes, but not unusual for dance.

IN DIR IST FREUDE
Irregular

In thee is glad - ness, A - mid all sad - ness, Je - sus,
By thee are giv - en The gifts of heav - en, Thou the

sun - shine of my heart. Our souls thou mak - est,
true Re - deem - er art. Our hearts are pin - ing

Our bonds thou break - est; Who trusts thee sure - ly hath built se -
to see thy shin - ing; Dy - ing or liv - ing, to thee are

cure - ly, And stands for - ev - er. Al - le - lu - ia!
cleav - ing; Naught can us sev - er. Al - le - lu - ia!

Text: Johann Lindemann, 1598; trans. by Catherine Winkworth, 1858
Tune: Giovanni Giacomo Gastoldi, 1593

Meth #169

Perspective: Dance

The introduction of the *balletto* by Vulpius and Gastoldi requires another comment related to dance. We have a danger here, which will get more pronounced with Crüger. The introduction of a dance rhythm to the congregation's song is ingenious and invigorating so long as it does not take over the whole musical context. Given the divide between congregational song and dance in the West, however, and the nature of Christian worship that tends to suspend earthbound regular pulsation, it is but a short step to superimposing a foreign object on the singing. The end of that scenario is to silence the singing unless it is allowed to assume its own inner dynamic. As long as congregational song remained unaccompanied, its inner dynamic was intact and protected. The central vocal character of the song could embrace all sorts of rhythmic patterns, including dance, and break them to the Word. When accompanying instruments were introduced, however, a new dynamic was at work with the ever-present temptation that instruments would take over and even silence the congregation rather than embrace it or help it to sing. With Vulpius and Gastoldi, in spite of their ingenuity and our gratefulness for it, this temptation is now on the horizon.

Breadth

Before we get to Crüger, three other tunes from this period need to be mentioned. They point to the long trajectory and broad associations involved here. VALET WILL ICH DIR GEBEN or ST. THEODULPH is by another Lutheran church musician named Melchior, this one Melchior Teschner (1584–1635). It is almost universally associated now with the Palm Sunday (or Passion Sunday) hymn "All Glory, Laud and Honor," an older text by Theodulph of Orleans (ca. 760–821), which gives the tune its more recent name. Originally Teschner wrote the tune for the text that first named it by Valerius Herberger, the pastor Teschner worked with. A similarity to William Byrd's more florid "Sellinger's Round" in the early seventeenth-century *Fitzwilliam Virginal Book* has been suggested.[7] Whether there is any relation between the two tunes or not, the communal character of the simpler hymn tune and the soloistic character of the more ornamented piece by Byrd are the significant items to note.

ST. THEODULPH
7 6 7 6 D

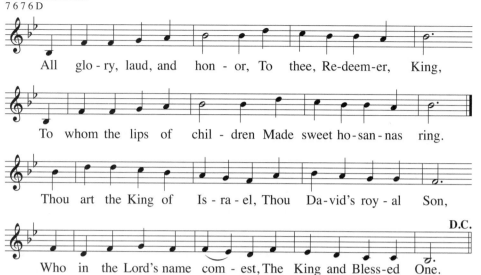

Text: Theodulph of Orleans, 8-9th c.; tr. John Mason Neale, 1851
Tune: Melchior Teschner, 1615

Meth #280

Structurally, ST. THEODULPH has been deformed, because it has been forced to accommodate a refrain. The original and natural shape of the tune repeats the first and last phrase groups, but does not use the first phrase group as a refrain. The uneasiness congregations feel when they sing this tune is not because of the tune itself, but because our deformation has made the middle into an end and the end into a middle—resulting in a muddle. Here is the tune as Zahn gives it, in its more natural state.

Zahn 5404a

LASST UNS ERFREUEN is a melody of much larger sweep, with possible origins in sixteenth-century Strassburg. It begins exactly like GENEVAN 68, which may have spawned it. It was shaped by Catholics in Cologne in hymnals of 1623 and 1625 and named for the text they put with it. Catholic hymnals kept it in play until it was filtered through Ralph Vaughan Williams in *The English Hymnal* (London, 1906) and linked there with "Ye Watchers and Ye Holy Ones."[8] This tune serves as another reminder of ecumenical connections. Then, as now, the musical being of the church transcended its divisions. Note also the long historical trajectory and shaping that attends tunes like this.

LASST UNS ERFREUEN
LM with alleluias

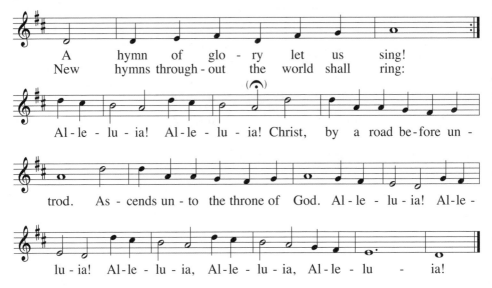

Text: *Hymnum canamus gloria;* Venerable Bede, 673-735; tr. *Lutheran Book of Worship,* 1978   Wor3 #469
Tune: *Geistliche Kirchengesange,* Cologne, 1623

HERR JESU CHRIST, DICH ZU UNS WEND, though printed in the *Cantionale Germanicum* (Gochsheim) in 1628, may come from much earlier. Its Moravian name HUS suggests it can be traced to the fifteenth-century reformer. Once more, the musical being of the church transcends its divisions and relates to a long trajectory. Like some Genevan tunes, this one repeats the same rhythm for each phrase. Its four phrases are paired so that the second answers the first— the first going up, the second going down—and the fourth answers the third in a similar fashion.

HERR JESU CHRIST, DICH ZU UNS WEND
LM

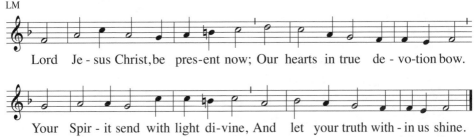

Text: Wilhelm II, 1598-1662; tr. Catherine Winkworth, 1829-1878, alt.   LBW #253
Tune: *Cantionale Germanicum,* Dresden, 1628

Johann Crüger

Johann Crüger (1598–1662) now comes into view. In addition to composing HERZLIEBSTER JESU (see Chapter III) and editing the *Praxis Pietatis Melica*, he edited other hymn collections, wrote musical treatises, and composed at least seventy-one tunes.[9] As the musician at the Nicolai Church in Berlin, he became a good friend of the chief hymn writer of the period, Paul Gerhardt, who was a deacon there.

Crüger's *Newes vollkömliches Gesangbuch Augsburgischer Confession* (Berlin) of 1640, the predecessor sometimes considered the "first edition" of the *Praxis*, was the first publication in which chorale melodies were arranged with a figured bass. As George Buelow says, this emphasized the importance of the organ for accompanying hymns in Berlin.[10] Crüger's tunes illustrate the underlying presence of the organ and a figured bass, though they have sufficient intrinsic melodic interest to stand on their own. As the next four examples illustrate, bar form is an important factor, though the tunes are "smoother" than their more rugged sixteenth-century predecessors.

NUN DANKET ALLE GOTT went with Martin Rinkhart's hymn of that name ("Now Thank We All Our God") and first appeared in the 1647 edition of *Praxis* (Berlin). Here it is in an isometric version. The figure at the B section (on the words "who, from our mothers' arms") skillfully repeats the opening notes at the fifth, but then proceeds up instead of down as at the beginning. A satisfying balance is achieved, which logically runs itself out to the end.

NUN DANKET ALLE GOTT
6 7 6 7 6 6 6 6

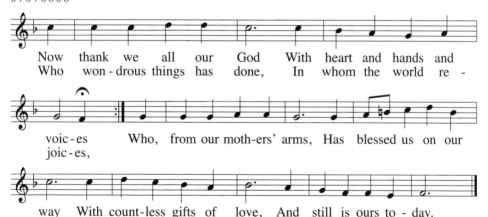

Text: Martin Rinkart, 1636; tr. Catherine Winkworth, 1858, alt.
Tune: Johann Crüger, 1647

Chal #715

JESU, MEINE FREUDE[11] went with Johann Franck's text of that name ("Jesus, Priceless Treasure") and first appeared in the 1653 edition of *Praxis*. Here the first phrase, which goes down by step, is balanced by the second, which goes up to conclude on the high tonic. At the B section the tune returns to the fifth where it started, but moves up before going down, then develops the color of the second phrase's A-natural after the A-flat, before concluding on the low tonic for whose return we have been waiting since the end of the first phrase.

JESU, MEINE FREUDE
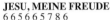
6 6 5 6 6 5 7 8 6

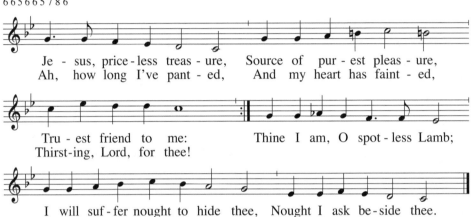

Text: Johann Franck, 1618-1677; tr. Catherine Winkworth, 1829-1878, alt.   LBW #457
Tune: Johann Crüger, 1598-1662

SCHMÜCKE DICH went with Johann Franck's text of that name ("Soul, Adorn Yourself with Gladness") in Crüger's *Geistliche Kirchen Melodien* (Leipzig, 1649). This quietly happy melody moves in slow waves and at the B section spins into threes rather than twos. The phrase with the threes repeats. Crüger's use of such repeats and his balanced structures illustrate his sensitivity to a congregation's capacities.

SCHMÜCKE DICH
LMD

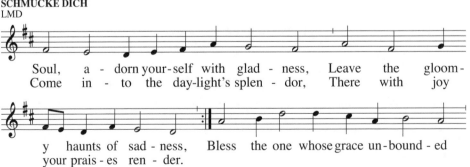

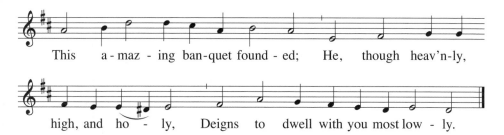

This a-maz-ing ban-quet found-ed; He, though heav'n-ly,

high, and ho - ly, Deigns to dwell with you most low - ly.

Text: Johann Franck, 1618-1677; tr. hymnal version, © 1978, *Lutheran Book of Worship*, admin. Augsburg Fortress
Tune: Johann Crüger, 1598-1662

LBW #224

Crüger adapted the melody we know as ERMUNTRE DICH MEIN SCHWACHER for his 1647 edition of the *Praxis*. Johann Schop (d. ca. 1665), an organist and violinist in Hamburg, wrote its initial version for the hymn that included as one of its stanzas the text we still use with it. It was further modified after Crüger to the form in which Bach received it. It is in that form and with the harmonization from his Christmas Oratorio that it is usually found today.

ERMUNTRE DICH MEIN SCHWACHER
Irregular

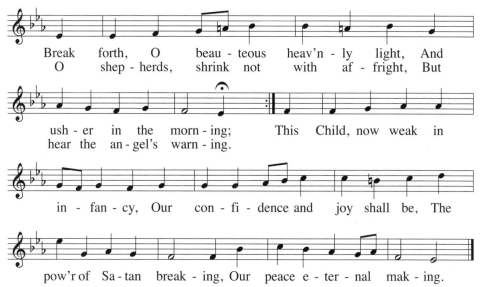

Break forth, O beau - teous heav'n - ly light, And
O shep - herds, shrink not with af - fright, But

ush - er in the morn - ing; This Child, now weak in
hear the an - gel's warn - ing.

in - fan - cy, Our con - fi - dence and joy shall be, The

pow'r of Sa - tan break - ing, Our peace e - ter - nal mak - ing.

Text: Johann Rist, 1607-1667
Tune: Johann Schop, c. 1590-1664

Bap #114

Perspective: Instruments and Conflict
　　1) **Instruments.** Crüger was a skillful writer of profoundly durable and congregational melodies, but a subtle and critical shift is going on here that he was probably not even aware of. It is related to his

use of figured bass and instruments. "Crüger claimed to be the first to add instrumental parts to chorale melodies."[12] This means adding instruments to the singing of the congregation, since vocal and instrumental parts of all kinds were commonplace for Lutherans in the stanzas choral and instrumental groups had been singing and playing in alternation with the congregation (and maybe, at least in some places, with the congregation after 1586[13]). Figured bass, organ, and other instrumental parts clearly have the capacity for delightful ornamentation, congregational support, and even exegetical aid. Once they are present, however, the temptation is strong for them to take over the congregation's vocal office rather than support it. When that happens, it is but a short step to a replay of the medieval problem—largely silent congregations.

2) **Conflict**. This period was not without conflict, which played into the hymnic story. The first part of Crüger's *Psalmodia sacra* (Berlin, 1658) points to it. There Lobwasser's psalms are set in four-part choral arrangements with instruments and figured bass. Ambrosius Lobwasser (1515–1585) was a Lutheran lawyer and teacher who translated the metrical psalms of Marot and Beza as literally as possible in their French meters so that they could be sung in German with the Genevan psalm tunes. Lobwasser seems to have done this as a personal devotional or literary exercise. He finished it by 1565, three years after the completion of the Genevan Psalter. His translations were published in 1573 (*Der Psalter dess Königlichen Propheten Davids* [Leipzig], with four voice settings by Goudimel) and almost universally adopted by the German Reformed Church for corporate worship until after the middle of the eighteenth century. They were repeatedly published, "coupled with other Protestant hymns in a second section of the book."[14]

Lobwasser's Psalter was strongly opposed by orthodox Lutherans. It stimulated Cornelius Becker (1561–1604), an orthodox Lutheran pastor and professor in Leipzig, to prepare another metrical psalter (*Psalter Davids Gesangweis* [Leipzig, 1602]) in order to "counteract crypto-Calvinism" and the influence of Lobwasser's German version of the Reformed metrical Psalter[15] with its "strange French melodies which ring sweetly in lascivious ears."[16] The effort was not successful. Lutherans were influenced. Becker's Psalter had its own influence, however. It entered the general stream of congregational hymnody and also stimulated choral settings by composers like Heinrich Schütz (*Psalmen Davids*, 1628 and 1661, SWV 97–256).

Georg Neumark

The devastation of the Thirty Years' War is part of the backdrop for this period. Georg Neumark (1621–1681) was among the many who suffered from its scourge—in his case by robbery, poverty, and fire—but who sang hymns of faith and hope into its horror anyway. With help from a pastor, he became a tutor in Kiel and later the librarian and poet for Duke Johann Ernst of Weimar. He wrote poetry and novels, but was also a viol player and composer who set some of his poetry to music. WER NUR DEN LIEBEN GOTT LÄSST WALTEN is a tune he wrote for his text of that name in his *Fortgepflanzter musikalisch-poetischer Lustwald* (Jena, 1657). As a simple congregational melody in bar form it has circulated widely.

WER NUR DEN LIEBEN GOTT

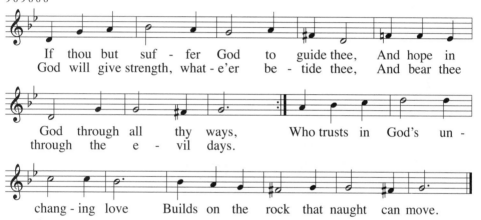

Text: Georg Neumark, 1657; trans. by Catherine Winkworth, 1863   Meth #142
Tune: Georg Neumark, 1657

Perspective: Tempo and Its Context

WER NUR DEN LIEBEN GOTT LÄSST WALTEN is an example of a tune that can be sung successfully at different tempos, from a one-beat-per-measure waltz to a three-beat-per-measure slow and stately procession. The meaning of the text will follow the tempo, from life as jubilant dance to life as more subdued and patient joy through sorrow.

The choice of tempo is not arbitrary. It relates to many variables—the specific hymn and its tune, the nature of the community singing, their performance practice, the nature of the worship service, the placement of the hymn in it, the day and time of year, events in the world and the people's lives, the acoustical frame in which the singing is taking place, and the leader's sensitivity to all of these factors.

There is no single right tempo, but there is a right tempo within a range of tempos for every hymn, tune, and occasion. It might be called "settling in," the way a good race horse "settles into" a race. The fundamental issue is breath and breathing. Communities know when they get it right, though they seldom, if ever, are able to articulate what is happening. Skillful leaders have the responsibility to sense all the factors and set tempos well.

Catholic Tunes

Already in the sixteenth century German Catholics produced important hymnals that interacted with Lutheran ones.[17] ES IST EIN' ROS is a tune from one of these sources. It is present in all the hymnals checked for this book and is almost always given in a setting by Michael Praetorius (ca.1571–1621), a prolific composer who wrote over one thousand pieces based on Lutheran chorales. This tune may date from the fifteenth or even the fourteenth century, but it comes to us through the *Alte Catholische Geistliche Kirchengeseng* published in Cologne in 1599. It is a melody in the shape AABA, where the B section is a short bridge back to A. It has the unusual capacity to lend itself equally well to both congregational and choral singing, with and without harmony in both cases.

ES IST EIN' ROS
7 6 7 6 6 7 6

Text: German, 15th c., tr. Theodore Baker, 1894; alt.
Tune: *Catholische Geistliche Kirchengesäng*, Cologne, 1599

NC #127

Catholic hymnal production continued in the seventeenth century during the Thirty Years' War, as LASST UNS ERFREUEN indicates. In the period after the Thirty Years' War another potent tune from this stream, O HEILAND REISS DIE HIMMEL AUF,[18] comes from the *Rheinfelsisches Deutsches Catholisches Gesangbuch* (Augsburg, 1666) where it went with the text which still goes with it and names it. (The text had previously been sung to CONDITOR ALME SIDERUM). This anonymous tune has the punch of FREUEN WIR UNS ALL IN EIN and the folk-like character of PUER NOBIS, but, unlike them (minor and major respectively), it is dorian. It migrated to Lutheran and Reformed hymnals.

O HEILAND, REISS DIE HIMMEL AUF
LM

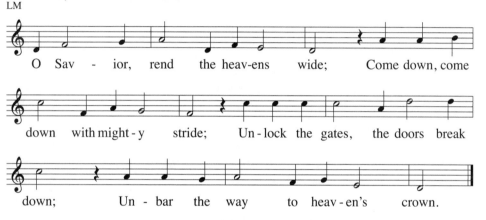

Text: Friedrich von Spee, 1591-1635, abr.; tr. Martin L. Seltz, 1909-1967, alt., © 1969, Concordia Publishing House   CW #22
Tune: *Rheinfelssisch Deutsches Catholisches Gesangbuch,* Augsburg, 1666

Joachim Neander, German Reformed, and Pietism

Joachim Neander (1650–1680) takes us on another path. His well-known hymn of praise, "Praise to the Lord, the Almighty," was first associated with the tune we call LOBE DEN HERREN in his *Alpha und Omega* (Bremen, 1680), but the tune reaches back in various versions before that, may have roots in a folk song, and took the form we have it around 1700.[19] As we have seen with other tunes, this one was shaped over time into a sturdy congregational version, once more in bar form and with soloistic elements rubbed out. (The following example is an update of LBW #543, an attempt to make the language more inclusive.)

LOBE DEN HERREN
14 14 4 7 8

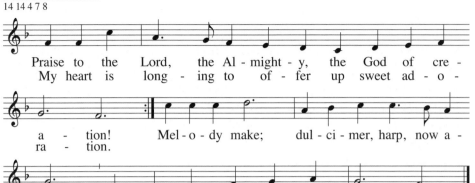

Praise to the Lord, the Al - might - y, the God of cre -
My heart is long - ing to of - fer up sweet ad - o -

a - tion! Mel - o - dy make; dul - ci - mer, harp, now a -
ra - tion.

wake. Sound forth your praise, ev - 'ry na - tion.

Text: Joachim Neander, 1650-1680; tr. composite; © 2000, Augsburg Fortress · Cong Song, p. 58
Tune: *Ernewerten Gesangbuch*, Strasland, 1655

As a text writer, Neander has been dubbed "the Paul Gerhardt of the German Reformed," that is, a hymn writer of the Calvinists on a par with Gerhardt for the Lutherans. Neander also wrote tunes. There he signals a shift that is not obvious in the forthright adoration of his text, "Praise to the Lord." One sees in Gerhardt and Crüger an introspection that has moved away from the bolder and less refined work of Luther. Neander, however, especially in his tune writing, signals more: not only the Calvinist move from psalm to hymn singing with its influence on German tunes, but also Pietism.

Neander was a Calvinist headmaster, poet, and composer. He was converted to Pietism and knew Philip Jacob Spener (1635–1705) whose *Pia desideria* (Frankfurt, 1675) was the Pietists' watchword. Two of Neander's tunes still in use, though both in traditional bar form, symbolize two important departures. First, UNSER HERRSCHER (which we use for various texts, but which took its name from Neander's "Unser Herrscher, Unser König" in *Alpha und Omega*) is the first tune we have encountered that employs a major sixth.

UNSER HERRSCHER
8 7 8 7 7 7

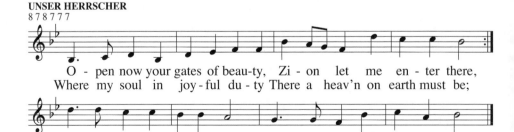

O - pen now your gates of beau - ty, Zi - on let me en - ter there,
Where my soul in joy - ful du - ty There a heav'n on earth must be;

O how bless - ed is this place, Filled with sol - ace, light, and grace.

Text: Benjamin Schmolck, 1672-1737; tr. Catherine Winkworth, 1827-1878, alt. · Cov #520
Tune: Joachim Neander, 1650-1680

Until now there have been leaps of thirds, fourths, and fifths, and a downward minor sixth (CAITHNESS), but never an upward major sixth. Pietism was characterized by small groups called *collegia pietatis*, which had emotional fire and the tendency, contrary to Spener's intent, to become divisive little churches within the church.[20] The larger interval of the upward major sixth apparently attracted such groups. It helped them express their emotional desires, as did a wider melodic range and upward reach. Here the upward motion across an octave and a third is traversed very quickly, with the major sixth forming a hole at the top of the line. (It is interesting to compare this tune with VALET WILL ICH DIR GEBEN, which, though it encompasses the same octave and a third and has some of the same fervor, manages to reach from the bottom to the top without the leap of a sixth.) This tune shows a private, less public face, where everyone is expected to have participated in the same experience and to have developed the same musical capacity. The capacity here is the vocal agility to move within three measures from the low part of the range (chest voice) to the high part of the range (head voice), without trying to force (or choke) the low voice into the high one.

Historically, the sixth was made possible by two musical developments—the gravitation toward "common practice harmony" of the seventeenth-century Baroque period and the use of the pipe organ to accompany congregational singing. The organ provided support to help congregations accommodate the larger interval. The musical developments coincided with the Pietistic ones. The private affair of the group that was in on the pious experience called in an external instrument for help. The public, intrinsic, inside-out character of the people's song was turned in a private, extrinsic, outside-in direction. This was not yet using tunes in emotive dress to attract people. That will come in the eighteenth and nineteenth centuries. It is rather another temptation to replay the medieval in-group that undercut the common people's song.

The point here is not that a major sixth is by arbitrary definition a bad thing. Context is critical. Once the sixth entered the vocabulary, it could be—and, as we shall see—was employed well. The point is that it related to a small group and called in external instrumental help, setting up a potential obstacle for the common believer.

Second, WUNDERBARER KÖNIG is the first tune we have seen where the harmony of organ or voices is as important, or more important, than the tune itself.

WUNDERBARER KÖNIG
6 6 8 6 6 8 6 6 6

God is tru - ly pres - ent; Let us come a - dor - ing And with awe
God is in the tem - ple; Let all earth keep si - lence, Bend - ing low

our God im - plor - ing. You a - lone God we own,
in deep - est rev - 'rence.

Sov - 'reign high, our Sav - ior; Praise we sing for - ev - er!

Text: Gerhard Tersteegen, 1697-1769; tr. composite, © 2001, *Congregational Song*, admin. Augsburg Fortress
Tune: Joachim Neander, 1650-1680

Text: Cong Song, p. 32
Tune: LBW #249

This music, with its slow harmonic rhythm, matches the meditative stasis of mysticism, which characterizes some facets of Pietism. Gerhard Tersteegen's text ("Gott ist gegenwärtig"—"God Is Truly Present"), usually associated now with this tune, points in the same mystic direction. (The tune originally went with Neander's "Wunderbarer König.") Teerstegen (1697–1769), along with Neander and Friedrich Lampe (1683–1729), is one of the foremost German Reformed hymn writers. He moved his church in a Pietistic direction away from the sole use of metrical psalms. Teerstegen actually stopped attending public church services and attracted a group of followers around his prayer meetings. His text and Neander's tune symbolize this mystic sprit of withdrawal from the church, albeit coupled with a concern for the poor, which is where the church and this version of the pious could still make common cause.

Musically, the boldly driving public and proclamatory character of earlier Germanic tunes is gone. It is replaced by a quieter, more inward-looking harmonic meditation rather than a melodic journey. The tune itself is quite accessible with its repeated notes and small intervals, but the temptation to an in-group activity—in this case singing in harmony—again presents itself. Those who cannot sing this way easily feel left out and, depending on the character of the community, come to regard those who can as the elite. In such a circumstance, the congregation outside the elite circle eventually stops singing, and we have yet another medieval replay.

The point here is not that harmony is by arbitrary definition a bad thing. Context is critical. Some communities have sung in harmony and interpreted that singing itself as a sign of community. Such a practice nurtured inclusively is to be prized, though Dietrich Bonhoeffer's opposite opinion needs careful pondering.[21] The point is that singing in harmony is not an option for many believers, and the temptation to shut them out is present here.

Harmony and the Organ

A cluster of tunes symbolically closes out the seventeenth century with interchangeable names, a harmonic conception, an organ underlay, and a common melodic palette with interchangeable parts. One of these is MUNICH, which comes from the *Neu-vermehrtes Gesangbuch* (Meiningen, 1693) and is apparently spliced together from pieces of tunes by the composer and organist Hieronymous Gradenthaler (1637–1700). It is sometimes called MENINGEN, for the place of the hymnal's publication, or O GOTT DU FROMMER GOTT, for the text by Johann Heermann that went with it. The tune as we have it is an altered version of the way Felix Mendelssohn (1809–1847) used it in the oratorio *Elijah* for "Cast Thy Burden upon the Lord."[22]

MUNICH
7 6 7 6 D

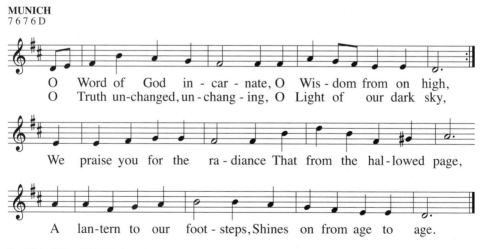

O Word of God in-car-nate, O Wis-dom from on high,
O Truth un-changed, un-chang-ing, O Light of our dark sky,
We praise you for the ra-diance That from the hal-lowed page,
A lan-tern to our foot-steps, Shines on from age to age.

Text: William W. How, 1823-1897, adapt., alt.
Tune: *Neu-vermehrtes...Gesangbuch*, 3rd ed., Meiningen, 1693, alt.

CW #279

MUNICH may be a variation on another tune called O GOTT, DU FROMMER GOTT, which also comes from the *Neu-vermehrtes Gesangbuch*.

O GOTT, DU FROMMER GOTT (II)
67676666

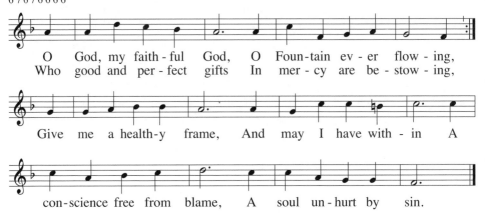

Text: Johann Heermann, 1585-1647, abr., adapt.; tr. Catherine Winkworth, 1827-1878, alt.   CW #459
Tune: *Neu-vermehrtes...Gesangbuch*, 3rd ed., Meiningen, 1693, alt.

O GOTT, DU FROMMER GOTT is the name of two other tunes. One of them was used for a hymn by Heermann in 1646.

O GOTT, DU FROMMER GOTT
67676666

Text: Johann Heermann, 1630; tr. Catherine Winkworth, 1858; alt.   Pres #277
Tune: *Neu ordentlich Gesangbuch*, 1646

The other one, possibly by Ahasuerus Fritsch (1629–1701), is also called DARMSTADT because it was published in Darmstadt in the *Geistreiches Gesangbuch* of 1698.

O GOTT, DU FROMMER GOTT (DARMSTADT)
67676666

O God, thou faith-ful God, Thou Foun-tain ev-er flow-ing,

With-out whom noth-ing is, All per-fect gifts be-stow-ing,

Grant me a health-y frame, And give me, Lord, with-in, A

con-science free from blame, A soul un-hurt by sin.

Text: Johann Heermann, *O Gott, du frommer Gott, Devoti Musica Cordis*, 1630; tr. Catherine Winkworth,   HWB #376
    Lyra Germanica, Series II, 1858, alt.
Tune: *Himmels-Lust und Welt-Unlust*, 1679

This tune is also called WAS FRAG ICH NACH DER WELT because of Wolfgang Dessler's text that went with it in the *Geistreiches Gesangbuch*.

All these tunes predictably modulate to the dominant or relative major. All except the last are in bar form, but they are more sedate than their sixteenth-century relatives. They all move in isometric fashion essentially by quarter notes until the ends of phrases, imply chord structures and progressions that fit easily under the hands and feet of organists, and give ample opportunity for non-harmonic embellishments by organists. The melodies are more interesting than WUNDERBARER KÖNIG, but there is the same harmonic center of gravity with the dangerous tendency to highlight the organ rather than the song of the congregation. An isometric mindset also folds the earlier rhythmic tunes into its grasp, with the same dangerous tendency at work.

The Darmstadt hymnal included SEELENBRÄUTIGAM (sometimes called DARMSTADT or other names), which, though it has characteristics similar to the preceding cluster, points in a little different direction.

SEELENBRÄUTIGAM
5 5 8 8 5 5

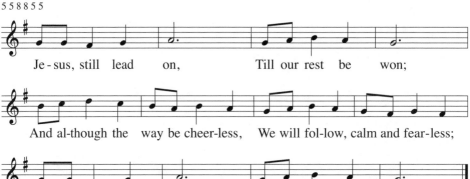

Text: Nicolaus Ludwig von Zinzendorf, 1721; tr. Jane Borthwick, 1846; alt.   NC #446
Tune: Adam Drese in *Geistreiches Gesangbuch*, Darmstadt, 1698

This tune is by the Pietist Adam Drese (1620–1701), a Kappelmeister and mayor who knew Georg Neumark. He wrote the tune for his hymn, "Seelenbräutigam, Jesu Gotteslamm," though we now associate it with "Jesus, Still Lead On," which comes from a later Pietist whom we will soon encounter, Nicolaus Ludwig von Zinzendorf (1700–1760). Drese studied Spener and Luther and opened his home to the meetings of Pietists. This tune breathes that spirit and the harmonic organ underlay of the period, but it is also close to chant-like and almost reminds one of JAM LUCIS (discussed in Chapter II). It uses two more pitches (six rather than four), but they move stepwise even between phrases with the exception of one major third. (JAM LUCIS also has only one third, a minor one). SEELENBRÄUTIGAM is not quite monotonic like JAM LUCIS, but a similar quality is replicated in the reiterated rhythm that begins phrases. Both tunes move forward to satisfying goals and are congregational in conception.

3. EIGHTEENTH CENTURY

In the manner of medieval sequences (see Chapter II), the hymns and tunes of the Pietists proliferated. At Halle, the center of Pietism, Johann Anastasius Freylinghausen (1670–1739) edited the *Geistreiches Gesangbuch* in two parts. The first one (1704) contained 683 hymns and 173 tunes, the second one (1714) 815 hymns and 154 tunes. Count Zinzendorf, who offered Moravians asylum on his estates and served as their cantor, outdid Freylinghausen. His *London Songbook* of 1753 and 1754 included 3,265 hymns and had to be published in two volumes. As for sequences, only a small fraction of the Pietist's output remains in use, tunes like MACHT HOCH DIE TÜR

MACHT HOCH DIE TÜR
8 8 8 8 8 8 6 6

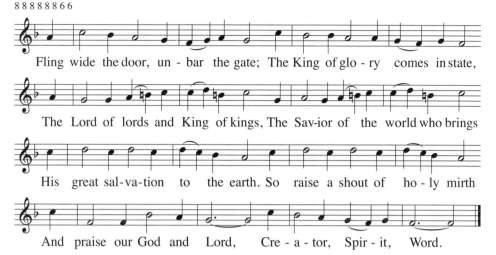

Fling wide the door, un - bar the gate; The King of glo - ry comes in state,
The Lord of lords and King of kings, The Sav-ior of the world who brings
His great sal-va-tion to the earth. So raise a shout of ho - ly mirth
And praise our God and Lord, Cre - a - tor, Spir - it, Word.

Text: Georg Weissel, 1590-1635; tr. Gracia Grindal, b.1943, © 1978, *Lutheran Book of Worship*   Mor #272
Tune: Johann A. Freylinghausen, *Geistreiches Gesang-Buch,* 1704, from *Orgelchoralbuch Württemberg,* © Gesangbuchverlag
   der Ev. Landeskirche Württemberg, Stuttgart

and GOTT SEI DANK.[23]

GOTT SEI DANK
7 7 7 7

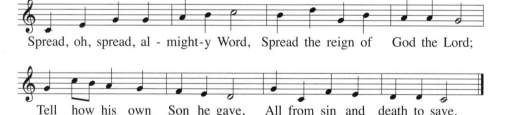

Spread, oh, spread, al - might-y Word, Spread the reign of God the Lord;
Tell how his own Son he gave, All from sin and death to save.

Text: Jonathan F. Bahnmaier, 1774-1841; tr. hymnal version, 1978, © 1978, *Lutheran Book of Worship,* admin. by Augsburg Fortress   LBW #379
Tune: J. A. Freylinghausen, *Geistreiches Gesang-Buch,* 1704

Both of these come from the *Geistreiches Gesangbuch.* The first rides along eagerly
in triplicate patterns. Its length is made accessible to congregations by two
skillful internal repetitions (measures 5–8 and 9–12). The second tune is bolder.
It takes singers on a short trip by triadic leaps and steps, from its initial low tonic
up to just past the high tonic and gradually back down.

     The eighteenth century continued to pass earlier tunes through its
isometric filter, but it provided only a few melodies still in common use. They
follow in the wake of the cluster of tunes like MUNICH, which closed out the
seventeenth century. In our usage, the first four of these have often gravitated to
F major, which requires a comment about keys before they are cited.

Perspective: Key and its Context

O DASS ICH TAUSEND ZUNGEN HÄTTE (DRETZEL), given below in F major, may have been sung in B-flat major.[24] Whether it was actually sung there is a good question. If so, it would have progressed up to an F″, though that may or may not have been our F″ in an A′ = 440 tuning, since pitch placement varied. B-flat major could have meant that altos in the congregation sang an octave lower with the tenors, and basses might have sung two octaves lower, forming an interesting three octave congregational ride. Basses who regularly sing hymns an octave lower automatically generate this three-octave texture.

The question of key, as in what is the "right" key for a given hymn tune, is raised here. So is equal versus unequal temperament—whether, for example, unaccompanied choirs and congregations invariably gravitate to unequal, as mentioned in Chapter II. These may seem like arcane matters, but they are immensely practical issues for congregational singing. They extend well beyond the obvious considerations of range, single historical periods, and contrasts between keys at any given service. They have to do with the nature of music, and, therefore, of the harmonic series, in our universe. Musicians regularly face these concerns. They are critical, but they are also mysterious. Though palpable, they are very difficult to understand with precision, even when their theory can be articulated, which explains why there is disagreement about them. As for F major, for example, which set off this discussion, at a conference I once quoted a student who said F major is the most boring key of all. An organist who played an unequally tempered organ responded that F major was beautifully colorful on it.

And then there is the matter of the room where you are singing. When a new organ was put in one church I served, the organ company told me our worship space was in D major, that is, its acoustical properties made D major and related keys resonate most successfully. Singing a D major hymn in that church was indeed different from singing one in E-flat major—which, of course, means that any sense of an arbitrary "right" key for a hymn tune is contextualized and modified by your room.

STUTTGART comes from an early eighteenth century hymnal, *Psalmodia sacra* (Gotha, 1715), compiled and edited by Christian F. Witt (ca. 1660–1716). Witt's father, Johann Ernst Witt, was a court organist who came from Denmark.

The younger Witt, working in Gotha as organist and teacher, composed a set of cantatas with biblical texts and chorales for the whole church year. He wrote other music as well, including many hymn tunes in *Psalmodia sacra*. STUTTGART was one of them. Zahn gives its original more florid version,[25] which Henry Gauntlett "put into its present . . . form for *Hymns Ancient and Modern* (1861)."[26] Though clearly shaped by the harmonic mold of its period, it is nonetheless a bold and sturdy congregational melody that stands on its own and bears repetition.

STUTTGART

Come, thou long-ex-pect-ed Je-sus, Born to set thy peo-ple free:

From our fears and sins re-lease us, Let us find our rest in thee.

Text: Charles Wesley, 1744   VU #2
Tune: *Psalmodia Sacra*, 1715

O DASS ICH TAUSEND ZUNGEN HÄTTE names two tunes that came to be associated with that text by Johann Mentzer. One tune was published in Kornelius Heinrich Dretzel's (1743–11775) *Des Evangelisches Zions Musicalisches Harmonie* (Nürnberg, 1731) and is identified by the parenthesis "(DRETZEL)."

O DASS ICH TAUSEND ZUNGEN HÄTTE (DRETZEL)
989888

Bap-tized in - to your name most ho - ly, O Fa - ther,
I claim a place, though weak and low - ly, A - mong your

Son, and Ho - ly Ghost, Bur - ied with Christ and
seed, your cho - sen host.

dead to sin, I have your Spir - it now with - in.

Text: Johann J. Rambach, 1693-1735; tr. Catherine Winkworth, 1829-1878, alt.   LBW #192
Tune: Kornelius Heinrich Dretzel, 1705-1773

The other was published a few years later in Johann Balthasar König's (1691–1758) *Harmonischer Liedersatz* (Frankfurt, 1738) and is identified with the parenthesis "(KÖNIG)."

O DASS ICH TAUSEND ZUNGEN HÄTTE (KÖNIG)
989888

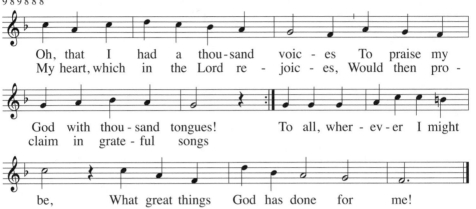

Text: Johann Mentzer, 1658-1734; tr. *The Lutheran Hymnal,* 1941, alt., © 1941, Concordia Publishing House   LBW #560
Tune: Johann B. König, 1691-1758

Longer than STUTTGART and not quite so solid, they both employ bar form with an eighteenth-century congregational zip—serious but playful, and probably slower than our zip. If DRETZEL really was sung in B-flat rather than F (see the above *Perspective*) and a three-octave ensemble was created, the tempo would obviously have been slower and the interest generated as much by the wide vocal range of the ensemble as by the tempo. The range of these tunes themselves is small, a fifth for DRETZEL and a sixth for KÖNIG.

GROSSER GOTT is an anonymous tune. It first appeared in the *Katholisches Gesangbuch* (Vienna, 1774), which the Hapsburg Empress Maria Theresa of Austria requested. It was joined to and named by the text of an anonymous German metrical setting of the *Te deum.* Taking many forms (HURSLEY[27] is one of its relatives) and possibly originating as a French folk song, it is an eminently congregational tune that has achieved wide circulation to the present day.[28]

GROSSER GOTT
787877

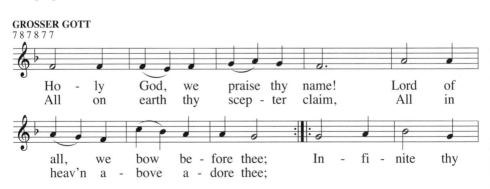

repeat ad lib

vast do - main, Ev - er - last - ing is thy reign.

Text: Ascr. to Ignaz Franz, 1719-1790; tr. Clarence Walworth, 1820-1900
Tune: *Katholisches Gesangbuch*, Vienna, c. 1774

Wor3 #524

Not everybody who sings this tune observes the repeat at the end.

AUSTRIA or AUSTRIAN HYMN comes from the end of the eighteenth century and was not conceived as a hymn tune. The Austrian composer Franz Joseph Haydn (1732–1809) wrote it in 1797 as the Austrian national anthem, extending it out of the first phrase of a Croatian folk song. Edward Miller (1731–1807), an English organist and student of the music historian Charles Burney, saw its potential as a hymn tune and in 1800 included it in his *Dr. Watts' Psalms and Hymns Set to New Music*. In many of our hymnals it has been paired with John Newton's text, "Glorious Things of Thee Are Spoken," as in the example given below. Haydn used the tune in a sublime way for a set of variations in the slow movement of his "Emperor" String Quartet (Op. 76, No. 3), but the Nazi thugs and criminals who sang "Deutschland, Deutschland über Alles" to it demonstrate how associations can defile a tune for many people.[29]

AUSTRIA
8 7 8 7 D

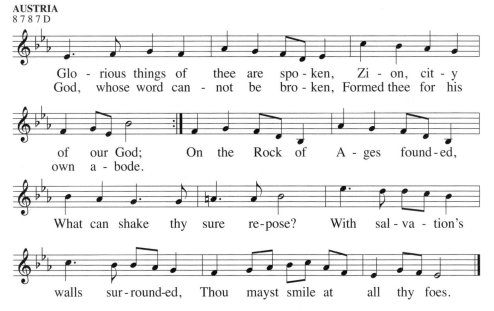

Glo - rious things of thee are spo - ken, Zi - on, cit - y
God, whose word can - not be bro - ken, Formed thee for his

of our God; On the Rock of A - ges found-ed,
own a - bode.

What can shake thy sure re-pose? With sal - va - tion's

walls sur-round-ed, Thou mayst smile at all thy foes.

Text: John Newton, 1779
Tune: Croatian folk song; arr. Franz Joseph Haydn, 1797

Meth #731

4. NINETEENTH CENTURY

Three motifs emerged in the nineteenth and twentieth centuries. One was the continuing progression to the sentimental begun by Pietism. It advanced with the support of a society increasingly controlled by the second motif, consumerism. Together these two created a culture of listening rather than singing, which for congregational song is the same as a death knell. The third motif was a reaction that sought to recover vital congregational singing 1) by retrieving the hymnody of the Reformation in its rhythmic forms (allied to a confessional renewal), 2) by eliciting new but isometric tunes from composers like Weyse and Lindeman, and 3) by harnessing again the music of folk cultures—which will be considered later.

Hymns in a Society of Consumers

Early in the nineteenth century, STILLE NACHT signals the second of these three motifs.

STILLE NACHT
6 6 8 9 6 6

Text: Joseph Mohr, 1792-1849; tr. John F. Young, 1820-1885
Tune: Franz X. Gruber, 1787-1863

Wor3 #379

This tune was composed by Franz Gruber (1787–1863), the parish organist at St. Nikolaus Church in Oberndorf, Germany, for the text of the same name, which the parish priest Joseph Mohr had written. When the organ stopped working on Christmas Eve 1818, Mohr decided to write a new hymn, and took it to Gruber, who wrote the tune. Priest, musician, and choir sang the hymn at the service that night, with Gruber accompanying them on a guitar. Twenty years later the hymn and its tune were published in the *Katholisches Gesang- und Gebetbuch* (Leipzig, 1838).

The origin of this tune points to its character. It is a soloistic piece with light guitar accompaniment. At the Christmas Eve service in 1818, the choir repeated the last two phrases in four-part harmony, which indicates the harmonic underlay and the choral possibilities that were implied. That is, the tune is not really quite congregational with its span of an octave and a fourth or its operatic upward glide over a static harmonic background, though many if not most congregations love it. They love "Silent Night," however, as much for what they hear as for what they sing, and their singing is often attuned to a nostalgic listening, which is less vocally engaged on this hymn than on more congregational ones (though it is interesting that adding a countermelody, like Daniel Kantor's "Night of Silence," makes STILLE NACHT more engaging). Erik Routley, though he is writing here about England, cuts to the heart of the matter by highlighting Western society, generally in the nineteenth century, and its impact on hymn singing.

> The Industrial Revolution, the first population explosion, and the growth of the new cities was already producing a society of consumers, which in music means a society of listeners. (The preaching houses were in their way a response to this.) More particularly, the idea of a *concert*, no longer a *consort* of chamber-musicians but a large event patronized by many listeners, had now become firmly rooted, and the corresponding cult of the conductor and virtuoso player, creating a market for music of a dramatically advanced kind, was part of the ordinary cultural scenery.[30]

Partly because of its popularity, STILLE NACHT can easily point to itself rather than beyond itself to the Word, though that is surely not what Mohr and Gruber intended. It is a harbinger of things to come, yet one more challenge to the congregation's song. This time, the challenge comes in the form of hymns treated as something to be listened to rather than sung, hymns for the spectator like concerts for the concertgoer.

The Sentimental, Children, and Manufactured "Volk"

The context of the consumer surrounded the sentimental and encouraged it. SO NIMM DENN MEINE HÄNDE is illustrative, though like all tunes that last from any period, it only hints at the excesses of its time and is not a bad tune. To see this motif and its trajectory in its own habitat, you have to look at a hymnal like the *Liederkranz für Sonntag-Schulen und Jugen-Vereine*[31] at the end of the century where the tune appears with others, which are more chromatic, have a goodly supply of dotted rhythms and compound background beats, and dropped from view long ago. SO NIMM DENN MEINE HÄNDE, however, does give the flavor of the time.

SO NIMM DENN MEINE HÄNDE
7 4 7 4 D

Lord, take my hand and lead me Up - on life's way;
Di - rect, pro - tect, and feed me From day to day.

With - out your grace and fa - vor I go a - stray;

So take my hand, O Sav - ior, And lead the way.

Text: Julie von Hausmann, 1825-1901; tr. hymnal version, © 1978, *Lutheran Book of Worship*, admin. Augsburg Fortress　　　LBW #333
Tune: Friedrich Silcher, 1789-1860

Like MUNICH, it moves in equal quarters that now slow to half notes at the ends of phrases, and it modulates to the dominant after the repeat of A. Not quite like MUNICH, it lends itself either to a harmonization that leads to a second inversion tonic in the second measure (*Liederkranz #227*)

or to a chromatically altered passing tone in the bass (LBW #333).

The inevitable seventh chord awaits

at the beginning of the last phrase. With less debilitating effect than other tunes from the period and with a relation to the broader stream from which it derives, it nonetheless plays with the clichés of the period without the skill of a Brahms or a Mendelssohn.

The text that came to be associated with it makes the picture clearer. The tune was written by Friedrich Silcher (1789–1860) for the third volume of his *Kinderlieder für Schule und Haus* (Tübingen, 1842) where it went with the text, "Wie könnt ich ruhig schlaffen,"[32] which prays for a pure heart. It joined "So nimm denn meine Hände" ("So take my hand and lead me"), a text by Julie Hausmann (changed to von Hausmann), in 1883 in the *Grosse Missionsharfe* (Gütersloh). The latter text in its original German assumes, but does not name God. That permitted brides and grooms at weddings to sing it as if addressed to one another.[33] Even when this generalized spirituality is replaced in translation by insertions of "Lord" and "Savior,"[34] the text still reflects a private and easily sentimentalized journey of the individual and God. Hymns like this can be meaningful when they live within the orbit of the common life of the liturgy and its song, so that their implied connotations have the faith's references. When they spin off into individual spiritual make-believe,[35] however, they lose their ballast and turn into sentimental solipsistic bubbles.

Note, finally, that this tune comes from a collection of children's hymns for school and home. The *Liederkranz für Sonntag-Schulen*, referred to above, was also a hymnal for youth groups. At the Reformation children were treated as human beings who could sing what everybody else sang and, because they were together in school, could learn new hymns and help their elders sing them at worship. In the nineteenth century children were singled out as a special cute class of objects and treated as if they had to be enticed by sentimental tactics with a manufactured "Volk" hymnody, designed specifically for them. Not only did that musically divide the body of Christ, but the title, *Missionsharfe*, signals the tie that was made between a faulty understanding of mission and hymnody, so that hymns began to be a means to the end of attracting people to the church, with children the first victims. We are still playing this game and its continuing price: when children grow up or adults wake up, they resent the contempt with which they were treated, recognize the church's dishonesty, stop singing, and leave the church. Sentimentality is a short-term fix and a long-term way to gut the faith and empty the church.

Felix Mendelssohn

The composer Felix Mendelssohn (1809–1837) enters the hymn tune story here, though not by his intention. We have already noted his use of the tune MUNICH in the oratorio *Elijah*. There he employed a pre-existing melody. Three other compositions by him with his melodies have been adapted for use as hymns, the first two with quite restricted use, the last with wide circulation. CONSOLATION[36] comes from a piano solo, *Lieder ohne Worte* ("Songs without Words"), Op. 30; and HEAVENLY LOVE[37] is from a choral piece, *Abschied vom Wald* ("Taking Leave of the Forest"), Op. 59. These are both nineteenth-century works by a skillful composer, but they are not congregational. This is true especially of HEAVENLY LOVE's penultimate phrase[38] which soars up to a high G and its last phrase which intersperses rests as in choral, but not congregational, music.

The tune that bears the composer's name, MENDELSSOHN, is another matter. It is the Christmas favorite that goes with Charles Wesley's text, "Hark! the Herald Angels Sing." Mendelssohn wrote the piece for men's chorus to celebrate the 400th anniversary of printing. He thought other words would be appropriate, but said "it will *never* do to sacred words."[39] William H. Cummings (1831–1915)—organist, singer, scholar, musical bibliophile, and admirer of Mendelssohn—thought differently and set Wesley's text to the melody. The marriage was published in 1857 in Richard R. Chope's *Congregational Hymn and Tune Book*. To date there has been no divorce.

MENDELSSOHN
7 7 7 7 D with refrain

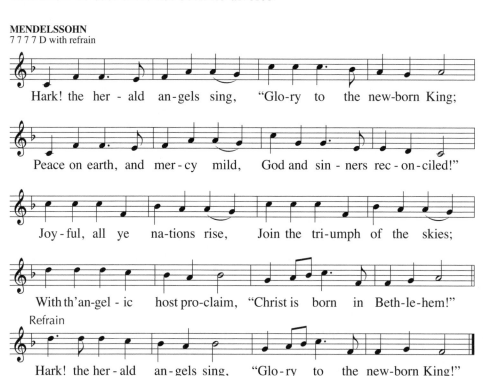

Text: Charles Wesley, 1739; alt. by George Whitefield, 1752, and others   Meth #240
Tune: Felix Mendelssohn, 1840

Though more examples could be given, the dimensions of these European continental trajectories from the sixteenth to the nineteenth centuries are clear enough to move on. In the next chapter, we will return to England at the beginning of the eighteenth century and pick up the narrative from the end of Chapter IV.

[1] For more detail, see Walter Blankenburg, Hans Heinsheimer, trans., "The Music of the Bohemian Brethren," in Blume, *Protestant Church Music*, 593–607. For textual matters see J. T. Mueller, "Bohemian Brethren's Hymnody," Julian, *A Dictionary of Hymnology*, I, 153–160.

[2] See *Luther's Works*, 53, 203.

[3] Correspondence from Robert Scholz, June 15, 2004.

[4] Walter Blankenburg, "Vulpius, Melchior," NGDMM, 20, 90.

[5] Chal #719, CW #s 333 and 606, HWB #426, H82 #s 295 and 356, LBW #263, Pres #s 179, 200, and 558, PsH #565, VU, page 783.

[6] Thomas Morley (ca. 1557–1602) also arranged the madrigal "Sing Wee and Chaunt it" from Gastoldi's tune.

[7] Carl Schalk, "Blest be the King Whose Coming," Glover H82C, 3A, 140; and Stulken, HCLBW, 208.

[8] *The English Hymnal with Tunes* (London: Oxford University Press, 1906), #519, hereafter, EH.

[9] George J. Buelow, "Crüger, Johannes," NGDMM 5, 70.

[10] Ibid., 69. Buelow also notes the simple practicality of the arrangements of these tunes for use in the home for private worship. There was nothing new, however, about use in the home. The new thing was the figured bass (figures beneath the bass that imply chords), which, no matter how simple, is more complex than the previous practice of tunes alone.

[11] On which J. S. Bach wrote a remarkable motet, BWV 227. Ludwig Lindeman wrote another tune that goes with this text, GUD SKAL ALTING MAGE (LBW #458).

[12] George J. Buelow, "Crüger, Johannes," NGDMM 5, 70.

[13] After 1586, when Osiander wrote harmonizations which moved the tune from the tenor to the treble voice, the congregation may well have sung in some places with the choir and instruments on its stanzas, which is the interpretation of Paul McCreesh with the Gabrieli Consort and Players, *Praetorius Christmette, Lutheran Mass for Christmas Morning as It Might Have Been Celebrated around 1620* (Hamburg: Deutsche Grammophon, 1994), Archiv 439 931-2.

[14] Walter Blankenburg, "Lobwasser, Ambrosius," NGDMM, 11, 103. Blankenburg details some of the adoptions beginning in the Palatinate and some of the numbers of publications.

[15] Walter E. Buszin, "Becker, Cornelius," *The Encyclopedia of the Lutheran Church* in 3 vols., ed. Julius Bodensieck (Minneapolis: Augsburg Publishing House, 1965), A–E, 202.

[16] Walter Blankenburg, "Becker, Cornelius," NGDMM, 2, 337. Marilyn Stulken [correspondence, June 17, 2004] notes the irony here—"that Lutherans should call the Calvinist tunes lascivious when the Calvinists considered them to be pious substitutes for other 'lascivious' music."

[17] See Carl Schalk, "German Hymnody, Stulken, HCLBW, 24, who notes two of them: *Ein new Gesangbüchlein geystlicher Lieder* (Leipzig, 1537) by Michael Vehe (ca. 1480–1539) and *Geistliche Lieder und Psalmen* (Bautzen, 1567) by Johannes Leisentrit (1527–1586).

[18] On which Johannes Brahms wrote a remarkable stanza-by-stanza choral setting (Op. 74, No. 2).

[19] See Robin Leaver, "Praise to the Lord, the Almighty," Glover, H82C, 3B, 738–740. On page 739 four versions of the tune from 1665 to 1680 are laid out side by side.

[20] See Theodore G. Tappert, "Introduction" to Philip Jacob Spener, trans. Theodore G. Tappert, *Pia desideria* (Philadelphia: Fortress Press, 1964), 19.

[21] Bonhoeffer emphasized the communal and spiritual importance of unison singing. See Dietrich Bonhoeffer, *Life Together* in *Dietrich Bonhoeffer's Works, Volume 5* (Minneapolis: Fortress Press, 1996), 66–68.

22   Cov #453 gives this text and its choral setting directly from *Elijah* and calls the tune CAST THY BURDEN.

23   For a version with more passing tones, see Pres #163. Another version is at H82 #47.

24   As in Zahn, MDEK, 2, # 2858.

25   Zahn, MDEK, 1, # 1353, also given by Robin Leaver, "Come, Thou Long-expected Jesus," Glover, H82C, 3A, # 66.

26   Brink/Polman, PsHH, 478.

27   Cov #658.

28   Johann Singenberger, *Orgelbuch* zu J. Mohr's "Caecilia" (Regensburg, Rome & New York: Friedrich Pustet, 1899), iv, refers to the popularity of this text and tune among nineteenth-century German Catholics in the United States.

29   For more detail see Robin Leaver and Nicholas Temperley, "Glorious Things of Thee Are Spoken," Glover H82C, 3B, 975–978.

30   Routley, MCH, 86A.

31   *Liederkranz für Sonntags-Schulen und Jugend-Vereine* (St. Louis: Eden Publishing House, 1898).

32   Ibid., #260, where no music is given, but SO NIMM DEN MEINE HÄNDE is referenced.

33   Haeussler, *The Story of Our Hymns*, 348.

34   As in LBW #333.

35   Or, as Routley said, "The hymnody of pietism . . . majors in solo religion." Erik Routley, *Christian Hymns Observed: When in Our Music God Is Glorified* (Princeton: Prestige Publications, Inc., 1982), 35.

36   Chal #416.

37   Cov #385 and HWB #613.

38   Omitted in Cov #385.

39   Robin Leaver, "Hark! the Herald Angels Sing," Glover, H82, 3A, 170.157

VI. Seventeenth- to Eighteenth-Century English Tunes

1. Overview

Restoration to Evangelical Revival

Erik Routley's overview of the late seventeenth and eighteenth centuries in England goes something like this. The English Restoration—that is, the return of the monarchy with Charles II in 1660 after the Puritan Commonwealth in 1649 and the Protectorate in 1653—"irrigated a church scene that puritan repressions had rendered somewhat arid." Church music was given over to the hands of professionals so that the "great psalm tunes of the puritan era stood alongside the splendor of Byrd and Gibbons," the latter a "more flexible, expressive, and subtle kind of music [that] took a great deal more handling." A gap developed between professionals and amateurs. "As the eighteenth century wore on," said Routley, "the crust of culture began to crack. . . The later eighteenth century produced very little professional music and a huge quantity of music associated with the evangelical revival."[1] That development brought with it "half-literate" composers whose piety rather than skill was in control, and "vulgarity" became a "serious concern."[2]

As usual, time has sorted out the wheat from the chaff of the eighteenth-century productions. What remains in use is the best of the various genres. For the excesses one has to go to the sources. The examples that follow in this and the next chapter will give the flavor through what remains. The order here will be quasi-historical, because the progression itself is not neat. It moves in this chapter from England to Germany to England at the end of the seventeenth century, then to English materials in the eighteenth century. The next chapter is eighteenth- and nineteenth-century English, with a short foray to France. But first we need to flesh out developments that threatened the people's singing in this period and then note the movement from metrical psalms to hymns.

Perspective: Threats to the People's Song

1) **Lining out**. In 1644 the Westminster Assembly, controlled by Puritans, authorized *A Directory for the Publique Worship of God*. It was a compromise between a liturgy and the absence of a common liturgical practice, "which outlined the main headings of worship, and described the substance of each element in such a way that 'by altering here and there a word, a man may mould it into prayer.'"[3] This *Directory* has been enormously influential among Protestants, not so much because of its specific content, but because it effectively gave control of worship to individual pastors and left congregations at their whim without the protection of the liturgy. Though many—probably most—pastors since then have tried to be responsible, some have bailed out altogether from any musical concern,[4] but have been equally quick to seize control whenever it suited their individual conceits to help or hurt congregational singing.

The Westminster *Directory* had another lasting effect. "Of Singing of psalms," it said this.

> That the whole congregation may join herein, everyone that can read is to have a psalm book; and all others, not disabled by age or otherwise, are to be exhorted to learn to read. But for the present, where many in the congregation cannot read, it is convenient that the minister, or some other fit person appointed by him and the ruling officers, do read the psalm, line by line, before the singing thereof.[5]

That is, a leader would speak or sing a line, and the congregation would sing it again. Though this "lining out" that the *Directory* describes could easily have been practiced earlier, Temperley thinks it "may have been a completely new idea" that the Assembly originated.[6] It modified psalm or hymn singing in three significant ways: 1) doubled the length because each line was repeated; 2) broke the text into separate fragments of individual lines which were difficult to relate to one another, undoing a hymn's meaning; and 3) created a new call-and-response form.

The original intention was laudable: to make it possible for those who could not read to sing. The historical development, however, led to a brand of singing with little or no connection to the original intention. The Westminster Assembly probably had no inkling of what it hatched (or affirmed). Lining out stimulated a slower and slower tempo in a call-and-response pattern, in which the response might be individually and cacophonously ornamented versions of the call (if it had been sung rather than spoken) or numerous completely different melodies all sung together at the same time. The result was yet another in-group activity in which only the initiated could participate, a gradual internal collapse of congregational song. It met resistance after the Restoration in England and in the United States early in the eighteenth century.

It should be noted that lining out, as in much of humanity's ironic experience, also stimulated a fecundity beyond the narrow confines of its origins in both white and black cultures. One can still find groups like the Old Regular Baptists from Blackey, Kentucky, mentioned in Chapter II, whose engaged vigor and rustic art are compelling. In black America, lining out went by various other names like metered singing or "Dr. Watts" hymns and exerted a lasting influence. Esther Rothenbusch Crookshank refers to the "beautified, cultural transformation of African-American lining out [which] came to bear [Watts'] name, and ultimately to permeate nearly every form of vernacular black musical expression to this day."[7] Developments of this sort are not only important historically, but deserve to be celebrated. For hymn singing generally, however, beyond its creative impact in specific groups, lining out caused problems and provoked a reaction.

2) **Slower singing.** The matter of slower singing is a phenomenon we have already noted in the chorale and Genevan psalm traditions. With lining out, psalm singing disastrously slowed. Temperley, relying on Samuel Pepys' judgment in 1661 that a psalm took an hour, estimates "the speed of singing would have been two or three seconds to a note."[8] In this case an external force did not bear down on the assembly's singing to silence it (unless one considers lining out an external force), but an internal collapse occurred that, unless countered, would lead to death. John Darwall, whom we will meet near the end of the eighteenth century, realized the problem. In a speech for an organ dedication in 1773, he

argued for reversing the trend. He said Psalm tunes should be "in quicker time than common [in order that] six verses might be sung in the same space of time that four generally are."[9]

3) **Organs and children**. Anglicans, like Lutherans, did not exclude organs from worship as Puritan separatists did, though congregational singing in both England and Scotland, also like the Lutheran practice, at first had "little or no help from choirs, organs, or other instruments."[10] In contrast to Lutherans, who supported eighteenth-century organ builders like Silbermann, English organs— destroyed during the Commonwealth—were not large or especially compelling projects. Peter Williams characterized commissions for English organs from 1550 to 1850 as "extreme miserliness."[11] Larger organs requiring advanced techniques of organ building only came into being in chapels of foreign embassies in the last half of the eighteenth century, then in Methodist churches and concert halls in the nineteenth century. The first separate Pedal division, for example, was not built in England until 1778.[12] Temperley comments on "the relative scarcity of organs, even in Anglican churches, until after 1700,"[13] when they could be found "in many of the larger town churches."[14]

After the Restoration, Temperley says, a reform of urban church music was generated by 1) a religious motive related to piety and morality and 2) an aesthetic motive related to the offensiveness of the old way of singing, which set in motion the new way of "regular singing," that is, singing by "note" rather than "rote." ("Old way" here meant the drawl of lining out.[15] It was a "new way" in the sense that it reversed the lively Reformation singing of psalm tunes. "Regular singing" was another "new way," set against the last "new way" that had become the "old way"!) In this reform "the main function of the organ [where it existed] was to provide a kind of musical whitewash, so that decorum could be attained."[16] The musical office of the people, expressed in their singing of the liturgy and psalms and hymns, took yet another hit. The liturgy was regarded as an introduction to the sermon, the sermon was the justification of "conventional morality,"[17] and the "common people could not rise to the new standards now required [and] the gentry would not so far demean themselves as to sing in church."[18]

In place of congregational song, endowed charity schools came to the rescue. Poor children were trained to sing what critics said they were too young to mean in music that was to be "treble-dominated and 'airy'"[19]—that is, the melody moved out of the tenor to the soprano. Here we have wealth paying for worship and turning it into entertaining decorum allied to a non-bodily sound. That sound, like the organ, has a very important place. In this context, however, it and the organ, with its potential for fancy façade and musical whitewash, joined to shut out the people's voice yet again. Temperley says it did not return until the Methodists rejuvenated it.[20]

It needs to be noted that children have played a very positive and important role in teaching and leading congregational singing. As Temperley notes, charity schools also functioned to teach children "to sing the psalms and then to lead the singing in the parish church."[21] So did the Sunday Schools "chiefly promoted by Evangelicals and dissenters."[22] Children have served as teachers and leaders in the same way at other times and places, including the sixteenth century among Lutheran and Reformed communities (as noted earlier). For children to be treated well and welcomed to the teaching and other roles in the community, which they can carry out so ably, obviously depends on the wisdom of the adults who are entrusted with their care.

Organists also have aided congregational singing, though their connection with hymn singing is later than that of children or other choral forces. Nineteenth-century developments tended to tie the organ, like other instruments, to solo performance. Organists who have led congregational singing well, therefore, have had to discipline themselves so that the resources under their control, especially as they became larger, did not usurp the congregation's role.

4) **West-gallery choirs and bands**. Around 1700 and in connection with getting rid of the "old way of singing" and the parish clerks who lined out the psalms, voluntary groups of singers formed. They developed into "predominantly or wholly male" choirs who used three- and four-part settings with the tune in the tenor.[23] "At first their function was to lead and regulate congregational singing of the old psalm tunes, but as time went on their music became increasingly elaborate."[24] They were given a special place, the "west gallery," and, in "the absence of organs, they began to be supported by bass viols and bassoons and eventually by full bands."[25] Instruments began to join worship in the middle of the eighteenth century,[26] and from

about 1780 to 1830, church bands were common. The center of the ensemble, whatever its makeup, was a bass instrument, usually a bassoon or cello.[27]

Both choirs and bands tended to exaggerate their importance. Choirs, who began as help for the congregation, often succumbed to the temptation to forget the congregation as they desired to sing "more ambitious music"[28] at the congregation's expense. Bands, who played for all the town's events that required music,[29] did not have the congregation's song uppermost in their minds either. It took another hit.

5) **Barrel organs**. Barrel organs are mechanical organs in which a barrel or wooden cylinder is rotated by a crank. A system of pins placed on the barrel at the right positions makes it possible to get wind to the specific pipes that need to speak. Barrel organs are very old. In England from the end of the eighteenth century and for the first half of the nineteenth they vied with choirs and bands in English churches, used not only for voluntaries, but to lead hymns as well.[30]

Barrel organs are delightful contrivances, but they deliver yet another blow to hymn singing if they are used to accompany it. As mechanical devices, they work against the incarnational character of the church, which is a group of human beings whose humanity, flesh and blood, breath, and all the marvelous contingencies of community, under the guidance of the Holy Spirit, modify the way a hymn is sung in each community each time it is sung. Here are some of the elements that make up a group of worshipers: health or sickness or a mix, younger or older ages or a mix, hot or cold temperature, low or high humidity, sun or clouds or snow or rain, beautiful or ugly surroundings, good or bad acoustical space or something in between, the occasion, the time of day, the season, the year, the presence or absence of warfare, and a funeral or wedding the day before. A mechanical device like a barrel organ forces a community into an artificially pre-determined and non-incarnational straitjacket of tempo and notes, giving it no space to be what it is.

As pipe organs and barrel organs were introduced, congregational song suffered one more sling, namely, the jealousy their introduction engendered among the choirs and instrumentalists who were "made redundant" by them.[31] Focus on the congregation's role took yet another backseat to petty squabbles about turf.

From Psalms to Hymns

Isaac Watts (1674–1748) was an Independent (today he would be called a Congregational) minister who challenged the exclusive use of metrical psalms. His freer paraphrases of the psalms and newly composed hymns were begun in the last decade of the seventeenth century and published in four collections during the first two decades of the eighteenth. They were resisted at first, but by the end of the eighteenth century and in the nineteenth Watts became dominant in English-speaking churches. He cast his texts mostly into Common Meter, Short Meter, and Long Meter so that the known psalm tunes could carry them. His texts gradually had a musical influence, but they did not require any new tunes.[32] He put up with lining out, a practice he said "cannot presently be reformed," but matched one complete thought with one line of poetry so that meaning was not so easily fractured.[33] He also pushed for a faster tempo in hymn singing.[34]

Charles Wesley (1707–1788) followed the lead of Watts by writing hymns. With more poetic grace, he wrote about ten times as many as Watts (about 700 for Watts and between 5,000 and 9,000 for Wesley) and used more meters. Wesley and his older brother, John, were the leaders in the Methodist movement. Its jubilant character and greater metrical variety had an influence on tunes, which will become apparent in the next chapter.

2. Tunes

Henry Purcell

Sometime in the early 1680s Henry Purcell (1659–1695), one of the finest English composers, who in 1679 succeeded John Blow as the organist at Westminster Abbey, wrote the anthem, "O God, Thou Art My God." In the nineteenth century, the end of the anthem was adapted by Ernest Hawkins as a hymn tune in Vincent Novello's *The Psalmist* (London, 1842), and in the twentieth century Sydney Nicholson named it WESTMINSTER ABBEY in the *Shortened Music Edition of Hymns Ancient and Modern* (London, 1939). Since then, it has become well known and much loved. Its origins fit here just before the beginning of the eighteenth century, but its general use as a hymn tune did not occur until the twentieth century.[35] It is a stately procession, not a waltz.

WESTMINSTER ABBEY
878787

Christ is made the sure foun-da-tion, Christ the head and cor-ner-stone,

Cho-sen of the Lord and pre-cious, Bind-ing all the church in one;

Ho - ly Zi - on's help for-ev - er, And her con - fi-dence a-lone.

Text: 7th c. Latin; trans. John Mason Neale, 1851, alt. 1861, 1972
Tune: Henry Purcell, 1659-1695, adapt.

Pres #416

(Purcell has another hymnic connection. Charles Wesley wrote "Love Divine, All Loves Excelling" as a "spiritual parody" on John Dryden's poem, "Fairest Isle, All Isles Excelling," which Henry Purcell set in his opera *King Arthur* (1691). In *Select Hymns with Tunes Annext* (1761), John Wesley set his brother's text to Purcell's melody.[36])

From Germany to England

What we now call WINCHESTER NEW started out in Germany as a popular but anonymous tune in 98 98 88 to go with "Wer nur den lieben Gott lässt walten" ("If You But Trust in God to Guide You"[37], a text known by us to the tune that names it discussed in Chapter V). It was printed in the *Musicalische Hand-buch der geistlichen Melodien* (Hamburg, 1690) that Georg Wittwe compiled. Here is that form of the tune.

Tune: George Wittwe's *Musicalische Hand-buch der geistlichen Melodien* Hamburg, 1690

Stulken, HCLBW, p.425

This melody morphed into 9 10 9 10 10 10 for Bartholomäus Crasellius's text, "Dir, dir Jehovah, will ich singen" in Freylinghausen's 1704 *Geistreiches Gesangbuch*. Here it is in one of its versions as DIR, DIR, JEHOVAH.[38]

DIR, DIR, JEHOVAH
9 10 9 10 10 10

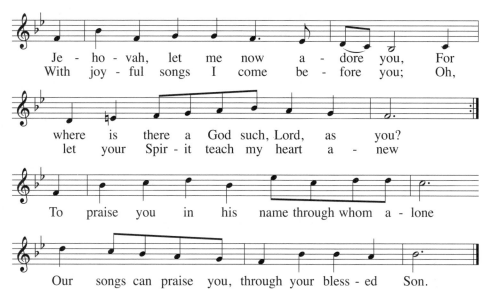

Je - ho - vah, let me now a - dore you, For
With joy - ful songs I come be - fore you; Oh,

where is there a God such, Lord, as you?
let your Spir - it teach my heart a - new

To praise you in his name through whom a - lone

Our songs can praise you, through your bless - ed Son.

Text: Bartholomäus Crasselius, 1667-1724, abr.; tr. Catherine Winkworth, 1827-1878, alt.   CW #189
Tune: *Musicalisch Hand-Buch der Geistlichen Melodien*, Hamburg, 1690, alt.

In England it turned into Long Meter. That is how Wesley gave it in his Foundery Collection, where it was called SWIFT GERMAN TUNE. The Foundery Collection will come up later in connection with the Methodists and the evangelical revival, but here is SWIFT GERMAN TUNE.

SWIFT GERMAN TUNE

"Foundery Collection," p. 34

The form of WINCHESTER NEW we generally use today is the version William Henry Havergal gave in *Old Church Psalmody* (London, 1847).

WINCHESTER NEW
LM

On Jor-dan's bank the Bap-tist's cry An - noun-ces that the Lord is nigh; A -

wake and heark-en,   for he brings Glad tid-ings of the   King of kings!

Text: Charles Coffin, 1736; tr. John Chandler, 1837, alt.   Pres #10
Tune: *Musikalisches Handbuch*, 1690

AMSTERDAM is another tune from Freylinghausen's 1704 *Geistreiches Gesangbuch*. It too will come up again when we get to Wesley's Foundery Collection. While WINCHESTER NEW begins up a fourth and then reverses direction, AMSTERDAM does just the opposite—begins down a fourth and then reverses direction. WINCHESTER NEW is a short tune that modulates to the dominant at midstream. AMSTERDAM is a longer tune in bar form that uses a modified repeat of A for the last phrase to get back home to the tonic.

AMSTERDAM
76767776

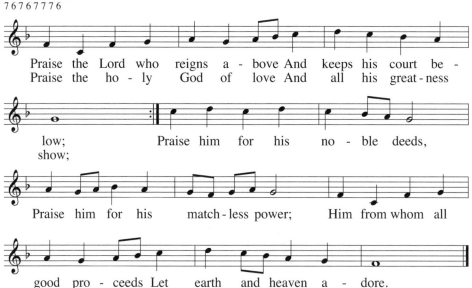

Praise the Lord who   reigns a - bove And   keeps his court be -
Praise the ho - ly   God of   love And   all his great - ness

low;   Praise him   for   his   no - ble deeds,
show;

Praise him for his   match - less power;   Him from whom all

good pro - ceeds Let   earth   and heaven a - dore.

Text: Charles Wesley, 1743   Meth #96
Tune: *Foundery Collection*, 1742

Jeremiah Clarke and Henry Playford's Divine Companion *(1707)*

Nicholas Temperley calls ST. MAGNUS (which has been known by at least ten other names) an "invigorating tune, typical of the revival of interest in hymnody in Queen Anne's reign (1702–1714)."[39] ST. MAGNUS was probably written by Jeremiah Clarke (ca.1674–1704), the organist and composer best known for his "Trumpet Voluntary," which is played at many weddings and sometimes wrongly ascribed to his contemporary Henry Purcell. ST. MAGNUS first appeared in 1707, after Clarke's death, in the second edition of Henry Playford's *Divine Companion* (London). Henry Playford (ca.1657–ca.1707) was a music publisher, the son of the Anglican music publisher John Playford (1623–1686) who was concerned about improving psalm singing,[40] and the godson of Henry Lawes (1596–1662) whom we shall meet shortly. Henry Playford "began a new tradition by commissioning the leading composers of the day to write original tunes in a contemporary style."[41] Up to this time, though individual composers might be enlisted for tunes and can sometimes be identified (the most obvious examples are Tallis and Gibbons), tunes generally had an anonymous character. Composers were more associated with their harmonizations.

Robert Bridges, the English poet laureate who died in 1930, called Clarke the "inventor of the modern English hymntune [sic]" and said, "his tunes are beautiful, and have the plaintive grace characteristic of his music and melancholy temperament. They are first in merit of their kind [and] are truly national and popular in style. . ."[42] (Bridges' comment about "melancholy temperament" probably reflects the person of Clarke more than his music. Clarke shot and killed himself, but his music exudes the cheerful style of this tune and his "Trumpet Voluntary.") Whether this effusive praise is quite accurate or not, what we can say about ST. MAGNUS is that it looks both backward and forward. It is related to the psalm tunes that preceded it, yet can be seen as "modern" and "popular" with a "plaintive grace" about it. Clearly in a major key without any modal hints at all, it modulates to the dominant at midstream like many other tunes we have encountered, but concludes with a new thing, a bold leap of an octave.

Until now, octave leaps have been between phrases and even then are rare. LASST UNS ERFREUEN and ES IST EIN' ROS have octaves going up between phrases, ST. THEODULPH going down. Such leaps remain rare. KUORTANE, from the nineteenth century, has an upward leap between phrases, and DISTLER, from the twentieth century has a most unusual downward octave on the last two notes. The octave leap in ST. MAGNUS works because it is prepared well by the span of the first two phrases and their outermost notes.

ST. MAGNUS
CM

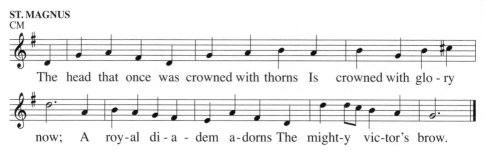

The head that once was crowned with thorns Is crowned with glo - ry now; A roy-al di - a - dem a-dorns The might-y vic-tor's brow.

Text: Thomas Kelly, 1769-1855
Tune: Jeremiah Clarke, 1670-1707

Wor3 #464

William Croft and the Supplement to the "New Version" (1708)

In 1696, after more than 130 years, the 1562 "Old Version" of the Psalter was finally challenged by *A New Version of the Psalms* (London) compiled by two Irishmen, Nahum Tate (1652–1715) and Nicholas Brady (1659–1726). *A Supplement to the New Version* (London) followed. In 1708, the year after Playford's *Divine Companion*, the sixth edition of this *Supplement* included seventy-five tunes.[43] We need to attend to three of them, HANOVER, ST. MATTHEW, and ST. ANNE.

HANOVER has often been attributed to William Croft (1678–1727) and sometimes to George Frederick Handel (1685–1759),[44] but neither Croft nor Handel was its likely composer.[45] Croft does figure in our story, however. In 1700, he and Clarke were together made "Gentlemen-extraordinary" of the Chapel Royal and in 1704 became joint organists there. When Clarke died in 1707, Croft held the post alone and was the primary Chapel Royal composer. A year later, he followed John Blow (1649–1708) as organist at Westminster Abbey. He contributed EATINGTON to Playford's *Divine Companion*. We do not use it.[46]

CROFT'S 136TH was also in Playford's book. Some of us use it. Though sometimes known as CROFT'S 148TH, in Playford it was the setting for Psalm 136. It extends the tension of movement away from the tonic from one to two keys by modulating to the dominant at midstream as had been customary, but then moving to the relative minor before getting back to the major home key.[47]

CROFT'S 136th
6 6 6 6 8 8 with refrain

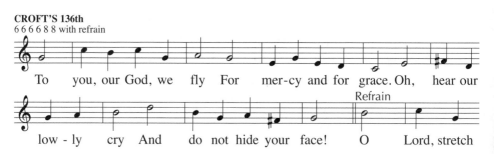

To you, our God, we fly For mer-cy and for grace. Oh, hear our low - ly cry And do not hide your face! O Lord, stretch

Refrain

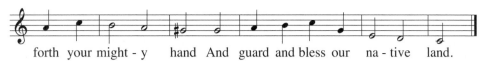

forth your might - y   hand And guard and bless our   na - tive   land.

Text: William W. How, 1823-1897, abr., alt.
Tune: William Croft, 1678-1727

CW #620

HANOVER is quite well known. Temperley tells us how well.

The popularity of this tune has been phenomenal throughout its history. Since about 1750 it has been in almost every major hymnbook in the English-speaking world. It was the sixth most frequently printed sacred piece in American tunebooks up to the year 1810. Second only to OLD 100TH, it was the tune most frequently found on English barrel organs in their period of widespread use (ca. 1790 to 1860).[48]

Whatever may account for its popularity, this is a jaunty tune. It hastens along with a balance of leaps and steps, drives to the reach of a minor sixth up to C and then to the held D that we long for after its touch in the first phrase, and concludes with leaps that gradually narrow back and forth around the final G.

HANOVER
10 10 11 11

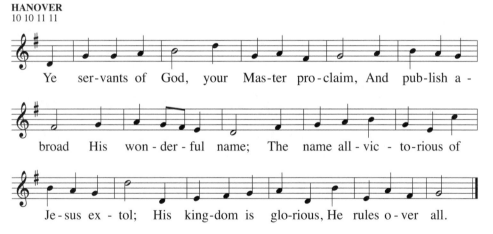

Ye   ser-vants of God,   your   Mas-ter pro-claim, And   pub-lish a -

broad   His   won - der - ful   name;   The   name all - vic - to-rious of

Je - sus ex - tol;   His   king-dom is   glo-rious, He rules o - ver all.

Text: Charles Wesley, 1744
Tune: Attr. William Croft, 1708; *A Supplement to the New Version of the Psalms,* 1708

Pres #477

ST. MATTHEW, like HANOVER with three beats to the bar, is almost twice as long and more meditative, with a journey to the relative minor in the third phrase group. A fine tune but not as well known as HANOVER, it too has probably been wrongly attributed to Croft.[49]

ST. MATTHEW
CMD

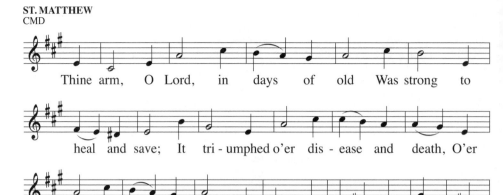

Thine arm, O Lord, in days of old Was strong to

heal and save; It tri - umphed o'er dis - ease and death, O'er

dark - ness and the grave. To thee they went, the blind, the

deaf, The pal - sied, and the lame, The lep - er set a -

part and shunned, The sick with fe - vered frame.

Text: Edward Hayes Plumptre, 1821-1891, alt.   H82 #567
Tune: *Supplement to the New Version of Psalms, Dr. Brady and Mr. Tate,* 1708

ST. ANNE is the best known of all the tunes by or attributed to Croft. He probably did write this one.[50] It is even more widely used than HANOVER. Routley calls it "the most celebrated of all English tunes."[51] It is almost always paired now with the text Isaac Watts fashioned for the first part of Psalm 90, "Our God, Our Help in Ages Past" ("Our God" is Watts' original; John Wesley changed it to "O God"), but in the 1708 *Supplement* it was used for Psalm 42, "As Pants the Hart."[52]

ST. ANNE
CM

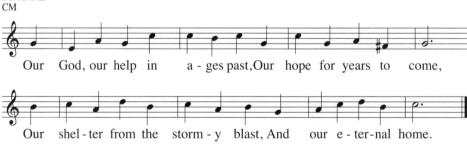

Our God, our help in a - ges past, Our hope for years to come,

Our shel - ter from the storm - y blast, And our e - ter - nal home.

Text: Isaac Watts, 1719; alt.   Pres #210
Tune: Attr. William Croft, 1708

Routley, though he did not disregard Croft as its "composer," thought ST. ANNE "was inspired" by "one of the great eccentrics of hymnody," Henry Lawes (1596–1662).[53] Lawes was a singer and composer who wrote some church music, but worked chiefly as a songwriter. Routley contrasted him with Gibbons, whom he saw "at the end of the long procession of great madrigalists who had adorned the Elizabethan age."[54] He regarded Lawes, on the other hand, as "one of the very first practitioners in England of the new music styles which had been developing in Europe since the beginning of the [seventeenth] century."[55] He thought Lawes, like Gibbons, wrote his tunes in short order and derived them from a stock of his own musical phrases. He knew Lawes' tunes, however, unlike those by Gibbons, never "achieved the first or even the second rank" of popularity and could not stand on their own the way Gibbons' could. That is, the congregation's native voice finds expression in Gibbons as it does not in Lawes.

> The difference is that most of the Gibbons tunes could be sung quite effectively in unison without accompaniment—the Lawes tunes, never.[56]

Because of their "unusual intervals," however, he called them "salty"[57] and thought their influence was greater than might have been expected.

Routley is on to something here. The "'saw-edge' profile"[58] of ST. ANNE is present in Lawes' tunes. The first phrase of his PSALM 9 is exactly the same as ST. ANNE (though this phrase also appears in unrelated fashion elsewhere, for example, G. F. Handel's sixth Chandos Anthem [HG xxxv, 98] and J. S. Bach's E-flat organ fugue [BWV 552, 2]). PSALM 9 predates ST. ANNE by seventy years, first appearing in George Sandys' *A Paraphrase upon the Divine Poems* (London, 1638).

PSALM 9
LM

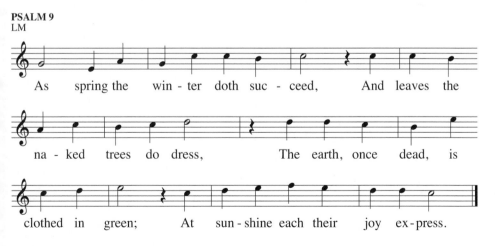

Text: Anne Bradstreet, 1657, alt.   HWB #568
Tune: Henry Lawes, *A Paraphrase upon the Divine Poems*, 1638

Furthermore, as Routley notes, Lawes wrote tunes that finish "on the high tonic."[59] That is true not only for PSALM 9, but for a more interesting tune by Lawes, FARLEY CASTLE, which first appeared in an earlier book of George Sandys', *A Paraphrase upon the Psalmes of David* (London, 1636).

FARLEY CASTLE
10 10 10 10

Here, O my Lord, I see you face to face; Here would I
touch and han-dle things un-seen, Here grasp with firm-er hand e -
ter - nal grace, And all my wea - ri - ness up - on you lean.

Text: Horatius Bonar, 1808-89, abr., alt.
Tune: Henry Lawes, 1595-1662

CW #315

Routley thought ending on the high tonic was "almost a 'first' in all hymnody."[60] The only other example he could think of was Luther's EIN NEUES LIED.[61] Luther wrote that tune for a text that was a celebrative and defiant polemic in response to the martyrdom of two Anabaptists.[62] Though it entered some hymnals, Luther wrote no other hymns like this ballad. He may not have intended the tune for worship; it stands in a less-than-intrinsic relation to the chorale stream and worship, and its final cadence was usually altered from the high tonic to the dominant.[63]

A tune written in 1645, more clearly in the chorale stream, also finishes on the high tonic, FREUET EUCH, IHR CHRISTEN ALLE.

FREUET EUCH, IHR CHRISTEN ALLE
8 7 7 8 7 7 with refrain

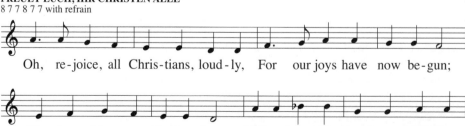

Oh, re-joice, all Chris-tians, loud - ly, For our joys have now be-gun;
Won-drous things our God has done. Tell a-broad his good-ness proud-ly,

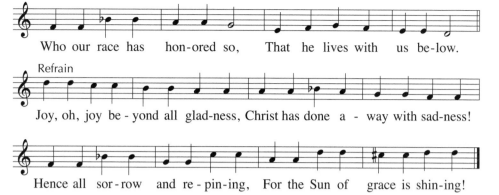

Who our race has   hon-ored so,   That he lives with   us be-low.

Refrain

Joy, oh, joy be - yond all glad-ness, Christ has done a - way with sad-ness!

Hence all sor - row   and re - pin - ing,   For the Sun of   grace is shin-ing!

Text: Christian Keimann, 1607-1662; tr. Catherine Winkworth, 1827-1878, alt.
Tune: Andreas Hammerschmidt, c. 1611-1675, alt.

CW #45

This is a high tonic ending from the same period as Lawes, where such an interest seems to be in evidence. (AUF, AUF MEIN HERZ by Johan Crüger, from a couple years later [the 1648 edition of the *Praxis Pietatis Melica*], is another example.[64]) The melody is by the popular Bohemian composer and organist Andreas Hammerschmidt (ca.1611–1675), found in his *Musikalische Andachten* (Freiberg, 1646) where it appeared with the text that named it by Christian Keimann. Though written for students in a 1645 Christmas play at Zittau,[65] it entered the chorale stream as a popular Christmas hymn. The tune has variants, finishing on the low tonic,[66] and its climbing use of sequence to get to the high tonic at the end taxes congregations—which may explain why it has fallen out of use.

Routley is probably right that Lawes' high tonic ending is a first in all hymnody or at least precedes by a decade what Hammerschmidt, probably without knowing Lawes' work, did in Germany. Routley explains this as part of the harmonic development of the Baroque period after 1600, by suggesting the melody is the "rhetorical principle and the bass the rational principle."[67] I take it he means to point to a partnership in which the melody is the persuasive partner and the bass the reasoned one. This suggests two things: 1) that tunes may be less chaste than earlier ones because they have the anchor of the bass line and its harmony to protect them and 2) for many of the tunes from the Baroque period on, especially in the nineteenth century, this partnership may be understood to imply that bass, harmony, and tune form a unit which needs to be cited with all its components.

Routley's insights are helpful. The underlying historical progression to the tonal logic of the seventeenth and eighteenth century Baroque that they presume, both in England and on the continent, is surely accurate.[68] Several other comments need to be added, however. First, ending on the high tonic is the exception that proves the rule. Generally such an ending is difficult for a congregation because it demands preparation and breath support, which people without vocal training cannot normally be expected to have. In the case of ST. ANNE, the saw-tooth edge of the melody, the short phrases, and the tessitura between the dominant and the high tonic set up an unconscious preparation. Second, there is a danger here again. Tunes that end on the high tonic but do not have the built-in preparation of ST. ANNE can easily silence congregations. Third, even if the melody is the rhetorical principle and the bass the rational one in an interlocking partnership, most people in most congregations will still be able to sing the melody, not the harmony. That means we still have to attend primarily to the tunes. From time to time, I will include the bass and harmony, but I will avoid that as much as possible in order to focus on the congregation's capacities in normal circumstances. Finally, Croft in ST. ANNE did what Luther did—took the musical materials that lay at hand and harnessed them well for congregational participation.

> In reality the composer's achievement lay in making a powerful new synthesis of preexisting elements . . .ST. ANNE, with its swinging "sawtooth" melodic line, is clearly modeled on some of the classic tunes of a century earlier, such as YORK, LONDON NEW, and ST. DAVID'S.[69]

YORK and ST. DAVID'S are "sawtooth" tunes that Samuel Sewall said Old South Church in Boston confused with one another, much to his discouragement (given in Chapter IV, under "The Precentor's Nightmare"). Here is the similar LONDON NEW.

LONDON NEW
CM

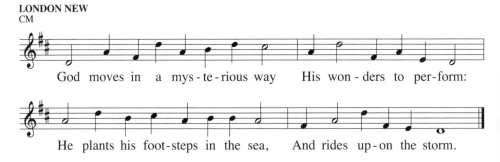

God moves in a mys-te-rious way   His won-ders to per-form:

He plants his foot-steps in the sea,   And rides up-on the storm.

Text: William Cowper, 1731-1800   H82 #677
Tune: *The Psalmes of David in Prose and Meeter*, 1635, alt.

EASTER HYMN *and* Lyra Davidica *(1708)*

Carlton Young regards EASTER HYMN (called SALISBURY TUNE and by numerous other names including CHRISTMAS DAY[70]) "as among the first of the hymn tunes composed in the emerging evangelical style. . . ."[71] Robin Leaver calls it "an extraordinary tune for its time, anticipating the more exuberant tunes of the Evangelical revival later in the century."[72] It comes from early in the eighteenth century—the same year as the *Supplement to the New Version* – in an anonymous publication called *Lyra Davidica* (London, 1708), whose tunes were intended to give "a little freer air than the grave movement of the Psalm-tunes."[73] In keeping with this intent, *Lyra Davidica* not only anticipated what was to come in England, but was also "the first English printing of several German hymn tunes."[74] EASTER HYMN was paired with an English version of a fourteenth-century Latin text for Easter that had gone through a fifteenth-century German translation,[75] structured so that melismatic "alleluias" break into the text.

EASTER HYMN
7 7 7 7 with alleluias

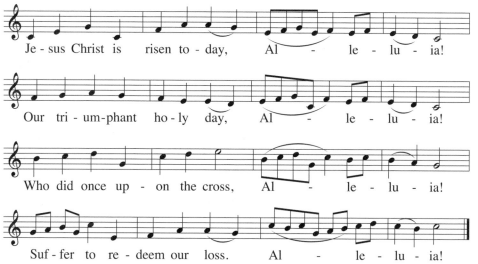

Text: Latin, 14th c.; tr. *Lyra Davidica*, 1708, alt.
Tune: *Lyra Davidica*, 1708; adapt. *The Compleat Psalmodist*, 1749, alt.

H82 #207

William Knapp and Sett of New Psalm Tunes and Anthems in Four Parts *(1738)*

Here is a perceptive analysis of WAREHAM, a tune that has migrated to many texts and has been widely used since it was written.

> WAREHAM is one of the most durable tunes produced by English country psalmists of the period of the west-gallery choirs and bands. Its almost exclusively conjunct motion is kind to congregations, and the gradual climb to a climax in the second half gives it an attractive warmth of feeling.[76]

This tune is named for the birthplace of its composer, William Knapp (ca.1698–1768), a glover, parish clerk, choir director, and compiler of church music collections (and maybe not the easiest person to get along with, unless a certain poetic reference to him is *only* humorous[77]). WAREHAM comes from his 1738 edition of a *Sett of New Psalm Tunes and Anthems in Four Parts* (London).

WAREHAM
LM

The church of Christ, in ev - 'ry age Be - set by change, but Spir - it led, Must claim and test its her - i - tage And keep on ris - ing from the dead.

Text: Fred Pratt Green, 1969, © 1971, Hope Publishing Co.   Mor #694
Tune: William Knapp, 1738

Thesaurus Musicus (1744 or 1745)

AMERICA (or NATIONAL HYMN or NATIONAL ANTHEM) has served more as a "national anthem" (official or not, for more than one country) than a hymn tune, but it needs to be mentioned if for no other reason than that it may be the best-known tune in the Western world.[78] Its composer is unknown. With origins perhaps in the seventeenth century, its first appearance in print seems to be the second edition of *Harmonia Anglicana* (London, 1744), called *Thesaurus Musicus* (London, 1744 or 1745).[79]

AMERICA
6 6 4 6 6 6 4

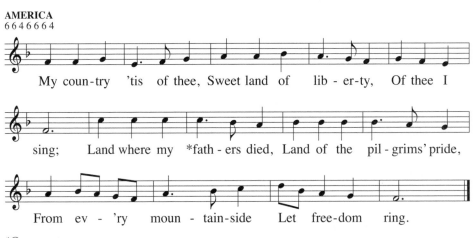

My coun-try 'tis of thee, Sweet land of lib - er - ty, Of thee I sing; Land where my *fath - ers died, Land of the pil - grims' pride, From ev - 'ry moun - tain-side Let free-dom ring.

*Or parents

Text: Samuel Francis Smith, 1831   Chal #721
Tune: *Thesaurus Musicus*, 1744

1   Erik Routley, *Church Music and the Christian Faith* (Carol Stream: Agape, 1978), 70.
2   Ibid., 70–71.
3   Bard Thompson, *Liturgies of the Western Church* (Cleveland: Meridian Books, 1961), 349.
4   See, for example, Nicholas Temperley, *The Music of the English Parish Church, Volume 1* (Cambridge: Cambridge University Press, 1979), 88.
5   Ibid., 81–82.
6   Ibid., 82.
7   Esther Rothenbusch Crookshank, "'We're Marching to Zion,': Isaac Watts in Early America," *Wonderful Words of Life: Hymns in American Protestant History & Theology,* ed. Richard J. Mouw and Mark A. Noll (Grand Rapids: William B. Eerdmans Publishing Company, 2004), 38.
8   Temperley, The Music of the English Parish Church, Volume 1, 92.
9   Quoted in Brink/Polman, PsHH, 568.
10 Temperley, "The Tunes of Congregational Song in Britain from the Reformation to 1750," Glover, H82C, I, 353.
11 Peter Williams, "Organ," NGDMM, 13, 747.
12 Ibid., 749–750.
13 Temperley, HTI, I, 48.
14 Ibid., 50.
15 Temperley, *The Music of the English Parish Church, Volume 1,* 100.
16 Ibid., 101.
17 Ibid., 100.
18 Ibid., 101.
19 Ibid., 102.
20 Ibid., 99.
21 Temperley, HTI, I, 22.
22 Ibid., 23. See also page 25.
23 Ibid., 9.
24 Ibid.
25 Ibid.
26 Temperley, *The Music of the English Parish Church, Volume 1,* 148–149.
27 Ibid., 197 where Temperley lists specific bands with their dates and instrumentation.
28 Ibid., 202.
29 Ibid., 201.
30 Ibid., 234–239, where Temperley gives a list of hymn tunes found on the barrel organs of this period and discusses matters like tempo.
31 Ibid., 235.
32 For more detail in summary form with sources, see, Westermeyer, *Te Deum,* 201–205.
33 Isaac Watts, "The Preface," *Hymns and Spiritual Songs* (London, 1709), reprinted in Music, *Hymnology: A Collection of Source Readings,* 118.
34 See Esther Rothenbusch Crookshank, "'We're Marching to Zion'. . .", *Wonderful Words of Life,* 24.
35 For the last two notes of the second measure, H82 #518 reverses the expectation and has a quarter note followed by a half, which "rescues the tune from waltzhood" (Marilyn Stulken, correspondence, June 17, 2004). At the eighth measure, some versions have a quarter note F-sharp in place of the two eighths, which angers those who oppose this "dumbing down."
36 Young, CUMH, 476.
37 LBW #453,
38 For others see Zahn, MDEK, #3067.

39 Nicholas Temperley, "The Christ Who Died but Rose Again," Glover H82C, 3B, 843.

40 See Temperley, HTI, I, 49.

41 Temperley, HTI, I, 31.

42 Stulken, HCLBW, 262. Three of his tunes, in addition to ST. MAGNUS, can be found in a few of our hymnals: BISHOPTHORPE at HWB #73 and VU, 811; ST. LUKE at CW #s 303, 308, and 519; and UFFINGHAM at H82 #148 and Meth #450.

43 For more detail, see John Julian, A Dictionary of Hymnology (New York: Dover Publications, Inc., 1957, reprint of 2nd rev. ed. with supplement), Vol. 1, A to O, 801–802.

44 For Handel's relationship to hymn tunes, see John Wilson, "Handel and the Hymn Tune: I, Handel's Tunes for Charles Wesley's Hymns," The Hymn 36:4 (October 1985): 18–23, and John Wilson, "Handel and the Hymn Tune: II, Some Hymn Tune Arrangements," The Hymn 37:1 January 1986): 25–31.

45 Nicholas Temperley, "O Worship the King, All Glorious Above," Glover, H82C, 3B, 728–731.

46 It can be found in EH at #639.

47 For a later rhythmic version than the one given here, see H82 #284.

48 Temperley, "O Worship the King . . . ," 731.

49 For details, see Nicholas Temperley, "Thine arm, O Lord, in Days of Old," Glover, H82C, 3B, 1053–1054.

50 For details, see Nicholas Temperley, "O God, Our Help in Ages Past," Glover, H82C, 3B, 1255–1258.

51 Routley, MCH, 53B.

52 Five stanzas of this text can be found at LBW #452 and the whole hymn at Robin Leaver, "As Longs the Deer for Cooling Streams," Glover H82C, 3B, 1206–1208.

53 Routley, MCH, 53B.

54 Ibid., 51B.

55 Ibid., 52B.

56 Ibid., 53B.

57 Ibid., 52B.

58 Ibid., 53A.

59 Ibid., 52B.

60 Ibid.

61 For this tune and its text, see Luther's Works, vol. 53, 214–216.

62 And part of a polemic against the cult of saints. See Rebecca Wagner Oettinger, Music as Propaganda in the German Reformation, 51–53 and 61–69.

63 Luther's Works, vol. 53, 214. See also Zahn, MDEK, #7245, and Rebecca Wagner Oettinger, Music as Propaganda in the German Reformation, 62, FN 19.

64 LBW #129.

65 Aufdemberge, CWH, 66.

66 See Zahn, MDEK, 4, #s 7880–7884.

67 Routley, MCH, 53A.

68 Figured bass, from a German influence, first entered English-language hymns in 1720. [Temperley, HTI, I, 53.]

69 Temperley, "O God, Our Help . . .," Glover, H82C, 3B, 1256. (See Chapter IV, under the "The Precentor's Nightmare.") LONDON NEW is at H82 #s 50, 251, and 677.

70 Young, CUMH, 281.

71 Ibid.

72 Robin Leaver, "Jesus Christ Is Risen Today, Alleluia," Glover, H82C, 3A, 419.

73 Ibid., 417.

74 Temperley, HTI, I, 35.

75   Leaver, "Jesus Christ Is Risen Today, Alleluia," Glover, H82C, 3A, 414–417, sorts this out.

76   Nicholas Temperley, "O Wondrous Type! O Vision Fair," Glover H82C, 3A, 276.

77   Stulken, HCLBW, 465, cites this poem by H. Price in the *London Magazine* (1742) about Knapp and George Savage—Knapp, the parish clerk, and Savage, the sexton of St. James's Church in Poole.

> From pounce and paper, ink and pen,
> Save me, O Lord, I pray;
> From Pope and Swift and such-like men,
> And Cibber's annual lay;
> From doctors' bills and lawyers' fees,
> From ague, and gout and trap;
> And what is ten times worse than these,
> George Savage and Will Knapp.

78   When I was auditioning college choirs and teaching college music appreciation classes (among students who were churchgoers and those who had nothing to do with the church), this was the only melody, with the possible exception of "Happy Birthday," I could find that everybody knew. (I think Quentin Faulkner at the University of Nebraska did a study and found the same thing.)

79   Temperley, HTI, I, 30, says it was sung in England (as the British national anthem, "God Save the King [or Queen]") "on public occasions from its first appearance in the 1740s. Especially in times of war or national crisis, it was frequently performed at the beginning or end of a play, opera, or concert."

VII. EIGHTEENTH- TO NINETEENTH-CENTURY ENGLISH TUNES

Methodists

Helmsley is a town in northern England where Richard Conyers, a friend of John Wesley, was the parish priest. After his "conversion" on Christmas Day in 1758, he introduced hymn singing into his parish.[1] His town names one of the hymn tunes that Temperley saw as "typical" of the Methodists"[2] and Routley said represented "early Methodist hymnody at its best."[3] Routley compared it with ST. ANNE, which he called "measured and stately," versus HELMSLEY, which he called "decorative and shamelessly jubilant."[4] He thought HELMSLEY showed "the universality of great melody" and noted its "association with one of the most solemn hymns in the language."[5] It provides an instructive study. Here it is as we have it today.

HELMSLEY
878747

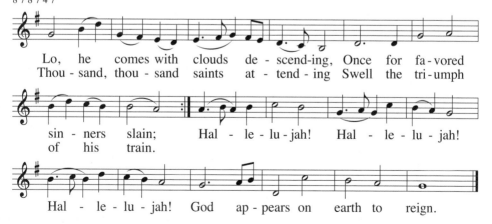

Lo, he comes with clouds de - scend-ing, Once for fa - vored
Thou - sand, thou - sand saints at - tend - ing Swell the tri - umph

sin - ners slain; Hal - le - lu - jah! Hal - le - lu - jah!
of his train.

Hal - le - lu - jah! God ap - pears on earth to reign.

Text: Charles Wesley, 1758
Tune: Trad. English melody, 18th cent.

Meth #718

John Wesley (1703–1791) included it in the 1765 edition of his *Sacred Melody* (London),[6] with the text just given by his brother, Charles (1707–1788). Here is the way it appeared there.

Stulken, HCLBW p. 127

Wesley attributed this tune to the preacher Thomas Olivers (1725–1799), who is said to have gotten it from a melody he "heard whistled on the street."[7] Since the first line resembles something the composer and violinist Thomas Arne (1710–1778) wrote for *Thomas and Sally, or The Sailor's Return* of 1761,

Stulken, HCLBW, p. 126

there has been speculation that Arne is the source for HELMSLEY, but Nicholas Temperley thinks Olivers probably heard HELMSLEY itself. He thinks it was "in print since 1763 and may have been in use for some years before that,"[8] presumably at Lock Hospital in London where Martin Madan (1726–1790) was the chaplain. Madan, a Calvinist Methodist convert of John Wesley, was an ordained Anglican priest like Wesley.

Lock Hospital was one of the charitable institutions of the time, like the Foundling Hospital, which Handel helped to support by his annual performances there. Charities and proprietary chapels were Anglican institutions, but not directly controlled by bishops. Supported by wealthy London citizens, they became centers of evangelical activity where new hymns and tunes were sung and collected, and where the children sheltered there sometimes formed choirs. Lock Hospital, which apparently could not sustain a choir,[9] was founded in 1746 for venereal patients.[10] After his ordination in 1758, Madan became the chaplain, supporting a chapel and its music with his own financial resources.[11] He compiled a *Collection of Psalms and Hymns Extracted from Various Authors* (London, 1760) and a tune book to go with it, a *Collection of Psalm and Hymn Tunes Sung at the Chapel of the Lock Hospital* (London, 1769). Temperley thinks HELMSLEY was printed in an earlier edition of this book in 1763.[12] Madan gave the tune in "the most up-to-date gallant style, with elegant melismas in thirds and sixths, pretty appoggiaturas, and trills,"[13] like this.

HELMSLEY

Lo, He comes with clouds de-scend-ing, Once for fa-vour'd sin-ners slain!

H82C, 1A, p. 110

Now, except for the version as we have it, these examples veer toward solo music. Such music can be sung for short periods of time in some fashion by groups of enthusiasts—enthusiasts both in the technical theological sense of persons or groups who presume to have direct possession of the Spirit and the more popular sense of persons or groups with ardent zeal often accompanied by emotive excess, but for the catholic community at large who is not part of such a group and who needs what is genuinely communal, this kind of music is out of reach.

These various versions reveal the birth pangs of a congregational melody. Its range of an octave and a third drives its lowest pitch a bit too low, its seventh near the end pushes the congregational envelope, and its repetitions verge on excess; but its overall ambit saves it, its sequence-like repetitions are not out of control, and they actually serve to prepare the seventh. The tune works, though it is a difficult one for congregations. Anglicans objected to HELMSLEY's potential for excess, partially because of its jubilant style, but also because in its decorated forms it could not be sung by normal people. It took Ralph Vaughan Williams[14] in the twentieth century to transform it for Anglicans, partially by his skillful use of harmony, but also because he studied folk song and was one of those unique composers who knew what a congregational melody looks like and how to harness musical materials for congregational singing.

This tension between a congregation's musical office and the entertaining emotive excess of the moment was Methodism's struggle and remains the struggle of all similar evangelical movements. Substituting one wrong for another is not helpful. Silent congregations or ones that barely sing (one wrong) are not helped by giving them music they cannot sing (another wrong), which is choral or soloistic in nature, no matter how appealing it may appear. Solos, duets, oratorios, and concerts all have a legitimate place, but they are not the musical office of the people at worship. When they are taken to be what they are not, the trouble begins. John and Charles Wesley understood this and the nature of the congregation's song. That is partly why John Wesley did not like florid and complex hymn tunes, was ambivalent about organs, worried about "vain repetitions," and understood the primal power of monophonic music.[15] That is partly why Charles Wesley "always deplored Lampe's involvement with theater music."[16]

John Frederick Lampe (1703–1751) was a bassoonist and composer mostly for the theater. He became a friend of Charles Wesley and composed soloistic tunes for his hymns.[17] Martin Madan at Lock Hospital tended toward a similar style. Madan's tune book was more about duets and trios than about congregational song,[18] with "a new type of church music based on the current idiom of opera and concert music,"[19] which explains the strong fare of musical concerts and oratorios at Lock Hospital as well as the necessity there for "congregational rehearsals."[20] Congregational rehearsals are not necessarily bad, but they are not a norm for the church as a whole. They are legitimately resisted by some congregants who are interested in congregational singing, but not in being treated as part of a choir that rehearses. When music based on a Lock Hospital model is exported as the norm for the church, trouble is near in the form of congregations gradually being silenced. This is true, even though, as in this case, there may be immense initial popularity.[21] The point here is not to fault Madan or anybody else who in a given locale works with the resources available, as in the possibility of rehearsing at Lock Hospital. The point is that such local models do not work as the norm for the whole church, and music used in such places cannot successfully be imported as congregational to the rest of the church.[22] This is especially true when part of the intent is to attract people and their money,[23] which over the long haul proves to be a counterproductive denial of the faith.

John Wesley, on the other hand, chose congregational tunes. His Foundery Collection,[24] though its title is hopeless ("Tunes, set to music"?) and its printing full of errors, nonetheless showed sound congregational judgment. The collection is named for the cannon factory that, after an explosion, had been rebuilt and used by the Methodists as a "preaching-house, school-room and living quarters."[25] It contains tunes John Wesley continued to use in future collections and points, as Carlton Young says, to his "ability to select solid tunes in a variety of meters."[26] We have already discussed some of them that we still use:

- AMSTERDAM (called AMSTERDAM TUNE, a "flawed variant"[27]), from Freylinghausen's 1704 *Geistreiches Gesangbuch*, encountered by Wesley among Moravians on board a ship on his way to Georgia where he was impressed by their hymn singing,

- HANOVER (called BROMSWICK TUNE and TALLY'S or TALLIS' because Wesley thought Tallis wrote it),
- WINCHESTER NEW (called SWIFT GERMAN TUNE),
- OLD 113TH (GENEVAN 68, called the 113TH PSALM TUNE),
- TALLIS' CANON (called CANNON TUNE or CANON),
- VATER UNSER (called PLAYFORD'S TUNE), and
- WER NUR DEN LIEBEN GOTT (in a version called SLOW GERMAN TUNE).

Wesley is another of the church's historic figures who is accused of raiding the bars and asking why the devil should have all the good tunes. While it is certainly true that, like Luther, he opposed what was dull and formal in the sense of deadly perfunctory and superficial[28]—and that he was attentive to the musical currents of his time, it is equally true that he affirmed the *Book of Common Prayer* (as breathing a "solid, scriptural, rational Piety"[29]) and the best hymn tunes of the church. Wesley wanted to do what the church at its wisest has continually done—use the best available musical resources, broken to a congregational shape around Word, font, and table. In any period like his when dryness without irrigation has set in, the use of new "secular" tunes will seem striking.[30] That is part of the story. The larger part is that Wesley, like the church before him, used the best sources that lay at hand, including "secular" ones, but he did not raid bars and assume the devil had all the good tunes.[31] Most of the tunes he used, and certainly the ones that have endured, came from churchly sources.

Perspective: Sacred and Secular

According to Nicholas Temperley, "It is sometimes claimed that the hymn tunes of the Reformation period were folksongs, and several sources suggest that Thomas Sternhold's metrical psalms were originally sung to existing ballad tunes or even dance tunes."[32] He goes on to say that "all attempts to link the tunes printed with early English psalm texts to specific folksongs have so far failed."[33] He points in the English tradition to what we might see as a sacred-secular linkage without a one-to-one identity, though the folk song itself is not exactly sacred or secular but lives in a symbiosis with both, and in the sixteenth century the distinction we make between sacred and secular did not apply.[34] In the Genevan and chorale traditions a similar circumstance prevailed with different details: psalm tunes that related to but were not either secular chansons or Gregorian chant, and chorale melodies that derived from both sacred and secular sources, always related to but were separate from the world. *Contrafacta* employed for worship in the chorale tradition broke secular associations to the Word. The Dutch *Souterliedekens* of 1540, which had tunes for 150 psalms, is a clearer example of borrowing secular melodies. It included "drinking songs, children's songs, hunting songs, mocking songs, etc."[35] Even there, however, the familiar folk song was at issue, not what we today might call "secular," and plainsong sources were employed as well. A sacred-secular linkage, applying the terms anachronistically, was at work via the folk song, which is simply what the people can sing in sacred or secular contexts.

Following the Reformation, this creative linkage disappeared, and a troublesome division developed. "In the course of time," says Temperley, the pace of singing "slowed to a drawl," psalm tunes were "set apart from other music" and "by 1700" were "a hallowed survival from the past, in stark contrast with popular styles."[36] Authorities even defended them "against the *'impious, lewd, and blasphemous* Songs' of the playhouses."[37] Notice what happened. A new and slower practice with lining out, quite unlike the original practice at the Reformation, was frozen into a museum-like "sacred" style. Methodists and Evangelicals made strong and legitimate objections by "borrowing from contemporary secular music, including operas and theatre pieces."[38] A false dichotomy was the result of this historical progression.

We are still in the throes of this faulty either/or that treats the people poorly by attempts to force them to identify either with a museum or a fad. The people know better, and, though they can be enticed momentarily in one direction or the other by the misguided efforts of their leaders, over time their wisdom prevails. The church as a whole no longer has either lining out or eighteenth-century theater music. It does have the best congregational tunes from many periods, among them ones John Wesley identified.

Thomas Olivers, Meier Leoni, and Jewish Influence

Thomas Olivers, the conduit for HELMSLEY, provided a similar role for the tune we call LEONI or YIGDAL. Olivers was an itinerant preacher for both George Whitefield and John Wesley. In addition to an elegy on Wesley's death, he wrote hymns. One of them is "The God of Abraham Praise," which he based on the *Yigdal* or Jewish articles of faith from Moses Maimonides (1130–1205), which Daniel ben Judah had versified around 1400. Olivers heard the cantor Meier Leoni (Meyer Lyon [1751–1797]) sing the *Yigdal* at the Great Synagogue in London and asked him to transcribe the melody for him. Olivers adapted it to his translation. The tune probably comes from the seventeenth century. It moves in a minor and then a major wave, stays in major at midstream, moves to the dominant of the original minor, and gets home by repeating and developing the first phrase.

LEONI
6 6 8 4 D

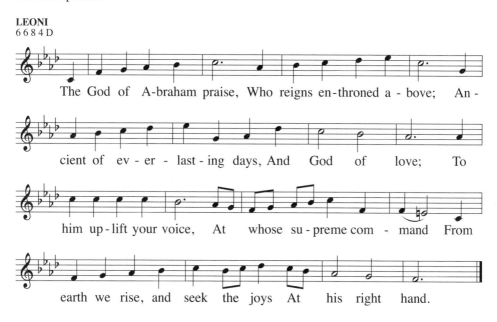

The God of A-braham praise, Who reigns en-throned a - bove; An-cient of ev - er - last-ing days, And God of love; To him up-lift your voice, At whose su-preme com - mand From earth we rise, and seek the joys At his right hand.

Text: *Yigdal Elohim Hai*; ascr. to Daniel ben Judah Dayyan, fl. 1400; para. by Thomas Olivers, 1725-1799, alt.   Wor3 #537
Tune: From the *Yigdal*; tr. Meyer Lyon, c. 1751-1797

Felice de Giardini, Italian Influence, and the Countess of Huntingdon

It may have occurred to the reader that tunes have been "found out" in families of the human race. It may have also occurred to the reader that there is no large Italian grouping. Some groups have influenced hymnody either in one period or through a body of hymns and hymn tunes. They logically group themselves together. Italians, however, have had a more sustained influence, part of a larger tapestry with threads that keep reemerging. They run from the hymns of Ambrose and Fortunatus and maybe the tunes associated with their texts, to musical stimuli in the Baroque, to the Italian Catholic priest and composer Giovanni Giacomo Gastoldi and his tune IN DIR IST FREUDE, to what Temperley calls the "smoothly Italianite" tunes of Jeremiah Clarke and William Croft,[39] and now to ITALIAN HYMN at Lock Hospital.

ITALIAN HYMN first appeared in Madan's 1769 *Collection of Psalm and Hymn Tunes Sung at the Chapel of the Lock Hospital*. It was written by Felice de Giardini (1716–1796) and is sometimes called MOSCOW because of the place where Giardini died, or TRINITY because of the text for which it was composed. Giardini was an Italian violinist who, as part of his extensive composing, worked with another composer on an oratorio for Lock Hospital. Giardini composed this tune for the text given here at the request of Selina Hastings, the Countess of Huntingdon (1707–1791). In Madan's *Collection*, this hymn was called "An Hymn to the Trinity." This tune has received wide circulation and is interesting because of its internal repetition at measures 9 through 12. Formally it is laid out *abcddef*.

The Countess of Huntingdon—who requested the tune—knew the Wesleys, protected Methodists in the Anglican Church, introduced the aristocracy to Methodism, supported a Calvinist (emphasis on election) version of Methodism, and in 1748 made the Calvinist Evangelical Revival preacher George Whitefield (1714–1770) one of her chaplains. She encouraged the writing of hymns and tunes and was instrumental in publishing numerous hymnals for her seminary called Trevecca House in South Wales and for her chapels, which she organized as the Countess of Huntingdon Connexion. Private proprietary chapels, loosely attached to the Established Anglican Church, were common in the late eighteenth century. Those of the Countess of Huntingdon were of this sort until they left the established church in 1782.[40]

ITALIAN HYMN
6 6 4 6 6 6 4

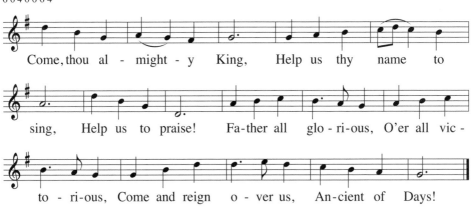

Text: Anonymous
Tune: Felice de Giardini, 1769

Meth #61

François Hippolite Barthélémon

Another violinist of this period brought a French and Irish influence. François Hippolite Barthélémon (1741–1808) was the son of a French father and an Irish mother. He gave up a career in the Irish brigade to become a violinist and conductor at Vauxhall Gardens in London. A man from Philadelphia named Jacob Duché (1737–1798) became chaplain at the Female Orphan Asylum in London. He requested MORNING HYMN from Barthélémon for Ken's "Awake, My Soul, and with the Sun," with which it is still associated. It first appeared in print in a Supplement to William Gawler's *Hymns and Psalms Used at the Asylum for*

Female Orphans (London, ca. 1785). Routley thought it was a children's tune.[41] Whether such distinctions can be made very successfully is a question, since children can sing fine hymn tunes as well as adults, and adults delight in singing what children also enjoy. It is developed out of its initial conjunct motive, which is soon turned upside down and then extended downward across a complete scale. The motive in its original form is then treated sequentially before it breaks into a triad on its way to the upside-down version and partial scale to the tonic.

MORNING HYMN
LM

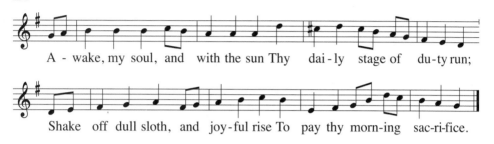

A - wake, my soul, and with the sun Thy dai-ly stage of du-ty run;

Shake off dull sloth, and joy-ful rise To pay thy morn-ing sac-ri-fice.

Text: Thomas Ken, 1637-1711, alt.   H82 #11
Tune: François Hippolyte Barthélémon, 1741-1808

Aaron Williams and John Darwall

ST. THOMAS (WILLIAMS) is a Short Meter tune to be distinguished from the one called ST. THOMAS (HOLYWOOD) with the meter 87.87.87 by John Francis Wade, which will come up momentarily. Like WAREHAM, ST. THOMAS (WILLIAMS) was written by the parish clerk, music teacher, and compiler of church music collections, Aaron Williams (1731–1776), who geared his music to "country choirs." ST. THOMAS (WILLIAMS) is even more common in our hymnals than WAREHAM, though Temperley is probably accurate when he calls it "undistinguished."[42] It is the second half of a longer tune, which first appeared in Williams' *The Universal Psalmist* (London, 1763).

ST. THOMAS (WILLIAMS)
6 6 8 6 (SM)

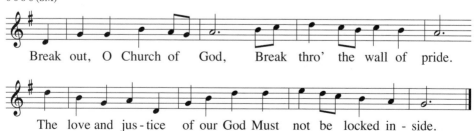

Break out, O Church of God, Break thro' the wall of pride.

The love and jus-tice of our God Must not be locked in - side.

Text: Wesley L. Forbis, 1930, © 1990, Broadman Press (SESAC). All rights reserved.   Text: Bap #401
Tune: Aaron Williams, 1731-1776   Tune: Bap #400

In his *Psalmody in Miniature, II* (London, 1769), and then again in his *A New Universal Psalmist* (London, 1770), Williams included a tune by John Darwall (1731–1789) that we call DARWALL'S 148TH or just DARWALL. Darwall (who championed faster hymn singing, as noted earlier) was an Anglican priest and musician. In addition to piano sonatas, he composed hymn tunes with bass, one for each of the 150 psalms in Tate and Brady's *New Version*. This widely used buoyant melody is the only one of Darwall's tunes that we remember. Originally for the praise of Psalm 148, "Ye boundless realms of joy," it begins with leaps that grow to an octave. The leaps are balanced by a downward stepwise walk across a seventh at the beginning, which turns into an upward one across a ninth at the end. (The midstream octave leap, nicely prepared here by the first phrase, had its precedent in Jeremiah Clarke's ST. MAGNUS.)[43]

DARWALL'S 148th
6 6 6 6 4 4 4 4

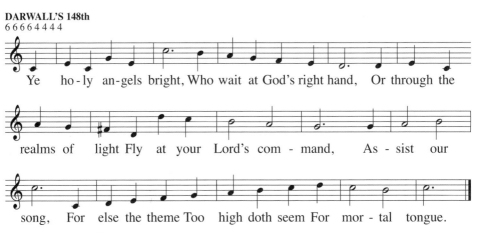

Ye ho - ly an-gels bright, Who wait at God's right hand, Or through the

realms of light Fly at your Lord's com - mand, As - sist our

song, For else the theme Too high doth seem For mor - tal tongue.

Text: Richard Baxter, 1615-1691; rev. John Hampden Gurney, 1802-1862   H82 #625
Tune: John Darwall, 1731-1789

John Francis Wade and Samuel Webbe

ST. THOMAS (HOLYWOOD) is used less than ST. THOMAS (WILLIAMS), but may well be a better tune if judged by its internal merits. It certainly evokes engaged congregational singing within the span of an octave. Sequence in the first two measures and gentle upward motion prepare for the high tonic in the fifth measure, and then gradual movement downward through a skillful repeat of the second through the fourth measures leads back to the low tonic at the end.

ST. THOMAS (HOLYWOOD)
8 7 8 7 8 7

Come a - dore this   won-drous pres - ence, Bow to Christ the source of grace.
Tan-tum er - go   Sa - cra-mén - tum   Ve - ne - ré - mur   cér - nu - i:

Here is kept the   an-cient prom-ise   Of God's earth-ly dwell-ing place.
Et an - tí - quum   do - cu - mén-tum   No - vo   ce - dat   rí - tu - i:

Sight is blind be - fore God's glo - ry, Faith a - lone may see his face.
Prae-stet fí - des   sup - ple - mén-tum   Sén - su - um   de - fé-ctu - i.

Text: Thomas Aquinas, 1227-1274; tr. James Quinn, SJ, b.1919, © 1969. Used by permission of Selah Publishing Co., Inc.   Wor3 #758
Tune: John F. Wade, 1711-1786

ST. THOMAS (HOLYWOOD) comes from the same source as the much more famous tune ADESTE FIDELES.

ADESTE FIDELES
Irregular

O   come,   all   ye   faith - ful,   joy-ful and tri - um - phant, O
A - des - te,   fi - de - les,   lae - ti   tri - um - phan - tes;   ve -

come   ye,   O   come   ye,   to   Beth   -   le - hem.
ni - te,   ve - ni - te   in   Beth   -   le - hem.

Come   and be - hold   him,   born the King of   an - gels;
Na - tum vi - de - te   Re - gem an - ge - lor - um.

Refrain
O   come, let   us   a - dore   him, O   come, let   us   a -
Ve - ni - te   a - do - re - mus, ve - ni - te   a - do -

dore   him, O   come, let   us   a - dore   him,   Christ   the Lord.
re - mus, ve - ni - te   a - do - re - mus,   Do - mi - num.

Text: John F. Wade, ca.1743; tr. Frederick Oakeley, 1841, and others   Meth #234
Tune: John F. Wade, ca.1743

These two tunes appeared in print in 1782 in *An Essay on the Church Plain Chant* (London), a collection "almost certainly"[44] made by Samuel Webbe, Sr. (1740–1816). Webbe, to whom we will return in more detail shortly, was a Roman Catholic organist who served both the Portuguese and Sardinian embassy chapels in London, where Roman Catholic worship was legal. He encountered these tunes at the Portuguese Embassy in a manuscript of John Francis Wade (ca.1710–1786), which Wade "may have begun between 1735 and 1740."[45] In this manuscript ST. THOMAS (HOLYWOOD) went with "Tantum ergo sacramentum," the fifth stanza of Thomas Aquinas' hymn, "Pange lingua gloriosi," which—with the doxology in the next stanza—has been peeled off as a separate hymn.[46] "Adeste fideles" went with the tune that now names it (formerly known as PORTUGUESE HYMN), though numerous other texts and translations were tried before it became so inseparably linked with the translation by Frederick Oakeley (1802–1860), "O Come, All Ye Faithful."[47]

Wade was an English Roman Catholic who lived most of his life in France at the monastery at Douay where exiles were welcomed. He taught Latin and church music there and made music manuscripts for use at worship. In the absence of other evidence, it is assumed that he wrote the tune ST. THOMAS (HOLYWOOD) for "Tantum ergo" and both the text and tune of "Adeste fidelis."[48] Again, as in so many tunes we have seen, ST. THOMAS (HOLYWOOD) may "be a reworking of earlier material; for example, the first line is almost identical with Heinrich Schütz's setting of Ps. 131 in his Becker Psalter of 1628."[49] The plainsong melody TANTUM ERGO SACRAMENTUM also bears resemblances.[50]

Routley thought the tune ADESTE FIDELES, with its repetition of "O come, let us adore him," was "quite remarkable as early as 1744,"[51] or earlier, whatever the date of the manuscript. It suggested to him "the style of the evangelical hymns, so often written in the metre 87 87 47 which was coined for this very purpose, to provide a repeatable short line near the stanza's end."[52] He opined that Wade did not know hymn tunes like this in the 1740s, but that "he knew the music of the light operas that became fashionable in the years around 1730." Routley suggested that the folk opera "textual expansion at the end of a 'number'" was the "common source for this gesture in Wade's tunes and for the cliché of repetition in evangelical hymns, especially in Wales."[53]

We come back now to Samuel Webbe. He was a writer of masses, motets, and glees—one of the best composers of glees (entertaining, homophonic pieces for three or more male voices, for which "glee clubs" are named)—and also wrote hymn tunes. His VENI SANCTE SPIRITUS[54] was written for the medieval sequence of that name and his TANTUM ERGO for the same text Wade used with ST. THOMAS. TANTUM ERGO has been known by a variety of other names. We know it as DULCE CARMEN. It is structured in three four-bar sets, each one consisting of a two-bar statement and a two-bar response.

DULCE CARMEN
878787

Text: *Alleluia, dulce carmen;* Latin, 11th C.; John M. Neale, 1818-1866
Tune: *Essay on the Church Plain Chant,* 1782

Wor3 #413

We do not use "Wade's" BENEVENTO. Routley said it was a "lunatic tune" with which Webbe "should not be libelled."[55] He referred to it as a "patchwork of phrases" from one of Webbe's motets and its presence in the *English Hymnal* (1906) "a mystery."[56] This sequence of pitches is indeed little more than a meaningless series of repetitions with clichés for cadences. Its harmonization with different positions of the same chord does not help. It points to harmony called in to rescue what cannot be rescued. Here is what a "lunatic tune" might look like.

BENEVENTO
7777D

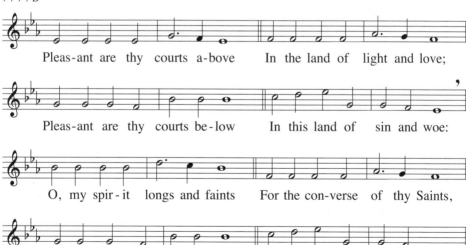

Text: H. F. Lyte, 1793-1847
Tune: Adapted from S. Webbe's *Motetts or Antiphons,* 1792

EH #469

Webbe's best-known hymn tune is MELCOMBE, often in English usage joined to John Keble's text given here.

MELCOMBE
8 8 8 8

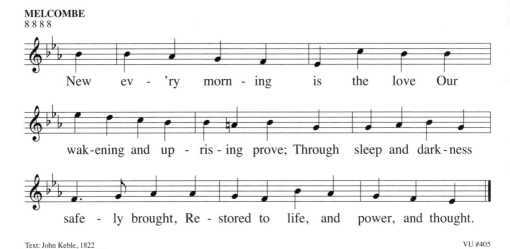

Text: John Keble, 1822   VU #405
Tune: Samuel Webbe, 1782

MELCOMBE was intended for "O salutaris hostia."[57] Because of its "persistent downward movement," Routley did not think the melody suggested morning and was not pleased, therefore, with the subsequent marriage to Keble's text that *Hymns Ancient and Modern* made in the nineteenth century.[58] However, the tune does not only move downward (there are significant upward reaches), that does not make much difference anyway, and many worshipers for the last century and more have found the marriage felicitous. Like DULCE CARMEN it is made up of statements and responses, in this case two of them with pickups, so that its measures could be diagramed (2 + 2) + (2 + 2).

Edward Miller's Psalms of David (1790)

ROCKINGHAM (or ROCKINGHAM OLD or CATON or COMMUNION) first appeared in *Psalms of David for the Use of Parish Churches* (London, 1790), a collection prepared by Edward Miller (1731–1807), where he paired it with five metrical psalms. The link with Watts' "When I Survey the Wondrous Cross" was made by *Hymns Ancient and Modern* in 1861. Miller apparently adapted it from a tune called TUNBRIDGE that first appeared in *Music Sacra* (Bath, ca. 1778) and then in Aaron Williams' *Psalmody in Miniature* (London, 1780).[59] For forty-one years Miller was the organist at an Anglican parish, Doncaster in South Yorkshire, northern England. Also a flutist, he studied with the music historian Charles Burney, published a number of books, composed music, and received a doctorate in music from Cambridge.

Temperley calls Miller's book "a landmark" of the "new ideal" bishops and clergy supported on behalf of the congregation's singing, in opposition to professionalizing it. The ideal "was for simple but musically literate and well-harmonized tunes, sung by the congregation, led by an organ and choir of children."[60] Here is an instance of common support for the congregation's singing—bishops, clergy, organ, organist, composer, and children together on behalf of the people and their song.

Robert Bridges thought the "grandeur" of Watts' text was "obscured" by this melody.[61] That it is nevertheless often appreciated by congregations suggests that, whatever its demerits, the congregational concern it represents was not entirely misplaced. Both Temperley and Routley give it high praise. Temperley calls it a "fine warm tune,"[62] and Routley refers to it as "the excellent and almost Mozartian LM."[63] Again with a balanced eighteenth-century symmetry, its measures could be diagramed (4 + 4) + (4 + 4). The second 4 of the first set carries the melody to the high tonic, and the first 4 of the second set returns there before moving to the dominant and to an ornamented modification of the opening motive at the end.

ROCKINGHAM
LM

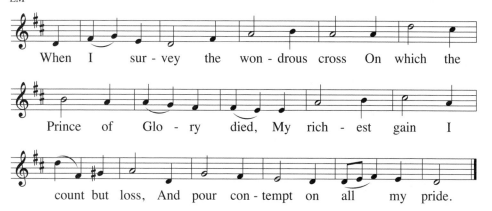

Text: Isaac Watts, 1707
Tune: Anonymous

Meth #299

The Evangelical Trajectory

The evangelical trajectory headed at the end of the eighteenth century to MILES LANE and then in the nineteenth century to SAGINA.[64] MILES LANE is one of the tunes associated with "All Hail the Power of Jesus' Name," better known in England than in the United States. William Shrubsole (1760–1806) wrote it when he was nineteen. It is the only music we have from him. The son of a blacksmith and a chorister at Canterbury Cathedral, in 1782 he was named organist at Bangor Cathedral. His tenure there was short lived. He was released in December 1793 because he associated with Methodists and Dissenters. From 1784 until his death, he was organist in London at Spafields Chapel, Clerkenwell, one of the chapels of Lady Countess of Huntingdon's Connexion.

He was a very good friend of Edward Perronet, who wrote the text with which this tune has been tied from its first publication in *The Gospel Magazine* (1779).

This tune represents, as Routley says, a "choral-congregational style," which is what "the Charity foundations [like Lock Hospital] encouraged."[65] Its repetitions of "Crown him" in the Refrain, which drive the melodic range to an octave and a fifth, were originally set up in the key of C as a pyramid for three different voices parts, the first on C' by the basses, the second on E' by the tenors, and the third on G' by the altos (or some mix of that sort). This was followed by a four-part texture in which both tenors (with the tune) and sopranos (with a descant) ended on the high tonic.[66] When everybody sings the melody, the tune has been lowered to B-flat, A, A-flat, or even G, which drives the low tonic at the fourth measure quite low so that it is sometimes altered to the third. Here it is with the low tonic and the octave and a fifth laid out for everybody.

MILES LANE
8 6 8 6

All hail the pow'r of Je - sus' name! Let an - gels pros-trate fall; Bring forth the roy - al di - a - dem, And crown Him, crown Him, crown Him, crown Him Lord of all.

Text: Edward Perronet, 1726-1792   Bap #201
Tune: William Schrubsole, 1760-1806

MILES LANE is structurally tight. Whether it can be called congregational for normal congregations who are not quasi-choral, like a charity foundation, is a legitimate question, but it is tight. SAGINA is another matter. Carlton Young says the evangelical style that began with EASTER HYMN "culminates in Thomas Campbell's SAGINA."[67] This culmination pushes toward the anti-congregational, in-group dangers of this style. Leaps are wide and untamed, and repetitions get out of control. Routley calls the tune "calamitous"[68] and "near profanity."[69] Marilyn Stulken sees it "as one of the 'growing pains' of a church that [was] finding its way out of some . . . anti-congregational . . . psalm-singing that had been dead for years."[70] It appeared in a collection Campbell published in 1825 called *Bouquet*, where twenty-three tunes were given the names of plants. ("Sagina" means "nourishment" and refers to a plant that "grew in the Roman Campagna and provided spring fodder for flocks of sheep."[71])

There are groups of believers who know SAGINA and sing it with vigor. As Paul Richardson says, they "are fluent in this idiom and find [it] easier than some [tunes] that are better constructed from a logical standpoint."[72] Or, as David Music says, there are "congregations that sing it with gusto. Surely that counts for something."[73] I do not mean to disparage them or their piety. I do mean to say that a syntax such as this cannot be a norm for the catholic whole.

SAGINA
8 8 8 8 8 8 with repeat

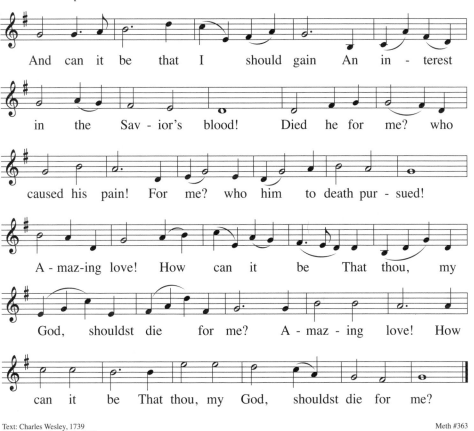

Text: Charles Wesley, 1739
Tune: Thomas Campbell, 1835

Meth #363

Three Well-known Tunes by Little-known Composers

TRURO was printed anonymously in Thomas Williams' *Psalmodia Evangelica* (London, 1789) with Isaac Watts' "Now to the Lord a Noble Song." The tune may be by Williams, a Congregational printer and musician possibly related to Aaron Williams, but his dates are not known. In any event, this melody takes just over an octave to proceed in two stately waves that congregations love to sing.

TRURO
8 8 8 8

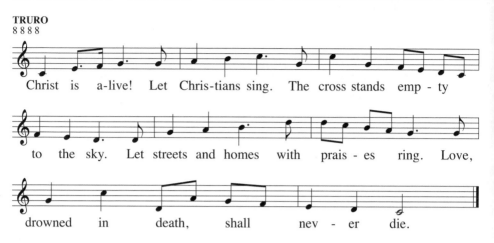

Christ is a-live! Let Chris-tians sing. The cross stands emp - ty to the sky. Let streets and homes with prais - es ring. Love, drowned in death, shall nev - er die.

Text: Brian Wren, 1968, alt.; © 1975, Hope Publishing Co.
Tune: Thomas Williams, 1789

VU #158

Opening with the same four pitches and rising to the top octave, DUKE STREET is cut from the same musical cloth as TRURO and, similarly, is as well-known as the composer to whom it is attributed is obscure.[74] John Hatton (d. 1793) lived on Duke Street in Lancaster (or Lancashire), England, and may have died in a stagecoach crash. The tune first appeared in Henry Boyd's *A Select Collection of Psalm and Hymn Tunes* (Glasgow, 1793) for Joseph Addison's version of Psalm 19, "The Spacious Firmament on High."[75] Like TRURO, this is a relatively short Long Meter tune that manages to be spacious within, rather than just over, an octave.

DUKE STREET
LM

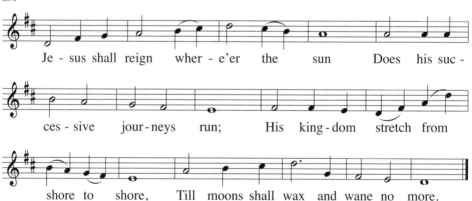

Je - sus shall reign wher - e'er the sun Does his suc - ces - sive jour-neys run; His king-dom stretch from shore to shore, Till moons shall wax and wane no more.

Text: Isaac Watts, 1674-1748, alt.
Tune: John Hatton, c. 1710-1793

Wor3 #492

MARTYRDOM (or AVON) was probably originally an eighteenth-century folk song. Hugh Wilson (1764-1824), a shoemaker and precentor in the Secession Church that broke from the Church of Scotland, made a duple version of it some time before the end of the eighteenth century. Robert A. Smith (1780–1829), precentor at St. George's Church in Edinburgh, published the three-to-a-bar version we use in his *Sacred Music Sung at St. George's* (Edinburgh, 1825). With the exception of the third note from the end of the third phrase (C-natural in the key given here), it is pentatonic. It has a curious mix about it: somewhat like earlier Common Meter "Common" tunes, somewhat like the white spirituals that are coming in Chapter XI (the pentatonic tune AMAZING GRACE, for example), and somewhat more Romantic than either of those with its slow lilt that cannot quite restrain itself to stay in a pentatonic discipline.

MARTYRDOM (AVON)
CM

Text: *A New Version of the Psalms of David*, ed. Nahum Tate and Nicholas Brady, 1696, alt.   NC #481
Tune: Hugh Wilson, 1825

Viennese Influences

Ludwig van Beethoven (1770–1827), though not intentionally, is one of the few famous composers who wrote a hymn tune. The melody we call HYMN TO JOY was composed by him for Schiller's "Ode to Joy," which he set for a chorus in the fourth movement of his Ninth Symphony (first performed in 1824) and can be found in his sketches as far back as 1797. In spite of its potential identification with the martial spirit of the French Revolution, it was adapted as a hymn tune by Elam Ives (1802–1862) in his *Mozart Collection* (New York, 1846) and by Edward Hodges (1796–1867) in his *The Trinity Collection of Church Music* (New York, 1864). Ives was a music teacher and church musician in Connecticut who also worked at the Philadelphia Music Seminary and started a music school in New York. He was influenced by Johann H. Pestalozzi (1746–1827) and influenced Thomas Hastings and Lowell Mason to whom we will come in Chapter XII. Hodges was an English organist who served Trinity

Church in New York from 1839 to 1859 before he returned to England. The tune was paired with "Joyful, Joyful We Adore Thee" in the early twentieth century, when Henry van Dyke chose HYMN TO JOY to go with his text.

This AA'BA' melody is built on the first five degrees of a major scale, with but one exception, the last note of the third line. There the melody descends momentarily to the lower dominant (D). It is followed immediately by a syncopated beginning of the last line, the second statement of A'. We have usually received this tune in hymnals with the last line squared up on the beat and the syncopation removed. This modification drains the tune of its life and destroys it. Congregations not only can handle rhythms like this, but delight in them. Squaring up the tune treats congregations badly and assumes there is an arbitrary, non-musical congregational template, rather than music that sings in its integrity. Fortunately, recent hymnals have restored Beethoven's rhythm, as in the example below. (Once the altered version is in a congregation's memory bank, to change it or not is a difficult pastoral issue—not unlike retrieving the verve of rhythmic chorales after congregations have learned isometric ones.)

There are those who "object strenuously" to my point of view here, among them no less an expert than Austin Lovelace, who thinks the "syncopation is a stumbling block to congregational singing and does nothing to make the hymn easier to sing or understand."[76] Such disagreement is the delight of the study of hymn tunes and their use (and the wondrous puzzle for editors and editorial committees).

HYMN TO JOY
8 7 8 7 D

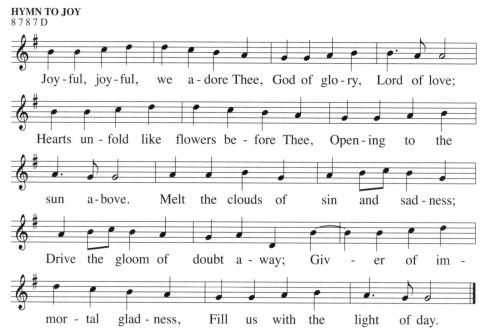

Joy-ful, joy-ful, we a-dore Thee, God of glo-ry, Lord of love;
Hearts un-fold like flowers be-fore Thee, Open-ing to the
sun a-bove. Melt the clouds of sin and sad-ness;
Drive the gloom of doubt a-way; Giv-er of im-
mor-tal glad-ness, Fill us with the light of day.

Text: Henry van Dyke, 1907; alt.
Tune: Ludwig van Beethoven, 1824

Pres #464

William Gardiner (1770–1853) began adapting Beethoven's music for hymn tunes earlier in the nineteenth century than Elam Ives or Edward Hodges. He was a manufacturer of stockings who played the viola, wrote about music, composed, edited, and loved Haydn, Mozart, and Beethoven. His *Sacred Melodies* (London, 1815) was the second volume of six published between 1812 and 1838 in which he popularly, but without clarity of sources, adapted the instrumental music of the Viennese composers and others to hymn tunes. One of these was GERMANY, which Gardiner attributed to Beethoven.

GERMANY
LM

Where cross the crowd - ed ways of life, Where sound the cries of race and clan, A - bove the noise of self - ish strife We hear your voice, O Son of Man.

Text: Frank Mason North, 1905, alt.
Tune: attr. to Ludwig van Beethoven in William Gardiner's *Sacred Melodies*, 1815

Mor #581

Another of Gardiner's contributions in *Sacred Melody* was LYONS, which is a fitting conclusion to this chapter. With HANOVER it brackets the period we're considering. It has the same opening line and meter as HANOVER and is used almost as much and with the same texts,[77] but it comes from a century later. Gardiner gave it the notation, "Subject Haydn." It has been attributed to Johann Michael Haydn (1737–1806), the composer and younger brother of Franz Joseph Haydn, though it was probably taken from a work composed in 1785 by Joseph Martin Kraus (1756–1792),[78] a German composer who worked in Sweden.

LYONS
10 10 11 11

O wor-ship the King,   all   glo-rious a - bove!   O   grate-ful - ly

sing God's   power and God's love;   Our shield and de - fend-er, the

An-cient of Days, Pa - vil-ioned in splen-dor and   gird-ed with praise.

Text: Robert Grant, 1833; alt.
Tune: Johann Michael Haydn, 1737-1806, alt.

Pres #476

These tunes work. GERMANY's first phrase going up is answered by its second phrase going down. Then a modified sequential line leaps gradually by a fourth, sixth, and fifth to climax on a high E-flat, after which the conjunct downward motion of the sequential figure leads home. The fifth to the high E-flat is diminished, not usually an easy congregational interval, but here the gradual movement upward to just a half step above the D is a simple matter, especially when supported by the harmony and its chromatic bass line.

LYONS is set up in two statements and responses, the second response an answer to the first. Then a repeated figure is extended to a four-bar phrase whose scale outlines a dominant seventh chord over the repeated root of the dominant in the bass, which propels the tune homeward to the tonic by means of a repeat of the second statement and answer. Again, in eighteenth-century symmetry, the tune can be easily diagrammed: (2 + 2) + (2 + 2) + 4 (which could be seen as a linked 2 + 2 on an extended dominant) + (2 + 2). Popular instrumental melodies, unless broken to a congregational idiom like these, are not necessarily congregational.[79]

1   Nicholas Temperley, "Lo! He Comes, with Clouds Descending," Glover H82C, 3A , 110.
2   Nicholas Temperley, *The Music of the English Parish Church, Volume 1* (Cambridge: Cambridge University Press, 1979), 212.
3   Erik Routley, *The Church and Music: An Enquiry into the History, the Nature, and the Scope of Christian Judgment on Music* (London: Gerald Duckworth & Co. Ltd., 1950), 160.
4   Erik Routley, *English Hymns and Their Tunes*, 8.
5   Young, CUMH, 468.
6   This was the second edition, the first published in 1761 with a separate title page in *Select Hymns*. See Oliver A. Beckerlegge, "The Development of the Collection, *"The Works of John Wesley, Volume 7, A Collection of Hymns for the use of the People called Methodists*, ed. Franz Hildebrandt, Oliver A. Beckerlegge, and James Dale (Oxford: Clarendon Press, 1983), 25.
7   Stulken, HCLBW, 126. *Select Hymns* of 1761 is where John Wesley gave his "Directions for Singing" which can be found in Meth, vii.
8   Nicholas Temperley, "Lo! He Comes, with Clouds Descending," Glover H82C, 3A , 109.
9   Temperley, HTI, I, 23. See also Nicholas Temperley, "The Lock Hospital Chapel and Its Music," *Journal of the Royal Musical Association* 118 (1993): 47.
10 In 1780, in a book called *Thelyphthora* (from the Greek for "female" and "destruction," probably meaning "the destruction of women"), Madan suggested that polygamy would solve the problems Lock Hospital represented. Though he was a popular preacher and composer, in Routley's words, "This abruptly ended his ministry at the 'Lock,' and he took no other. He died in 1790 in obscurity" (Routley, *The Musical Wesleys* (New York: Oxford University Press, 1968], 73). Nicholas Temperley, "Madan, Martin," NGDMM, 11, 453, suggests that Madan and his book influenced Samuel Wesley and may "have had some indirect responsibility for the birth of Samuel Sebastian Wesley," who was born out of wedlock.
11 See Temperley, "The Lock Hospital Chapel and Its Music," *Journal of the Royal Musical Association* 118 (1993): 50–51.
12 Temperley, "Lo, He Comes," 109.
13 Ibid.
14 EH (1906), #7.
15 See John Wesley's "Thoughts on the Power of Music," given in Carlton R. Young, *Music of the Heart: John & Charles Wesley on Music and Musicians* (Carol Stream: Hope Publishing Company, 1995), 84–88, followed by Young's "Commentary," 88–93.
16 Roger Fiske, "Lampe, John Frederick," NGDMM, 10, 421.
17 John F. Lampe, *Hymns on the Great Festivals* (London, 1746). (Carlton Young notes that the tunes appear with figured bass, and that one of the 24 texts in this volume is not by Charles, but by his oldest brother, Samuel Wesley, Jr. [Correspondence, May 31, 2002.])
18 Westermeyer, *Te Deum*, 233.
19 Temperley, HTI, I, 23.
20 Ibid.
21 The *Lock Hospital Collection* was reprinted more than any other book in the period, and its tunes "were especially popular among Methodists and dissenters" in England and in the United States (Temperley, HTI, I, 34).
22 Though one could draw some parallels between Lock Hospital and a parish church, as Temperley does (Temperley, "The Lock Hospital Chapel and Its Music," *Journal of the Royal Musical Association* 118 [1993]: 48), the two are fundamentally different—as Temperley's article makes abundantly clear (54–55, for example).
23 Temperley, "The Lock Hospital Chapel and its Music," *Journal of the Royal Musical*

Association 118 (1993): 63.

24   *A Collection Tunes, Set to MUSIC, As they are commonly SUNG at the FOUNDERY* (London: A. Pearson, 1742, reprinted by Bryan F Spinney, 1981).

25   Ibid., 2.

26   Young, CUMH, 50.

27   Ibid., 557.

28   See Nicholas Temperley, "John Wesley," NGDMM, 20, 357.

29   James F. White, ed., *John Wesley's Sunday Service of the Methodists in North America* (Bristol, 1784, reprinted by The United Methodist Publishing House, 1984), A1.

30   See Nicholas Temperley, "John Wesley," NGDMM, 20, 357, and Temperley, HTI, I, 18.

31   See Westermeyer, *The Church Musician*, 131–135 and Young, *Music of the Heart*, 104.

32   Temperley, HTI, I, 36.

33   Ibid.

34   As indicated in Chapter III. (See Rebecca Wagner Oettinger, *Music as Propaganda in the German Reformation*, 2.

35   Leaver, *Ghoostly Psalmes and Spirituall Songs*, 93.

36   Ibid.

37   Ibid.

38   Ibid. Temperley (36–37; 37, FN1) notes a close connection of early Methodism to high-church religious societies, and points out that the Methodists were "anticipated, strangely enough," by Arthur Bedford (1668–1745). He was a clergyman who attacked the London theatres and appended easy grave tunes to his *The Excellency of Divine Musick* (1733). In his *Divine Recreations*, "probably intended" for the high-church societies, he gave a "sacred parody" that became "the basis of a hymn tune."

39   Temperley, HTI, I, 8.

40   Ibid., 12. (See also page 19.)

41   Routley, MCH, 77B.

42   Nicholas Temperley, "Williams, Aaron," NGDMM, 20, 432.

43   For more about John Darwall, see John Wilson, "John Darwall and the 148th Metre," *The Hymn Society of Great Britain & Ireland Occasional Paper* Second Series No. 5 (April 2002).

44   Routley, MCH, 81A.

45   John Stephan, *The "Adeste Fideles": A Study of Its Origin and Development* (South Devon: "PUBLICATIONS," Buckfast Abbey, 1946), 17.

46   As H82 #330 and Wor3 #758. The full text of "Pange lingua" with its chant tune of the same name is given at Wors3 #813.

47   For more detail see Nicholas Temperley, "O Come, All Ye Faithful," Glover, H82C, 3A, 160–162.

48   For more detail see Robin Leaver, "Lo! He Comes, with Clouds Descending," Glover, H82C, 3A, 111; Nicholas Temperley, "O Come, All Ye Faithful," Glover, H82C, 3A, 161–162; Nicholas Temperley, "Wade, John Francis," Glover, H82C, 2, 647–648; and John Stephan, *The "Adeste Fideles,"* where much of the spade work was done.

49   Leaver, "Lo! He Comes. . .," 111. Leaver gives the reference in Zahn, MDEK, #4601.

50   It can be found at H82 #330 and in the *Liber Usualis*, 1852.

51   Routley, MCH, 81B.

52   Ibid.

53   Ibid.

54   EH, #155.

55   Routley, MCH, 81A.

56   Ibid.

57   This text and its translation can be found at Wor3 #757.

58   Routley, MCH, 81A.

59 Nicholas Temperley has chased down the sources. See his "When I Survey the Wondrous Cross," Glover, H82C, 3B, 892.

60 Temperley, HTI, I, 13.

61 See Young, CUMH, 692–693.

62 Temperley, "When I Survey," 892.

63 Routley, MCH, 72A.

64 For nineteenth-century tunes used by Methodists in the United States in the nineteenth century, see Fred Kimball Graham, *With One Heart and One Voice": A Core Repertory of Hymn Tunes Published for Use in the Methodist Episcopal Church in the United States, 1808–1878* (Lanham: the Scarecrow Press, 2004).

65 Routley, MCH, 75B.

66 See Nicholas Temperley, "All Hail the Power of Jesus' Name!," Glover H82 C, 3B, 855.

67 Young, CUMH, 281.

68 Routley, MCH, 156A.

69 Ibid., 84A.

70 Marilyn Stulken, correspondence, June 17, 2004.

71 Young, CUMH, 213, quoting Wesley Milgate.

72 Correspondence with Paul Richardson, June 2, 2004.

73 Correspondence with David Music, June 8, 2004.

74 Paul Richardson points out (correspondence, June 2, 2004) that ANTIOCH (see Chapter X) "opens with a complete descending octave, the complement to TRURO and DUKE STREET."

75 This text can be found at H82 #409.

76 Correspondence, August 28, 2004.

77 Pres #s 476 and 477 print them back to back, which is one way to avoid the potential for confusion.

78 Brink/Polman, PsHH, 588.

79 A good illustration is FINLANDIA (Meth #534, NC #607), which comes from Jean Sibelius' tone poem of the same name. An attractive orchestral melody, its long notes at cadences are not especially congregational.

VIII. Welsh Tunes and French Diocesan Tunes

1. Welsh

Characteristics

The Welsh have provided the church some strong and durable tunes. With earlier roots, these tunes essentially come from the second half of the eighteenth century and beyond.[1] Alan Luff described them as having these characteristics:

- an eighteenth-century style,
- nothing archaic about them,
- written in meters that owe more to hymns of the Evangelical Revival in England than to Welsh models,
- with Welsh influences present nonetheless,
- in major and sometimes minor keys—but not modal,
- built by careful juxtaposition of leaps and stepwise motion,
- much indebted to the ballad tradition of earlier English tunes, and
- often in a common AABA pattern.[2]

Luff says that "especially in the later years of the nineteenth century and the early years of the twentieth century" there is "nothing distinctively Welsh about them." He regards them as "essentially folksong" fashioned for worship,[3] which is why they have proven to be so exportable. Though Routley is surely right that Welsh tunes go "closely with the Welsh language and the Welsh vocal style with its abundance of rich tenor sound, and many of the finest Welsh tunes lose a good deal as soon as they are exported,"[4] they nonetheless function very well in their exported state. Because of translation problems, the world beyond Wales knows basically only one Welsh hymn, William Williams' "Guide Me, O Thou Great Jehovah," which will be given with the tune that concludes this Welsh survey, but it knows many Welsh tunes used with a variety of non-Welsh texts.

Edmwnd Prys

We encountered the Welsh archdeacon and poet Edmwnd Prys (1544–1623) in connection with his collection, *Llyfr y Psalmau* (London, 1621) where SONG 67 appeared and may be by him. (See Chapter IV.) It is one of the common tunes, which found its way to George Wither's *Hymnes and Songs of the Church* (London, 1623), for which Orlando Gibbons provided the bass line.

Prys was the first to publish tunes with Welsh words. The tunes he used were the well-known English and Scottish ones, like WINDSOR, DUNDEE, and OLD HUNDRETH.[5] Though the Welsh were "always natural folk singers,"[6] in Prys' times they had not yet harnessed their musical idiom for the church's congregational song. That came with the evangelical revival in Wales that began in the mid-1730s with Howel Harris and Daniel Rowland, just before the beginnings made in England by George Whitefield and the Wesleys.[7]

Eighteenth Century

William Williams, Pantycelyn[8] (1717–1791), is for Welsh hymnody what Paul Gerhardt is for German and Isaac Watts for English. A "Calvinistic Methodist" inspired by the preaching of Howel Harris, he wrote about eight hundred Welsh hymns (plus some English ones). The English-speaking world knows him for "Guide Me, O Thou Great Jehovah." He did not write hymn tunes, but is important to our story because of the tunes that were used with his hymns. Prys' metrical Psalter was one source for the tunes. The others were harp melodies of Welsh folk music, which could yield a meter like 87 87 87 for a tune like RHUDDLAN (developed from 87 87 47 with the 4 repeated, as mentioned in connection with ADESTE FIDELES). This bar form tune may be an old Welsh harp melody that Williams used to create a text with its meter. The words of Williams' first hymn in this meter begin with "Come to the Battle." They are "the first words of the Welsh War Song that Edward Jones (Bardd y Brenin—that is, "The King's Bard") published in the second edition (1794) of *Musical and Poetical Relicks of the Welsh Bards*."[9] RHUDDLAN "dropped out of use in Wales" and was rediscovered after it was included in the *English Hymnal* of 1906.[10] Its A section is in two-bar phrases where the second two answer the first with the same dotted beginning. Then, sequence is used to spell first a tonic triad and then a dominant seventh, which propels the tune back to the dotted figure from the beginning, now fitted out with the complete tonic triad.

RHUDDLAN
8 7 8 7 8 7

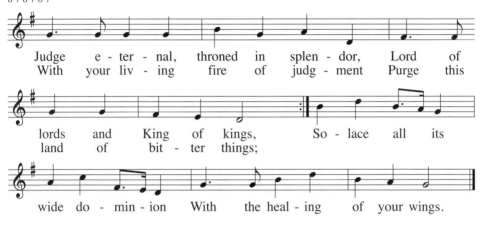

Judge e - ter - nal, throned in splen - dor, Lord of
With your liv - ing fire of judg - ment Purge this

lords and King of kings, So - lace all its
land of bit - ter things;

wide do - min - ion With the heal - ing of your wings.

Text: Henry S. Holland, 1847-1918   LBW #418
Tune: Welsh, 18th c.

AR HYD Y NOS appeared in the first edition of Edward Jones' *Musical and Poetical Relicks of the Welsh Bards* (1784) with harp variations, which give us an insight into the harp tunes[11] that were popularized outside Wales in the seventeenth, eighteenth, and nineteenth centuries.[12] The harp is the national instrument of Wales, associated with poetry and bards. The "triple harp" with three rows of strings was used by Welsh harpists before the pedal harp.[13] On it, chords could be played to support the melody as well as passage work above the chords.

In Jones' version of AR HYD Y NOS, half note chords of tonic, subdominant, secondary dominant, and dominant accompany the melody until the cadence when quarter note chords begin. In the B section of this AABA tune, a dominant pedal point supports the melody that sits on top of parallel thirds and sixths. The B section is set a fourth above the A section and runs essentially by step for four measures to a longing dominant on the doorstep of the final repeat of A. The melody is utmost simplicity, but imparts meditative import to worthy texts. Fred Pratt Green's "For the Fruit of All Creation" is one of the texts often used with this tune. The text given here is by Reginald Heber and may have been stimulated when Heber heard a Welsh harper playing the tune. Heber's text concludes with the line of a secular text by which the tune is also known.

AR HYD Y NOS
8 4 8 4 8 8 8 4

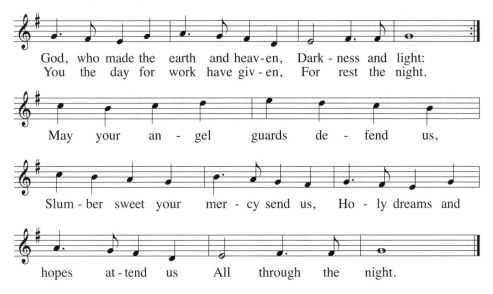

God, who made the earth and heav-en, Dark-ness and light:
You the day for work have giv-en, For rest the night.

May your an - gel guards de - fend us,

Slum - ber sweet your mer - cy send us, Ho - ly dreams and

hopes at - tend us All through the night.

Text: Reginald Heber, 1783-1826
Tune: Welsh

LBW #281

ASH GROVE (or THE ASH GROVE) is another early Welsh harp melody, though the printed source comes from the late nineteenth century.[14] Tonic, dominant, and subdominant chords support the melodic structure. The harmonic simplicity, rhythmic regularity, and AABA pattern of ASH GROVE, where each section is eight bars long, may be expected to yield boredom, but congregations repeat this hardy tune with delight.

ASH GROVE
6 6 11 6 6 11 D

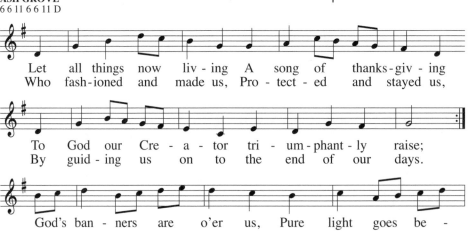

Let all things now liv-ing A song of thanks-giv-ing
Who fash-ioned and made us, Pro - tect - ed and stayed us,

To God our Cre - a - tor tri - um - phant - ly raise;
By guid-ing us on to the end of our days.

God's ban - ners are o'er us, Pure light goes be -

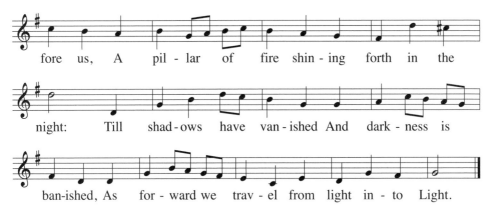

fore us, A pil - lar of fire shin - ing forth in the

night: Till shad - ows have van - ished And dark - ness is

ban-ished, As for - ward we trav - el from light in - to Light.

Text: Katherine K. Davis, 1892-1980, © 1939, E.C. Schirmer Music Co.   Wor3 #559
Tune: Welsh

Alan Luff classes ST. DENIO as of probable eighteenth-century origin.[15] The version we use has the same regular three to a bar rhythm as ASH GROVE, though in its first printed use as a hymn tune (John Roberts' *Caniadau y Cyssegr*—"Songs of the Sanctuary" [Denbigh, 1839]) it was less regular. Here the 6s of ASH GROVE's meter are not present, only four lines of 11 in the characteristic AABA pattern. Harmonically this tune is something of a curiosity, because its first three notes spell not the tonic but the subdominant triad. That may be expected to snare a congregation, but by leading so naturally to the dominant and then to the tonic the result is rather to increase the interest and engender a happy surprise.

ST. DENIO
11 11 11 11

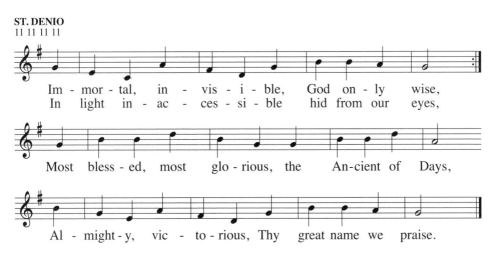

Im - mor - tal, in - vis - i - ble, God on - ly wise,
In light in - ac - ces - si - ble hid from our eyes,

Most bless - ed, most glo - rious, the An-cient of Days,

Al - might - y, vic - to - rious, Thy great name we praise.

Text: Walter Chalmers Smith, 1867; alt. 1987   Pres #263
Tune: Welsh folk melody; adapt. in *Caniadau y Cyssegr*, 1839

All the tunes we have cited so far are major, the Welsh norm, popular impressions notwithstanding.[16] LLANGLOFFAN is in one of the less normal though powerful minor tunes, which, in an ambiguously ambidextrous fashion the Welsh seem to favor, also can be found in a major key as LLANFYLLIN (where the sheen of LLANGLOFFAN's dark luster turns to a smooth white).[17] LLANGLOFFAN is anonymous. Its first appearance in print so far as anybody has yet discovered is *Llwbrau Moliant*—"The Paths of Praise" (Wrexham, 1872). Luff thinks it is of probable eighteenth-century origin.[18] Its form is not quite as predictable as the other tunes we have seen, though similar: ABCB with B an outgrowth of A. It has the power to handle prophetic texts like the one by G. K. Chesterton given here.

LLANGLOFFAN

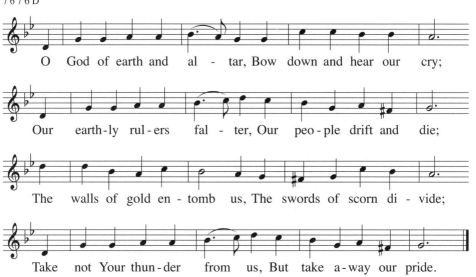

Text: Gilbert Keith Chesterton, 1906   Pres #291
Tune: Welsh folk melody; Evans' *Hymnau a Thonau*, 1865, as in *English Hymnal*, 1906

Nineteenth and Twentieth Centuries

LLANFAIR takes us back to a major key. It comes from the early nineteenth century. We think we know its composer. All the composers of the more recent tunes we now have to consider are even more certain than this one. LLANFAIR was probably written by a blind basket maker named Robert Williams (ca. 1781–1821). It first appeared with the name BETHEL in John Parry's *Peroriaeth Hyfryd*—"Sweet Music" (Chester, 1837) and may be traceable to a manuscript of Robert Williams from 1817.[19] In characteristic AABA form, B begins with the motive from A, now a third higher, where it can easily move to the dominant. The tune happily assumes the "Alleluias," which all have the same rhythm.

LLANFAIR
7 7 7 7 with alleluias

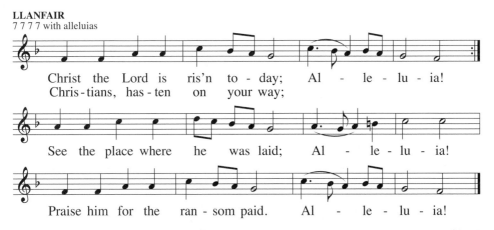

Christ the Lord is ris'n to - day; Al - le - lu - ia!
Chris - tians, has - ten on your way;

See the place where he was laid; Al - le - lu - ia!

Praise him for the ran - som paid. Al - le - lu - ia!

Text: Latin sequence, 11th c., abr.; tr. Jane E. Leeson, 1807-1872, alt.
Tune: Robert Williams, c. 1781-1821

CW #150

HYFRYDOL, another tune in a major key, was written by Rowland Hugh Prichard (1811–1887) and first published in his *Cyfaill y Cantorion*— "The Singer's Friend" (Llanidloes, 1844), though he is credited with writing it over a decade earlier, that is, by the time he was twenty. He worked at the Welsh Flannel Manufacturing Company in Holywell, but was also a precentor and composer of hymn tunes. This one, the only one of his that remains with us, is by far the most-used tune in the fourteen hymnals we surveyed for this book.[20] In the bar form shape AAB, it is skillfully constructed within the range of a fifth, except for one push to a sixth in the last phrase. It needs the right tempo, which only becomes apparent with the eighth notes that follow the sequence in the second last phrase of the B section.

HYFRYDOL
8 7 8 7 D

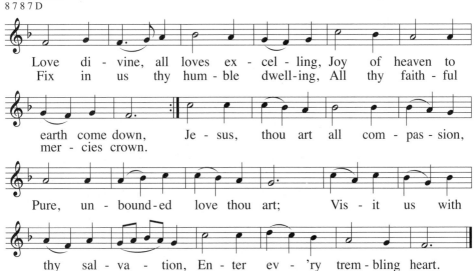

Love di - vine, all loves ex - cel - ling, Joy of heaven to
Fix in us thy hum - ble dwell - ing, All thy faith - ful

earth come down, Je - sus, thou art all com - pas - sion,
mer - cies crown.

Pure, un - bound - ed love thou art; Vis - it us with

thy sal - va - tion, En - ter ev - 'ry trem - bling heart.

Text: Charles Wesley, 1747
Tune: Rowland H. Prichard, ca. 1831

VU #333

RHOSYMEDRE (also known as LOVELY) was written by J. D. Edwards (1805–1885) who was the rector at Rhosymedre near Wrexham in North Wales. It was published in the periodical *Y Drysorfa*—"The Treasury" (May, 1838) and then in the "first collection of music for the established church in Wales,"[21] *Original Sacred Music* (London?, ca. 1839), which Edwards composed and arranged. A member of the clergy, he was constructively concerned about singing congregations. He also happened to be among those who wrote music, more music than RHOSYMEDRE, but we justly remember him for this one tune. Routley called it "a meditative stepwise tune majoring in repeated notes."[22] Its curve in bar form sensitively sets the following text (though this text also goes with LOVE UNKNOWN which works equally well—see Chapter XIV[23]) and nicely handles the repeated words at the end.

RHOSYMEDRE
6 6 6 6 8 8 8

My song is love un-known, My Sav-ior's love to me,
Love to the love-less shown, That they might love-ly be.
Oh, who am I, that for my sake My Lord should take frail
flesh and die? My Lord should take frail flesh and die?

Text: Samuel Crossman, c. 1624-1683   LBW #94
Tune: John D. Edwards, 1806-1885

BRYN CALFARIA takes us to a minor key again. It is by William Owen of Prysgol (1814–1893), from the second volume of his *Y Perl Cerddorol*—"The Musical Pearl" (Caernarvon, 1852[24]). Owen worked in the Penrhyn slate quarry in North Wales from the time he was ten, listened to the organist at the church of St. Anne near his home, became a musician himself, and began to compose at an early age. Though more of his tunes were popular in his time, BRYN CALFARIA is the one for which he is still known. The drive of this tune tempts singers to a tempo that can easily destroy the bar form's B section. There, the key to the tempo is revealed as the tune spins into even more critical eighth notes than in HYFRYDOL. The A section at the beginning requires a speed that will accommodate the B section with exuberant breadth (unless, as in some Welsh performance practice, there is a big ritard at the eighth notes, which poses its own problems of staying together and resetting the former tempo).

Carl Daw, the executive director of the Hymn Society in the United States and Canada, points to the telling link between this tune and its name.

> BRYN CALFARIA means "Mount Calvary," and both the halting rhythm and melodic shape of the A section suggest Christ's struggle in climbing the hill bearing his cross. This is a classic example of how a hymn tune name can provide information that enhances the appreciation of the tune.[25]

BRYN CALFARIA
8 7 8 7 4 4 4 7 7

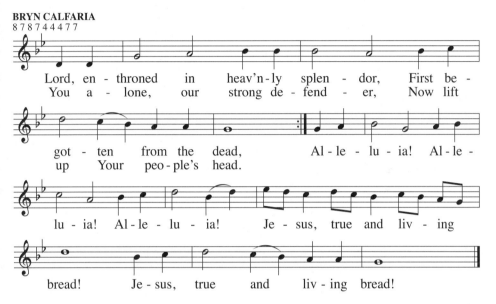

Lord, en - throned in heav'n - ly splen - dor, First be -
You a - lone, our strong de - fend - er, Now lift

got - ten from the dead, Al - le - lu - ia! Al - le -
up Your peo - ple's head.

lu - ia! Al - le - lu - ia! Je - sus, true and liv - ing

bread! Je - sus, true and liv - ing bread!

Text: George Hugh Bourne, 1874, alt.
Tune: William Owen, 1852   Pres #154

ABERYSTWYTH by Joseph Parry (1841–1903) is one of the best-known Welsh tunes and probably one reason (with EBENEZER and BRYN CALFARIA) that Welsh tunes are all popularly perceived to be in minor keys. Though reared as a poor child laborer in a coal mine and iron works in Merthyr Tydfil, Parry was, nonetheless, exposed to a high level of musical culture. He moved with his family to a Welsh community in Danville, Pennsylvania, scraped together enough money to attend the Royal Academy of Music in London from which he graduated, became professor of music at the University of Wales at Aberystwyth, and held other professorial appointments thereafter. He composed a good deal of music, including 400 hymn tunes, and was well known in his lifetime, but is probably best remembered now for this one tune he wrote in 1876.[26] It was first published in Edward Stephen's *Ail Lyfr Tonau ac Emynau*—"The Second Book of Tunes and Hymns" (Wrexham, 1879). It starts as if it will be in bar form, but what begins as a repeat of A turns out to be an answer. Sequence then rides the tune up to its climax on the top octave, and the last two measures come back to the home we always knew but now as if for the first time.

ABERYSTWYTH
7 7 7 7 D

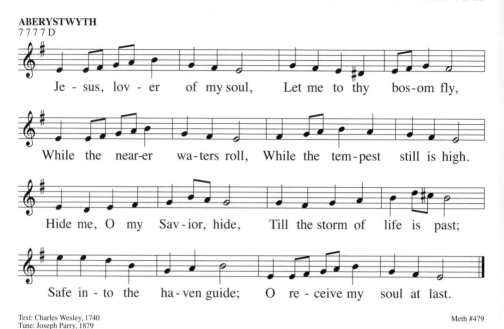

Je - sus, lov - er of my soul,   Let me to thy   bos-om fly,

While the near-er wa-ters roll,   While the tem-pest   still is high.

Hide me, O my Sav-ior, hide,   Till the storm of   life is past;

Safe in - to the ha-ven guide;   O re - ceive my   soul at last.

Text: Charles Wesley, 1740   Meth #479
Tune: Joseph Parry, 1879

    EBENEZER is a tune Ralph Vaughan Williams classed with the world's finest one hundred.[27] Formally it is quite usual: AABA with B moving to the relative major. The triplet is less usual though not unknown to the Welsh.[28] Luff says that "in the Welsh idiom, the triplet is sung heavily and deliberately and there is no great care taken to distinguish between it and the dotted figure."[29] EBENEZER was composed by the organist and choirmaster Thomas John Williams (1869–1944) in 1890 or 1896, first for an anthem and then turned into a hymn tune.[30] It has nothing to do with being washed up in a bottle on the coast in North Wales. That nonsense came after it was published in the *Baptist Book of Praise* (ca. 1900) and unfortunately gave the tune its alternate name TON-Y-BOTEL ("The Bottle Tune").

EBENEZER
8 7 8 7 D

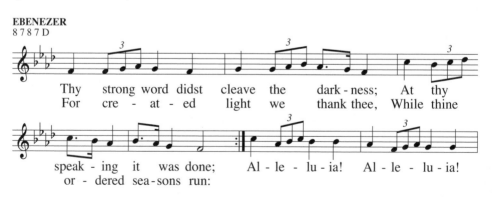

Thy strong word didst cleave the dark - ness; At thy
For cre - at - ed light we thank thee, While thine

speak - ing it was done;   Al - le - lu - ia! Al - le - lu - ia!
or - dered sea-sons run:

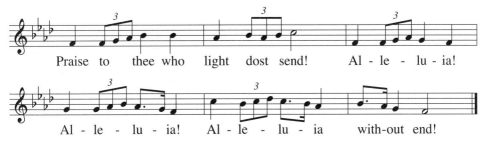

Praise to thee who light dost send! Al - le - lu - ia!

Al - le - lu - ia! Al - le - lu - ia with-out end!

Text: Martin H. Franzmann, 1907-1976, alt.; © 1969, Concordia Publishing House   Wor3 #511
Tune: Thomas J. Williams, 1869-1944

We conclude the Welsh survey with CWM RHONDDA, another well-known tune, this one in a major key, and yet again the only tune we still know from its composer, John Hughes (1873–1932). He wrote it for a Baptist Welsh singing festival (*Cymanfa Ganu*) in 1903.[31] It was first published in a bilingual hymnal of the Calvinistic Methodist Church in the United States, *Cân a Mawl: Song and Praise* (Chicago, 1918), with the hymn, "Angels from the Realms of Glory."[32] Hughes worked at the Glynn Colliery at Llanilltyd Faerdref, but was also a Baptist deacon and precentor. "The value of the tune," says Luff, "lies in its immense vigor and what can only be described as its vulgar appeal (not necessarily a bad thing in a hymn)."[33] Its structure is ABC. B is both an outgrowth of and an answer to A, and C employs sequence to lead to the high dominant and then a repeat of the end of B. C gives the opportunity to drive home the text by powerful repetitions.

CWM RHONDDA
8 7 8 7 8 7 7

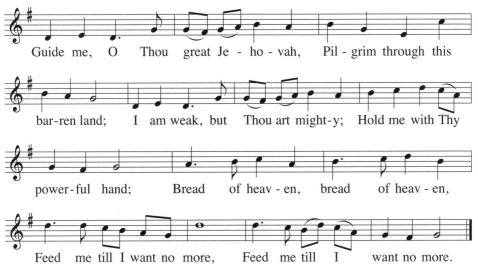

Guide me, O Thou great Je - ho - vah, Pil - grim through this

bar-ren land; I am weak, but Thou art might-y; Hold me with Thy

power-ful hand; Bread of heav - en, bread of heav - en,

Feed me till I want no more, Feed me till I want no more.

Text: William Williams, 1745; tr. Peter Williams, 1771   Pres #281
Tune: John Hughes, 1907

2. FRENCH DIOCESAN TUNES

In the sixteenth, seventeenth, and eighteenth centuries, in the midst of considerable "Neo-Gallican" dispute and ferment among Roman Catholics, breviaries in various dioceses—therefore the name "Diocesan"—were "modernized" and Office hymns recast. New tunes began to appear in Neo-Gallican missals in the second half of the seventeenth century for the new Office hymns.[34] They moved into modern "measured rhythm" and major and minor tonal frames. While there is reason to have qualms about what happened to texts and chant in this process, the tunes that were produced represent a "serious attempt to preserve the use of unison and melodic singing in liturgical worship at a time when it was decaying in Western Christianity."[35]

A creative concern for congregational song was at work. Even when monks or a choir rather than the whole church were the primary singers, a congregational concern was still the underlying force. The practice confirms this. It was complete with the church's instinct to combine a congregational part with more rehearsed possibilities. Alternation of stanzas gave the congregation the simpler form, and embellishments called *machicotage* gave chanters more complex possibilities.[36] François de La Feilée's *Method nouvelle pour apprendre parfaitement les règles du plain-chant* (Poitiers, 1775) provided rules for the embellishments. Some of these tunes passed into the English-speaking world through François de La Feilée's *Method* by way of *The Hymnal Noted* (1851) of John Mason Neale and Thomas Helmore.

Congregational song was challenged on two fronts. The eighteenth-century "theatrical" music "developed by the Viennese school of musicians affected church music more and more" so that the Opera House became the paradigm. In the nineteenth century, Solesmes (for more about the significance of the monastery at Solesmes, see the beginning of the next chapter) rightly objected, but their monastic grounding left the congregation out: the machicotage for the trained group that effectively by alternation preserved the simpler part for the congregation seems to "have been suppressed" by Solesmes' reforms.[37] Nonetheless, tunes were composed that have entered the church's repertoire and may turn out to be one of the most durable legacies of the period.

As usual, rhythm is the most disputed issue about the original performance practice of these tunes. They were written in square-note notation on a four-line staff, as was standard practice in the liturgical books in which they were printed. They looked like chant and, therefore, may have some sources in chant, but they were attuned to more modern major and minor musical currents with regular bar lines and were performed in a more "measured" way than chant. Pocknee regarded the four differently shaped neumes as having distinct values and resulting in a measured rhythm lacking a "regularly recurrent accent,"[38] while Routley thought there was "no consistency" about the values of the neumes so that they fell into our "modern form."[39] Whatever may have happened in their "original" performance practice, we tend to regularize the rhythm with regularly recurring accents expressed by bar lines. Here are some of these tunes in the form we use them.

O FILII ET FILIAE is attached to the Easter text that names it. It began outside a liturgical usage and later joined the "diocesan tunes." Its text was printed in the early sixteenth century and usually is said to be by the Franciscan monk Jean Tisserand who died in 1494, though Jeffrey Wasson suggests it is by the Dominican bishop Jehan Tisserand.[40] The first printed source we have for the tune is in *Airs sur les hymns sacrez, odes et noels* (Paris, 1623). It may be a fifteenth-century French folk noel melody, but sometimes chant has been seen as its source. Though the *Liber Usualis* includes it,[41] it is given there in modern notation with a meter signature and a five-line staff rather than the *Liber's* normal four-line staff with chant notation. Stulken and Salika point out that "it falls into triple meter" no matter how you notate it. It ranges across an octave from fifth to fifth around the tonic.

O FILII ET FILIAE
8 8 8 with alleluias

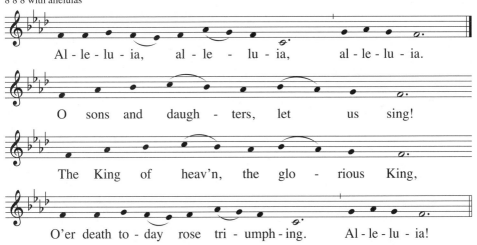

Text: *O filii et filae;* Jean Tisserand, d.1494; tr. John M. Neale, 1818-1866, alt.   Wor3 #447
Tune: Mode II

CHRISTE SANCTORUM comes to us via the 1782 edition of François de La Feilée's *Method*, but its sources are in the previous century, where it began its association with many texts. It is found in the *Paris Antiphoner* (1681) with the hymn "Ceteri numquam nisi vagiendo" for the Visitation of the Virgin Mary and in the *Cluny Antiphoner* (1686) with the hymn "Mille quem stipant" for the commemoration of St. Michael. It is named for yet another hymn, "Christe

Sanctorum." Its well-known link with the hymn for Matins from the tenth century, given here, is traceable to the *English Hymnal* of 1906. In our hymnals, it has been set to still other texts, sometimes by altering its Sapphic meter with the addition or subtraction of notes on one syllable. (Sapphic meter is 11 11 11 5, where each 11 is 5 plus 6, the 5 a dactyl [long, short, short] and a trochee [long, short] and the 6 three trochees.)

CHRISTE SANCTORUM is clearly in a major key and utilizes common practice harmony by moving to the dominant to set up the longing for the home of the tonic. Within the span of an octave, this time from the low tonic to the high tonic, it highlights the fifth where it begins and the third where the second phrase begins. At the end of the fourth phrase, it modulates to the dominant and then emphasizes the supertonic as part of the dominant chord at the end of the second to last phrase before it returns home to the major triad. Motives are unobtrusively repeated so that the melody is easily sung, even though it is structured with no repeated sections.

CHRISTE SANCTORUM
11 11 11 5

Fa - ther, we praise thee, now the night is o - ver, Ac - tive and watch - ful, stand we all be - fore thee; Sing - ing we of - fer prayer and med - i - ta - tion: Thus we a - dore thee.

Text: Latin, 10th c.; tr. Percy Dearmer, 1867-1936, © Oxford University Press   H82 #1
Tune: melody from *Antiphoner*, 1681

O QUANTA QUALIA comes through the same sources as CHRISTE SANCTORUM, though from a later edition of François de La Feilée's *Method*, in 1808. Thomas Helmore, in the second part of *The Hymnal Noted* (London, 1854), set it to John Mason Neale's translation (given here) of Abelard's "O quanta, qualia" with the rhythm we now use.[42] This is a stately tune in a major key that moves from fifth to fifth around the tonic. It modulates to the dominant already by the end of the second phrase where it reaches its melodic peak, then moves downward to the low fifth rather than upward before it goes back to the upper fifth at the beginning of the last phrase.

O QUANTA QUALIA
10 10 10 10

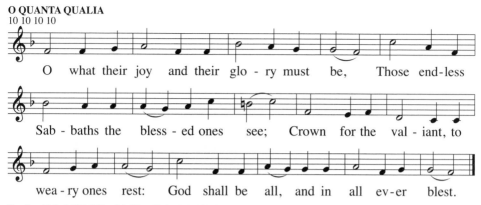

O what their joy and their glo - ry must be, Those end - less

Sab - baths the bless - ed ones see; Crown for the val - iant, to

wea - ry ones rest: God shall be all, and in all ev - er blest.

Text: Peter Abelard, 1079-1142; tr. John Mason Neale, 1818-1866, alt.   H82 #623
Tune: *Antiphoner*, 1681

ADORO DEVOTE (or ADORO TE DEVOTE) is from the *Paris Processional* of 1697, where it was paired with a Neo-Gallican processional text for the Feast of Corpus Christi, "Adoro te supplex," a variation of "Adoro te devote," which is usually attributed to Thomas Aquinas and has its own variant as "Adoro devote."[43] Though the tune is closely associated with this Eucharistic hymn, it has been used with other texts as well. Some of these texts, including some translations of "Adoro te devote," have, as for CHRISTE SANCTORUM, changed the tune's natural meter by the addition or subtraction of notes on a single syllable.

Once again, this is a tune in a modern major key within the span of an octave from tonic to tonic. The tonic triad is set up at the beginning, after which the movement is almost entirely conjunct. The first two phrases repeat as in bar form, the fifth and sixth phrases (counting the repeat of the first two) move to the dominant, and the last two phrases return to the tonic. Rhythmically the melody is less able to be regularized with bar lines than CHRISTE SANCTORUM or O QUANTA QUALIA and shows the influence of chant in delightfully irregular successions of twos and threes. (Pocknee gives the tune and its first phrase in an embellished version.[44])

ADORO DEVOTE
11 11 11 11

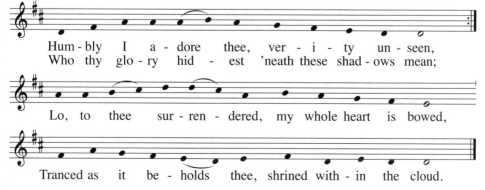

Hum - bly I a - dore thee, ver - i - ty un - seen,
Who thy glo - ry hid - est 'neath these shad - ows mean;

Lo, to thee sur - ren - dered, my whole heart is bowed,

Tranced as it be - holds thee, shrined with - in the cloud.

Text: Att. Thomas Aquinas, 1225?-1274; tr. *Hymnal 1940*   H82 #314
Tune: French church melody, Mode 5, *Processionale*, 1697

ISTE CONFESSOR comes from the *Poitiers Antiphoner* of 1746 where it went with the hymn for a confessor, "Iste Confessor,"[45] an eighth-century text probably written for the patron saint of France, St. Martin of Tours (ca. 335–397). Today the tune tends to be associated with the ninth-century hymn, "Only Begotten, Word of God Eternal."

ISTE CONFESSOR lives once more within the span of an octave from tonic to tonic, but in this case in a minor key. The tonic triad is spelled immediately. The third phrase repeats the first as if the fourth will also be a repeat, but instead the melody stays on the fifth and moves naturally a fifth higher to the dominant. That sets up a gentle leap to the high tonic, which prepares for a gradual descent to the low one where we began. Like all of these melodies, this one also is thoroughly congregational.

ISTE CONFESSOR
11 11 11 5

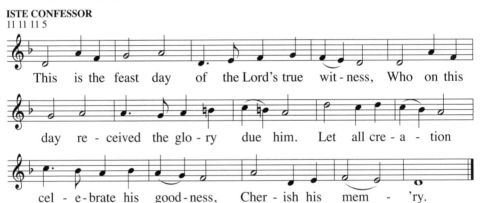

Text: *Iste confessor Domini, colentes;* Latin, 8th c.; tr. Peter J. Scagnelli, b.1949, ©
Tune: Rouen Church Melody

Wor3 #717

DEUS TUORUM MILITUM (or GRENOBLE) comes from the *Grenoble Antiphoner* of 1753. It is the most vigorous of the French tunes we have encountered, the first one in Long Meter, and the first to expand the range to an octave and a third. In triple time, it immediately sets up the tonic chord and then glides around it with the predictable modulation to the dominant at the end of the second phrase.

This tune is named for the text that accompanied it in the *Grenoble Antiphoner*, an Office hymn for martyrs. That text is not in common use. We join the tune to a variety of other hymns.

DEUS TUORUM MILITUM
LM

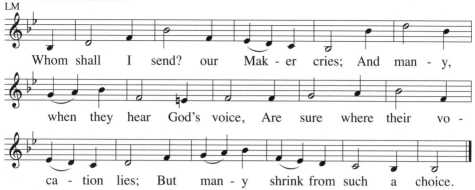

Whom shall I send? our Mak-er cries; And man-y,
when they hear God's voice, Are sure where their vo-
ca-tion lies; But man-y shrink from such a choice.

Text: Fred Pratt Green, 1970, © 1971, Hope Publishing Company
Tune: *Grenoble Antiphoner,* 1753; adapt. by Ralph Vaughan Williams, 1906

Meth #582

1   Alan Luff, *Welsh Hymns and Their Tunes* (Carol Stream: Hope Publishing Co., 1990), 130.
2   Ibid., 236–237.
3   Ibid., 238.
4   Routley, MCH, 120B.
5   Ibid., 131.
6   Routley, MCH, 118A.
7   For this history and its context in the fuller history of Christianity in Wales, see Luff, *Welsh Hymns,* 52–84.
8   That is, William who must have had an ancestor named William, which gave him the surname Williams who lived at a farm called "Pantycelyn." See Luff, *Welsh Hymns,* 19.
9   Luff, *Welsh Hymns,* 139.
10 Ibid.
11 For a reproduction of the page from *Musical and Poetical Relicks,* see *The Hymnal* 1940 Companion, 126.
12 Luff, *Welsh Hymns,* 26.
13 Ibid., 26–27. For pictures and a description see Joan Rimmer, "Triple harps," NGDMM, 8, 201–203.
14 Given in Luff, *Welsh Hymns,* 27, from John Owen (Owain Alaw), *Gems of Welsh Melody,* 1873.
15 Luff, *Welsh Hymns,* 155.
16 Ibid., 130.
17 Arfon (found in Welsh and French resources) is another tune with both minor and major versions. See Pres 99 for minor, VU 244 for major.
18 Luff, *Welsh Hymns,* 160–161.

[19] See Alan Luff, "Hail the Day That Sees Him Rise," Glover, H82C, 3A, 435. Stulken, HCLBW, 227 and Aufdemberge, *Christian Worship Handbook*, 151 both refer to Robert McCutchan, *Hymn Tune Names*, 93–94, who gives the village "Llanfair" as an abbreviation "of one of the longest words in any language: 'Llanfairpwllgwyngyllgogerychwyrndrobwllllantysiliogogogoch' . . . 'Church of St. Mary in a hollow of white hazel near the rapid whirlpool of the Church of St. Tysillio by the red cave.'" Luff, 436, seems less sure. He treats the name of "St. Mary's Llan (Llan signifies a Christian settlement)" as so commonplace as needing additions, but wonders which one this is. If the tune "is rightly ascribed to Robert Williams, then it is likely to be Llanfairynghornwy in Anglesey."

[20] It appears in all fourteen hymnals, used 44 times. The second most-used tune is OLD HUNDRETH (GENEVAN 134), which also appears in all fourteen hymnals, used 32 times.

[21] Luff *Welsh Hymns*, 165.

[22] Routley, MCH, 119A.

[23] For yet another engaging tune for this text, see *Baptist Hymnal* (Nashville: Convention Press, 1975), #486, listed by James Bigelow, pseudonym for William J. Reynolds.

[24] Stulken, HCLBW, 249, says 1886, and Stulken and Salika, *Hymnal Companion to Worship – Third Edition* (Chicago: GIA Publications, Inc., 1998), 307, say 1890.

[25] Correspondence from Carl Daw, May 28, 2004.

[26] From Parry's *Autobiography*, reported in Luff, *Welsh Hymns*, 213. For more detail about Parry and differing appraisals of his work, see Alan Luff, "Joseph Parry," *Hymn Society of Great Britain and Ireland Bulletin* 235 17:2 (April 2003): 41–43.

[27] Luff, *Welsh Hymns*, 221.

[28] Luff, *Welsh Hymns*, 222.

[29] Alan Luff, "Thy Strong Word Did Cleave the Darkness," Glover, H82C, 3A, 708.

[30] Stulken, HCLBW, 311, says 1890, from Moffatt's *Handbook to the Church Hymnary*. Luff, *Welsh Hymns*, 221, says 1896 from an article in 1940, which is Moffatt's source. Stulken (correspondence, June 17, 2004) notes that, in handwritten form, 1890 and 1896 can easily be mistaken for one another.

[31] Alan Luff, "God of Grace and God of Glory," Glover, H82C, 3B, 1095, says 1903, and Alan Luff, *Welsh Hymns*, 223, says 1905. Stulken, HCLBW, 397, says 1905 or 1907.

[32] Stulken, HCLBW, 397.

[33] Alan Luff, "God of Grace and God of Glory," Glover, H82C, 3B, 1096.

[34] Cyril E. Pocknee, *The French Diocesan Hymns and Their Melodies* (London: The Faith Press, 1954), 22. Pocknee gives a careful, concise discussion of this history with comments about their composers on pages 23–24.

[35] Pocknee, *The French Diocesan Hymns*, 26.

[36] Ibid. For more about "machicotage," see Mary Berry, "Machicotage", NGDMM, 11, 437–438. It is named for singers of the lower clergy called machicots.

[37] Pocknee, The French Diocesan Hymns, 26.

[38] Ibid., 37.

[39] Routley, MCH, 79A–B.

[40] Jeffrey Wasson "Alleluia, Alleluia, Alleluia! O Sons and Daughters," Glover, H82C, 3A, 409.

[41] *Liber Usualis*, 1875.

[42] Suggestions for earlier rhythms are given in Robin Leaver, "Lord, We Have Come at Your Own Invitation," Glover H82C, 3A, 649.

[43] See Pocknee, 162, and, for the textual variations of the latter, Joseph Herl "Humbly I Adore Thee, Verity Unseen," Glover, H82C, 3A, 592–593.

[44] Pocknee, 34.

[45] Pocknee, 162.

IX. Nineteenth-century English Tunes 1

1. Overview

In Chapter V, three nineteenth-century motifs were isolated: 1) a continuing progression toward the sentimental, 2) consumerism, and 3) a push against these on behalf of congregational singing by retrieving the rhythmic chorale, writing new isometric but congregational tunes, and re-harnessing the music of folk cultures. That is part of the story. The push against the negatives of the culture, however, had larger components in three other movements: the Caecilian[1] Society in Germany, the monastery at Solesmes in France, and the Oxford-Cambridge movement in England.[2] These movements are sometimes dismissed as backward-looking aspects of Romanticism. Such an understanding is not altogether unwarranted. The Caecilian and Oxford-Cambridge trajectories in their later years did sometimes get snared by antiquarianism or nostalgic sentimentality and cliché, but those were cultural perversions that avoided the movements' underlying intentions and countercultural essence.

In eighteenth-century Vienna and Passau a "Caecilian-Bündnisse" had sought to maintain unaccompanied singing against the temper of the times. It was not successful, but in 1869 Franz Xaver Witt (1834–1888) organized the Caecilian Society at Bamberg, Germany, with more success. Pius IX recognized it in 1870. Gregorian chant, Renaissance polyphony, and congregational singing were set as ideals against what was regarded as "impure church music," namely, the theatrical, orchestral, and non-congregational. As the Caecilian movement unfolded, the congregational concern took a backseat to the choral one. In his book *Dies Irae*, Robert Chase[3] notes the impact of the Caecilian ideals on large choral works. John Baptist Singenberger (1848–1924), a Caecilian who came to Milwaukee from Switzerland, illustrates their impact on smaller choral music for parish use. Singenberger's Organ-book[4] points to the Caecilian support for congregational singing, but the Society did not produce a durable body of congregational music or have a congregational impact comparable to the choral one.

Neither did the Benedictine monastery at Solesmes, but for a different reason. Solesmes stands as a witness to liturgical renewal against control by the culture or state. After its suppression in 1791, it was refounded in 1833 by Prosper Guéranger (1805–1875). For the rest of the century, it housed the study, singing, and publishing of Gregorian chant. Solesmes is a remarkable symbol of the church that resists collapse into the culture's bondage, but since it was centered in monastic chant it largely stands outside our congregational story.

The Oxford-Cambridge movement, however, had a profound congregational concern and impact. The year 1833 is usually taken to be the date of its genesis also, when John Keble (1792–1866) preached his assize sermon at Oxford on "National Apostasy." The immediate issue was the proposed suppression of ten Irish bishoprics, but the deeper concern was whether the church ought to be subject to governmental control. The Oxford-Cambridge movement breathed new life into what the Wesleyans saw as Anglican aridity, but it stands more broadly as another tribute to the church's integrity against bondage to the state and its culture.

While the Oxford-Cambridge partisans began with a prejudice against hymns nurtured by the Methodist excess that SAGINA (see Chapter VII) represents, they embraced congregational song when they came to the realization that hymns were integrally related to the Breviary and the church's Daily Prayer. In 1827, six years before Keble preached his assize sermon, his *The Christian Year* (Oxford) and Reginald Heber's *Hymns Written or Selected for the Weekly Church Service of the Year* (London) were published (the latter completed in 1820 and published posthumously). These books infused hymns and the rhythm of the church's weekly and yearly life with a new authority. After that, John Mason Neale (1816–1866) began to make his remarkable English translations of Latin and Greek hymns, Thomas Helmore (1811–1890) provided the musical expertise, and together they published *The Hymnal Noted* (London, in two parts, 1851 and 1854). Though it supplied some of the staples of English hymnody we know, as in "O Come, O Come, Emmanuel," for example, its four-line staff and Gregorian notation seemed too antiquarian to engage the popular imagination. However, the editors of *Hymns Ancient and Modern* (London, 1861)—Henry W. Baker (1821–1877), William Henry Monk (1823–1889) and their advisors, including Keble and Neale, brought together Latin and German translations, the German ones stimulated by the pacesetting work of Catherine Winkworth (1827–1878), as well as new texts and tunes. This paved the way for the broad ecumenical spectrum that characterizes our modern hymnals. *Hymns Ancient and Modern* also made perceptively long-lasting pairings of texts and tunes. The book was the filter through which much of our English-speaking hymnody has passed. It is the model of a modern hymnal, and, in Temperley's view, the vehicle for hymn tunes that brought all parties together in a new folk song.[5]

Since the English in the nineteenth century settled on a common musical language that *Hymns Ancient and Modern* represents and, since we know the composers, it is logical to let them lead us. This chapter and the next are restricted to composers born before mid-century. They are organized by a quasi-alphabetical ordering of their tunes under the headings of the composers, beginning here with the "quintessential" AURELIA and beginning in the next chapter with the "archetypal" NICAEA.

2. Composers and Their Tunes

S. S. Wesley

Samuel Sebastian Wesley (1810–1876) wrote what has sometimes been dubbed the quintessential Victorian hymn tune, AURELIA. The grandson of Charles Wesley and the son of Samuel Wesley and his housekeeper, Sarah Suter, he was named for his father and for the composer who was his father's passion, Johann *Sebastian* Bach. S. S. Wesley was an outstanding cathedral organist and composer who wrote many hymn tunes, but AURELIA is the only one that remains in general circulation. (A few of his other tunes can be found here and there, but only AURELIA regularly appears in virtually every English hymnal.) Routley suggested it might be his "most uncharacteristic tune."[6] Temperley thinks its "melodic shape, with two high lines between two low ones, recalls a typical form of English folk song."[7] The tune implies its nineteenth-century harmonic envelope, but, perhaps because of its English folk song "recall," the melody has the stamina to stand alone. Composed in 1864 and used with numerous texts, it was married to "The Church's One Foundation" in 1868 in the Appendix to *Hymns Ancient and Modern* (London).

AURELIA
7 6 7 6 D

The Church's one foun - da - tion Is Je - sus Christ her Lord;

She is his new cre - a - tion By wa - ter and the word:

From heaven he came and sought her To be his ho - ly bride;

With his own blood he bought her, And for her life he died.

Text: Samuel John Stone, 1839-1900
Tune: Samuel Sebastian Wesley, 1810-1876

H82 #525

HEREFORD makes a good comparison with AURELIA. Instead of two high lines between two low ones, its undulating curves gradually make their way up and then down to form an arch. Routley calls it "delectable,"[8] and in the later twentieth century Wesley's second most popular tune in Britain. It first appeared in S. S. Wesley's *The European Psalmist* (London, 1872).

HEREFORD
LM

O thou who cam - est from a - bove The fire ce -
les - tial to im - part, Kin - dle a flame of sa - cred
love Up - on the al - tar of my heart.

Text: Charles Wesley, 1707-1788, alt.
Tune: Samuel Sebastian Wesley, 1810-1876

H82 #704

George Elvey

Sir George Elvey (1816–1893) may not have been the musician S. S. Wesley was, but he beat Wesley with an anthem for the Gresham Prize in 1834[9] and the next year was chosen instead of Wesley as organist at St. George's Chapel, Windsor. He remained there until he retired in 1882. Though most of his music is forgotten, two of his hymn tunes can be found in virtually every English hymnal today. ST. GEORGE'S WINDSOR, named for the place of his employment, was first published in 1858 in E. H. Thorne's *A Selection of Psalm and Hymn Tunes* (London) with Montgomery's "Hark, the Song of Jubilee." In *Hymns Ancient and Modern* it was joined to "Come, Ye Thankful People, Come," where it has remained. A few years later, for the 1868 Appendix to *Hymns Ancient and Modern*, Elvey wrote DIADEMATA for "Crown Him with Many Crowns," with which it too has remained. Unlike S. S. Wesley's AURELIA, Elvey's tunes are more aligned to the eighteenth century.

ST. GEORGE'S WINDSOR is developed from a dotted quarter and an eighth. The first phrase is repeated, the dotted figure is then repeated in close proximity, and the melody smoothes out to the dominant. The motive from the beginning now comes in the dominant, works its way up in sequence, turns upside down for the close repeats of the dotted figure, and modifies the move to the dominant at the middle just enough to make a satisfying conclusive answer in the tonic. Though not consciously aware of its construction, congregations are nonetheless helped because the tune is structured in two eight bar halves, each of which has exactly the same rhythm.

ST. GEORGE'S WINDSOR
7 7 7 7 D

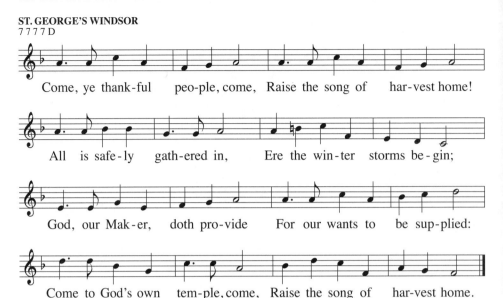

Text: Henry Alford, 1810-1871
Tune: George J. Elvey, 1816-1893

Bap #637

DIADEMATA also is structured in two eight bar halves. The first half modulates to the dominant, but the two are not rhythmic duplicates of each other. Like ST. GEORGE'S WINDSOR, however, the second employs sequence to drive to a climax on the top tonic, after which a modified downward scale leads home.

DIADEMATA
SMD

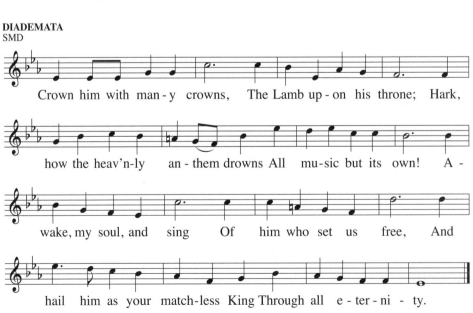

Text: Matthew Bridges, 1851, alt.
Tune: George Job Elvey, 1868

Mor #405

William Henry Monk

DIX started its life as a tune in Germany, composed by Conrad Kocher (1786–1872), a musician who founded a School of Sacred Song in Stuttgart in 1821, pushed for part-singing by congregations, and was influenced by Haydn, Mozart, Clementi, and Palestrina. The original version of the melody was published in 1838 in *Stimmen aus dem Reiche Gottes* (Stuttgart) for the text, "Treuer Heiland, wir sind hier." William Henry Monk (1823–1889), the musical editor of *Hymns Ancient and Modern*, shortened it and joined it to "As with Gladness Men of Old." It turns out to be a brief AAB tune that spans an octave from fifth to fifth and is easily sung in harmony.

DIX
777777

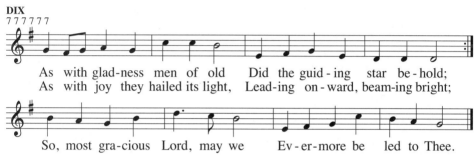

As with glad-ness men of old   Did the guid - ing   star be - hold;
As with joy they hailed its light,   Lead-ing on - ward, beam-ing bright;

So, most gra-cious Lord, may we   Ev - er-more be   led to Thee.

Text: William Chatterton Dix, c.1858
Tune: Conrad Kocher, 1786-1872; abr. by William Henry Monk, 1861
Pres #63

Monk adapted much earlier music by Giovanni Pierluigi Palestrina (1525–1594). From the *Gloria* of Palestrina's Tone 3 *Magnificat*, he constructed the tune we know as VICTORY for the first edition of *Hymns Ancient and Modern*, possibly following the lead of someone who had made an earlier version for the *Parish Choir; or Church Music Book* (London, 1851). VICTORY is sung widely by congregations at Easter, but it is not the most congregational of tunes.

VICTORY
8 8 8 with alleluias

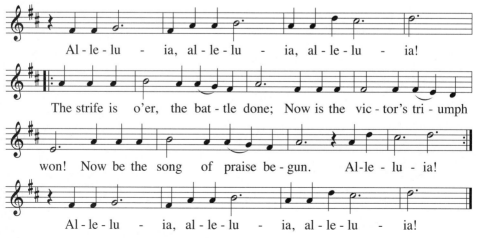

Al - le - lu - ia, al - le - lu - ia, al - le - lu - ia!

The strife is o'er, the bat - tle done; Now is the vic - tor's tri - umph

won! Now be the song of praise be - gun. Al-le - lu - ia!

Al - le - lu - ia, al - le - lu - ia, al - le - lu - ia!

Text: *Symphonia Sirenum*, Köln, 1695; tr. Francis Pott, 1832-1909
Tune: Giovanni P. da Palestrina, 1525-1594, adapt.
LBW #135

Monk himself wrote EVENTIDE, for "Abide with Me." The tune pushes toward the sentimental and exposes that nineteenth-century hazard. Monk was an organist who championed congregational singing and daily choral services. Several of his hymn tunes are still used, this one most widely. Routley regarded Monk as writing "serviceable" tunes "to order" for specific texts—tunes which did their work and then faded and were "never vulgar, never extravagant, often distractingly dull." He thought EVENTIDE was Monk's "most characteristic tune."[10] Like AURELIA, it moves a fifth away to the dominant (at the end of the fourth phrase) and another fifth away to the supertonic (at the end of the sixth phrase) before it comes back home via the dominant (at the beginning of the seventh phrase). Its harmonization is not quite as dissonant as Wesley's, which, along with the dominant seventh chord at the seventh phrase (AURELIA has a dominant without the seventh) leads it along a more sentimental path. Also like AURELIA, though it presumes the harmonic framework, the tune can stand alone.

EVENTIDE
10 10 10 10

Text: Henry F. Lyte, 1847
Tune: W. H. Monk, 1861

Meth #700

Edward John Hopkins

ELLERS was written by Edward John Hopkins (1818–1901) and first published in the third edition of *The Supplemental Hymn and Tune Book* (London, 1869). It probably is titled by a nickname for John Ellerton, who wrote the text that goes with it. From 1843 until 1898, Hopkins was the organist at the Temple Church in London, a church that called him to introduce the regular choral service in a building that had been restored to Gothic splendor just before he came. Though not in Barnby's sentimental and entertaining style that we shall soon encounter, the practice at the Temple Church nonetheless matched what happened in Barnby's church: "the choir sang while the people listened."[11] Hopkins had an interest in congregational song, however, as ELLERS demonstrates (even though its original harmonizations may have been chorally conceived) and as he expressed more obviously toward the end of his life in his editing of hymnals and harmonizing of tunes for Methodists, Presbyterians, and Congregationalists. (His theories about tune writing in relation to the Hexachord and Octochord were probably congregational only insofar as they may have translated themselves into good congregational ranges.[12]) What should be noted here is a difference of opinion and practice among Oxford-Cambridge movement congregations. Some sang. Some did not. Also note that this tune has the problem of long notes at the ends of phrases, which may stem from Hopkins's choral conception. Choirs can practice to stem these textual and musical breaks (whether or not they literally hold them over without a breath into the next phrase). Congregations cannot.

ELLERS
10 10 10 10

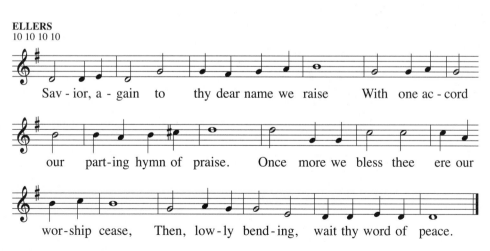

Sav - ior, a - gain to thy dear name we raise With one ac - cord our part-ing hymn of praise. Once more we bless thee ere our wor-ship cease, Then, low - ly bend - ing, wait thy word of peace.

Text: John Ellerton, 1826-1893, alt.
Tune: Edward J. Hopkins, 1818-1901

CW #321

Richard Redhead

Sentimentality was one nineteenth-century pitfall. Carlton Young isolated another one when he said of PETRA (also known as GETHSEMANE, REDHEAD, REDHEAD 76, REDHEAD NO. 76, and AJALON) that it "expresses prevailing mid-nineteenth century Anglo-Catholic perceptions that to recapture the spirit of antiquity is to compose reserved, understated, if not cheerless, hymn tunes."[13] Then he affirmed Routley's opinion that the tune's composer Richard Redhead (1820–1901) "did better work when he was not composing."[14] When not composing, he was serving admirably as organist and choirmaster at two Oxford movement churches in London, first Margaret Street Chapel (All Saints' Church), from 1839 to 1864, and then St. Mary Magdalene, Paddington, until 1894, the latter with rector Frederick Oakeley who translated "Adeste Fideles." He trained boy choirs and played services very well. Redhead prepared a plainsong Psalter with Oakeley and several collections of hymn tunes. PETRA is number 76 in his *Church Hymn Tunes, Ancient and Modern* (London, 1853).

Though Young and Routley may be right, congregations have not generally shared their jibes about this tune, which lives within the relatively narrow gambit of leading tone to sixth. Congregations find it a good fit with Montgomery's text, given below. That is probably why it is in thirteen of the fourteen hymnals we consulted. Its fault, starting every phrase on the same note, may be part of what commends it to congregations. Its structure is three phrase groups, each a set of two bars answered by two bars. The middle set is simply a repeat, an exact repeat when there is no contrasting dotted rhythm at bar 8 as some versions have it. The last set repeats the first with a concluding modification of the answer.

PETRA
7 7 7 7 7 7

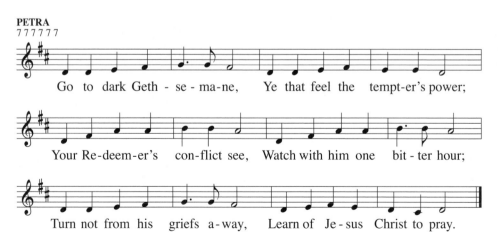

Go to dark Geth - se - ma-ne, Ye that feel the tempt-er's power;

Your Re-deem-er's con-flict see, Watch with him one bit - ter hour;

Turn not from his griefs a-way, Learn of Je - sus Christ to pray.

Text: James Montgomery, 1771-1854
Tune: Richard Redhead, 1820-1901   H82 #171

Henry J. Gauntlett

Every Christmas since 1918, "Once in Royal David's City" has been used with IRBY as the processional at the annual King's College, Cambridge, festival of lessons and carols. Countless people who may never have sung this hymn know it, therefore, from broadcasts or recordings and associate it with IRBY, which Henry J. Gauntlett (1805–1876) wrote for it in 1849 and published in a little booklet called *Christmas Carols* (London). Gauntlett moves us outside of the Oxford-Cambridge circle to the more evangelical wing of the church. Gauntlett's father, Henry Gauntlett, was the priest at the church in Olney of John Newton fame, and from the age of ten to twenty, Henry J. was the organist there. The father wanted him to become a lawyer, a profession he pursued for fifteen years, but his considerable musical talents would not be denied. He served a number of churches as organist and choirmaster, was a superb player, designed English organs and extended their compass, lectured, published books of and about church music, had a wide range of interests from chant to Bach fugues, and wrote thousands of hymn tunes (maybe ten thousand![15]). Mendelssohn celebrated his achievements with praise. Irby is the only one of his tunes in wide circulation. It is unusual in that it gravitates to the tonic, or in one instance to the third of the tonic chord, at the end of every phrase. This would not normally work, but the AAB melody is saved by the subdominant that begins the two phrases of B and by the eighth notes that move naturally and seamlessly out of the initial motive.

IRBY
8 7 8 7 7 7

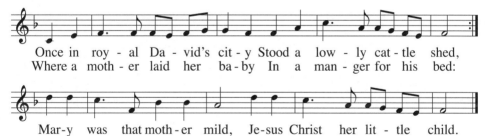

Text: Cecil F. Alexander, 1848, alt.   Chal #165
Tune: Henry John Gauntlett, 1849

C. Hubert H. Parry

C. Hubert H. Parry (1848–1918), not to be confused with the Welshman Joseph Parry (1841–1903) considered in Chapter VIII, came just a bit later than the other nineteenth-century English composers we have met. He worked with George Elvey and played the organ as a youth, but never became a church organist. His niche was as a composer and congenial teacher who set high musical and scholarly standards, wrote a biography of Bach, and was invited by

George Grove to help with the *Dictionary of Music and Musicians*. He was a remarkably able tunesmith. Four of his melodies, mined partly from non-hymnic sources, illustrate his skill.

REPTON comes from an oratorio called *Judith* that Parry wrote in 1888. The diminished fifth to the A-flat in the third phrase, which could easily be a problem, fits nicely into a gradually rising line and is prepared by the A-flat that is remembered from the strong leap of a fourth to it at the beginning of the second phrase. Nevertheless, without accompaniment this tune poses problems for congregations. This points to yet another pitfall of the nineteenth century, the heavy reliance on harmony. Parry is exceedingly melodic, so in his tunes the harmony does not obscure the melody; but there is nonetheless an undertow of harmonic importance without which (even in Parry) nineteenth-century tunes do not exist. As Robert Scholz says, however, this integration of melody and harmony can make "a wonderful union like a good marriage with two solid partners."[16]

The matter of what texts and tunes are used together is worth noting here. It is not an arbitrary matter and requires thought about structure (as well as what is sometimes called "tone"). As Austin Lovelace points out, REPTON fits "How Clear Is Our Vocation, Lord," very well, but because of the necessity to repeat the last line of the text, it does not work well for "Dear Lord and Father of Mankind" with which it is sometimes paired.[17]

REPTON
8 6 8 8 6 6

238

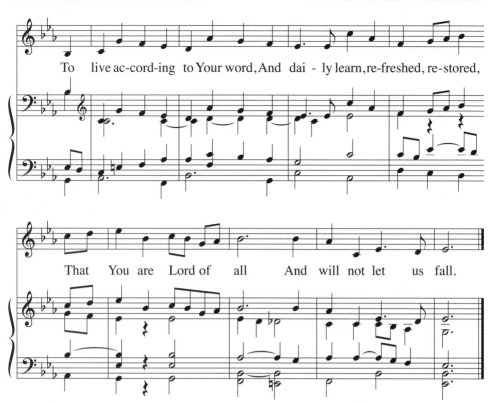

To live ac-cord-ing to Your word, And dai - ly learn, re-freshed, re-stored,

That You are Lord of all And will not let us fall.

Text: Fred Pratt Green, 1981, © 1982, Hope Publishing Co.
Tune: C. Hubert H. Parry, 1888

Pres #419

LAUDATE DOMINUM is taken from the anthem "Hear My Words," which Parry wrote in 1894. Here the opening interval of an upward major sixth sets in motion a congregational tune with a jubilant lift. It is a symmetrical tune that can be easily diagramed: (2 + 2) + (2 + 2) + 4 + (2 + 2). The opening motive receives an answer. Its modification and answer (the second 2 + 2) in turn answer the first four bars. The shorter and more disjunct motives now stretch to a more conjunct four-bar phrase. Its initial motive is repeated a third higher in the last phrase group and answered by the opening motive, which, though now shrunk a half step to a minor sixth, reaches nevertheless to the highest point, the climax note on E-flat, before turning for home.

LAUDATE DOMINUM
10 10 11 11

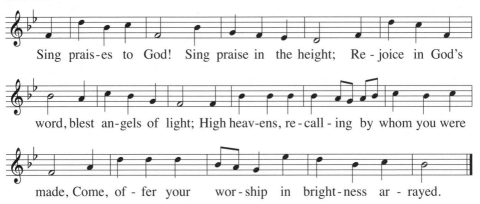

Sing prais-es to God! Sing praise in the height; Re-joice in God's
word, blest an-gels of light; High heav-ens, re-call-ing by whom you were
made, Come, of-fer your wor-ship in bright-ness ar-rayed.

Text: Henry Williams Baker, 1875, et al.   VU #228
Tune: C. Hubert H. Parry, 1887

RUSTINGTON, named for the town where Parry died, was written for the *Westminster Abbey Hymn-Book* (London, 1897). It sings easily in a gradually rising progression that Parry nurtures well both melodically and harmonically.

RUSTINGTON
8 7 8 7 D

God, whose giv-ing knows no end-ing, From your rich and end-less store:
Na-ture's won-der, Je-sus' wis-dom, Cost-ly cross, grave's shat-tered door,
Gift-ed by you, we turn to you, Of-f'ring up our-selves in praise;

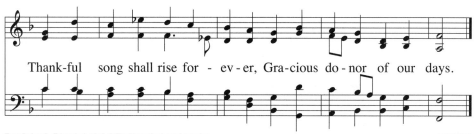

Thank-ful   song shall rise for - ev-er, Gra-cious do-nor of our days.

Text: Robert L. Edwards, b.1915, © The Hymn Society of America.   LBW #408
Tune: C. Hubert H. Parry, 1848-1918

JERUSALEM is the tune for which Parry is perhaps most famous. Routley heaps lavish praise on it, as breaking the rules yet a "flawless piece of melodic engineering" that "ordinary people are glad to sing," constructed "not by repetition but by intellectual development," and "the last great vulgar tune (in the most exalted sense) in music history."[18] Well, maybe. It is surely a fine melody, but some Americans resist it. Is that because of the Anglophilia of William Blake's poem "Jerusalem" ("And did those feet in ancient time") for which Parry wrote it in 1916? Carl Daw's text solves that problem, but may not remove the associations. At a more substantive level, is the melody finally more orchestral than congregational, with problems of length, range, and rhythm?

JERUSALEM
LMD

O day of peace   that dim-ly   shines   Through all our hopes and

prayers and   dreams, Guide us to   jus - tice, truth and love, De-liv-ered

from   our self - ish   schemes. May swords of   hate   fall from   our

hands,   Our hearts from   en - vy find re - lease,   Till by God's

grace   our war-ring world   Shall see Christ's prom-ised reign of peace.

Text: Carl P. Daw, Jr., *The Hymnal 1982*, 1985, Copyright © 1982, Hope Publishing Co.   HWB #408
Tune: Charles H. H. Parry, 1916

Henry Thomas Smart

Henry Thomas Smart (1813–1879), son of the violinist Henry Smart and nephew of George Smart, who was organist and composer at the Chapel Royal, moved in Presbyterian circles. Another excellent organist, improviser, and organ designer who gave up law to pursue a musical vocation, he wrote LANCASHIRE in 1836 for a mission festival to celebrate the 300th anniversary of the Reformation at the church he was serving, the Blackburn Parish Church in Lancashire.

LANCASHIRE
7 6 7 6 D

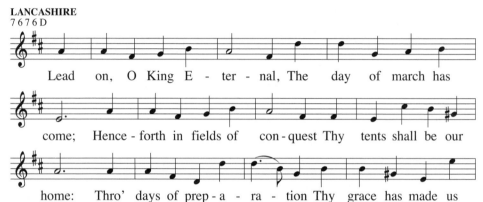

Text: Ernest W. Shurtleff, 1862-1917   Bap #621
Tune: Henry T. Smart, 1813-1879

LANCASHIRE was published along with another of Smart's vigorous tunes, REGENT SQUARE, in the Presbyterian hymnal *Psalms and Hymns for Divine Worship* (London, 1867). REGENT SQUARE was named for the next church Smart served, the "Presbyterian cathedral" of London, St. Philip's Regent Square Church. He and his pastor there edited *Psalms and Hymns*.

REGENT SQUARE
8 7 8 7 8 7 with refrain

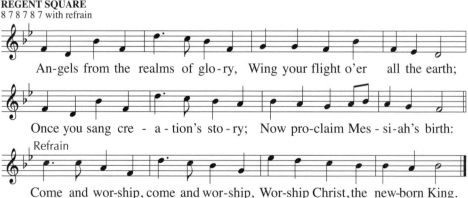

Text: James Montgomery, 1771-1854, abr., alt.   CW #80
Tune: Henry T. Smart, 1813-1879

Smart was regarded very highly in his time. He composed a number of other tunes that still appear in a few hymnals, but none so extensively as LANCASHIRE or REGENT SQUARE. Routley rightly calls him a "good congregational writer."[19]

John Goss

John Goss (1800–1880), son of the organist Joseph Goss, followed his teacher Thomas Attwood as organist at St. Paul's Cathedral and was himself followed there by John Stainer—the three comprising almost a century of service to that cathedral. (Attwood was at St. Paul's from 1796 until his death in 1838, Goss stayed until he retired in 1872, and Stainer resigned in 1888 because of his failing eyesight.) Goss taught harmony at the Royal Academy of Music, wrote a textbook to aid his teaching, and compiled church music publications in the typical "ancient and modern" line like *Chants, Ancient and Modern* (London, 1841). His tune PRAISE, MY SOUL (also called LAUDA ANIMA and BENEDIC ANIMA) was composed in 1868 for the text given below. It was published in Robert Brown-Borthwick's *Supplemental Hymn and Tune Book* (London, 1869) and entered the 1875 edition of *Hymns Ancient and Modern*. It has been praised as one of the finest, if not *the* finest of the Victorian hymn tunes, and certainly one of the most satisfying for congregations.[20] Though it may be perceived as symmetrical, its phrases are not quite parallel, which probably helps to account for its interest. The first phrase has five bars, the other ones four.

PRAISE, MY SOUL
878787

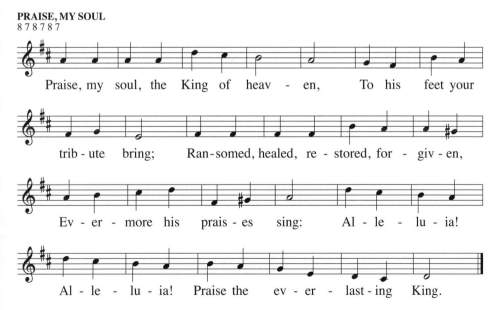

Text: Based on Psalm 103, Henry F. Lyte, 1793-1847, alt.   Cov #35
Tune: John Goss, 1800-1880

Joseph Barnby

On the surface, Joseph Barnby (1838–1896) appears to represent the Oxford-Cambridge point of view, but actually expresses a different mindset. A historical sketch of contrasts is needed to explain this.

When Barnby was but five years old in 1843, W. J. E. Bennett became the rector at St. Paul, Knightsbridge. Imbued with Oxford-Cambridge ideals, Bennett presided over a vigorous round of liturgical worship there[21] and also challenged his wealthy congregation on behalf of the poor. At the edge of his parish, next to the Thames River, there was a slum district called Pimlico. Bennett proposed that his people build a church for their neighbors. He thought the church should identify with the neighborhood by actually housing a college of priests, and he wanted a splendid example of what he deemed to be the finest architecture, furnishings, worship practices, and music of the period. His project was supported more amply than he expected, and, on June 11, 1850, the day of the commemoration of St. Barnabas, for whom the new church was named, an elaborate consecration took place. It was followed by a week of choral services with sermons by the Anglican Church's finest leaders—John Keble, Archdeacon Henry Edward Manning, John Mason Neale, Edward Pusey, and Bishop Samuel Wilberforce. Thomas Helmore was responsible for leading the music of both choir and congregation. The congregation was gently but surely invited to sing—which it did.[22]

Not all the Oxford-Cambridge partisans thought the people should sing, or at least were not agreed on what they should sing.[23] Helmore was committed to the congregation's singing of chant. He was not enamored by modern hymn tunes because he felt they smacked too much of cultural temptations.[24] He established a remarkable track record of helping congregations sing chant. It is not surprising that St. Barnabas in Pimlico, which shared his ideas, chose him to lead the music at the consecration.

Soon after St. Barnabas was consecrated, England was plunged into an anti-Roman Catholic agitation, "conditioned by centuries of misrepresentation," which confused "piety with patriotism."[25] When a Roman Catholic pastoral letter in October 1850 announced the "re-establishment" of twelve actual sees in England (instead of a vicars general who had been presiding over the few Roman Catholics in London as if they lived in an imaginary district), there was an outcry that mistakenly viewed this as a grab for real estate.[26] When the prime minister joined the fray, he worried more about the danger from within rather than from without and turned the protest from Rome to the Church of England. "At once the wrath of popular clamor was diverted from the Pope—who was safely out of reach—to the more accessible and vulnerable Tractarians."[27] St. Barnabas now became the symbol of what was to be attacked. On November

10, riots began in Pimlico. On December 8 they "reached a peak" when mobs broke down the doors of St. Barnabas and occupied "the church during the morning service."[28]

Thirteen years later, Benjamin Webb, the rector at St. Andrew's (Wells Street) appointed Joseph Barnby, in his twenties in 1863, to be the organist at this wealthy church. Benjamin Webb, along with John Mason Neale and E. J. Boyce, had been one of the founders of the undergraduate Cambridge Camden Society (later the Ecclesiological Society) in 1839. At the time, he had disapproved of Neale's interest in hymns,[29] and he and Neale did not follow parallel paths later.[30] Webb determined to give his people music and art comparable to what they heard in concert settings around them, at the Royal Academy or Covent Garden, for instance.[31] The result was an embrace of the trappings of the Oxford-Cambridge movement, even though Webb was not a ceremonialist, without its underlying ideals. Barnby and Webb developed "lavish choral services, which were really in the nature of sacred concerts."[32] A large paid and robed choir sang "fully choral" services of Roman Catholic Mass and motet music mostly by Charles Gounod, with "the words translated by Webb, and the music adapted by Barnby."[33] When Barnby went to St. Anne's, Soho, "despite a complete absence of Tractarian influence"[34] there, he continued these "on a still more ambitious scale" so that his services "soon gained the popular nickname of 'The Sunday Opera.'"[35] John Spencer Curwen, a music publisher who wrote a two volume set called *Studies in Worship Music*, reported that beyond "'a quiet hum'" there was "no congregational singing" at St. Anne's and a "'small stampede' after the anthem, as people left the church without attending the remainder of the service."[36]

Nevertheless, Barnby did write hymn tunes, albeit with choirs in mind. He consciously allied himself[37] to what he called the "modern feeling," the "natural style and idiom, so to speak, of our own time" even if it were "maudlin."[38] He was "shamelessly sentimental."[39] Not unexpectedly, as Routley points out, "few Victorian hymn tune writers wrote so much that has perished so quickly."[40] Or perhaps one should say Barnby is an example of how quickly so much that seems so popular at the moment perishes over time. Among his large musical output were 246 hymn tunes. They have proven more durable than his choral music which, after a period of popularity, disappeared. Like so many other writers, a few of his tunes are scattered here and there in one or two hymnals, but only one, LAUDES DOMINI, is in all fourteen of the hymnals we consulted. Though "in the style of a nineteenth-century part-song"[41] as was characteristic for Barnby, it is nonetheless one of his least typical and most congregational tunes, though it ends on the high tonic. He wrote it for the following text in the 1868 Appendix to *Hymns Ancient and Modern*.

LAUDES DOMINI
666666

When morn-ing gilds the skies, My heart a-wak-ing cries, May

Je-sus Christ be praised! A - like at work and prayer, One

pur-pose I de - clare: May Je - sus Christ be praised!

Text: *Katholisches Gesangbuch*, 1828, tr. Edward Caswall, 1854, alt., © 1992, The Pilgrim Press
Tune: Joseph Barnby, 1868   NC #86

MERRIAL (or EVENING or EMMELAR) shows how nineteenth-century chromatic harmony and a choral pillow inform Barnby's tunes. In the third measure, the chromaticism enters the tune itself, which is virtually a harmonic component rather than a melody. MERRIAL is attractive at first hearing, but singing it for six stanzas gets tedious and reveals its non-melodic and non-congregational character. Barnby published it in his *Original Tunes to Popular Hymns, for Use in Church and Home* (London, 1869) for the text given with it here.

MERRIAL
6565

Now the day is o - ver; Night is draw - ing nigh;

Shad-ows of the eve-ning Steal a-cross the sky.

Text: Sabine Baring-Gould, 1834-1924, alt.
Tune: Joseph Barnby, 1838-1896

LBW #280

O PERFECT LOVE
11 10 11 10

O per-fect Love, all hu-man thought tran - scend - ing,

Low - ly we kneel in prayer be - fore thy throne,

That theirs may be the love which knows no end - ing,

Whom thou in sa - cred vow dost join in one.

Text: Dorothy F. Gurney, 1883, alt.
Tune: Joseph Barnby, 1889

PsH #580

O PERFECT LOVE (or SANDRINGHAM) on the preceding page, started in 1889 as the first part of an anthem on the text that names it. It was composed for the Duke and Duchess of Fife and then entered hymnals as a hymn tune. (SANDRINGHAM was the name of the royal residence.) It is a testimony to Barnby's willingness to be "shamelessly sentimental," dependent on its harmonic envelope of chromatic movement and seventh chords—what, in Routley's definition of sentimental, could be termed a "short-cut to sensation that bypasses responsibility."[42] Sentimentality and other issues Barnby raises are addressed in the *Perspective* at the end of the next chapter.

H. Percy Smith

MARYTON "is a serviceable but generic nineteenth-century hymn tune"[43] that requires harmony, composed by the Church of England priest H. Percy Smith (1825–1898). It was originally paired with John Keble's hymn "Sun of My Soul, Thou Saviour Dear" in *Church Hymns with Tunes* (London, 1874). Washington Gladden chose this tune for his text, given below. The two are mostly known together.

MARYTON
LM

Text: Washington Gladden, 1879
Tune: H. Percy Smith, 1874

Meth #430

1   Named for St. Caecilia, an obscure early Christian martyr, who in the late fifteenth century began to be venerated as the patron saint of music and musicians.

2   This movement is often called the "Oxford Movement." I am using "Oxford-Cambridge," since Cambridge University had as strong a part as Oxford, especially via John Mason Neale and the Ecclesiological (late Cambridge Camden) Society.

3   Robert Chase, *Dies Irae: A Guide to Requiem Music* (Lanham: The Scarecrow Press, Ltd., 2003.

4   Johann Singenberger, *Orgelbuch zu J. Mohr's "Caecilia"* (Regensburg, Rom & New York: Friedrich Pustet, 1899).

5   Temperley, *The Music of the English Parish Church*, I, 314. See also Harry Eskew and Hugh T. McElrath, *Sing with Understanding* (Nashville: Church Street Press, 1995), 156–158, Routley's assessment in MCH, 92A–94B, and Young's summation in Young, CUMH, 15.

6   Routley, MCH, 105A. He also thought it was one of Wesley's "most commonplace and dreary tunes" (Nicholas Temperley, "The Church's One Foundation," Glover H82C, 3B, 984).

7   Temperley, "The Church's One Foundation," Glover H82C, 3B, 984.

8   Routley, MCH, 106A.

9   Elvey's anthem was "Bow Down Thine Ear," and Wesley's was "The Wilderness."

10   Routley, MCH, 98B–99A.

11   Bernarr Rainbow, *The Choral Revival in the Anglican Church* (1839–1872) (London: Barrie & Jenkins, 1970), 40.

12   See Routley, MCH, 100B–101A.

13   Young, CUMH, 361.

14   Ibid. (Routley, MCH, 91A.)

15   Routley, MCH, 99B.

16   Robert Scholz, correspondence, June 15, 2004.

17   Correspondence, August 31, 2004.

18   Ibid., 112A.

19   Ibid., 100B.

20   For more detail about Goss and PRAISE, MY SOUL, see Patrick Little, "Two Hymn Tunes by Sir John Goss," *Hymn Society of Great Britain and Ireland Bulletin* 235 17:2 (April 2003): 44–51.

21   Rainbow, *The Choral Revival in the Anglican Church*, 151, details this.

22   Ibid., 156.

23   John Jebb identified "choral service" with "cathedral service" at which the choir did the singing and not the "roar of the congregation" which he "felt to be opposed to propriety." Jebb thought unison psalm tones "exemplified the defects, not the advantages of antiquity." Frederick Oakeley, on the other hand, supported "Gregorian tones not only for their seemly antiquity, but because their simplicity made them available to all the people" (Rainbow, 31–32). He and Helmore stood against many professional musicians of the period, including S. S. Wesley and Henry Smart, who felt chant was a "retrogression to be resisted sternly" (Rainbow, 274f.).

24   Rainbow, *The Choral Revival in the Anglican Church*, 300.

25   Ibid., 145.

26   Ibid.

27   Ibid., 146.

28   Ibid., 160.

29   For a sketch of this history and Webb's part in it see Paul Westermeyer, "The Hymnal Noted: Theological and Musical Intersections," Church Music 73:2: 1–9 (especially 3–5).

30   See Rainbow, *The Choral Revival in the Anglican Church*, 276–277.

31   Ibid., 277.

32   Nicholas Temperley, "Barnby, Sir Joseph," GDMM 2, 166.

33   Ibid.

34   Rainbow, *The Choral Revival in the Anglican Church*, 279.

35   Nicholas Temperley, "Barnby, Sir Joseph," GDMM 2, 166.

36   Rainbow, *The Choral Revival in the Anglican Church*, 279.

37   Routley, MCH, 101–102, gives a good overview of his perspective with quotations from Barnby himself.

38   Ibid., 101B.

39   Ibid., 102B.

40   Ibid., 101A.

41   Raymond Glover, "When Morning Gilds the Skies," Glover, H82C, 3B, 801.

42   Routley, *Church Music and the Christian Faith*, 94.

43   Brink and Polman, PsHH, 749.

X. NINETEENTH-CENTURY ENGLISH TUNES 2

John Bacchus Dykes

John Bacchus Dykes (1823–1876) stands at the center of Victorian hymn tunes. In 1861 all seven of the tunes he submitted to *Hymns Ancient and Modern*—among them two of his most famous, NICAEA and MELITA—were included. In the 1875 edition, the number had risen to 57, "an eightfold multiplication," as Routley notes, "while the hymnal itself expanded by 75 percent, from 273 to 473 hymns."[1] After his death 276 of his tunes were published. Haeussler says he wrote 300.[2] A remarkable number of them remain in use, though somewhat fewer of late. Dykes provided "the largest single source of hymn tunes" for the Episcopal *Hymnal 1940*, where twenty-two of his tunes were used with twenty-seven texts.[3] In the Episcopal *Hymnal 1982*, ten of his tunes were used with twelve texts,[4] still a substantial number. In the fourteen hymnals we consulted, there are nineteen tunes by Dykes used eighty-nine times,[5] also a substantial number—among them BEATITUDO,[6] DOMINUS REGIT ME,[7] O QUANTA QUALIA,[8] ST. CROSS,[9] and VOX DILECTI.[10] "He captured the secret for which congregations were waiting as surely as Luther captured the secret of the Reformation," says Routley, and then adds that "the further we get from him in time the more impressive his place in history becomes."[11]

By the time he was ten, Dykes was the organist at the church where his grandfather was the vicar, St. John's, Hull. In 1849 he became minor canon and precentor at the Durham Cathedral, and, from 1862, vicar at St. Oswald's in Durham. Like John Mason Neale and W. J. E. Bennett, he was a Tractarian who was treated badly by his bishop. He lived in the north of England, not in London as one might expect, and he wrote for the parish, not the cathedral.

If S. S. Wesley's AURELIA is the "quintessential" Victorian tune, NICAEA is the "archetypal" one.[12] Those adjectives may seem synonymous, but "quintessential" suggests the most concentrated embodiment, whereas "archetypal" suggests the pattern from which copies are made. Those descriptions accurately fit the two tunes. In AURELIA, S. S. Wesley embodied the style of the period, whereas NICAEA typifies it as a template. NICAEA is probably Dykes' best-known tune, but also his least typical. Routley suggested "it is the only tune of Dykes which in any sense reaches back into history," the one for which he drew on "the common coin of hymnody, which elsewhere he hardly ever does."[13] Written for Heber's "Holy, Holy, Holy," and named for Nicaea where the Nicene Creed was formulated in 325, its opening triad (related tonally by some to the Trinity) has reminded commentators of WAUCHET AUF. Leaver points to its similarities with Psalm Tone 5 and two contemporaneous tunes.[14] Structurally it

Tone 5

consists of two two-phrase groups that modulate to the dominant and two two-phrase groups that go back to the tonic, the second set beginning like the first and concluding with material that answers the midstream dominant: ([2 + 2] + [2 + 2, dominant]) + ([2 + 2] + [2 + 2, tonic]).

NICAEA
11 12 12 10

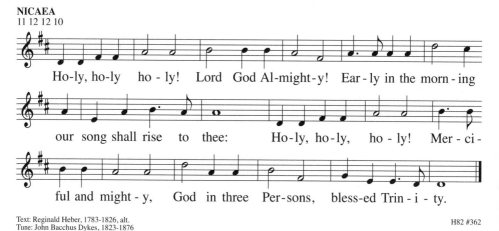

Ho-ly, ho-ly ho - ly! Lord God Al-might-y! Ear - ly in the morn - ing our song shall rise to thee: Ho-ly, ho-ly, ho - ly! Mer - ci-ful and might - y, God in three Per-sons, bless-ed Trin - i - ty.

Text: Reginald Heber, 1783-1826, alt.
Tune: John Bacchus Dykes, 1823-1876

H82 #362

MELITA is the name of the island where Paul was shipwrecked (Acts 28:1–2). It was written for William Whiting's "Navy Hymn." Though there are brief occurrences of octaves (as in ST. CROSS and VOX DILECTI, for example[15]) that serve as contrasts in the part-song-like hymns Dykes constructed, MELITA stays in four parts throughout. Dykes' tunes are not unlike what Barnby wrote. Chromaticism even sneaks into the melody of MELITA. Dykes was clearly a Romantic, as LUX BENIGNA[16] demonstrates even more obviously than MELITA, and he did not escape one of the Romantic snares that Routley isolated so well, writing "'listener's music' . . . better performed by a choral group than a congregation."[17] Routley also gave the clue to the difference in Dykes, however, when he said,

> What is remarkable about Dykes, when one investigates the church music by which he was surrounded, is not his extravagance, but his restraint. If sometimes he does side-slip, surprisingly often what he celebrates is the more lovable qualities of romanticism.[18]

In Routley's view, Dykes, unlike Barnby, was not "shamelessly sentimental."

Though a four-part choral underlay is at work here, the conception is fundamentally congregational. As Marilyn Stulken says, "the whole harmonic package" of a tune like this, including the color of its chromaticism, "does not impede congregational singing [but] enhances it."[19] It is structured in three two-phrase groups.

MELITA
8 8 8 8 8 8

E - ter - nal Fa - ther, strong to save, Whose arm has bound the rest - less wave, Who bade the might - y o - cean deep Its own ap - point - ed lim - its keep: O hear us when we cry to Thee For those in per - il on the sea.

Text: William Whiting, 1860; alt.
Tune: John Bachus Dykes, 1861

Pres #562

253

ST. AGNES, composed for "Jesus, the Very Thought of Thee," first appeared in *A Hymnal for Use in the English Church* (London, 1866) before it entered the *Appendix* to *Hymns Ancient and Modern* in 1868. This sweet tune moves in a more sentimental direction than the other two. Routley's definition of sentimental as a "short-cut to sensation that bypasses responsibility"[20] is not quite applicable to this tune, which might be seen as having the more "lovable" qualities of Romanticism and is not badly crafted, but the move toward quiet "sensation" is nonetheless present. The diminished fifth worms itself around the tonic at the end of the first phrase, the three repeated notes serve to make the upward leap of a major sixth emotive in the second, and the downward scale of the third phrase around the ubiquitous Romantic dominant seventh sets up the precious character of the final phrase.

ST. AGNES, like MERRIAL and MARYTON at the end of the last chapter, all point up a "Victorian habit of starting out with a lot of repeated notes."[21] In a tune like LEOMINSTER,[22] this habit can be tedious.

ST. AGNES
CM

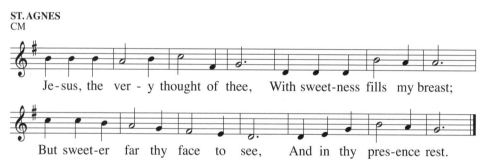

Je-sus, the ver - y thought of thee,   With sweet-ness fills my breast;

But sweet-er far thy face to see,   And in thy pres-ence rest.

Text: Attr. Bernard of Clairvaux, 12th c.; tr. Edward Caswall, 1849
Tune: John B. Dykes, 1866

Chal #102

John Antes and John Wilkes

The outlines of nineteenth-century tunes that come from or through England are clear now. Additional examples will add color to the picture. MONKLAND comes through the first edition in 1861 of *Hymns Ancient and Modern* but is an eighteenth-century tune with a circuitous history and several arrangers, not a single composer. It started in Freylinghausen's *Geistreiches Gesangbuch* (1704), was modified by the Moravian John Antes (1740–1811) around 1800, passed through John Lees in the Moravian hymnal called *Hymn Tunes of the United Brethren* (1824), and was further simplified by John Wilkes (d. 1882). Wilkes was the organist of the Monkland parish where he knew Henry W. Baker, the vicar there and the editor who put MONKLAND in *Hymns Ancient and Modern*.

MONKLAND
7 7 7 7

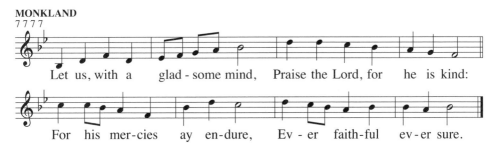

Let us, with a glad - some mind, Praise the Lord, for he is kind:

For his mer-cies ay en-dure, Ev - er faith-ful ev - er sure.

Text: John Milton, 1608-1674
Tune: melody from Freylinghausen's *Geistreiches Gesanbuch*, 1704; adapt. John Antes, 1740-1811   H82 #389

Johann Werner

RATISBON is a tune that came through the first (1861) edition of *Hymns Ancient and Modern* and was passed to other English hymnals. It is usually traced to the German organist Johann Werner (1777–1822), who published it in his *Choralbuch zu den neuen fächsichen Gesangbüchern vierstimmig für die Orgel* (Leipzig, 1815). As Robin Leaver has shown, however, it is "a good illustration of the way in which new tunes are created from old ones and how a tune in one tradition is modified when taken over for use in another."[23] Leaver traces it as follows. Its origins are in a fifteenth-century German Marian folk hymn, which Luther, leaving the melody unchanged, adapted to a Trinitarian hymn, "Gott der Vater wohn uns bei." Luther's text named the melody. The hymn and tune remain in the Lutheran repertoire[24] and had English versions in Coverdale's *Goostly Psalmes* (London, ca. 1536) and Jacobi's *Psalmodia Germanica* (1722). Werner took the A part of the AABBC melody, wrote a new B section, and made a bar form tune. Henry Havergal (1793–1870), an Anglican priest who sought to improve congregational song and brought German chorales to England, simplified Werner's work and published it in *Old Church Psalmody* (London, 1847). From there it passed into *Hymns Ancient and Modern* and beyond.

RATISBON
7 7 7 7 7 7

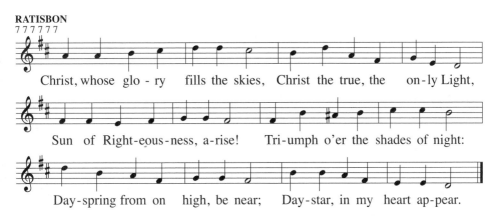

Christ, whose glo - ry fills the skies, Christ the true, the on-ly Light,

Sun of Right-eous-ness, a-rise! Tri-umph o'er the shades of night:

Day-spring from on high, be near; Day-star, in my heart ap-pear.

Text: Charles Wesley, 1707-1788
Tune: *Geystliche gesangk Buchleyn*, 1524; adapt. att. William Henry Havergal, 1793-1870   H82 #7

Frederick Cook Atkinson

MORECAMBE (originally HELLESPONT) is characteristic once more of a nineteenth-century single hand, Frederick Cook Atkinson (1841–1896). Though we usually use the tune for the hymn given below, he wrote it in 1870 to go with "Abide with Me" for "the church in Manningham, England" where he was the organist.[25] It first appeared in the *Congregational Church Hymnal* (London, 1887).

MORECAMBE
10 10 10 10

Spir - it of God, de - scend up - on my heart; Wean it from earth; thro' all its puls-es move; Stoop to my weak-ness, might-y as Thou art, And make me love Thee as I ought to love.

Text: George Croly, 1780-1860
Tune: Frederick C. Atkinson, 1841-1897

Bap #245

Frederick C. Maker

Frederick C. Maker (1844–1927), a chorister at the cathedral in Bristol, became the organist at Milk Street Methodist Free Church, Clifton Downs Congregational Church, and Redland Park Congregational Church in that city. He also taught at Clifton College. Two of his tunes are still in use, REST and ST. CHRISTOPHER.

"Dear Lord and Father of Mankind" has recently been viewed as sexist, but the more basic question is whether it should be a hymn at all, mined as it is from John Greenleaf Whittier's "The Brewing of Soma" (and having what is a deeper problem, the line that refers to "the silence of eternity"[26]). If you think the hymn belongs in the repertoire, the quietly chromatic tune REST fits it. It raises the usual nineteenth-century problems of harmony, choral conception, and push toward the sentimental. Text and tune were set together in the *Congregational Hymnal* (London, 1887), but the tune apparently comes from its composer's earlier collection, *The New Tune Book for Special Hymns* (n. d.) where it went with "There Is an Hour of Peaceful Rest."

REST
86886

Dear Lord and Fa - ther of man - kind, For -

give our fool - ish ways; Re - clothe us in our

right - ful mind, In pur - er lives thy

serv - ice find, In deep - er rev - erence, praise.

Text: John Greenleaf Whittier, 1872
Tune: Frederick C. Maker, 1887

Meth #358

ST. CHRISTOPHER was written for Elizabeth Cecilia Clephane's text for the 1881 Supplement to *The Bristol Tune Book* (Bristol, 1863). In it harmony is completely in control, not only by way of chromaticism, but with an augmented fourth that has now found its way into the tune itself at the beginning of the last line. An augmented fourth, even in a nineteenth-century harmonic context, is no easy matter for congregations. It works here because Maker has driven the melody up to B-flat near the end of the third line in such a way that the longing for the C-natural above it forms a completion that runs through the augmented fourth.

257

ST. CHRISTOPHER
76868686

Be - neath the cross of Je - sus I long to take my stand;

The shad - ow of a might - y rock With - in a wea - ry land,

A home with-in a wil - der-ness, A rest up - on the way,

From the burn-ing of the noon-tide heat And bur-dens of the day.

Text: Elizabeth Cecilia Clephane, 1868, alt.
Tune: Frederick C. Maker, 1881

Mor #329

Henri Hemy and James Walton

ST. CATHERINE is tied to the text, "Faith of Our Fathers," which has been popular among Protestants even though the "Fathers" its author celebrated were probably understood as persecuted English Roman Catholic priests. The tune comes from the second part of *Crown of Jesus Music* (London, 1864), edited by Henri F. Hemy (1818–1888), who was the organist at St. Andrew's Roman Catholic Church in Newcastle. James G. Walton (1821–1905) took the first part of the melody, added new material, and published it as altered in his *Plainsong Music for the Holy Communion Office* (London, 1874). Though not the best of the nineteenth-century tunes, it is a buoyant product of the period.

ST. CATHERINE
LM with refrain

Faith of our fa - thers! liv - ing still In spite of dun - geon,
fire and sword: O how our hearts beat high with joy,
When-e'er we hear that glo - rious word: Faith of our fa - thers,
ho - ly faith! We will be true to thee till death.

Text: Frederick W. Faber, 1814-1863, alt.   Wor3 #571
Tune: Henry F. Hemy, 1818-1888; adapt. James G. Walton, 1821-1905

Clement Cotterill Scholefield

ST. CLEMENT, which Routley calls "an obstinately immortal tune,"[27] begins with an upward major sixth. That opening interval and the whole tune are regarded by some as archetypically cloying. What makes an upward major sixth and a tune more or less emotive and more or less objectionable is partly a matter of context and partly a matter of opinion. I see the sixth here—followed immediately up a second, then back down a second, and then up to the octave (and not preceded by repeated notes in order to prepare for a passionate leap)— as setting up a sweeping arc rather than creating an emotively open upward hole.

ST. CLEMENT
9 8 9 8

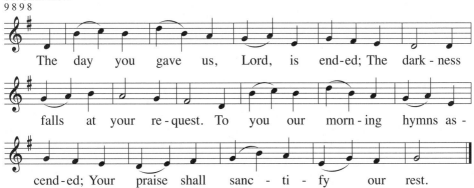

The day you gave us, Lord, is end-ed; The dark - ness
falls at your re - quest. To you our morn - ing hymns as -
cend-ed; Your praise shall sanc - ti - fy our rest.

Text: John Ellerton, 1826-1893, abr., alt.   CW #594
Tune: Clement C. Scholefield, 1839-1904

Its repetition is answered in the second half by a satisfying modification of the first answer. This melody was written for John Ellerton's text, included in *Church Hymns with Tunes* (London, 1874), and the next year passed into *Hymns Ancient and Modern*. Its composer, Clement Cotterill Scholefield (1839–1904), was the son of a member of parliament, a parish priest, and a composer of numerous hymn tunes.

Arthur Sullivan

Arthur Sullivan (1842–1900), who, with the librettist William Gilbert (1836–1911) is famous for "Gilbert and Sullivan operettas," was the son of a bandmaster. He became a prolific composer and conductor as well as a church organist (at St. Michael's, Chester Square, London, and St. Peter's, Cranley Gardens). He also wrote tunes for hymns, fifty-nine of which found their way into his *Hymn Tunes* (London, 1902). ST. GERTRUDE was written in 1871 for Baring-Gould's unfortunate "holy war" text and fits it too well. This successful pairing gives credence to C. S. Lewis' sense that hymnody represents the gang songs of the church (or, in Routley's characterization, having a "good shout"[28]). Routley sees ST. GERTRUDE as "a first-rate march for a choir of local Lestrades," since Sullivan was "an energetic choirmaster in his London churches [who] built up a choir from almost nothing by recruiting men from the local police force."[29] Sullivan was also a skillful and leading composer of his day. He studied with Thomas Helmore and John Goss, though his hymn tunes recall the stage rather than what one associates with those teachers. FORTUNATUS[30] is another of his tunes.

Routley is not complimentary about Sullivan, whom he regarded as related to show business. He called his tunes "as a group . . . by far the worst, the least sincere, the most pretentious and misconceived, of any written by a major Victorian composer."[31] Temperley has a different idea. He calls ST. GERTRUDE "one of the greatest of all hymn tunes in its ability to arouse feeling and high spirit."[32] The difference of opinion here is partly about how one understands craft and partly about what one thinks hymn tunes ought to do.

ST. GERTRUDE
6 5 6 5 D with refrain

On - ward, Chris - tian   sol - diers,   March - ing   as   to   war,

With the cross of Je - sus Go - ing on be - fore.

Christ, the roy - al mas - ter, Leads a - gainst the foe;

For - ward in - to bat - tle See his ban - ners go!

Refrain

On - ward, Chris - tian sol - diers, March - ing as to war,

With the cross of Je - sus Go - ing on be - fore.

Text: Sabine Baring-Gould, 1865, alt.   PsH #522
Tune: Arthur S. Sullivan, 1871

In order to "elucidate how much of the attraction of the hymn derives from the tune," Carl Daw suggests an instructive comparison of ST. GERTRUDE with the tune HAYDN, which is paired with Baring-Gould's text in *The English Hymnal*.[33]

HAYDN
6 5 6 5 Ter.

On-ward, Christ-ian sold-iers, March-ing as to war, With the Cross of

Je - sus Go-ing on be - fore. Christ the ro-yal Mas-ter Leads a-

gainst the foe; For-ward in - to bat - tle, See, his ban-ners go!

Text: S. Baring-Gould, 1834-1924
Tune: Adapted from F. J. Haydn, 1732-1809

EH #643

"The ABA structure of the tune [HAYDN, adapted from F. Haydn]," says Daw, "keeps it from having much forward movement. ST. GERTRUDE, by contrast, uses the stanza settings to build anticipation (like marching in place) before the vigorous movement of the refrain."[34] The marching in place is generated by the bass line of the accompaniment as much as by the tune. One might add that HAYDN is more childlike (the hymn written was for children), which takes away the text's sense of killing the enemy, counter to Jesus' instruction in Matthew 5:44 and Luke 6:27. One can, of course, as in Ephesians 6:10–17, interpret the warfare as not against flesh and blood, but against cosmic powers and spiritual forces; but when a hymn like this is sung to a tune like ST. GERTRUDE, such distinctions are easily lost, especially in times of war when they are most needed. Hymns like "A Mighty Fortress" have been misused in the same way.

Alexander Reinagle

ST. PETER is a little off the nineteenth-century beaten path and looks more to the eighteenth century. In so doing it points to the breadth *Hymns Ancient and Modern* encompassed. Its composer, Alexander Reinagle (1799–1877), was born in Brighton, East Sussex, but came from an Austrian musical family. He was the organist in Oxford at St. Peter-in-East. He wrote this tune around 1830 for Psalm 118, then reharmonized it for inclusion in the 1861 edition of *Hymns Ancient and Modern*.

ST. PETER
8 6 8 6

How sweet the name of Je-sus sounds In a be-liev-er's ear! It soothes the sor-rows, heals the wounds, And drives a-way all fear.

Text: John Newton, 1779, alt.   VU #344
Tune: Alexander Robert Reinagle, ca. 1830

John Stainer

THE FIRST NOEL (or THE FIRST NOWELL) is again off the nineteenth-century beaten path, but affords a chance to mention John Stainer (1840–1901), who harmonized it. The tune was paired with its well-known text in William Sandys' *Christmas Carols, Ancient and Modern* (London, 1833) and is generally assumed to be from the eighteenth century. It is an unusual tune in that it repeats the same material twice, then starts to repeat it again in the refrain and only veers off slightly before continuing the repeat. It ends curiously on the third, not the tonic. Some commentators have suggested it is a piece of another tune or may be a descant that turned into a tune. Since John Stainer harmonized it for *Christmas Carols New and Old* (London, 1871), it has been widely used.

THE FIRST NOEL
Irregular with refrain

The first No - el, the an - gel did say, Was to cer-tain poor
In fields where they lay keep-ing their sheep, On a cold win-ter's

shep - herds in fields as they lay   No - el, No -
night that was so deep.

Refrain

el, No - el, No - el, Born is the King of Is - ra - el.

Text: English carol, *Some Ancient Christmas Carols*, 2nd ed., 1823   HWB #199
Tune: English carol, *Christmas Carols*, 1833

Stainer, though sometimes best known and maligned for his "God So Loved the World" from *The Crucifixion*, was a respected musician, composer, and musicologist. He made necessary reforms when he became organist at St. Paul's Cathedral; created a fine choir there; taught at Oxford University; wrote books on harmony, the history of music, and music in relation to the Bible and the emotions; and edited a number of books, including *Hymns Ancient and Modern* after 1870. Routley calls him modest in contrast to Sullivan.[35] He wrote over 150 hymn tunes—published in *Collected Hymn Tunes* (London, 1900)—but only a few of them appear occasionally in our hymnals today. PER RECTE ET RETRO is not likely ever to be found in any hymnal, but testifies to Stainer's skill. As its name suggests ("Through leading straight and back"), it is a musical palindrome. Both melodically and harmonically it is exactly the same going forward as going backward, possibly the only such hymn tune in existence. It serves as a useful reminder that the nineteenth century was not only a Romantic stew that Stainer represented, but included skillful craftspersons whom Stainer also represented.

PER RECTE ET RETRO

Tune: J. Stainer, c. 1898   MCH Ex. 340 (corrected)

Robert Jackson

TRENTHAM, a nondescript tune mildly representative of the late nineteenth-century chromatic harmonic tradition, is a good place to end. It was named for a village in Staffordshire, England, near its composer's birthplace. Robert Jackson (1842–1914) wrote it for Henry Baker's "O Perfect Life of Love," and the two were published together in *Fifty Sacred Leaflets* (1888). In the United States it has usually been paired with "Breathe on Me, Breath of God." (The length of service Jackson and his father gave as organists at St. Peter's in Oldham, England, is pretty remarkable. Robert was there for forty-six years, from 1868 to 1914, and his father there for the previous forty-eight.)

TRENTHAM
6 6 8 6

Breathe on me, Breath of God, Fill me with life a-new, That I may love what Thou dost love, And do what Thou wouldst do.

Text: Edwin Hatch, 1835-1889
Tune: Robert Jackson, 1840-1914

Bap #241

Perspective: Further Threats to the People's Song

Translations of old hymns plus newly written ones made nineteenth-century *hymns* ancient as well as modern. Though chant and other older tunes were not forgotten, the center of gravity for nineteenth-century *tunes* tended to be mostly modern, with the defects of their period that have been noted—mired in Romantic harmony and a choral model or beset by dullness, nationalism, militarism, and show business. Many of them, nonetheless, were well crafted and have done yeoman service, for which the church needs to be grateful. The nineteenth-century composers whose hymn tunes we still use forged melodies that have helped the church sing in widely scattered places and in various ways. Though nineteenth-century English tunes have controlled and still control too much of the musical vocabulary of hymn singing in the English-speaking world, we owe their composers our gratitude. However, the nineteenth century has also passed defects on to us. Joseph Barnby, whom Routley calls "perhaps the most notorious 'Victorian' of them all," signals them most obviously. These defects are deeper threats to the people's singing than Barnby's alone, however, and bigger than any single person. They need to be faced and named.

1) In Barnby we encounter the same problem Lock Hospital posed in the eighteenth century, only then it was in an evangelical wing of the church among Methodists. Here it is in a liturgical wing among Anglicans. The problem is the same: the congregation's musical office versus the emotive and entertaining excess of the moment, which denies that office. The fundamental question has to do with the nature of Christian worship. Congregational hymn tunes and their texts bring with them the presupposition that Christian worship is about the baptized people who take up their priestly office and sing around font,

Word, meal, and daily prayer. Barnby starts from another presupposition, that the people are to be entertained as largely silent spectators at worship.

The question is posed not only by Barnby in the nineteenth century or by Lock Hospital and Madan in the eighteenth, but by village bands and choirs in the eighteenth, by some organists and choir directors in many periods, by clergy in many periods, by medieval priests and choirs before the Reformation, and by similar movements in our day where worship is treated as entertainment and a means to attract people.[36] Though the musical styles differ, the presuppositions are the same. In our "postmodern" period, the case is repeatedly made that we inhabit a new paradigm with attractive, entertaining worship forms that have never been tried before. This assumption is false. There may be a difference in degree because of the ferocity of our consumerism, but there is nothing new here. The English poet Alexander Pope (1688–1744) isolated this point of view long ago when he said, "Some to church repair, Not for the doctrine, but the music there."[37] In nineteenth-century dress the same perspective was expressed with this sarcasm.

> If pulpit utterance won't suffice
> To win the people from their sins,
> You'll find a method more concise
> Than preaching: play on violins.
> Or, if you see devotion sinks
> Beneath the organ's solemn tones,
> Increase th' attractions of your jinks,
> And to the fiddles add trombones.[38]

With such intentions the people are mistreated and silenced.

2) The sentimental, as Routley says, a "short-cut to sensation that bypasses responsibility,"[39] is an inevitable component of this perspective, at least from the nineteenth century onward. It lands us perilously close to the "lies and cunningly devised fables" that Paul says Christians have renounced.[40] There are exceptions where Christians sing the sentimental and still remember who they are and what they have to do, but the perspective itself has the danger of "cunningly" seducing and silencing them. It all too easily makes them forget their baptismal birthright along with their responsibility for the widow and the orphan. Both musicians and congregation become objects for false manipulation and comfortable insulation. The Christian Gospel expressed in congregational song frees them from just such manipulation and insulation.

3) Barnby, for all his sentimentality, performed some remarkably fine music—Handel's oratorios and Beethoven's *Missa Solemnis*—for which he is to be congratulated. The problem, as for Lock Hospital, comes when this or any music is used as a concert to substitute for worship. (To substitute for worship is at issue here, not concerts, which have their own value.) Barnby also performed Bach's Passions. Turning Bach's church music into a concert, while certainly possible and valuable, nonetheless brings its own problems: it avoids the music's proclamatory character as part of the liturgy and hides the congregational hymnic underlay Bach presumed.

4) Sentimentality brings with it the importance or even the centrality of feelings, so that Christianity stands or falls on how people feel, a most uncertain foundation. Music becomes the means to induce the feelings and the congregation a silent receptacle for them.

5) Wealth is an inevitable component of Barnby's perspective. Money can be used to support both the finest music and the finest congregational participation as in Bach's congregations in Leipzig (though Bach legitimately complained at times about a lack of the resources he needed). Too often, however, those with ample supplies of money shut out those without money and shut out the song in the process. It is the wealthy nineteenth- or twentieth-century city church, or the wealthy suburban one in our period, where the temptation has been strongest for worship to become a concert (in various styles, all of which operate from the same underlying presupposition), where musical entertainment takes away the people's song. The church's confession stands against this practice: people with and without ample supplies of money are welcomed to the feast of the church's worship and to its song. All that is needed are water, words about the incarnate Word, a morsel of bread, a sip of wine, and some simple unison lines. When wealthy, in-group musical activity used for entertainment takes that away, congregations are silenced.

It is difficult to untangle the forces that propelled the mob at Pimlico, as it is to disentangle all group violence. Prejudice against Roman Catholics and pent up anger of one class against another were certainly involved. Though they invariably affect it, issues like that are not basically about hymn singing, and causes are complex. One cannot but observe, however, that the violence took place in a financially poor neighborhood where the Oxford-Cambridge posture worked itself out in its characteristic support for the neighborhood's people and their singing as part of the church catholic. In Barnby's wealthy congregation a few years later, the absence of congregational song allied with entertainment and the trappings, but not the undergirding, of the Oxford-Cambridge ideals provoked no demonstrations. That is, support of the people's song, as of the poor and dispossessed, is not necessarily popular and may well engender the same antagonism the Christian Gospel itself engenders. As the Oxford-Cambridge people discovered—just like Benedictines, Lutherans, Calvinists, and other parts of the church[41]—the people's song requires discipline and work from a congregation and its leaders,[42] not unlike the discipleship of the rest of the Christian life. The middle class, or any class, can view congregational participation and discipleship as beneath them[43] and can un-do their very own birthright.

6) Organs and choirs in this period, just like bands and choirs in the eighteenth century, were tempted to take over the people's song. The original Oxford-Cambridge idea was for choirs to help the congregation sing.[44] As pipe organs replaced west gallery bands and barrel organs in the second half of the nineteenth century, they, along with choirs, often substituted for the congregations as at St. Andrew's. Bishop Charles Gore was finally driven to say, "In most parishes we have fallen, I know not how, under the despotism of choirs."[45] Nineteenth-century English hymn tunes do not have to imply that despotism, but they have not always been used as their congregational presuppositions imply. The church today is still not free from this or the other perversions noted here.

7) It might be argued that Barnby and Webb, or medieval priests and choirs, retained the liturgy and, therefore, in a curious way, not only called into question their own wealth, but supported the people's singing no matter what their practice looked like on the surface. There is some truth in that argument. When the liturgical bones of the church's worship remain, the lectionary keeps telling the whole story, words related to the lessons make the Incarnate Word hard to avoid, the ecumenical creeds point to the center of the faith, sacraments bring with them an inevitable incarnational dimension that calls forth a concern for the physical needs of the world, and the people's song is presupposed even though it may be denied in practice. The Protestant temptation to forget the liturgy has all too often highlighted the pastor or musician at the expense of the people, obliterated lessons and ecumenical creeds, turned the word into travelogues or inner psychological journeys, pushed sacraments into the background, and shut out the people's song even when the rhetoric has said otherwise. In short, it is true that the liturgy

does provide protections for the people and their singing, at least in principle. Fair enough, but none of that justifies hijacking the liturgy and the people's musical office for purposes of entertainment or anything else.

8) Power politics are often associated with the kinds of movements that entertain. Those who propel them (since motives can never be sorted out, we have to assume that their concerns are genuinely directed beyond themselves) think that by their efforts they can attract people, remake the church into their image, and save it. This faulty ecclesiological assumption leads entertainers to force their wills on others. The song of the church catholic always leads to more humility than that.[46] The church is always constrained not only to champion worship but to acknowledge a lack of certainty about any schemes and programs—musical or otherwise—because it realizes that all of them are shot through with sin. That is why it seldom wins the battles of power politics, but instead goes on quietly about its business of singing and caring for the neighbor in the certainty that in Christ the war has already been won. That the church has continued to sing in the midst of the hostile conflicts that have torn it apart, even when its voice has been weak and weary, is itself a testimony to the grace of God. As Paul knew, "Power is made perfect in weakness."[47]

---

1   Routley, MCH, 98A–B.
2   Haeussler, *The Story of Our Hymns*, 636.
3   "Dykes, John Bacchus," Glover, H82C, 409.
4   Ibid.
5   Here is a comparison, which also shows how often we use Victorian tunes:
      Barnby, 11 tunes used 49 times,
      Elvey, 3 tunes used 51 times,
      Gauntlett, 6 tunes used 19 times,
      Goss, 4 tunes used 31 times,
      Monk, 9 tunes used 33 times,
      Redhead, 3 tunes used 22 times,
      Smart, 9 tunes used 60 times,
      Stainer, 4 tunes used 7 times,
      Sullivan, 8 tunes used 31 times,
      C. H. Parry, 5 tunes used 49 times, and
      S. S. Wesley, 7 tunes used 41 times.
6   PsH #551.
7   Cov #84.
8   LBW #337.
9   VU #136.

10 Bap #551.

11 Routley, MCH, 95A.

12 Robin Leaver, "Holy, Holy, Holy! Lord God Almighty!" Glover, H82C, 3A, 668.

13 Routley, MCH, 97A.

14 Leaver, "Holy, Holy, Holy!" 669–670.

15 This characteristic is not only present in Dykes' tunes. Either Dykes (Routley, MCH, 85B) or Monk (Carl Schalk, "We plow the field and scatter," Glover H82C, 3A, 562) arranged WIR PFLUGEN (H82 #291) that way for Hymns Ancient and Modern.

16 VU #640. Arthur Hutchings compares it with Barnby's Sweet and Low [Arthur Hutchings, "Dykes, John Bacchus," NGDMM, 5, 794].

17 Routley, MCH, 96B.

18 Ibid., 96A.

19 Marilyn Stulken, correspondence, June 17, 2004.

20 Routley, Church Music and the Christian Faith, 94.

21 Correspondence with Austin Lovelace, August 28, 2004.

22 LBW 489, Mor 604.

23 Robin Leaver, "Christ, Whose Glory Fills the Sky," Glover, H82C, 3A, 11.

24 CW #192, LBW #308. (The first line is exactly the same as RATISBON.)

25 Fred D. Gealy, Austin Lovelace, Carlton R. Young, and Emery Stevens Bucke, Companion to the Hymnal: A Handbook to the 1964 Methodist Hymnal (Nashville: Abingdon, 1970), 379.

26 Robert W. Jenson says there is no "silence of eternity" because the Trinity is "eternally speech" (correspondence, September 30, 2004). He also argues that God is "eternally music." See Robert W. Jenson, Systematic Theology, Volume 1, The Triune God (Oxford: Oxford University Press, 1997), 234–236.

27 Routley, MCH, 107B.

28 Erik Routley, "Correspondence with an Anglican Who Dislikes Hymns," The Presbyter 6:2 (Second Quarter 1948): 17.

29 Routley, MCH, 104A.

30 LBW #153.

31 Routley, MCH, 104B.

32 Nicholas Temperley, "Onward, Christian Soldiers," Glover, H82C, 3B, 1040.

33 Correspondence from Carl Daw, May 28, 2004.

34 Ibid.

35 Routley, MCH,104A.

36 Routley, Church Music and the Christian Faith, 68, has an interesting comment about using music to attract "the uncoverted." It "is likely," he says, "to fall into the same error we find in the person who, in order to make users of bad language feel at home, uses bad language himself."

37 Quoted in Rainbow, 278.

38 Ibid.

39 Routley, Church Music and the Christian Faith, 94.

40 See 2 Corinthians 4:2.

41 See, for example, Witvliet, Worship Seeking Understanding, 210.

42 See Rainbow, 266 and 278.

43 Ibid., 266.

44 Rainbow, 269.

45 Ibid., 280. Routley, MCH, 141A, attests to the same problem.

46 See Rowan Williams, "Augustine and the Psalms," Interpretation 58:1 (January 2004): 17–27, where Williams continually notes in Augustine's understanding of the psalms—which are the womb of the church's song—the recurrent theme of humility.

47 See 2 Corinthians 12:9b.

XI. American Spirituals

1. White Spirituals[1]

In the early part of the eighteenth century New England ministers like Thomas Walter (1696–1725), Thomas Symmes (1677–1725), and John Tufts (1689–1750) became concerned about the state of congregational singing. They viewed the results of lining out with alarm. The pace of hymn singing had slowed so much that two breaths were sometimes required per note. The phrases and musical lines of the tunes had all but disappeared. The members of the congregation improvised flourishes on each note and drove the volume louder and louder so that individuals could hear themselves in what had become a cacophonous sea of meaningless sound. Walter said tunes were "miserably tortured, and twisted and quavered . . . into an horrid Medley of confused and disorderly Noises. . . something so hideous as is beyond expression bad."[2] These reformers argued for a return to "singing by note" or "regular singing" rather than "singing by rote."[3] Their work stimulated singing schools with itinerant and often self-taught singing masters who, along with their jobs as farmers or carpenters or civic officials, published hundreds of tunebooks over the next century and a half. These tunebooks, oblong in shape, were laid out as music theory instruction manuals followed by anthologies of hymn tunes, "fuging" tunes, and anthems.[4]

During this same period, the hymns of Isaac Watts and then of Charles Wesley were overtaking metrical psalmody, partly in association with the preaching of the Anglican George Whitefield (1714–1770) who made seven visits to the American colonies as part of a revival of religious interest known as the "Great Awakening." The theologian and Congregational minister in Northampton, Massachusetts, Jonathan Edwards (1702–1758), was part of this same movement. Some cooperation was engendered, and Watts became common fare along with the musical activity of singing schools and their tunebooks; but intense schism and conflict resulted as well. A "Second Great Awakening" came at the turn of the century. It, too, created conflict in both its more sedate form associated with Timothy Dwight (1752–1817) at Yale and its fierier version in camp meetings like the one at Cane Ridge, Kentucky, in 1800.

In 1801 William Smith and William Little published a book called *The Easy Instructor* (Philadelphia) in which they used four shapes for note heads[5]—a triangle for fa (or faw), a circle for sol, a square for la (or law), and a diamond for mi (or me). The shapes and their names were repeated, so that a major scale from the tonic to the tonic, or from what we would call do to do, looked like this:

fa   sol   la   fa   sol   la   mi   fa

Out of this context, using the shapes Smith and Little had provided, came an indigenous American group of hymn tunes, with musical materials from the British Isles. They are often called "white spirituals" or American folk hymn tunes, and their singers, largely Baptists and Methodists, the "fasola folk." These tunes took printed form in the nineteenth century in shape-note tunebooks, often given in three parts with parallel fifths, octaves, and unisons, and no concern for European conventions about part-writing. In the early twentieth century, George Pullen Jackson did the pacesetting research about these melodies.[6] Later, they became part and parcel of the church's denominational hymnals. They are largely gapped, pentatonic (the black keys of the piano give the arrangement of pitches), anonymous, rustic, and rugged folk melodies that are profoundly memorable and congregational. Though they can be accompanied, they easily stand alone in unison and also often work well in canon. Here are some of the more widely used ones in alphabetical order.

BEACH SPRING

BEACH SPRING is a gapped pentatonic tune in the form AABA' where A' completes the climax of B and then quickly returns to A. It is attributed to Benjamin Franklin White (1800–1879) who with Elisha J. King (ca. 1821–1844) published *The Sacred Harp* (Philadelphia, 1844) where it was paired with "Come, Ye Sinners, Poor and Wretched." White was a largely self-taught singing school teacher from South Carolina. He moved to Hamilton, Georgia, where he became a newspaper editor, court clerk, and mayor and served in the Georgia militia. The tune is named for the Beach Spring Baptist Church there. *The Sacred Harp* became the most widely used book in four-shape notation. It has gone through many editions right up to the present day when it is still used in "Sacred Harp Sings."[7]

BEACH SPRING
8 7 8 7 D

Lord, whose love in hum-ble serv-ice Bore the
Who up-on the cross, for-sak-en, Worked your

weight of hu-man need, We, your ser-vants, bring the
mer-cy's per-fect deed:

wor-ship Not of voice a-lone, but heart; Con-se-

crat-ing to your pur-pose Ev-'ry gift which you im-part.

Text: Albert F. Bayly, 1901-1984, alt., © The Oxford University Press   LBW #423
Tune: *The Sacred Harp*, Philadelphia, 1844

DETROIT

DETROIT (first spelled DETROYT) passed with alterations through *The Sacred Harp*, but appeared earlier in Ananias Davisson's *A Supplement to Kentucky Harmony* (Harrisonburg, Virginia, 1820),[8] attributed to "Bradshaw." With one minor exception (the eighth note from the end) it is pentatonic.

DETROIT
CM

"For-give our sins as we for-give," You taught us, Lord, to pray, But

you a-lone can grant us grace To live the words we say.

Text: Rosamund E. Herklots, 1905-1987, © Oxford University Press   Wor3 #754
Tune: Supplement to *Kentucky Harmony*, 1820

DOVE OF PEACE

DOVE OF PEACE is like DETROIT in that it is pentatonic with but the single (and similar) exception of a passing tone. In DETROIT it is on the sixth degree of a minor key. Here it is on the fourth degree of a major key (the thirteenth note from the beginning). DOVE OF PEACE has the character of a jubilant little dance with a compound background. It comes not from *The Sacred Harp*, but from another four-note shape book called *The Southern Harmony* (Spartanburg, South Carolina, 1835),[9] compiled by Benjamin White's brother-in-law, William Walker (1809–1875).[10] It, too, was very popular and still remains in use. (White and "Singin' Billy" Walker not only were singing teachers who generated very popular songbooks. They were also prolific parents. Benjamin White and Thurza Golightly had fourteen children—Benjamin himself was one of fourteen children—and William Walker and Amy Golightly had ten.)

DOVE OF PEACE
8 6 8 6 6

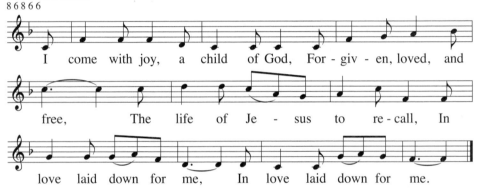

I come with joy, a child of God, For-giv-en, loved, and free, The life of Je - sus to re-call, In love laid down for me, In love laid down for me.

Text: Brian Wren, 1968; rev. 1982, 1994, © 1977, Hope Publishing Co.   NC #349
Tune: *Southern Harmony*, 1835

FOUNDATION

FOUNDATION (also known by other names that include PROTECTION, BELLEVUE, and BRETHREN) is another anonymous pentatonic tune, this one first printed in Joseph Funk's *Genuine Church Music* (Winchester, Virginia, 1832). Joseph Funk (1778–1862) was a Mennonite who settled near Harrisonburg, Virginia, in a community that came to be known as Singer's Glen (which named an opera by Alice Parker). Like White and Walker, Funk was the father of a large family (five children with his first wife, nine with his second). In addition to farming, he taught music, composed it, and compiled tune books. In the fifth edition (1851) of *A Compilation of Genuine Church Music* (re-titled *Harmonia Sacra*) he moved from four-shape to seven-shape notation.[11] FOUNDATION is one of the most widely used gapped tunes. It sings easily but with a remarkable durability in the formal shape of AA'BA'. (Another version of this tune[12] has a G in place of the A at measures 3 and 11, which increases the already heavy emphasis on the tonic and avoids the color the supertonic provides at those points.)

FOUNDATION
11 11 11 11

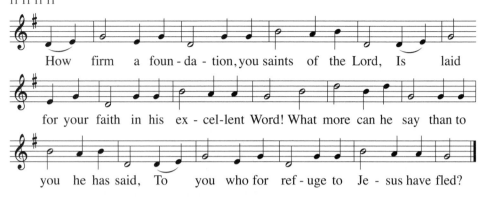

How firm a foun-da-tion, you saints of the Lord, Is laid
for your faith in his ex-cel-lent Word! What more can he say than to
you he has said, To you who for ref-uge to Je-sus have fled?

Text: J. Rippon's *Selection of Hymns*, 1787, alt.   PsH #500
Tune: J. Funk's *A Compilation of Genuine Church Music*, 1832

HOLY MANNA

HOLY MANNA is a similar pentatonic tune with a little less breadth but perhaps more élan. In the form AABA, the A parts are at a lower pitch range, B higher, the two interlocking at the tonic with A a fourth below and B a fifth above. The tune presumably comes from the hand of William Moore, who printed it in his *The Columbian Harmony* (Cincinnati, 1825). Little is known of Moore, except that he lived in Wilson County, Tennessee, and compiled this tunebook.[13] HOLY MANNA was paired there with, "Brethren, We Have Met to Worship," but it has also found a home with other texts, among them "God Who Stretched the Spangled Heavens."[14]

HOLY MANNA
8 7 8 7 D

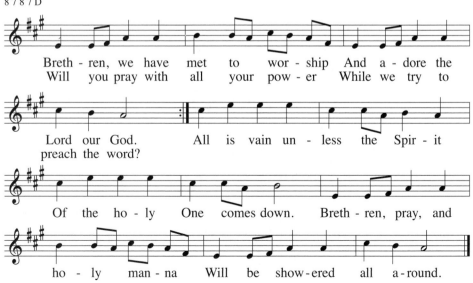

Breth-ren, we have met to wor-ship And a-dore the
Will you pray with all your pow-er While we try to
Lord our God. All is vain un-less the Spir-it
preach the word?
Of the ho-ly One comes down. Breth-ren, pray, and
ho-ly man-na Will be show-ered all a-round.

Text & Tune: *The Columbian Harmony*, 1825   HWB #8

KEDRON

KEDRON eventually passed through shape-note books, but it was first published at the end of the eighteenth century in round notes before the other tunes given here. It is found in one of the earliest books to include folk tunes, Amos Pilsbury's (1772–1812) *The United States' Sacred Harmony* (Charleston, 1799).[15] Pilsbury was a school teacher and singing school teacher, clerk in the Presbyterian Church, and compiler of tunes. In John Wyeth's *Repository of Sacred Music, Part Second* (Harrisburg, 1813) KEDRON's composer is given as Elkanah Kelsay Dare (1782–1826), a Methodist minister who was probably the musical editor of Wyeth's *Repository*. KEDRON is not a pentatonic tune. In the version given below, it has a Scotch snap (the eighth followed by the dotted quarter), which, as we will see, is characteristic of black spirituals, cousins to the white spirituals.

KEDRON
LM

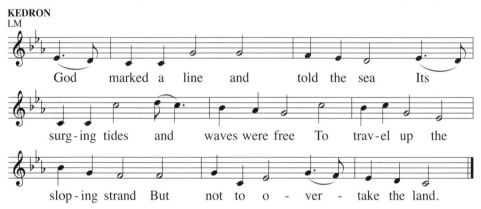

Text: Thomas H. Troeger, 1986, © 1989, Oxford University Press
Tune: Attr. Elkanah Kelsay Dare in Amos Pilsbury's *United States Harmony,* 1799
NC #568

LAND OF REST

The "originally pentatonic tune"[16] called LAND OF REST was linked with "O Land of Rest, for Thee I Sigh!" in the 1836 Appendix of Samuel Wakefield's shape-note tunebook book called *The Christian Harp* (Pittsburgh, 1832). As we have it, the fourth degree of the scale is used twice—once as a passing tone (measure 5) and once in a more accented fashion (four notes from the end)—to make the tune hexatonic.

LAND OF REST

8 6 8 6

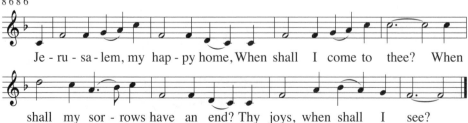

Text: Joseph Bromehead, 1747-1826
Tune: American folk hymn; arr. Annabel M. Buchanan, 1889-1983, © 1938, renewed 1966, J. Fischer and Bro.
Bap #517

MORNING SONG

MORNING SONG (or CONSOLATION), according to Marion Hatchett, is a variation of "Old King Cole."[17] Hatchett relates it to a stream of English folk ballads that began to appear in print from the end of the sixteenth century.[18] He found its first appearance in Andrew Law's *Sixteen Tune Settings* (Philadelphia, 1812) where Law printed it as if on a staff but without one, with Little and Smith's shapes for fa and la reversed.[19] It is a haunting tune that works very well for "O Holy City, Seen of John," for which it is often used. Though it employs all the pitches of the scale and is basically conjunct, the jump from the seventh degree down to the fifth (measures 2, 6, and 10) gives it a bit of a gapped character.

MORNING SONG
8 6 8 6 8 6

Text: Walter Russell Bowie, 1909   Meth #726
Tune: Wyeth's *Repository of Sacred Music, Part Second*, 1813

NETTLETON

NETTLETON has a repeated rhythm. Most of the time in this repertoire repeated rhythms generate interest, and the melodies are usually hardy enough to withstand considerable latitude in performance practice. NETTLETON, however,—even though George Pullen Jackson says it was quite popular, and it is found in all the hymnals we consulted—requires careful treatment with the right tempo and accents. If the tempo and accents are faulty, the singing becomes either monotonously bland or monotonously thumpy. First published in *Wyeth's Repository of Sacred Music: Part Second* (Harrisburg, 1813) with the text given below, the tune's name there was HALLELUJAH. A number of other names have been used, NETTLETON first in Darius E. Jones' *Temple Melodies* (New York, 1852), apparently in honor of Asahel Nettleton (1783–1844), a Congregational evangelist who edited a popular collection of hymns called *Village Hymns for Social Worship* (New York, 1824).

NETTLETON
8 7 8 7 D

Come, thou fount of ev-'ry bless-ing, Tune my heart to sing thy grace.
Streams of mer-cy, nev-er ceas-ing, Call for songs of loud-est praise.

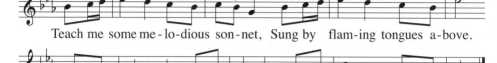

Teach me some me-lo-dious son-net, Sung by flam-ing tongues a-bove.

Praise the mount, I'm fixed up-on it, Mount of God's un-chang-ing love.

Text: Robert Robinson, 1758, *A Collection of Hymns,* 1759
Tune: American folk melody, J. Wyeth's *Repository of Sacred Music, Part Second,* 1813   HWB #521

AMAZING GRACE

AMAZING GRACE (or NEW BRITAIN) is probably the best known of these tunes, because of its association with the popular hymn, "Amazing Grace." Text and tune were first joined in William Walker's *The Southern Harmony* (New Haven, 1835), but the tune appeared earlier with different names and different texts in other books, the earliest as both ST. MARY'S and GALLAHER in Benjamin Shaw and Charles H. Spilman's *Columbian Harmony* (Cincinnati, 1829).[20]

AMAZING GRACE
CM

A - maz - ing grace! How sweet the sound That

saved a wretch like me! I once was lost, but

now am found; Was blind, but now I see.

Text: John Newton, 1779
Tune: 19th c. USA melody   Meth #378

PLEADING SAVIOR

PLEADING SAVIOR is AABA, with no variations of A. It first appeared in the *Christian Lyre* (New York, 1830) of Joshua Leavitt (1784–1873), a New England lawyer and Congregational minister. Though its repetitions make it accessible, this is a tune of which congregations can quickly tire. As Marilyn Stulken points out, it "has six repeats of the same phrase-start in one stanza alone"[21] (first, third, fifth, seventh, thirteenth, and fifteenth measures—counting the repeat of A as measures 5 through 8).

PLEADING SAVIOR
8 7 8 7 D

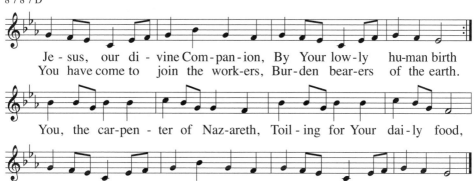

Je - sus, our di - vine Com - pan - ion, By Your low - ly hu - man birth
You have come to join the work - ers, Bur - den bear - ers of the earth.

You, the car - pen - ter of Naz - areth, Toil - ing for Your dai - ly food,

By Your pa - tience and Your cour - age You have taught us work is good.

Text: Henry van Dyke, 1909; alt.   Pres #305
Tune: American melody, 1830

RESIGNATION

RESIGNATION is like PLEADING SAVIOR in its formal shape, but is not driven on the beat by such a strong pulse. Its pickup and triple meter, with length rather than strength on the beat, make it more meditative and reflective. First attached to Watts' "My Shepherd Will Supply My Need" in J. W. Steffey's *Valley Harmonist* (Winchester, 1836), it appeared earlier in Freeman Lewis' *Beauties of Harmony* (Pittsburgh, 1814).[22]

RESIGNATION
CMD

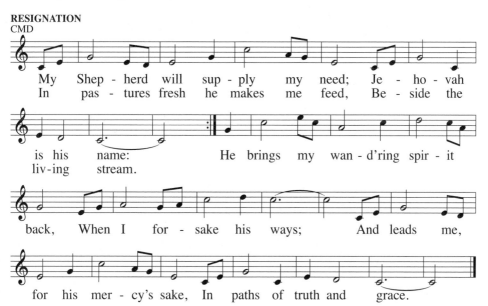

My Shep - herd will sup - ply my need; Je - ho - vah
In pas - tures fresh he makes me feed, Be - side the

is his name: He brings my wan - d'ring spir - it
liv - ing stream.

back, When I for - sake his ways; And leads me,

for his mer - cy's sake, In paths of truth and grace.

Text: Based on Psalm 23; Isaac Watts, 1674-1748, alt.   Cov #91
Tune: William Walker's *Southern Harmony*, 1835

WONDROUS LOVE

We conclude these white spirituals with a hauntingly beautiful one, WONDROUS LOVE. Sometimes related to the Captain Kidd ballad (not without dispute[23]), it was joined to the text given below in the 1840 edition of William Walker's *The Southern Harmony* (Philadelphia). Its form is ABA, not the more usual AABA that has been in evidence. The A section has the curiously ambiguous capacity to lead forward after its first statement and yet to conclude after its last statement, though its conclusion perfectly matches the "through eternity . . . sing on" character of the final stanza. The B section is a brief bridge that leads seamlessly back to A. The tune is in the almost pentatonic class. It uses the sixth degree only twice, once as the fifteenth note of each A section. Here is the tune by itself, followed by a setting with the tune in the tenor as it appeared in a characteristic three-part arrangement in *The Southern Harmony*. (The three-part arrangement assumes that at least the melody is sung by men and women in octaves, if not other parts as well. There is no gap of more than an octave between the melody and the upper voice.[24] The four notes on the opening chord include the "alto" D, which "is actually a 'choosing note' in the soprano."[25])

WONDROUS LOVE
12 9 12 12 9

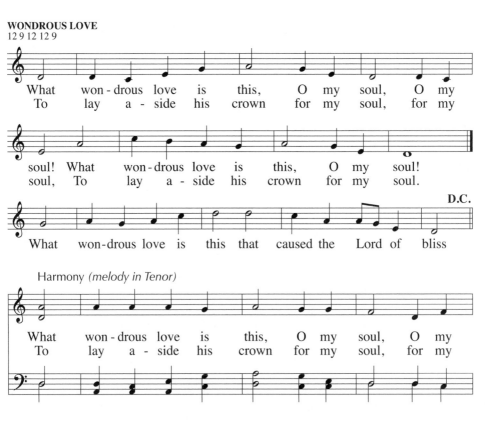

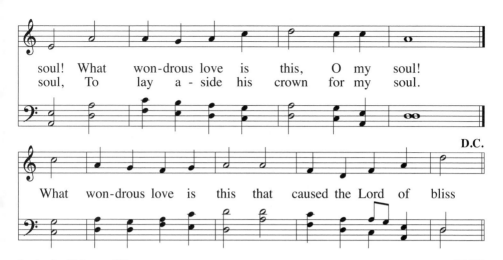

soul!   What   won-drous love   is   this,   O   my   soul!
soul,   To   lay   a - side   his   crown   for   my   soul.

What   won-drous love   is   this   that   caused the Lord   of   bliss

D.C.

Text: American folk hymn, ca. 1835
Tune: from *The Southern Harmony*, 1835

H82 #439

2. BLACK SPIRITUALS

The context sketched at the beginning of this chapter was the same one African Americans inhabited in the United States, but, as slaves, they were in it yet shut out of it. They had little choice but to learn to speak English and to adjust to life on plantations. They managed to worship in praise houses that were presumably out of white sight and range. There, singing was accompanied by shuffling "ring-shouts," which developed in circular dances with hand-clapping and bodily percussive effects. The slaves took music they heard and ran it through their own African call-response and improvisatory idioms. Black spirituals developed. Born of the African experience and pressed through the torture of slavery's oppression, these spirituals sing the death, resurrection, comfort, hope, and prophetic power of the Christian faith with poignancy. They also included multiple meanings and subliminal signals that communicated outside worship about the Underground Railroad or where to meet. Their relationship to white culture raises issues that we will discuss at the end of this chapter.

Here are some black spirituals that have passed into common use, in alphabetical sequence.[26]

BALM IN GILEAD

BALM IN GILEAD, as is typical for black spirituals, comes anonymously from an oral tradition. It is pentatonic, but not with a gapped pentatonic scale as in the black keys of the piano, but with the first five degrees of a major scale. Probably formed in the early part of the nineteenth century, it passed into print in *Folk Songs of the American Negro* (Nashville, 1907). This book was authored by two brothers—African Americans at work on their heritage—John Wesley Work II (1873–1925) and Frederick Jerome Work (1880–1942).

281

John Wesley Work was a composer, singer, teacher, administrator, and conductor. He taught Latin and history at Fisk University for twenty-five years and served as president of Roger Williams University in Nashville, Tennessee. He made Fisk a center of African American studies and did considerable research himself (in *Folk Songs of the American Negro*, Nashville, 1915, not to be confused with the similar title he published with his brother in 1907). Frederick Jerome Work was also a composer, scholar, and teacher. He taught at colleges in Missouri and Arkansas and at Roger Williams University.

At Fisk University, John Wesley Work championed the Fisk Jubilee Singers. They are important because they moved spirituals out of their native habitat and began to tour the United States and Europe with them in the 1870s (when John Wesley Work was but a baby). The Fisk Jubilee Singers took them from their congregational environment and adapted them as choral arrangements. Such arrangements became regular parts of choral concerts and worship services around the world.[27]

BALM IN GILEAD is structured like many tunes that come from an oral culture, with stanzas and a refrain. The stanzas (or verses) presume a single singer who can add additional ones and can as a soloist easily alter the rhythm and number of syllables per note. The refrain presumes the whole group can respond with text and music, which remain the same (although not quite the same—see the end of this chapter) so that everybody has equal access to it. Over time, once the spiritual is known, everybody tends to sing the verses, too, but the implications of the underlying structure continue to suggest that the verses are for an individual and the refrain for everybody.

BALM IN GILEAD
Irregular

Text: Afro-American Spiritual
Tune: Afro-American Spiritual

Wor3 #608

BREAK BREAD

Whether the text that goes with BREAK BREAD (or LET US BREAK BREAD or BREAK BREAD TOGETHER) was originally associated with gathering and protest or also related to Holy Communion will probably never be clear, but that it now carries associations with Communion is clear. Whether "Lord, have mercy" was derived from the church's *Kyrie eleison* or its biblical antecedents will also never be clear, but the text, nonetheless, pulls together for Christian congregations the historic associations from affirmation about God in Christ who has mercy to penitential cries before that same God. Whether falling on one's knees and facing the rising sun relates to pagan or Islamic traditions or turning toward Jerusalem,[28] Christians probably think either of the latter or of facing the sun in the morning when they are most likely to take Communion. All of this is carried in a few simple words by a tune with an unusually wide range—an octave and a third. (An octave and a fourth is employed when the tune is taken up an octave and modified for the third stanza.[29]) The melody highlights the major seventh degree. It works up gradually from a fourth below the low tonic and (at measure 6) jumps to the high seventh by the leap of a third with a Scotch snap (eighth followed by a dotted quarter). The Scotch snap also characterizes GIVE ME JESUS and GO DOWN, MOSES.

Boyer located an altered version of break bread in *Old Plantation Songs* (Boston, 1899) and "its first full-length appearance" in the Work brothers' *Folk Songs of the American Negro* (Nashville, 1907). He considers it slow, sustained, and "most effective [when] one voice or group . . . states the lead line of each succeeding stanza."[30]

BREAK BREAD
Irregular

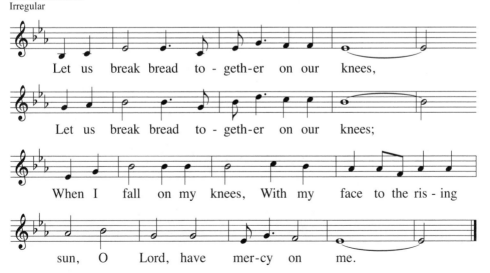

Let us break bread to-geth-er on our knees,

Let us break bread to-geth-er on our knees;

When I fall on my knees, With my face to the ris - ing

sun, O Lord, have mer-cy on me.

Text: Negro Spiritual   Bap #366
Tune: Negro Spiritual

GIVE ME JESUS

GIVE ME JESUS appears in only two of the hymnals we consulted; but it has found its way into supplements, and its verses title Andrew Ward's history of the Fisk Jubilee Singers.[31] It was printed in the first collection of their music—*Jubilee Songs as Sung by the Jubilee Singers* (New York, 1872). The melody is major and hexatonic with the fourth scale degree omitted.

There are variants of hymn tunes like this one, not at all surprising since they come from an oral tradition. Printing them freezes them into a form that does not reflect the continual lively shifts they have in actual performance from place to place and time to time.

GIVE ME JESUS
7 7 7 4 with refrain

Text: Afro-American Spiritual
Tune: Afro-American Spiritual

Mor #573

GO DOWN, MOSES

According to Horace Clarence Boyer, GO DOWN, MOSES is the first black spiritual "published with its music"—in 1861.[32] Sometimes referred to as a "Sorrow Song," Erskine Peters considers its text one of the "Lyrics of Deliverance."[33] Text and tune are structured in a call-and-response fashion. With the freedom of the soloist, a leader sings the call, "When Israel was in Egypt's land" and the rest of the story phrase by phrase. That is followed in each case by the response of the whole assembly, which in this case is an urgent plea, "Let my people go." After two such calls and their responses, a longer refrain—which adds to the front of the urgent plea and comes back to it—is sung by everybody. In slow but relentless fashion the story of Israelite oppression and deliverance is told, with obvious relevance to the singers themselves, who can continue for a long time with many additional verses in which they are pulled into the story with Moses, the Israelites, other biblical figures, and themselves.[34] The music matches the oppression by proceeding at a slow and mournful pace, like the toil of a work song. Here is another hexatonic melody, this time in a minor key with the sixth degree of the scale omitted.

GO DOWN, MOSES
Irregular

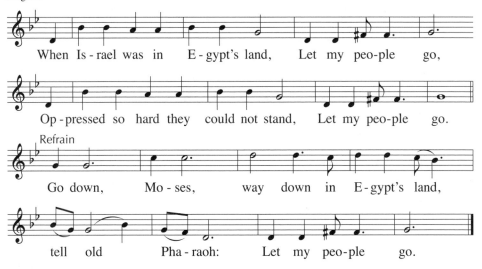

Text: Afro-American spiritual
Tune: Afro-American spiritual

PsH #476

GO, TELL IT

GO, TELL IT, almost universally considered a Christmas "carol," is faster and has more rhythmic drive. Its various versions can "swing" freely with triplets. Like BALM IN GILEAD, it is pentatonic, or almost so, but here the five notes are gapped. (They can be played on the black keys of the piano.) The exception is the last note of each verse which, like the last note of each verse in BALM IN GILEAD, employs the fourth degree of the scale (which can be viewed as providing contrast for or ameliorating the sturdiness of these tunes). Horace Boyer says that the performance practice for GO, TELL IT gives the verses to the entire congregation,[35] and indeed such a performance practice works very well because all the syllables for every verse fall in exactly the same way in good congregational fashion. This melody first appeared in print in R. Nathaniel Dett's *Religious Folk Songs of the Negro* (Hampton, 1927).

GO, TELL IT
78767676

Go, tell it on the moun-tain, O-ver the hills, and ev - 'ry-where;

Go, tell it on the moun - tain That Je - sus Christ is born.

While shep-herds kept their watch-ing O'er si - lent flocks by night,

D.C.

Be - hold, through-out the heav-ens There shone a ho - ly light.

Text: African-American Spiritual, c. 19th c., refrain; John W. Work, 1873-1925, stanza, alt.; from *American Negro Songs & Spirituals,* © 1940   CW #57
Tune: African-American Spiritual, c. 19th c., alt.

MCKEE

MCKEE immediately sets up a major key and then travels in it, except for the second measure, where there is the surprise of a mixolydian flatted seventh. This is another tune with a Scotch snap-like figure (in the second to last measure), but its history and arranger are even more interesting because they point to the breakdown of ethnic barriers. Charles Stanford said the melody was adapted by African Americans from a tune by Irish immigrants to the United States. The Fisk Jubilee Singers sang it as "I Know the Angel's Done Changed My Name," which is how it appeared in J. B. T. Marsh's *The Story of the Jubilee Singers with Their Songs* (London, 1876). In 1939 Henry T. Burleigh (1866–1949) adapted the tune for "In Christ There Is No East or West," written by the Englishman "John Oxenham" (pseudonym for William Dunkerley). It appeared in *The [Episcopal] Hymnal* 1940, and from there it has been widely circulated beyond the African American community. Burleigh named it for Elmer M. McKee, rector at St. George's Episcopal Church in New York City, where for fifty-two years he was the baritone soloist. In addition to singing, Burleigh was an African American composer, editor, and arranger. "Deep River" is one of his several hundred compositions. He was befriended and influenced by Antonin Dvořák, for whom he may have provided themes for the *New World Symphony*.

MCKEE
CM

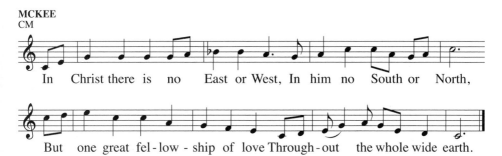

In Christ there is no East or West, In him no South or North,

But one great fel-low-ship of love Through-out the whole wide earth.

Text: John Oxenham, 1852-1941, alt.
Tune: Afro-American spiritual; adapt. Harry T. Burleigh, 1866-1949, © 1940, Henry T. Burleigh

H82 #529

WERE YOU THERE

WERE YOU THERE is another slow and sustained spiritual, found with BREAK BREAD in *Old Plantation Songs* and present in all the hymnals consulted for this book. It is a meditation on the crucifixion with a trembling wail for the refrain. Though strongly triadic as if in a major key, it is actually almost totally pentatonic. There is only one occurrence of the fourth scale degree (the A-flat near the end) and no leading tone (seventh degree).

WERE YOU THERE
10 10 with refrain

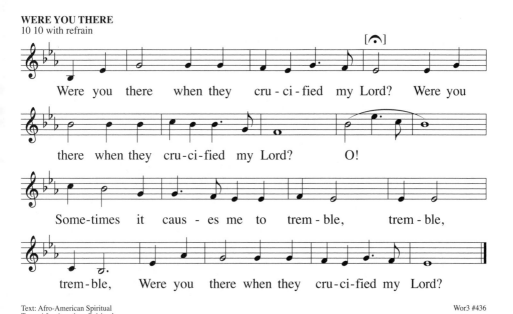

Were you there when they cru-ci-fied my Lord? Were you

there when they cru-ci-fied my Lord? O!

Some-times it caus-es me to trem-ble, trem-ble,

trem-ble, Were you there when they cru-ci-fied my Lord?

Text: Afro-American Spiritual
Tune: Afro-American Spiritual

Wor3 #436

Perspective: Ethnicity, Performance Practice, Meaning, Silence

1) Ethnicity. It becomes clear from a study like this that families of peoples in their ethnic identities have sung together, generating tunes in the process. The term "ethnic" of late has often been restricted to African Americans, and Sunday morning has been referred to as the most segregated hour of the week—which has meant essentially that blacks and whites have not normally worshiped together. While that is true, it is just as true that Italians, Spaniards, Irish, Germans, French, Norwegians, Swedes, Danes, Hungarians, Russians, Serbs, Croats, Japanese, Chinese, and Koreans have not normally worshiped together even when they have lived in close proximity to one another in the United States and have adopted a common English language. (And woe to the German who walked into a Polish tavern, or the reverse, in late nineteenth century Chicago.) Precise ethnicity can also be murky. Some whites who may not be able to tell you their "ethnic" heritage may initially find white spirituals foreign. They live in their "ethnic" identity, however that identity is defined for them. Certain musical styles like white spirituals, for example, may not be part of it.

That is, ethnicity is broader than black and white,[36] though of late in the United States it has been interpreted as fundamentally black and white. In part, ethnic groups simply flock together the way familial groups always do in their common heritage, language, history, and being. This togetherness reflects a positive and healthy sense of identity—and in the process generates "musical tunes." An unfortunate negative chokes the positive, however, when the familial or ethnic becomes a wall and weapon rather than a hospitable welcome.

What we are dealing with here is not fundamentally a black and white matter. The truth is that xenophobia, racism, and hatred have been as strong and pernicious between white folks as they have been from whites to blacks. The difference is that societal constraints in the United States have generally kept whites from enslaving and lynching one another, while no such restraints kept them from treating blacks in such horrible ways. On the contrary, societal norms and pressures have allowed and even encouraged whites to savage blacks with injustice and discrimination.

This has had hymnic implications. While musical currents move between ethnic groups, the music of black folks has put whites in a quandary. The fervor of black song has at once repelled and attracted them, and white guilt has compounded the problem. Is singing "black" music regarded as slumming by whites, is it born of white guilt, or is it genuine acceptance of and gratitude for the gift of another ethnic tradition? The answers are mixed, contradictory, and have differed from place to place and time to time.

This much is clear. Musical currents, over time—time is the critical factor here—seep through all the barriers human beings erect. Tunes that are worth singing are finally sung with delight by people of various ethnic backgrounds who may have no idea where they come from. For example, some years ago a seminary student told me she was shocked to discover BREAK BREAD was not a Lutheran chorale. Since it was in the *Lutheran Book of Worship*, she simply assumed it had to be a Lutheran chorale. It and other African American spirituals have found their way into all of our hymnals. That poses the potential for both a logjam and for new streams of life.

2) Performance Practice, Meaning, and Silence. When music moves from the ethnic group that produced it to another one who receives it, the context obviously changes. In the receiving group, the music is filtered through a different performance practice and set of meanings. The receiving group can sing what it receives only through its communal performance practice and understanding—its language and sense of melodic and rhythmic flow, for example, perceived through its own shared history and experience. This is complicated when a *white* spiritual enters a white group that has not known it, but it is more complicated when a *black* spiritual enters a white group because the movement then is from the oppressed to the oppressor.

Several responses in the receiving white community have been clear, though they have seldom lived in isolation. One, as noted above, is to regard the borrowing as slumming, but a duty nonetheless. This is usually born of guilt or a "multi-cultural" necessity regarded as politically correct or demanded by a legalistic sense of what the commandments require. Where this response is general in a community, the singing of black spirituals by white congregations is often perfunctory and includes hidden hostility.

A second response is liberation. To enter the song of the oppressed allows the oppressors to sing a new song. They can live into the story of the injustice their sisters and brothers have experienced and in so doing receive the song as gift and prophetic insight, which breaks open a new awareness, concern, and action. Whites are seldom likely to sing a spiritual so that it sounds "black," because they cannot be black.

They have to sing it through their "white" performance practice, but it nonetheless can come to life in meaningful ways that are profoundly authentic and by no means perfunctory (just the same as black or other American choirs can sing Bach cantatas in German and not sound like Germans, but nonetheless be profoundly authentic).[37]

The two extremes just isolated are the exceptions. Most of the time there is a muddier middle at work in which a mix of responses are not sorted out or consciously formed. In these cases black spirituals among whites live at many points on a spectrum between the two extremes. They can be perceived as sentimental and less than honest when there is little or no identification with the black experience and where hope born of suffering is absent. Hope born of privilege misreads the spirituals by avoiding Christian realism and turning (hopelessly) to what can be manufactured by human effort. In black culture that has not been seduced by consumerism (a rarer and rarer phenomenon for African Americans and all the world's peoples), spirituals have a sturdy prophetic character that nerves the oppressed for life they know may turn brutal at any moment, with the Christian affirmation that honestly acknowledges but sees beyond the brutality to an interrelated world in the hands of God.

Performance practice reflects the different meanings. In white culture, tempos that are too fast impart a perfunctory character to black spirituals, while attempts to manufacture emotion turn spirituals into empty sentimental exercises. In authentic black cultural contexts, spirituals settle into their natural tempos with a backbeat. Bodily rhythm and communal pulsation join, and a template is established to which layers of variations and intensity are added with each successive repetition. When whites are allowed to sing into this natural musical freedom on their own (which is not always easy because of the white tendency to clap on the beat), they alter it but nonetheless get at its essence. When leaders try to force whites to move and by so doing shame them, their very musical being is denied so that they cannot really sing. Here is yet another unfortunate and misguided, though probably unintentional, way congregations are silenced. The leader's shaming erects a block that keeps congregations from engagement, literally stops their song, or forces them to sing with phony smiles through clenched teeth. Time and compassionate musical leadership solve this dilemma, but it is enormously convoluted.

It is even more convoluted when white congregations sing black spirituals as entertaining "fun" songs without meaning, then add applause as if worship were a show. This is not only a white temptation. Blacks have done as well as whites at turning their worship into a commercial and profitable enterprise. Worship is always "fun" in the sense of holy play; but when it is turned into an amusement without *gravitas*, sometimes for commercial purposes and profit, its essence is altered. The prophetic cry of Amos is not far away.[38]

---

1 "White spirituals" tend to be called "folk hymns" today, but, in order not to confuse them with "folk tunes," which titles another chapter, I have kept "white spirituals" here.

2 Thomas Walter, *The Grounds and Rules of Music Explained: Or, An Introduction to the Art of Singing by Note, Fitted to the Meanest Capacities* (Boston: Benjamin Mecom [1760], 1st ed., 1721), 5.

3 Temperley, HTI, I, 8, says there were "efforts to get rid of the 'old way of singing' by training a voluntary group to sing from notes . . . in many English sources on either side of 1700." In HTI, I, 14, he says that "Singing by note, and the new styles, repertories and choirs that came with it, were first introduced in the Presbyterian Scottish churches at Monymusk, near Aberdeen, in 1753; from there they quickly spread over the country." And in HTI, I, 49, he notes that the English reform movements of the late seventeenth century had "'regular singing' as their main goal" and "spawned a dramatic increase in hymn-tune publications beginning about 1697."

4 Their English "ancestor" was Francis Timbrell's *The Divine Musick Scholars Guide* (1714). [Temperley, HTI, I, 50.]

5 The source of this system, according to Temperley, HTI, I, 48, is the notation John Day initiated in 1569, a solmization syllable next to each note, the first two (ut and re) little-used.

6 George Pullen, Jackson, George Pullen. *White Spirituals in the Southern Uplands: The Story of the Fasola Folk, Their Songs, Sings, and "Buckwheat Notes"* (New York: Dover Publications, Inc. 1965, republication of 1st ed., 1933).

7 For a reprint with a historical introduction, see B. F. White and E. J. King, *The Sacred Harp* (facsimile of the third edition, 1859), with "The Story of the Sacred Harp" by George Pullen Jackson (Nashville: Broadman Press, 1968). Two recent editions give separate streams: *The Sacred Harp, 1991 Edition* (Chelsea: Sacred Harp Publishing Co.) and *The B.F. White Sacred Harp, Revised Cooper Edition, 2000* (Samson: Sacred Harp Book Co.)

8 For a reprint of *Kentucky Harmony* with an introduction by Irving Lowens, see A. Davisson, *Kentucky Harmony* (facsimile edition of the first edition of 1816) (Minneapolis: Augsburg Publishing House, 1976).

9   Austin Lovelace (correspondence, August 28, 2004) supplied me with the date of the
    edition (1835) and page (89) from which DOVE OF PEACE first came. For a reprint of a later
    edition with a historical introduction, see William Walker, *The Southern Harmony and
    Musical Companion* (reproduction of the 4th printing of the 1854 edition), ed. Glenn C.
    Wilcox (Lexington: University of Kentucky Press, 1987).

10 The lore says that the first edition in 1835 was compiled by Walker and White; since White
    received no credit for it when it was published, a familial split was caused. Harry Eskew
    (conversation, October 1, 2004), says that though there may be some evidence for this it is
    not found in any church records—where at this time it would likely be found—that he has
    combed.

11 The first seven-shape system of notation was published by Jesse B. Aikin in *Christian
    Minstrel* (Philadelphia, 1846). For an overview of shape-note hymnody, see Harry Eskew,
    "Shape-note Hymnody," NGDMM, 17, 223–228.

12 As in Pres #361.

13 See David Music, "William Moore's *Columbian Harmony* (1825)," *The Hymn* 36:2 (April
    1985): 16–19, where Music reports "four men bearing the name William Moore, any one of
    whom could have been the tunebook compiler" (page 16). Music has contributed a number
    of studies of shape-note tunebooks to *The Hymn*.

14 LBW #463.

15 For a description of this book see Karl Kroeger, "A Yankee Tunebook from the Old South:
    Amos Pilsbury's the UNITED STATES HARMONY," *The Hymn* 32:3 (July 1981): 154–162.

16 Marion Hatchett, "I Come with Joy to Meet My Lord," Glover, H82C, 3A, 580.

17 Marion Hatchett, "Not Here for High and Holy Things," Glover, H82C, 3A, 21.

18 Ibid., 18.

19 Ibid., 16.

20 Marion Hatchett, "Amazing Grace! How Sweet the Sound," Glover, H82C, 3B, 1238–1240.

21 Marilyn Stulken, correspondence, June 17, 2004.

22 See Marion Hatchett, "My Shepherd Will Supply My Need," Glover, H82C, 3B, 1220–1223
    for the details.

23 Compare, for example, Stulken, HCLBW, 427, and Eskew, "Shape-note Hymnody,"
    NGDMM, 17, 224. ("The only relation to the Captain Kidd ballad," says Stulken, "is the
    unusual meter," correspondence, June 17, 2004).

24 See, for example, the description of the *Southern Harmony* "Big Singing" by Glenn C.
    Wilcox, "Introduction," William Walker, *The Southern Harmony* (reproduction of the 4th
    printing of the 1854 edition), x–xi.

25 David Music, correspondence, June 8, 2004.

26 For a more complete compilation of these, see the *African American Heritage Hymnal*
    (Chicago: GIA, 2001).

27 For a recent account with extensive detail about the Fisk Jubilee Singers, see Andrew Ward,
    *Dark Midnight When I Rise: The Story of the Fisk Jubilee Singers, How Black Music Changed
    America and the World* (New York: Amistad, 2000).

28 Carl Daw says that "seeing the rising sun while on one's knees probably relates" to
    "Anglican churches (especially in Virginia) [which] had a clear glass window over the altar
    at the east end…Slaves were frequently required to attend early church services (so they
    could be at home preparing the principal midday Sunday meal while the white folks were at
    the later service). [They] would often receive Communion [therefore] while facing the rising
    sun" (Correspondence from Carl Daw, May 28, 2004).

29 As in Pres #513.

30 Horace Clarence Boyer, "Let Us Break Bread Together on Our Knees," Glover, H82C,
    3A, 614.

31 Ward, *Dark Midnight When I Rise*.
32 Horace Clarence Boyer, "When Israel Was in Egypt's Land," Glover, H82C, 3B, 1188.
33 Erskine Peters, ed., *Lyrics of the Afro-American Spiritual* (Westport: Greenwood Press, 1993), 166.
34 Ibid., 166–167, for example.
35 Horace Clarence Boyer, "Go Tell It on the Mountain," Glover, H82C, 3A, 192.
36 See, for example, Temperley's discussion in HTI, 1, 6.
37 As Carl Schalk points out, "All hymnic music of any kind is always filtered through the performance practice of any given time" (correspondence, June 1, 2004), by which he means even within a single tradition, so that a given chorale in one period does not sound the same as it did in another period. This means that performance practice as defined by initial group or period, while important, is not the whole story. Performance practice as defined by the group singing at a given moment is equally or even more important, and the essence of hymn singing is not located in a historic artifact.
38 See Amos 5:21–24.

XII. Eighteenth- to Nineteenth-century American Tunes

1. The Eighteenth Century

The composed and folk traditions from the European colonization plus the eighteenth-century singing schools yielded American composers in two streams. One was typified by William Billings (1746–1800), a tanner without much musical training who was nonetheless consumed by music. He taught, composed, published, and promoted it—and produced what Temperley calls a "spectacular. . . one-man tune-book with no less than 116 tunes of his own. . . the largest number of new tunes by one composer in any single book in the entire repertory [of the English-language hymn tunes which Temperley surveys from 1525 to 1820]."[1] He is known for his fuging tunes, psalm tunes with imitative sections. (In England fuging tunes were "the culminating development" of "Anglican country psalmody . . . in the period 1740–90."[2]) His music is fundamentally choral and rustic, without a concern for European musical conventions. Paradoxically, the two of his hymn tunes that still have a little use among us are neither fuging nor especially rustic.[3] Here is one of them, LEWIS-TOWN—hexatonic and natural minor, with smooth conjunct motion balanced by triadic leaps. (The other is the canon WHEN JESUS WEPT.[4])

LEWIS-TOWN
CM

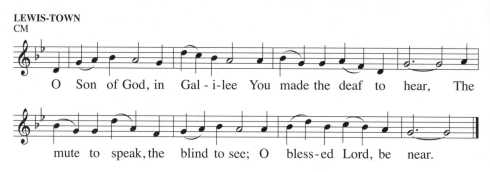

O Son of God, in Gal-i-lee You made the deaf to hear, The

mute to speak, the blind to see; O bless-ed Lord, be near.

Text: Anna Hoppe, 1889-1941, alt., © Lutheran Church in America
Tune: William Billings, 1746-1800

Wor3 #748

Other composers were attuned to more "chaste" European models. Hans Gram (1754–1804), Samuel Holyoke (1762–1820), and Oliver Holden (1765–1844) produced the *Massachusetts Compiler* (Boston, 1795), a notable collection of European music that espoused European theory. Of these three, Holden is most important for our story[5] since his hymn tune CORONATION is the oldest American hymn tune still widely-used. It has been printed and sung more often than any other eighteenth-century American tune. It may also be the only tune that can be harmonized so well with horn fifths (in the third phrase).

Holden was trained as a carpenter, but he became a wealthy general store owner and real estate dealer. From 1818 to 1833 he was a member of the Massachusetts House of Representatives. Though he had little musical training (two months' instruction in a singing school in 1783 was his own assessment[6]), he taught music, composed it, compiled musical collections, and directed what was apparently a fine choir at First Baptist Church in Boston. His tune CORONATION was first published in his *Union Harmony* (Boston, 1793). It went with Perronet's hymn in a four-part setting, where the tune migrated briefly from the tenor to the soprano, as if it would be a fuging tune. (MILES LANE is regularly used with this text in Great Britain, CORONATION in the United States.)

CORONATION
CM with repeat

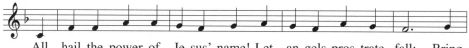

All hail the power of Je-sus' name! Let an-gels pros-trate fall; Bring

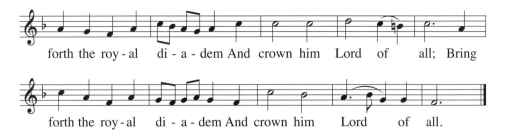

forth the roy-al di-a-dem And crown him Lord of all; Bring

forth the roy-al di-a-dem And crown him Lord of all.

Text: Edward Perronet, 1726-1792; alt. John Rippon, 1751-1836, alt. Wor3 #494
Tune: Oliver Holden, 1765-1844

Oliver Shaw (1779–1848), another American composer and conductor — one of the world's many blind organists—stood in the Gram-Holyoke-Holden line. He worked as a church organist, singing teacher, and owner of a music store in Providence, Rhode Island. A popular songster but not interested in fuging tunes, he "was one of the first and foremost supporters of the 'chaste' musical style."[7] He is important here because he was also one of Lowell Mason's teachers. Lowell Mason "said he was indebted to him [Shaw] for his start in life, that he owed all to him." Much of the nineteenth-century American story of hymn tunes revolved around Mason, to whom we now turn.

2. THE NINETEENTH CENTURY

i. Mason to Bradbury

Lowell Mason

Lowell Mason (1792–1872) worked as a church musician, teacher, composer, and writer, beginning in Savannah, Georgia. He introduced music into the public school system in Boston, which served as an example for other schools that followed suit. He spent his life trying to improve the church's musical life by teaching everyone to read music. Working from what he considered the "chaste" European model, he was neither happy with rural, self-educated singing instructors who were cobblers and carpenters, nor enamored with what was sometimes referred to as their "dunce notes" or "buckwheat" notation. He set out to make a "scientific improvement" using round notes, do-re-mi-fa-sol-la-ti-do solmization, and more "correct" tunes. Among his voluminous publications were perhaps as many as 1,697 melodies for hymns.[8] In the fourteen hymnals we consulted, 15 of these are used 55 times, three of them—the next three examples—generally.[9]

ANTIOCH is the well-known tune associated with Watts' text "Joy to the World," heard yearly with other "Christmas carols." It appeared in 1836 in No. 3 of Lowell Mason's booklets, *Occasional Psalm and Hymn Tunes.* Mason is usually given credit for arranging it from two pieces in Handel's *Messiah*, "Glory to God" and "Comfort Ye." John Wilson, an exacting sleuth in these matters, has shown that the roots and metamorphosis of this tune are considerably more complicated than that. Mason's role seems to have been "changing four notes of the melody" and "allying it with Watts' appealing text."[10] The second half, in spite of the Shaw-Mason antipathy to it, is in a "fuging tune" style where one part follows another imitatively.

ANTIOCH
CM with repeat

Text: Isaac Watts, 1719
Tune: Attr. George Frederick Handel, 1741; arr. Lowell Mason, 1848

Chal #143

HAMBURG was constructed by Mason from the first Gregorian Psalm Tone. He published it in the third edition of his *The Boston Handel and Haydn Society Collection of Church Music* (Boston, 1825).[11] Carol Pemberton calls it "an impressive, durable piece of music."[12] Routley says that "as a hymn tune it has no merit whatever and claims none: the attempt to square up Gregorian chant into a regular 4/2 rhythm and to harmonize it with straight chords was fatal to the enterprise."[13] (Then, to exonerate Mason, Routley adds this quip, "But in an age whose best historian was Charles Burney, what else could one expect?"[14]) The truth is probably somewhere between those opposing opinions. The tune employs five notes, the first five notes of the scale, not those of the gapped tunes, in the form ABAC where C develops the head of B and the tail of A. It is less interesting than the four notes of JAM LUCIS or the pentatonic tunes we have encountered and probably fits in the category with PETRA—dull to the analyst, but often appreciated by congregations.

HAMBURG
LM

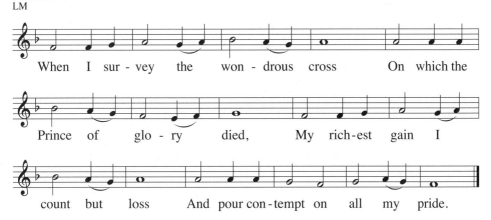

Text: Isaac Watts, 1674-1748, abr., alt.
Tune: Lowell Mason, 1792-1872

CW #125

Mason wrote OLIVET for Ray Palmer's text that almost invariably goes with it. He modified it to the form we use in his *Modern Psalmist* (Boston, 1839), but it first appeared a little differently in 1832 in *Spiritual Songs for Social Worship* (copyrighted in 1831), which Mason compiled with Thomas Hastings (1784–1872). Thomas Hastings, like Mason, was interested in improving the quality of church music. His extensive writings include a *Dissertation on Musical Taste* (Albany, 1822), over 600 hymns, and 1,000 hymn tunes. One of his tunes, TOPLADY,[15] still has some use. We will consider the influence of Hastings' *Dissertation* in the next *Perspective*.

OLIVET
6 6 4 6 6 6 4

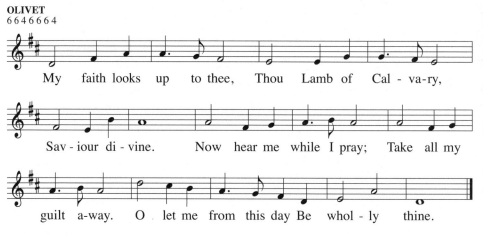

My faith looks up to thee, Thou Lamb of Cal - va - ry,

Sav - iour di - vine. Now hear me while I pray; Take all my

guilt a - way. O let me from this day Be whol - ly thine.

Text: Ray Palmer, 1830
Tune: Lowell Mason, 1831

VU #663

George J. Webb

Mason had a hand in numerous other tunes that he arranged or included in the publications he edited with associates. George J. Webb (1803–1887)—not to be confused with Benjamin Webb, the nineteenth-century rector who appointed Joseph Barnby, or Samuel Webbe, the eighteenth-century composer of glees and DULCE CARMEN—was one of these associates. Webb was born in England, where he became an organist, then moved to Boston as organist at Old South Church. He worked closely with Mason. In 1837, the two published *The Odeon: A Collection of Secular Melodies* (Boston), a book named for the former theater where Mason and Webb housed their Academy of Music. In that book, Webb's tune, which we now call WEBB, first appeared. It was turned into a hymn tune in *The Wesleyan Psalmist* (Boston, 1842) to go with "The Morning Light Is Breaking." William Bradbury, whom we shall meet shortly, linked it to "Stand Up, Stand Up for Jesus" in *The Golden Chain* (New York, 1861). That linkage "is too heavy handed."[16] The original association with "'Tis Dawn, the Lark Is Singing" and a quick tempo gave the tune a lighter and less militaristic cast.[17]

WEBB
7 6 7 6 D

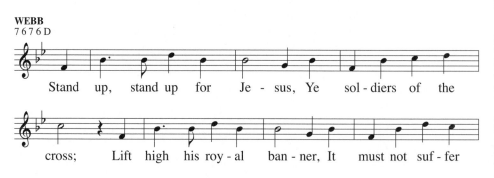

Stand up, stand up for Je - sus, Ye sol - diers of the

cross; Lift high his roy - al ban - ner, It must not suf - fer

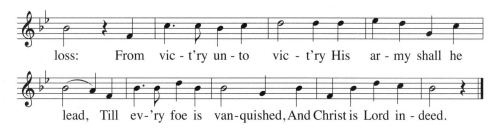

loss: From vic - t'ry un - to vic - t'ry His ar - my shall he
lead, Till ev-'ry foe is van-quished, And Christ is Lord in - deed.

Text: George Duffield, 1858
Tune: George J. Webb, 1837

Chal #613

Carl G. Gläser

AZMON is an arrangement Mason made of a melody by Carl G. Gläser (1784–1829), which he heard on one of his trips to Europe. Gläser was a music teacher and composer who owned a music store in Barmen, Germany. Mason published AZMON in his *Modern Psalmist* (Boston, 1839) and named it for a biblical place, as he often did, in this case the one mentioned in Numbers 34:4–5 and Joshua 15:4. Since the *Hymnal of the Methodist Episcopal Church* (New York and Cincinnati, 1878), this melody has been linked to "O For a Thousand Tongues to Sing," a text by Charles Wesley, which, with but three exceptions,[18] has been the first hymn in official Methodist hymnals since *A Collection of Hymns for the Use of People Called Methodists* (London, 1780).[19]

AZMON
CM

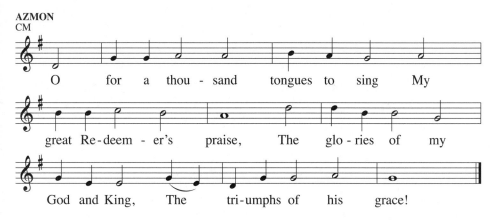

O for a thou - sand tongues to sing My
great Re - deem - er's praise, The glo - ries of my
God and King, The tri - umphs of his grace!

Text: Charles Wesley, 1739
Tune: Carl G. Gläser; arr. Lowell Mason, 1839

Meth #57

Hans Georg Nägeli

Mason and George Webb (see below) joined in editing another collection called *The Psaltery* (Boston, 1845). There the tune DENNIS was attributed to Hans Georg Nägeli (1773–1836), a Swiss music educator who influenced Mason. (See the next "Perspective" for more about the connection with Nägeli.) DENNIS may have been suggested by a melody for "O selig, selig, wer vor dir," which Nägeli included in his *Christliches Gesangbuch* (1828).[20] Routley thinks the tune as we have it is "really Mason's composition."[21]

DENNIS
SM

Blest be the tie that binds Our hearts in Chris-tian love; The
u - ni - ty of heart and mind Is like to that a - bove.

Text: John Fawcett, 1740-1817, alt.
Tune: Johann G. Nägeli, 1773-1836, adapt.

LBW #370

Perspective: Pestalozzi, Hastings, Feelings

Hans Georg Nägeli's influence on Mason relates to a larger cluster. Nägeli was influenced by the methods of a Swiss educator named Johann Heinrich Pestalozzi (1746–1827), and Pestalozzi may have been influenced by a more famous Swiss/French philosopher, Jean-Jacques Rousseau (1712–1778).[22] After 1830 Mason adopted Pestalozzian principles where he advocated an inductive model of teaching—from experience or "particular facts" to "general laws."[23] What influence this educational theory had on hymn tunes is beyond the scope of this study, but it does raise this question: was Mason's inductive method at odds with his more deductive intention to raise standards on a European model?

A related and more critical matter is the emphasis on feelings at the time, which perhaps can be traced to Rousseau. This emphasis is certainly evident in another of the people whose work influenced Mason, Thomas Hastings and his *Dissertation on Musical Taste*. Hastings thought that music was "a language of sentimental feeling, and the excellence of any music is directly proportional to the effect it produces in the listener."[24] This theory took musical shape in the hymn tunes of Mason and those who were influenced by him. To compare those tunes with the other genres we have encountered is to hear a different mind-set. Hymn tunes like spirituals, chorales, psalm tunes, Welsh tunes, French "Diocesan" tunes, and chant tunes all have a hardy character. They do not avoid feelings—they are, in fact, vehicles for deep emotional expression, but they are not calculated to evoke them. The Mason cluster often sets out to evoke them. That, coupled with the attempt to be "correct," may be why some call them by comparison a fairly pale set of pieces. Even more important, once again the problem of silencing congregations surfaces, in spite of the opposite intent. Starting with

302

feelings turns the attention of the singer inward toward him- or herself. Once that happens and the focus is no longer *soli Deo gloria*—to the glory of God alone—but on the singer, a self-absorbed, inward implosion is inevitable. This leads to a theological mistake that exalts the self instead of God. The direction and communal nature of the congregation's song—and ultimately the song itself—pay the price.

William Bradbury

The *Zeitgeist* just described included William Bradbury (1816–1868), one of Mason's students. He studied in Leipzig and became a church musician, editor, composer, and teacher. His tunes do not exhibit the improvement of church music on a European model that his teacher espoused, but they do suggest the more superficial attempts to evoke feelings. Bradbury wrote over 800 tunes. Ten of them are used sixty-five times in the fourteen hymnals we consulted, four generally.[25] Here are those four. As soon as we scan them, it will become clear where Bradbury leads.

Bradbury gave Joseph Gilmore's text a refrain and published the newly formed text with his tune HE LEADETH ME (or AUGHTON) in *Golden Censer* (New York, 1864).

HE LEADETH ME
8 8 8 8 with refrain

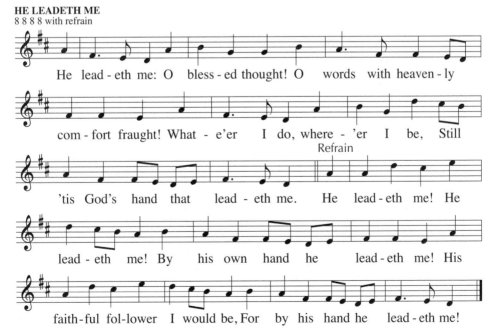

He lead-eth me: O bless-ed thought! O words with heaven-ly com-fort fraught! What-e'er I do, where-'er I be, Still 'tis God's hand that lead-eth me. He lead-eth me! He lead-eth me! By his own hand he lead-eth me! His faith-ful fol-lower I would be, For by his hand he lead-eth me!

Text: Joseph Henry Gilmore, 1862
Tune: William B. Bradbury, 1864

VU #657

Bradbury added a refrain to Anna Warner's text and set the tune JESUS LOVES ME (also known as CHINA) to it in *Golden Shower* (New York, 1862).

JESUS LOVES ME
7 7 7 7 with refrain

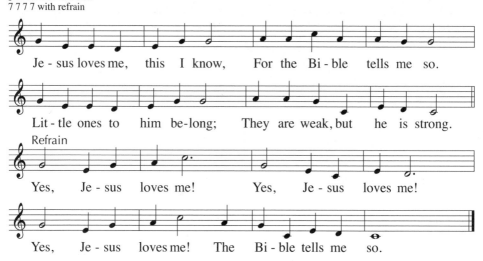

Je - sus loves me,   this   I   know,   For the Bi - ble   tells me   so.

Lit - tle ones to   him be-long;   They are weak, but   he   is strong.

Refrain

Yes,   Je - sus   loves me!   Yes,   Je - sus   loves me!

Yes,   Je - sus   loves me!   The   Bi - ble tells me   so.

Text: Anna B. Warner, 1859
Tune: William B. Bradbury, 1861

PsH #571

SOLID ROCK (or THE SOLID ROCK) was another tune with a refrain given in *The Golden Censer*, this one for Edward Mote's text.

SOLID ROCK
8 8 8 8 with refrain

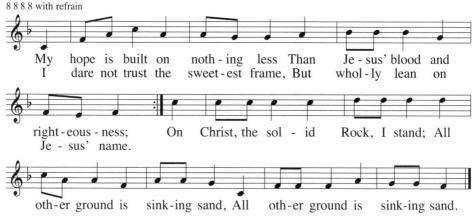

My   hope is built on   noth - ing less Than   Je - sus' blood and
I   dare not trust the   sweet - est frame, But   whol - ly lean   on

right - eous - ness;   On   Christ, the sol - id   Rock, I stand; All
Je - sus' name.

oth - er ground is   sink - ing sand, All   oth - er ground is   sink - ing sand.

Text: Edward Mote, 1797-1874
Tune: William B. Bradbury, 1816-1868

Bap #406

WOODWORTH, the most prevalent of these four tunes by Bradbury, is the exception that has no refrain, though its repetitions produce the same effect. It appeared in a collection Bradbury edited with Thomas Hastings called the *Mendelssohn Collection* (New York, 1849) where it was paired with Elizabeth Scott's text, "The God of Love Will Sure Indulge." Bradbury later adapted it to Charlotte Elliott's text in his *Eclectic Tune Book* (Philadelphia, 1860).

WOODWORTH
LM

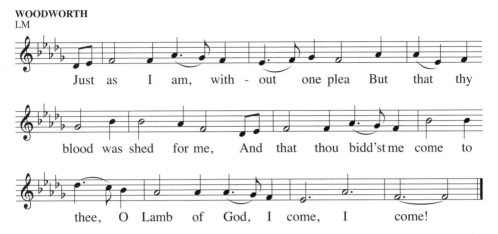

Just as I am, with-out one plea But that thy blood was shed for me, And that thou bidd'st me come to thee, O Lamb of God, I come, I come!

Text: Charlotte Elliott, 1789-1871, alt.
Tune: William B. Bradbury, 1816-1868

Cov #331

ii. White Gospel

As the examples of Bradbury's tunes illustrate, to Mason's and Hastings' predictable harmonies and melodies Bradbury added catchy tunes and refrains characteristic of camp meetings. He introduced his products as Sunday school hymns in profuse collections with names like *Golden Chain* (New York, 1861), *Golden Shower* (New York, 1862), and *Golden Censer* (New York, 1864)—and then the whole works together in *Golden Trio* (New York, 1866). Others, like the Baptist layman William Doane (1832–1915) and the Baptist pastor Robert Lowry (1826–1899), continued to write, compile, and edit hymns and tunes in the same style. (Lowry wrote one of the better pieces of this genre, "Shall We Gather at the River" and the tune HANSON PLACE that goes with it.[26]) As these were carried, contrary to most of their composers' intentions, by adults from Sunday Schools to urban revivals and church services, they became known as "gospel hymns."

Bradbury's work was done after what might be called a third phase of the "Awakening," spearheaded by Charles Grandison Finney (1792–1875). Finney was a teacher and lawyer who felt he had "a retainer from the Lord Jesus to plead his cause." He thought "New Measures" techniques like "the anxious bench"— a bench in the front of a church where, amidst loud crying and excitement, individuals were addressed and convicted—could convert people. By 1835 he wearied of the divisiveness he had caused among Eastern Presbyterians and retreated to teach and become president of Oberlin College, which, as Paul Richardson says, was "in the vanguard of social change."[27] Later, after Bradbury, Dwight Moody (1837–1899), a shoe salesman turned evangelist in Chicago with a big business mentality but less blatant techniques than Finney, conducted revivals in the United States and England.

In 1870 Ira Sankey (1840–1908) joined Moody as his musician and popularized gospel hymns with his baritone voice and harmonium. Sankey and Philip Bliss (1838–1876) began to publish these in 1875. George McGranahan (1840–1907) and George C. Stebbins (1846–1945) replaced Bliss when he died in 1876, and in 1895 they and Sankey published *Gospel Hymns Nos. 1 to 6 Complete* (New York) with 739 entries. Most, but not all of these, were gospel hymns. OLD HUNDRETH and some chants, for example, were included.

Gospel hymns have been enthusiastically embraced and fiercely resisted, which requires comments in the concluding *Perspective*. Not surprisingly, as with all the periods and movements we have observed in this study—in spite of enthusiastic embraces and fierce opposition—a few gospel hymns that avoided the excesses of the genre have gained some common currency, like the following examples given in alphabetical order by tune names.

Phoebe Palmer Knapp

ASSURANCE was written by Phoebe Palmer Knapp (1839–1908), a friend of Fanny Crosby (1820–1915), the prolific writer of over 8,500 gospel hymns. Knapp was the daughter of a Methodist evangelist, the wife of the founder of the Metropolitan Life Insurance Company, and a generous philanthropist. She wrote this melody and asked Fanny Crosby what it said to her. Crosby responded with the text that now goes with it. The two were published together in John Sweney's *Gems of Praise* (Philadelphia, 1873). The slow harmonic rhythm and repeated bass notes impart a mantra-like character. This is one of the gospel hymns that elicits deep divisions. Some sing it with fervor, while others are offended by what they perceive as smug and self-assured inwardness.

ASSURANCE
9 10 9 9 with refrain

Text: Fanny J. Crosby, 1873
Tune: Phoebe P. Knapp, 1873

PsH #490

William Marion Runyan

FAITHFULNESS is the latest tune of this set of gospel hymns. It comes from the early twentieth century, from the hand of William Marion Runyan (1870–1957), who composed it in 1923 for the text his friend Thomas O. Chisholm wrote in the same year. Runyan was already an organist as a young boy. He became a Methodist minister and evangelist who worked for the Moody Bible Institute and Hope Publishing Company. This text and tune were sung regularly at the Moody Bible Institute and used by Billy Graham in his crusades. Though the characteristic refrain, dotted rhythms, and chromaticism provide a somewhat subjective envelope, the tune is sturdier than many of this genre, and the text (based on Lamentations 3:23) is about God's faithfulness, not human effort.

FAITHFULNESS
11 10 11 10 with refrain

Great is thy faith-ful-ness, O God my Fa-ther, There is no

shad-ow of turn-ing with thee; Thou chang-est not, thy com-

pas-sions they fail not; As thou has been thou for-ev-er wilt be.

Refrain

Great is thy faith-ful-ness! Great is thy faith-ful-ness! Morn-ing by

morn-ing new mer-cies I see; All I have need-ed thy

hand hath pro-vid-ed; Great is thy faith-ful-ness, Lord, un-to me!

Text: Thomas O. Chisholm, 1923
Tune: William M. Runyan, 1923
Text & Music © 1923, Renewal 1951, Hope Publishing Co.

Mor #460

William H. Doane

TO GOD BE THE GLORY was composed by William H. Doane for another of Fanny Crosby's texts. The two appeared together in Doane's *Songs of Devotion* (1870)[28] and Doane and Lowry's *Brightest and Best* (Chicago, 1975), were imported to England via Moody's campaigns there, then reimported to the United States in the middle of the twentieth century in Billy Graham's crusades. Doane was a Baptist layman trained musically in New England where he grew up, a successful industrialist and civic leader in Cincinnati, and a supporter of Moody and Sankey's work. He wrote many tunes for Fanny Crosby's texts[29] and compiled collections with Robert Lowry.

TO GOD BE THE GLORY
11 11 11 11 with refrain

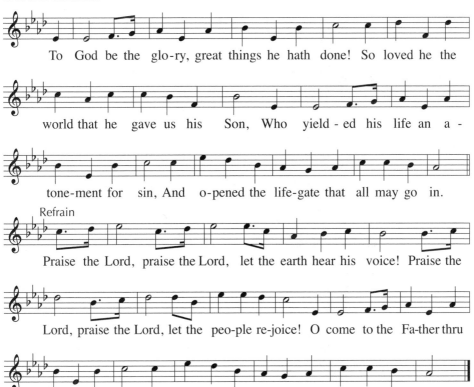

To God be the glo-ry, great things he hath done! So loved he the
world that he gave us his Son, Who yield-ed his life an a-
tone-ment for sin, And o-pened the life-gate that all may go in.

Refrain
Praise the Lord, praise the Lord, let the earth hear his voice! Praise the
Lord, praise the Lord, let the peo-ple re-joice! O come to the Fa-ther thru
Je-sus the Son, And give him the glo-ry, great things he hath done!

Text: Fanny J. Crosby, 1875
Tune: William H. Doane, 1875

Meth #98

Philip P. Bliss

In 1873, after his wife was saved but his four daughters died at sea on the French liner called the *Ville du Havre*, Horatio G. Spafford, a Chicago lawyer and professor of medical jurisprudence, wrote "When Peace Like a River." Philip P. Bliss (1838–1876), a family friend, composed the tune VILLE DU HAVRE (named after the ship, but also called IT IS WELL after the text.) Text and tune were published together in Sankey and Bliss' *Gospel Hymns No. 2* in 1876, the year Bliss died in a train wreck in Ashtabula, Ohio. For a couple of years before his death, he had joined Major D. W. Whittle as a singing evangelist. This tune pushes toward the sentimental hazards of chromatic harmony with seventh chords, the insistent upward sequence from the pickup of measure 7 through the first beats of measure 11, and the echo in the refrain. Its high tonic endings for both the stanzas and the refrain are not especially friendly toward congregations. These factors prompt emotive choral settings.

VILLE DU HAVRE
Irregular

Text: Horatio G. Spafford, 1828-1888
Tune: Philip P. Bliss, 1838-1876

Bap #410

310

iii. Black Gospel: Thomas Dorsey

Though individual hymn tunes in the black gospel style that developed in the twentieth century have entered some Anglo-European churches, as a whole few have found their way there. There is one exception, PRECIOUS LORD, which has an antecedent in MAITLAND.

PRECIOUS LORD is another instance of common coinage in hymn tunes. Thomas Dorsey (1899–1993), not to be confused with the trombonist Tommy Dorsey, is often called the "father" of black gospel. He organized the first gospel choir at Ebenezer Baptist Church in Chicago, founded the National Convention of Gospel Choirs and Choruses, toured with Mahalia Jackson, and composed at least two hundred gospel songs plus other music. After his wife died in childbirth, Dorsey wrote the text of "Precious Lord" and consciously or unconsciously adapted the tune MAITLAND to it.

MAITLAND was composed by George N. Allen (1812–1877) for the text "Must Jesus Bear the Cross Alone." It first appeared in 1844 in his *The Oberlin Social and Sabbath School Hymn Book*. Allen was a student of Lowell Mason. He taught sacred music, geology, and natural history at Oberlin College. Two of his students founded the Oberlin College Conservatory of Music.

Both MAITLAND (below) and PRECIOUS LORD (next page) contain the characteristic scotch snap. Here are the two tunes, though PRECIOUS LORD, as is typical for black gospel, seldom sounds as it appears on the printed page. An improvisatory realization is its normal state, with eighth notes often swung in triplets.

MAITLAND
8 6 8 6

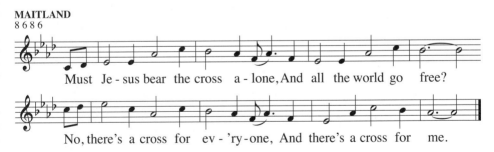

Must Je - sus bear the cross a - lone, And all the world go free?

No, there's a cross for ev - 'ry-one, And there's a cross for me.

Text: Thomas Shepherd, 1665-1739
Tune: George N. Allen, 1812-1877

Bap #475

PRECIOUS LORD
Irregular

Text: Thomas A. Dorsey, 1899-1993
Tune: George N. Allen, 1812-1877; adapt. Thomas A. Dorsey, 1899-1993
© 1938 Hill & Range Songs, Inc., renewed by Unichappell Music, Inc.

Bap #456

iv. Other Protestant Currents
Ithamar Conkey

Ithamar Conkey (1815–1867) was born in Massachusetts into a Scottish family. He wrote RATHBUN in 1849 and named it for soprano soloist Mrs. Beriah S. Rathbun, who was in his choir at Central Baptist Church in Norwich, Connecticut, where he served as organist. He later became the bass soloist and conductor of the quartet-choir at Madison Avenue Baptist Church in New York. Quartet choirs were fixtures in many late nineteenth and early twentieth century churches and suggest the conception of the period—and of tunes like RATHBUN, which depend on the trained tone color of quartet soloists to mask what Routley calls their "melodic stagnation."[30] RATHBUN was first published in H. W. Greatorex's *Collection of Psalm and Hymn Tunes, Chants, Anthems, and Sentences* (Boston, 1851), with the text, "Saviour, Who Thy Flock Art Feeding."

RATHBUN
8787

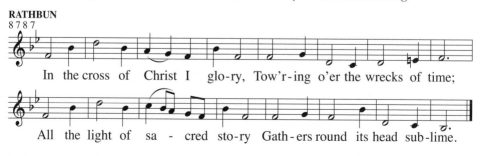

Text: John Bowring, 1792-1872
Tune: Ithamar Conkey, 1815-1867

Cov #221

Henry W. Greatorex

Henry W. Greatorex (1813–1858), in whose *Collection* RATHBUN first appeared, was an English organist and composer from a family of organists and composers. He moved to the United States in 1836 as a church organist. His *Collection* contained hymn tunes by him, his father (Thomas), and his grandfather (Anthony). It also contained what may be the most often used tune from this period, GLORIA PATRI (or GREATOREX). It is the setting for the "Lesser Doxology," known simply as the "Doxology" in many churches, where it has been used every Sunday, year after year, throughout the twentieth century.

GLORIA PATRI (GREATOREX)
Irregular

Text: Anonymous, 4th c.
Tune: Henry W. Greatorex, 1813-1858

Bap #252

Charles Meineke

If Greatorex's tune is not the most used one from this period, then the one by Charles Meineke (1782–1850)—which apparently provided Greatorex's rhythmic template—is. Meineke was a German organist who moved to England and then to Baltimore, where he served St. Paul's Episcopal Church from 1820 until he died. In his *Music for the Church* (Baltimore, 1844), he included what we know as MEINEKE, a setting of the Lesser Doxology, which, like Greatorex's, has been used in some churches each Sunday week after week and year after year.

MEINEKE
Irregular

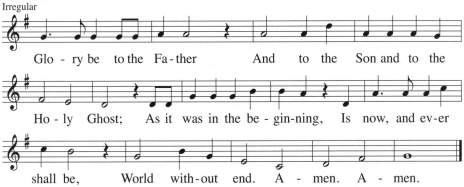

Text: Lesser Doxology, 3rd-4th century
Tune: Charles Meineke, 1844

Meth #70

Richard Storrs Willis

Richard Storrs Willis (1819–1900) was a Yale graduate who went to Germany to study, becoming a student and friend of Felix Mendelssohn, of whom he wrote a biography. He returned to this country as a newspaper music critic, but also published works related to church music. In *Church Chorals and Choir Studies* (New York, 1850), he published a tune for "See Israel's Gentle Shepherd Stand." Ten years later, he reworked it to fit "While Shepherds Watched Their Flocks by Night," and then in the *Hymnal of the Methodist Episcopal Church* (New York and Cincinnati, 1878) it was used with "It Came Upon the Midnight Clear." We know the tune as CAROL. It consists of four sets of two-bar phrases, each set in a question-and-answer sequence. The sets are grouped in twos, and each eight-bar group moves from dominant to tonic: (2 + 2 [dominant]) + (2 + 2 [tonic]) + (2 + 2 [dominant]) + (2 + 2 [tonic]). The second set starts like the first, but modifies it to get to the tonic; the third set provides a contrast, and the last set provides closure by repeating the second. The lilting 6/4 meter and conjunct melismas make for a peaceful ride, set off by a sixth, which in this case has no repeated notes before it to gather strength for an emotive show.

CAROL
CMD

It came up-on the mid-night clear, That glo-rious song of old,

From an-gels bend-ing near the earth To touch their harps of gold:

"Peace on the earth, good will to all, From heav'n's all-gra-cious king."

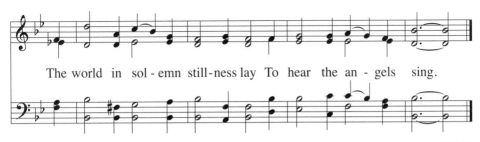

The world in sol-emn still-ness lay To hear the an - gels sing.

Text: Edmund H. Sears, 1810-1876, alt.
Tune: Richard S. Willis, 1819-1900

LBW #54

Adapted from Robert Schumann

The melody we call CANONBURY was adapted from Robert Schumann's *Nachtstücke*, Op. 23, No. 4 (1839) and published as a hymn tune in J. Ireland Tucker's *Hymnal with Tunes, Old and New* (1872). Routley implies that Mason or his influence had something to do with it (it "seems to have been in wide use since the days of Lowell Mason, and is still, obstinately surviving"[31]). He said, rightly, that it is "a particularly bad example of a poor tune being made out of a beautiful melody, since the four phrases in the hymn tune are only the *exordium* of a much longer melody, and by themselves they are a shapeless torso, with no climax at all."[32]

CANONBURY
LM

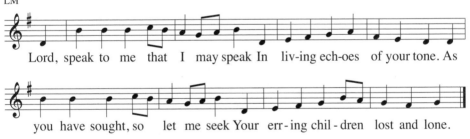

Lord, speak to me that I may speak In liv-ing ech-oes of your tone. As

you have sought, so let me seek Your err-ing chil-dren lost and lone.

Text: Frances R. Havergal, 1872, alt.
Tune: Arr. from Robert Schumann, 1839

Mor #646

Louis Henry Redner

ST. LOUIS was written by Louis Henry Redner (1831–1908) for Phillips Brooks' hymn "O Little Town of Bethlehem." As a lad in his teens, Redner was already an entrepreneur in real estate. He became a wealthy real estate broker, but that did not deter him from serving both as organist at several Philadelphia churches and as an unusually responsible and successful Sunday school teacher and superintendent at Holy Trinity Episcopal Church. He was the organist there when Phillips Brooks was the rector (before Brooks went to Trinity Church in Boston). ST. LOUIS was sung at Christmas 1868 while Brooks was still in Philadelphia. Text and tune were published later in *The Church Porch* (New York,

1874), an Episcopal Sunday School hymnal prepared by an Episcopal priest in Massachusetts, William R. Huntingdon, who named the tune. Routley is not too happy with this tune either. Like ALL SAINTS NEW,[33] he refers to its melody line as "broken-backed and paralytic."[34] While admittedly not the greatest tune in the world, those words may be a bit strong for what neither Brooks nor Redner expected to "live beyond that Christmas of 1868."[35]

ST. LOUIS
86867686

Text: Phillips Brooks, 1835-1893
Tune: Lewis H. Redner, 1831-1908

H82 #79

John Zundel

Routley gave BEECHER higher marks than it deserves, though he thought it is "ruined by its stagnant and sticky bass." He felt the tune could "be greatly improved, without losing any of its character, by radical rewriting of the bass counterpoint."[36] The yowl of the reiterated upward major sixth, set up by repeated notes before it, cannot be helped by the bass line, though taking the slow tempo its composer John Zundel (1815–1882) had in mind *might* (and might not) ameliorate that problem (assuming you can tolerate the tempo). He thought the tune should take sixty-five seconds, which means a quarter note would last about a second,[37] much slower that than our generation's norm. Whatever one may think about any of that, this is a melody that comes out of a context where hymn singing was prized (in spite of the title of the book where it first appeared). That context deserves to be described after the tune is cited. It was composed in 1870 for Charles Wesley's text, "Love Divine, All Loves Excelling" and published in Zundel's *Christian Heart Songs, A Collection of Solos, Quartets and Choruses of All Metres* (New York, 1870).

BEECHER
8 7 8 7 D

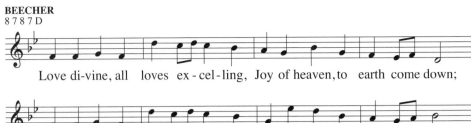

Love di-vine, all   loves   ex - cel-ling, Joy of heaven, to   earth   come down;

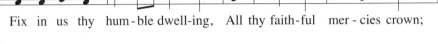

Fix   in   us   thy   hum - ble dwell-ing,   All thy faith-ful   mer - cies crown;

Je-sus, thou art   all   com-pas-sion, Pure, un-bound-ed   love   thou art;

Vis - it   us with   thy   sal - va-tion,   En-ter ev-'ry   trem - bling heart.

Text: Charles Wesley, 1743
Tune: John Zundel, 1870

Chal #517

After working in Germany as an organist and bandmaster, Zundel came to the United States in 1847, joined the staff of Plymouth Congregational Church in Brooklyn, New York, in 1850, stayed there for nearly thirty years, did a brief stint at Central Methodist Church in Detroit, retired, and returned to Germany. Henry Ward Beecher, the pastor for whom the tune is named, was the son of Lyman Beecher and the brother of Harriet Beecher Stowe. He served Plymouth Church from 1847 until his death in 1887. (Note the two lengthy tenures. Hymn singing takes time and trustworthy leadership. It does not happen with quick fixes.) In addition to being a popular preacher who plunged into social issues, opposed slavery, and sponsored the African American Fisk Jubilee Singers on their tour, one of Beecher's "oddities"[38] was a concern for hymn singing.

He was serious about it. When he came to Plymouth Church in 1847, he found that the choir did the singing, as in many if not most mainline Protestant churches where quartet choirs and soloists were common. He convinced his director of music, Darius E. Jones (1815–1881), who had associations with Lowell Mason, to prepare a hymnal with tunes the congregation would be able to sing. Beecher managed to get the publishing firm of Lowell Mason's sons to underwrite the project. In 1851 *Temple Melodies* (New York) appeared, the first hymnal in the United States to print text and tune on the same page as became customary.[39] Jones thought the hymnal with its two hundred tunes and nearly five hundred hymns did its job well, but Beecher wanted a larger book with more breadth. So, with his brother Charles and his new director of music, John

Zundel—who also had associations with Mason (he taught organ at Lowell Mason's first Normal Institute)—the *Plymouth Collection of Hymns and Tunes for the Use of Christian Congregations* (New York, 1855) with over 1,300 entries was prepared. It followed Jones' format, printing a tune above texts whose meters fit the given tune. Though Beecher and Zundel were criticized for selecting a wide range of hymnody that included German and Roman Catholic resources, the book was quite popular. It was printed from 1855 until 1870, used beyond 1870, and adapted by other churches. Baptists, for example, published their own version as *The Baptist Hymn and Tune Book: Being "The Plymouth Collection" Enlarged, and Adapted to the Use of Baptist Churches* (New York, 1867).

Mason's concern for congregational singing was obviously influential here. In 1866 a Hook and Hastings organ was installed in the church.[40] With Zundel leading from the organ, people flocked to the church not only to hear Beecher preach and Zundel play, but to sing hymns. "The hearty singing of the vast congregation became almost as much of an attraction as [Beecher's] preaching."[41] (Whether hymn singing, organ playing, or preaching should serve as an attraction is, of course, a very good question, but that does not necessarily detract from the hymn singing itself.)

William Fiske Sherwin

In 1874 Bishop John H. Vincent, secretary of the Methodist Sunday School Union, with help from Lewis Miller in Akron, Ohio, set up the first Chautauqua Assembly on Lake Chautauqua in New York. In the late nineteenth and early twentieth centuries these assemblies continued. They were meant for Sunday school teachers, providing biblical study, teaching methods, plays, concerts, and worship services. For the services, Vincent requested hymns from one of his assistants, Mary A. Lathbury, who wrote "Break Thou the Bread of Life." In 1877, when he was music director at Chautauqua, William Fiske Sherwin (1826–1888) wrote BREAD OF LIFE for her text. He was a student of Lowell Mason who taught at the New England Conservatory. With Lowry and Doane, he served as a musical editor for Biglow and Main after Bradbury's death. His tune and harmony partake of his teacher's "correct" but dull stagnation.

BREAD OF LIFE
6 4 6 4 D

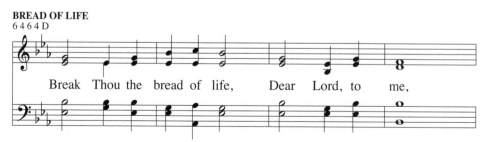

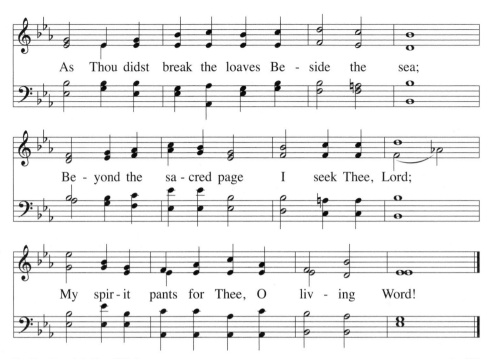

As Thou didst break the loaves Be - side the sea;

Be - yond the sa - cred page I seek Thee, Lord;

My spir - it pants for Thee, O liv - ing Word!

Text: Mary Artemesia Lathbury, 1877; alt.
Tune: William Fiske Sherwin, 1877, alt.   Pres #329

James R. Murray

It is possible to make a strong case for running one cultural "folk" idiom through the filter of another one. In a sense, that's the only choice you ever have. But playing loose with the truth is not acceptable. The tune called AWAY IN A MANGER that goes with the text of the same name is from James R. Murray's *Dainty Songs for Little Lads and Lasses*, published in Cincinnati in 1887.[42] It was headed "Luther's Cradle Hymn," followed by this parenthesis, "(Composed by Martin Luther for his children, and still sung by German mothers to their little ones)," with the initials J. R. M. beneath the parenthesis to the right.

AWAY IN A MANGER

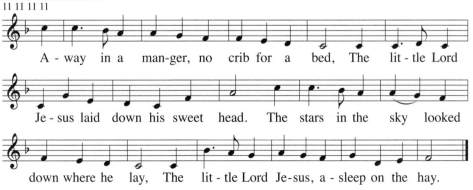

A - way in a man-ger, no crib for a bed, The lit - tle Lord

Je - sus laid down his sweet head. The stars in the sky looked

down where he lay, The lit - tle Lord Je - sus, a - sleep on the hay.

Text: Anon. (Luke 2:7)
Tune: James R. Murray, 1887   Meth #217

James Murray (1841–1905) came from a Scottish family in Massachusetts and studied with Mason, Webb, and Bradbury. He became a public school teacher in Massachusetts and then an editor for Root and Cady in Chicago and the John Church Company in Cincinnati. He let sentimentality (note the title of the book where this tune is found) and its sales pitch ally carry him away with a little white lie, one of sentimentality's temptations. German Lutheran mothers in the United States may have sung this text and tune after 1887, but they have nothing to do with Martin Luther, who never wrote a text of this sort[43] or composed a melodic minor seventh (measures 12–13) or a hymn tune built around the nineteenth-century harmonic frame of tonic and dominant seventh chords. The piece may commend itself as a nineteenth-century creation in the United States, but to give it the pretense of a Luther folk hymn from Germany is to tell a lie, which then permeates the culture. Mistakes are obviously possible. In fairness to Murray, he may have thought the text was by Luther, and he included his initials so that the possibility was present for discerning who wrote the tune; but the impression was nevertheless given that Luther was the author of both, since text and tune merge in the popular imagination. The church has the responsibility to check things out and be honest. Many people still assume "Away in a Manger" was "Luther's Cradle Hymn" and that he wrote the tune. Current "slanders" about Martin Luther raiding bars for his tunes fit the same scheme, tar the church with the reputation of not being trustworthy, and prime people to hear the church's message itself as a fabrication. (It is worth noting, again in fairness to Murray, that he made some good comments in the Preface about healthy singing for children,[44] though, as Austin Lovelace points out, he also included doggerel.[45])

Arthur Henry Messiter

Arthur Henry Messiter (1834–1916) worked in the United States as an Anglican in the English cathedral tradition—which, with the next two tunes from the Episcopal Church, indicates the wide breadth of traditions and practices that were developing in this country. Trained in England, Messiter came to the United States in 1863, volunteered in the choir at Trinity Church in New York, moved to Philadelphia to play at churches there, and then in 1866 came back to Trinity in New York as organist and choirmaster following Henry Cutler (who had pretty much reduced the congregation to "mere spectators"[46]). He developed an exemplary choir of men and boys in the Oxford-Cambridge movement mold, adding the novelty of an orchestra to Trinity's services. He edited a Psalter, choir office book, musical edition of the 1892 *Hymnal*, and in 1906 wrote a *History of the Choir and Music of Trinity Church* (New York). MARION was written in 1883 for "Rejoice, O Pilgrim Throng!", a hymn that in 1868 had been included in the Appendix to *Hymns Ancient and Modern*. This is a stately tune which moves to the dominant at the second phrase and to the supertonic at the fourth before repeating the dominant five times at the refrain to propel the tune forward on its way home to the tonic.

MARION
SM with refrain

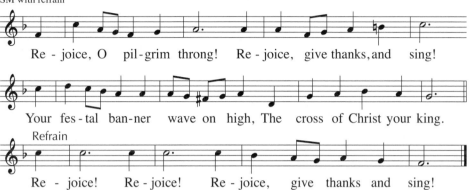

Re - joice, O   pil-grim throng!   Re - joice,   give thanks, and   sing!

Your fes - tal ban-ner   wave on high, The   cross of Christ your king.

Refrain

Re - joice!   Re - joice!   Re - joice,   give   thanks and   sing!

Text: Edward H. Plumptre, 1821-1891, abr., alt.   CW #540
Tune: Arthur H. Messiter, 1834-1916

William H. Walter

FESTAL SONG first appeared in J. Ireland Tucker's *The Hymnal with Tunes Old and New* (New York, 1872) for the text "Awake and Sing the Song." *The Pilgrim Hymnal* (Boston, 1912) matched it to William Merrill's hymn given below. William H. Walter (1825–1893) wrote this tune. He was the organist at Presbyterian and Episcopal churches in Newark, New Jersey, his birthplace, and studied with Edward Hodges,[47] the English organist at Trinity Church in New York City who preceded Henry Cutler and was one of the adaptors of Beethoven's HYMN TO JOY. (Hodges was a high churchman, but he did not agree with Cutler's emphasis on the choir at the expense of the congregation.) Walter became the organist at the Church of the Epiphany and Columbia University in New York City. FESTAL SONG proceeds in four stately phrases in which the second moves to the dominant and the last modifies it to the tonic.

FESTAL SONG
SM

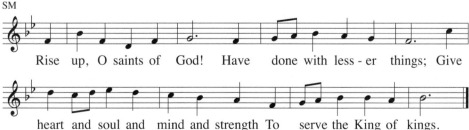

Rise up, O saints of God!   Have   done with less - er   things; Give

heart and soul and mind and strength To   serve the King of kings.

Text: William P. Merrill, 1911, alt.   Chal #611
Tune: William H. Walter, 1894

George William Warren

We conclude with NATIONAL HYMN and the danger it represents. In 1876 Daniel Roberts, rector at St. Thomas Church in Brandon, Vermont, wrote the text we associate with this tune for Brandon's centennial celebration of the Declaration of Independence. In 1892 it was chosen for New York City's celebration of the adoption of the United States Constitution. George William Warren (1828–1902) wrote the tune for that celebration, held at St. Thomas Episcopal Church where he was the organist for thirty years, from 1870 to 1900. In 1894 the text and tune were published together in Tucker's and Rousseau's *Hymnal Revised and Enlarged*.

NATIONAL HYMN
10 10 10 10

God of our fa - thers, whose al-might-y hand   Leads   forth in beau - ty all the star-ry band   Of shin-ing worlds   in   splen-dor through the   skies,   Our   grate-ful songs be - fore your throne a - rise.

Text: Daniel C. Roberts, 1841-1907
Tune: George W. Warren, 1828-1902

Wor3 #764

Routley called NATIONAL HYMN "a pretentious piece of bombast."[48] Especially when trumpet fanfares are used as introduction and interludes, he is not far from the mark. The martial strains of this tune can too easily interpret the text to mean that "this free land" is the only free land at the expense of all other lands and peoples. Nineteenth-century dangers like this still lurk nearby.

1   Temperley, HTI, I, 33.

2   Temperley, HTI, I, 11.

3   Another composer in Billings' mold was Daniel Read (1757–1836), whose fine tune WINDHAM still can be found in a couple hymnals (LBW #344 and PsH #64).

4   Chal #199, HWB #234.

5   That does not mean he was the best musician of the group. Hamilton C. MacDougall, *Early New England Psalmody: An Historical Appreciation, 1620–1820* (Brattleboro: Stephen Daye Press, 1949), 81. thought "Holyoke was more of a musician than Billings, Read, or Holden; by that is meant he had thought more about the management of voices as regards variety and effect, having also due regard to the rules of harmony. . ."

6   David W. Music, "Oliver Holden," in Harry Eskew, David W. Music, and Paul A. Richardson, *Singing Baptists: Studies in Baptist Hymnody in America* (Nashville: Church Street Press, 1994), 19.

7   Carol A. Pemberton, *Lowell Mason: His Life and Work* (Ann Arbor: UMI Research Press, 1985), 5.

8   It is not clear how many hymn tunes Lowell Mason wrote. The total of 1,697 comes from the counting his grandson Henry Lowell Mason made, which included 1,210 originals and 487 arrangements; but these totals have been called into question. See Pemberton, *Lowell Mason*, 184–185.

9   Two others are used more than once or twice: BETHANY—Bap #458, and BOLYSTON—Meth #413. Routley, MCH, 123A, thought Mason's best tune was ELTON (*Pilgrim Hymnal* [Boston: The Pilgrim Press, 1958], #449). It has no currency among us.

10 John Wilson, "Handel and the Hymn Tune: II, Some Hymn Tune Arrangements," *The Hymn* 37:1 January 1986): 31. For more detail see John Wilson, "The Evolution of the Tune 'Antioch'," *The Hymn Society of Great Britain and Ireland Bulletin* 166 11:5 (January 1986): 107–114.

11 For the relation of Mason's tunes to Gregorian Psalm tones, see J. Vincent Higginson, "Notes on Lowell Mason's Hymn Tunes," *The Hymn* 18:2 (April 1967): 37–42. A chant setting of the Lord's Prayer called GREGORIAN can be found at Meth #270.

12 Pemberton, *Lowell Mason*, 192.

13 Routley, MCH, 122B–123A.

14 Ibid., 123A.

15 Found at Bap # 342 and Meth # 361 and in several other hymnals. Hastings has eleven entries in the fourteen hymnals we consulted.

16 Marilyn Stulken, correspondence, June 17, 2004.

17 Ibid.

18 Correspondence with Austin Lovelace, August 29, 2004. Lovelace gives the three exceptions as 1932, 1935, and 1939 "where it was replaced by 'Holy, Holy, Holy,'—created quite a ruckus!" (For "unofficial" Methodist hymnals and books of Methodist groups who broke from one another, the picture is more complex.)

19 Hymn #57, the source for this example, is the first hymn in Meth.

20 Stulken, HCLBW, 418, gives it.

21 Routley, MCH, 123A.

22 William Channing Woodbridge, Elam Ives (mentioned in connection with Beethoven's HYMN TO JOY), and Mason were among those influenced by Pestalozzi and Nägeli. Carol Pemberton, *Lowell Mason*, 62–71, gives some of this detail. She tells me she did not uncover any connection to Rousseau in her research. Mark K. Smith, "Johann Heinrich Pestalozzi," http://www.infed.org/thinkers/et-pest.htm, 1, however, says Pestalozzi "took up Rousseau's

ideas and explored how they might be developed and implemented."

23 Pemberton, *Lowell Mason*, 67.

24 James E. Dooley, "Introduction," *Thomas Hastings, Dissertation on Musical Taste or General Principles of Taste Applied to the Art of Music* (New York: Da Capo Press, 1974, republication of the 1st ed., 1822), xiv.

25 Three others are used more than once: BRADBURY (or SHEPHERD)—Meth #381, OLIVE'S BROW—Chal #194, and SWEET HOUR—Bap #445.

26 Bap #518, Chal # 701, Meth #723. According to Paul Richardson (correspondence, June 2, 2004), Lowry viewed his tune HANSON PLACE as brass band music, which did not overly please him in spite of its popularity.

27 Correspondence, June 2, 2004.

28 This reference seems only to be given by Aufdemberge, CWH, 415.

29 Gealy, et al., *Companion to the Hymnal*, says over 2,200 tunes; Haeussler, *The Story of Our Hymns*, 627, says 2,200 compositions; William Reynolds, et al., *A Survey of Christian Hymnody* (Carol Stream: Hope Publishing Company, 1999, 4th ed.), 118, says over 2,000 tunes; and Mel R. Wilhoit, "Doane, William H(oward)," *New Grove Dictionary of American Music*, ed. H. Wiley Hitchcock and Stanley Sadie (London: Macmillan Press Limited, 1986), 1, 636, says over 1,000 tunes.

30 Routley, MCH, 124A.

31 Ibid., 86B.

32 Ibid., 86B-87A.

33 LBW #183.

34 Routley, MCH, 124B.

35 Aufdemberge, CWH, 86.

36 Routley, MCH, 124A–B.

37 Harry Eskew, "There's a Wideness in God's Mercy," Glover, H82C, 3B, 886.

38 Louis F. Benson, *The English Hymn: Its Development and Use in Worship* (Richmond: John Knox Press, 1962, reprinted from the 1915 edition), 471.

39 See Paul A. Richardson, "Hymnody in the United States through the Mid-Nineteenth Century," *The New Century Hymnal Companion: A Guide to the Hymns*, ed. Kristen L. Forman (Cleveland: The Pilgrim Press, 1998), 119.

40 Mason thought the primary role of the organ was to support congregational singing. See Barbara Owen, "Lowell Mason and the Organ," *The American Organist* (July, 1992): 49. See also Pemberton, *Lowell Mason*, 9, 148, 162–171.

41 Benson, *The English Hymn*, 474. People were attracted to other churches because of their congregational singing, non-Episcopalians to an Episcopal church in Minnesota, for example. See Jane Rasmussen, *Musical Taste as a Religious Question in Nineteenth-Century America* (Lewiston: The Edwin Mellon Press, 1986), 89–91.

42 James R. Murray, *Dainty Songs for Little Lads and Lasses* (Cincinnati: The John Church Co., 1887), 110.

43 Stulken, HCLBW, 170, gives the history of the text, which precedes Murray's Dainty Songs.

44 Murray, *Dainty Songs*, 2.

45 Correspondence with Austin Lovelace, August 28, 2004.

46 John Ogasapian, *English Cathedral Music in New York City: Edward Hodges of Trinity Church* (Richmond: The Organ Historical Society, 1994), 170.

47 For detail about Hodges, see Ogasapian, *English Cathedral Music in New York City*.

48 Brink and Polman, PsHH, 775.

XIII. FOLK TUNES AND FOLK INFLUENCES

A longside the recovery of the rhythmic chorale and the writing of new tunes, the music of folk cultures was harnessed in the nineteenth century. This continued in the twentieth century. Ralph Vaughan Williams, whose work is considered in the next chapter, was among those who sought out folk music. Folk tunes had been a part of the hymnic vocabulary, as with the German, Welsh, English, and African American sources already mentioned, but in the nineteenth and twentieth centuries they were part of a keen general folk interest. It was partly stimulated as a way to get around the heavy Romanticism of the late nineteenth century, but by the end of the twentieth century it had also become a means to get around the heavy hand of Western influence and control. Here are some examples of folk tunes and folk influences from various periods.

Argentine

Pablo Sosa (b. 1933) is a Methodist pastor and musician who was a professor at the National Conservatory of Music in Buenos Aires, Argentina. He gradually became more and more interested in the oral tradition of Hispanic music and poetry, especially in his country, and he sought to give it expression in worship. CENTRAL was composed in 1960, before this interest had developed fully, but the tune has had time to appear in some of our hymnals and represents the composer's native musical tongue with a driving rhythm allied to a typically twentieth-century slightly asymmetrical shape. It was written for Nicolás Martínez's text, which Fred Kaan translated into English, and is named for the Central Methodist Church in Buenos Aires.

CENTRAL
8 7 8 7 D

¡Cris - to vi - ve, fue - ra_el llan - to, Los la - men - tos y_el pe-
Ni la muer - te ni_el se - pul - cro Lo_han po - di - do su - je-
Christ is ris - en, Christ is liv - ing, Dry your tears, be un - a -
Death and dark - ness could not hold him, Nor the tomb in which he

sar! No bus - quéis en - tre los muer - tos Al que
tar.
fraid! Do not look a - mong the dead for One who
lay.

siem-pre_ha de vi - vir, ¡Cris - to vi - ve! es - tas

lives for - ev - er - more; Tell the world that Christ is

nue - vas Por do - quier de - jad o - ír.

ris - en, Make it known he goes be - fore.

Text: Nicolás Martínez, 1960; tr. Fred Kaan, 1972
Tune: Pablo D. Sosa, 1960, © 1962, Metho Press, Ltd.; tr. © 1974, Hope Publishing Co.

Meth #313

Brazilian

CANTAD AL SEÑOR from Brazil gives congregations a chance to dance the delight of the new song in Christ[1] in a vigorously happy minor tune, with four phrase groups of the 2 + 2 variety. A repeat of the initial motive at midstream spins into the material from the end of the first half a step higher where it can drive to a happy conclusion in the home key. Gerhard Cartford (b. 1923), a Lutheran church musician, teacher, and missionary who heard this Brazilian tune with a Portuguese text, translated the text into Spanish and then into English. He brought the text and tune to the United States, where they first appeared in *Songs of the People* (Minneapolis, 1986).

CANTAD AL SEÑOR
5 6 5 6 5 6 5 5

Can - tad al Señ - or   Un   cán - ti - co   nue - vo. Can - tad al Señ -
Oh, sing to our God,   Oh,   sing out a   new song.Oh, sing to our

or   Un cán - ti - co nue - vo. Can - tad al Señ - or   Un   cán - ti - co
God, Oh, sing out a   new song.Oh, sing to our God,   Oh,   sing out a

nue - vo. ¡Can - tad al Señ - or,   Can - tad al Señ - or!
new song. Oh, sing to our God.   Oh, sing to our God.

Text: Brazilian folk song; tr. Gerhard Cartford, alt., © Gerhard Cartford
Tune: Brazilian folk song, *Songs for the People*, 1986.

VU #241

Chinese

Asian materials have not been and still are not in great supply in Western hymnals. Western congregations have tried to use them in recent years, but they are the most difficult of all styles for Westerners to notate, teach, and learn. Their range, ornaments, and non-Western modal frames are hard for congregations to assimilate, and the temptation to force Western common practice harmonies and heavy accompaniments on them is destructive and counterproductive. When learned as they are and left to stand in their native dress, they introduce a beauty that reminds Westerners of a world made by one God but perceived through many human prisms. They work well in unison, though light percussion or simple accompaniments are also possible.

Here is MAN-CHIANG-HUNG, a Chinese tune. In spite of its wide range, leaps, and ornament at the end, it is accessible to Western congregations because, though pentatonic with leaps unlike other pentatonic tunes we have encountered, it deploys triadic melodic patterns in ways that—until the final— make it feel as if it derives from a major scale. I-to Loh (b. 1936) arranged this Chinese melody as a hymn tune in his *Hymns from the Four Winds* (Nashville, 1983), a supplement to *The Methodist Hymnal* of 1966. I-to Loh is an ethnomusicologist who studied at Tainan Theological College in Tainan, the School of Sacred Music at Union Seminary in New York City, and the University of California in Los Angeles. He was professor of church music and ethnomusicology at the Asian Institute for Music in Manila and at Tainan Theological College and Seminary in Taiwan. His interest in indigenous Asian music has led him to spend his life collecting and making Asian musical materials accessible for Christian worship.[2]

327

MAN-CHIANG-HUNG
7 7 7 7 7 7 with refrain

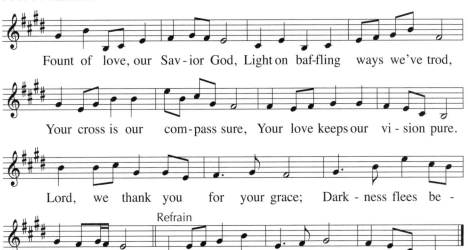

Fount of love, our Sav-ior God, Light on baf-fling ways we've trod,

Your cross is our com-pass sure, Your love keeps our vi-sion pure.

Lord, we thank you for your grace; Dark-ness flees be -

Refrain

fore your face. Fount of love, our Sav-ior God, be our guide.

Text: Ernest Y. L. Yang, 1934, *Hymns of Universal Praise*, 1977; tr. Frank W. Price, 1953, alt.   HWB #354
Tune: Chinese verse melody; adapt. by Ernest Y. L. Yang, 1933, © 1977, The Chinese Christian Literature Council, Ltd.

Dutch

The Dutch Reformed use of Genevan psalm tunes precluded a Dutch hymn tune heritage. But several Dutch folk melodies have nonetheless been adapted as hymn tunes and distributed throughout the church.

We use IN BABILONE, an attractive AABA tune with the danger of too many repetitions (the A section three times), for a wide variety of texts. It was matched to Christopher Wordsworth's Ascension text, "See the Conqueror Mounts in Triumph," in 1906 in *The English Hymnal*. Vaughan Williams, while he was working on the hymnal, accessed this tune through Julius Röntgen, who would later publish *Old Dutch Peasant Songs and Country Dances Transcribed for the Piano* (London, 1912). Röntgen's source was a large collection called *Oude en Nieuwe Hollantse Boerenlities in Contradansen* (Amsterdam, 1710).

IN BABILONE
8 7 8 7 D

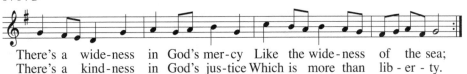

There's a wide-ness in God's mer-cy Like the wide-ness of the sea;
There's a kind-ness in God's jus-tice Which is more than lib-er-ty.

There is plen-ti-ful re-demp-tion In the blood that has been shed;

There is joy for all the mem-bers In the sor-rows of the Head.

Text: Frederick W. Faber, 1814-1863, alt.
Tune: *Oude en Nieuwe Hollanste Boerenlities*, c. 1710

Wor3 #595

KREMSER, firmly linked to the hymn used in the United States at Thanksgiving—"We Gather Together" or its replacement, "We Praise you, O God"—has the widest distribution of any of the Dutch tunes. It comes from a set of Dutch patriotic songs that Adriaan Valerius collected called *Nederlandtsch Gedenck-Clanck* (Haarlem, 1626).[3] The hymn "Wilt heden nu treden," translated by Theodore Baker as "We Gather Together," comes from the same source. "We Praise You, O God" is by Julia Buckley Cady Cory, who wrote it at the request of J. Archer Gibson to replace the older text. Gibson was the organist at Brick Presbyterian Church in New York City where Cory's text was first sung at Thanksgiving in 1902. The tune is named for Edward Kremser (1838–1914), the director of the Männergesangverein in Vienna, who published it with other pieces from the *Gedenck-Clanck* in *Sechs Altniederländische Volkslieder* (Vienna, 1877). It is a bit more introspective than IN BABILONE and drapes the text out in a flowing canopy.

KREMSER
12 11 12 11

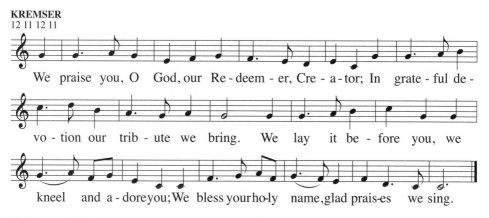

We praise you, O God, our Re-deem-er, Cre-a-tor; In grate-ful de-

vo-tion our trib-ute we bring. We lay it be-fore you, we

kneel and a-dore you; We bless your ho-ly name, glad prais-es we sing.

Text: Julia C. Cory, 1902, alt.
Tune: A. Valerius, *Nederlandtsch Gedenckclanck*, 1626

PsH #237

VRUECHTEN (also VRUCHTEN) comes from a popular seventeenth-century Dutch tune that went with the love song, "De liefde Voortgebracht" ("The Love Brought Forth"). Joachim Oudaen used in it his *David's Psalmen* (Amsterdam, 1684) for "Hoe groot de Vruechten zijn" ("How Great the Fruits"), which has named it. The tune appeared with George Woodward's text given below in Charles Woods' *The Cowley Carol Book* (London, 1902). Of the three Dutch tunes given here, VRUECHTEN is the most exuberant. Its range and melismas make it the least congregational, but it always seems to sing well.

VRUECHTEN
6767D

This joy-ful East-er-tide A-way with sin and sor - row!
My love, the Cru-ci-fied, Has sprung to life this mor - row:

Had Christ, who once was slain, Not burst his three-day pris-on, Our faith had been in vain: But now is Christ a-ris-en, a-ris-en, a-ris-en; But now has Christ a-ris - en!

Text: George R. Woodward, 1848-1934
Tune: Oudaen's *David's Psalmen*, 1685

Wor3 #449

English

The AGINCOURT HYMN or DEO GRACIAS is a tune that comes to us as it was adapted in *The English Hymnal* of 1906. Its origins lie in the fifteenth century for a text to celebrate King Henry V's victory at the Battle of Agincourt in 1415. When used with words like those of Thomas à Kempis, the tune's drive tells the story, celebrates the breaking of evil, and breaks out in doxology.

DEO GRACIAS
LM

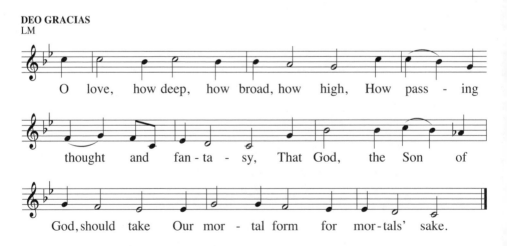

O love, how deep, how broad, how high, How pass - ing thought and fan-ta-sy, That God, the Son of God, should take Our mor-tal form for mor-tals' sake.

Text: Attr. Thomas à Kempis, 1380-1471, tr. Benjamin Webb, 1819-1885, alt.
Tune: Based on the Agincourt Song, England, c. 1415, E. Power Biggs, 1906-1977, © 1947, Mercury Music Corp.

Cov #204

KINGSFOLD is an English folk song named for the town in Surrey where Ralph Vaughan Williams heard it. He also found it in *English Country Songs* (London, 1893). Its form is AABA with slight adjustments on the repeats of A. They flow so naturally, however, that they cause no problems. They seem innately imbedded in the tune, which sings as if known before the singer knew it—as Vaughan Williams perceptively recognized.[4]

KINGSFOLD
CMD

Text: Howard C. Robbins, 1876-1952, © Morehouse-Barlow Co., Inc.   LBW #391
Tune: English folk tune, *English Hymnal,* © Oxford University Press

In *The English Hymnal* Vaughan Williams gave KINGSFOLD with a different rhythm from the one given above.[5] At measure 10 the previously established rhythm with pickups is broken. The last quarter and two eighths in that measure become a half note. That sets up a new phrase on the first beat of the next measure and puts two syllables on the following eighths rather than one, like this.

KINGSFOLD, alt. line 3

Both of these versions appear in our books.[6] The one Vaughan Williams used has the value of breaking the tune's potential for monotony with a surprise, though it can trip up a congregation's expectations.

FOREST GREEN was notated by Vaughan Williams in 1903 after he heard it sung by a man named Garman from Forest Green near Ockley, Surrey. It was paired with "O Little Town of Bethlehem" in *The English Hymnal,* but has since been used with many other texts.

Except for the half note that begins the final A section at measure 12, as below, which is how Vaughan Williams gave it[7], this tune is AABA without variations. When the half note is a quarter note following a dotted half,[8] there is an exact repeat of A. The version Vaughan Williams used again has the advantage of stemming monotony with surprise, but introducing the potential for minor congregational confusion.

FOREST GREEN
CMD

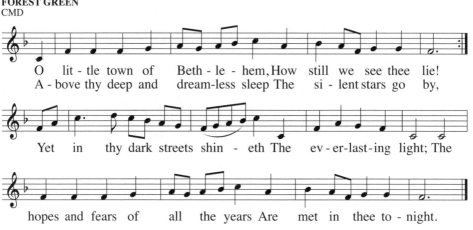

Text: Phillip Brooks, 1868
Tune: English folk melody

Pres #43

Cecil Sharp (1859–1924) was a Cambridge graduate who went to Australia to help run a music school and play the organ at Adelaide Cathedral. In 1892 he moved back to England, was involved with a couple of music schools there, and then became the most important collector of English folk songs. He came to the United States and collected English folk songs in Appalachia. He had a significant influence on composers like Vaughan Williams. Between 1904 and 1906 he transcribed three versions of O WALY WALY. The one given below was published in the third of five volumes of *Folk Songs from Somerset* (London, 1904–1909). It is an engaging musical line developed by three arches that gradually move higher by step—to the third, the fourth, and finally the high dominant. From there it winds down to the lower dominant and back up to the tonic. The tune's name is from a Scottish ballad, "Waly, Waly, Up the Bank."

O WALY WALY
LM

When love is found and hope comes home, Sing and be
glad that two are one. When love ex-plodes and fills the
sky, Praise God and share our Mak-er's joy.

Text: Brian Wren, b.1936, © 1983, Hope Publishing Co.   Wor3 #745
Tune: English

Finnish

KUORTANE (also known as NYLAND) comes from Finland.

KUORTANE
7 6 7 6 D

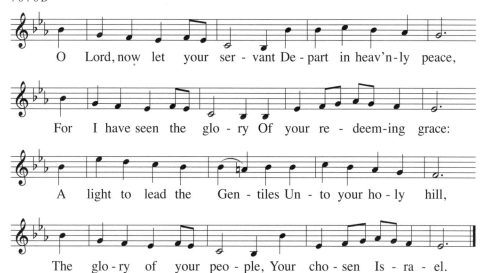

O Lord, now let your ser-vant De-part in heav'n-ly peace,
For I have seen the glo-ry Of your re-deem-ing grace:
A light to lead the Gen-tiles Un-to your ho-ly hill,
The glo-ry of your peo-ple, Your cho-sen Is-ra-el.

Text: Ernest E. Ryden, 1886-1981, alt., © Board of Publication, Lutheran Church in America   LBW #339
Tune: Finnish folk tune, 19th c.

Nyland, a province in Finland, has generally named the melody, but it probably comes from the province of Kuortane, which accounts for the more accurate name. It first entered a Finnish hymnal in 1909 (in the Appendix to *Suomen Evankelis Luterilaisen Kirken Koraalikirja*, Helsinki) and English hymnody in *The Revised Church Hymnary* (Edinburgh) of 1927. Armin Haeussler made valiant efforts to trace its origins, but came up empty.[9] It is a delightful tune that congregations sing heartily. Though the slight melodic modifications here and there might seem to cause trouble, it generates interest instead. At first glance it appears to be in bar form, but it is actually a melodic journey of AA'BA''. The second half of A' nicely complements the second half of A instead of introducing confusion, B moves up easily to the climax even though it reaches an octave and a fourth away from the lowest note, and in the second half of A'' the octave leap from A is used without a problem instead of a unison as in A'.

There are several less well-known but equally engaging Finnish tunes. One is NYT YLÖS, SIELUNI, which comes from southwest Finland and was found by Berndt Mikael Nyberg and Ilmari Krohn in 1890. It is a longer, broadly striding melody in the shape AABA'. The second half of B is the same as A except for the slight melodic adjustment before the telling half note on B-natural in the middle. The B section moves by conjunct motion to the B-natural, now a quarter note rather than a half note, then repeats the latter half of A. The same rhythmic modification is propelled into A' and moves toward home. The stride around the tonic triad and the repeated material set up more meditative stasis than KUORTANE's melodic journey.

NYT YLÖS, SIELUNI
PM

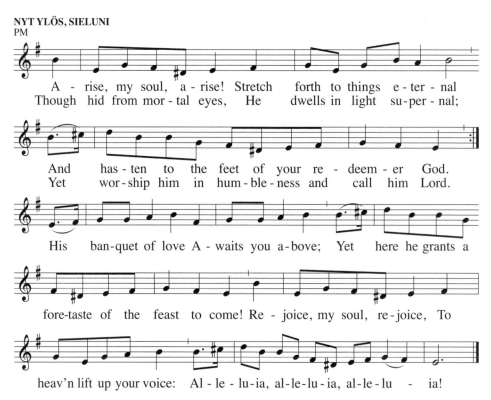

Text: Johan Kahl, 1721-1746; tr. Ernest E. Ryden, 1886-1981, alt., © 1958, *Service Book & Hymnal*, admin. Augsburg Fortress
Tune: Finnish folk tune

LBW #516

NOORMARKKU, also collected by Nyberg, is of the more meditative variety. It is an unusually beautiful phrygian melody that alternates 5 and 4 pulse measures in the span of an octave and in the shape AABB'.

NOORMARKKU
7 6 7 6 D

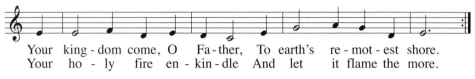

Text: Kauko-Veikko Tamminen, 1882-1946; *Laudamus*, tr. Ernest E. Ryden, 1886-1981, alt., © 1970, Lutheran World Federation   LBW #384
Tune: Finnish folk tune

LOST IN THE NIGHT comes from a collection of Finnish folk tunes published in 1857. "The original text was secular and quite erotic."[10] The text given here, Olav Lee's version of a Finnish (and somewhat Norwegian and Swedish?) hymn, receives a haunting minor sixth to initiate it and an equally haunting melody to support the plaintive cry for help.

LOST IN THE NIGHT
11 11 11 5 5

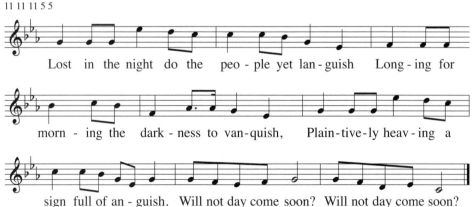

Text: Finnish song; tr. Olav Lee, b.1859, alt., © Augsburg Fortress   LBW #394
Tune: Finnish folk tune

French

In the 1928 edition of the *Oxford Book of Carols*, the traditional French Christmas text (the text Marcel Dupré had in mind in 1922 when he wrote his organ *Variations on an Old Noël*, Op. 22) was given for the tune called NOEL NOUVELET, but only *after* an *Easter* text was inter-lined with the music.[11] In the English-speaking world the Easter text, "Now the Green Blade Rises," has overtaken the Christmas text and been married to this tune.[12]

NOEL NOUVELET quotes the beginning of the chant melody for "Ave, Maris Stella" and was, according to Keyte and Parrott, linked to the Christmas text "Noel Nouvelet" in the seventeenth century.[13] Jeffrey Wasson, noting that some have assigned a medieval origin to it, thinks it comes from the eighteenth century or later.[14] The melody consists of one phrase repeated three times with a bridge before the final repetition. Though it engages congregations because of its raised sixth degree, the Easter text regularly trips them up because the second phrase of ten syllables undoes the expectation of the first phrase of eleven by putting two notes on the first syllable. *The Covenant Hymnal* prints the tune in two versions, the problematic Easter one and the Christmas one adjusted with eleven syllables on the second phrase. Here are both versions. (The metrical designation of the second one is correct here, wrong in the hymnal.)

NOEL NOUVELET
11 10 10 11

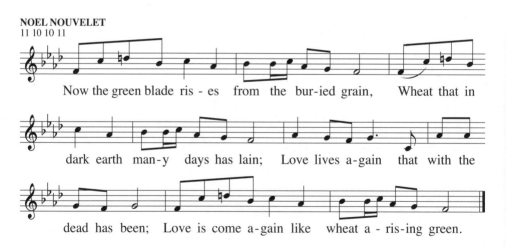

Now the green blade ris - es   from the bur-ied grain,   Wheat that in dark earth man-y   days has lain;   Love lives a-gain   that with the dead has been;   Love is come a-gain like   wheat a - ris-ing green.

Text: J.M.C. Crum, 1872-1958
Tune: French carol, *Oxford Book of Carols*

Cov #244

NOEL NOUVELET
11 11 10 11

Sing we now of Christ-mas, sing we here No-el! Of our Lord and Sav-ior we the tid-ings tell. Sing we No-el! For Christ is born, No-el! Sing we now of Christ-mas, sing we here No-el!

Text: *Noel Nouvelet,* tr. Richard Zgodava, © 1966, Augsburg Fortress
Tune: French carol, *Oxford Book of Carols*

Cov #177

PICARDY comes from the region for which it is named, possibly from the seventeenth century. It was printed in *Chansons populaires des provinces de France* (Paris, 1860), taken down from Mme. Pierre Dupont as she remembered it from her childhood. The folk text that went with it, "Jésus-Christ s'habille en pauvre," has Jesus searching for charity as a poor man. The master of the house chases him, the wife feeds him, her charity fills the bedroom with light, and Jesus tells her in three days she will go to paradise while her husband will burn in hell. This absorbing text on behalf of the poor, with a works righteousness twist, has been replaced by "Let All Mortal Flesh" from the Orthodox Liturgy of St. James. The tune interprets it well. A minor melody in AAB form, it spans an octave and moves largely by conjunct motion. It gets to the high tonic in the penultimate phrase and repeats that figure in the last phrase. None of these formal details accounts for its serious and profoundly engaging character, which has commended it to a wide range of congregations. All the hymnals we surveyed include it.

PICARDY
8 7 8 7 8 7

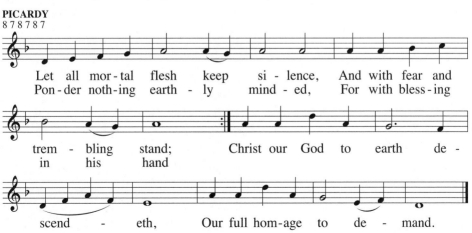

Let all mor-tal flesh keep si - lence, And with fear and
Pon-der noth-ing earth - ly mind - ed, For with bless-ing
trem - bling stand; Christ our God to earth de -
in his hand
scend - eth, Our full hom-age to de - mand.

Text: *Liturgy of St. James,* 4th c.; tr. Gerard Moultrie, 1864
Tune: French carol, 17th c.

Chal, #124

GLORIA is a sprightlier but equally well-known French folk tune. It goes exclusively with "Angels We Have Heard on High," whose earliest printed source is *Choix de cantiques sur des airs nouveaux* (1842) followed by *Nouveau recueil de cantiques* (1855). The text is assumed to be from the eighteenth century and the tune older "since it was usual for such texts to be written to existing tunes (no newly composed *noël* tune is known from the whole of the eighteenth century)."[15]

The stanzas tell the story in a straightforward way with a simple tune that has a modified inner repeat at measures 1 and 3, a motivic repeat at measures 2 and 4, and then a full-scale repeat of the first four measures. A single narrator or small choir is the implied singer of the stanzas. The people's response follows in the refrain, which is also a repeated structure, but this time much more melismatic and developed by sequence, which glides along the "Gloria" in a jubilant yet eminently congregational vocalise.

GLORIA
7 7 7 7 with refrain

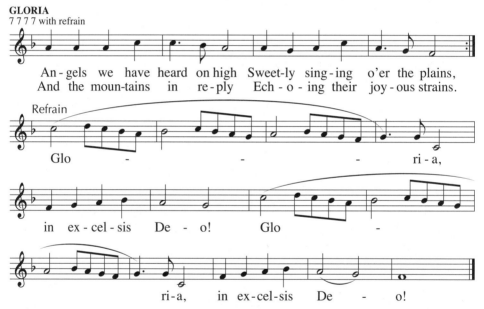

An - gels we have heard on high Sweet-ly sing-ing o'er the plains,
And the moun-tains in re-ply Ech - o - ing their joy-ous strains.

Refrain
Glo - - - ri - a,
in ex - cel - sis De - o! Glo -
ri - a, in ex - cel - sis De - o!

Text: Trad. French carol; trans. *Crown of Jesus*, 1862, alt.   Meth #238
Tune: French carol melody

Ghanaian

CHEREPONI is a tune from the town of that name in Northern Ghana, West Africa, where Tom Colvin (b. 1925) found it. Colvin was a missionary from Scotland who encouraged Africans to sing their own music, which he collected. This tune and its text were first published by the Iona Community in *Free to Serve: Hymns from Africa* (1968). (The Iona Community, from Scotland, is discussed below.) With a 6/8 lilt and considerable use of sequence, CHERIPONI is accessible and engaging for virtually any congregation and has generated considerable traction. It is too soon to tell whether that will last.

CHEREPONI
Irregular with refrain

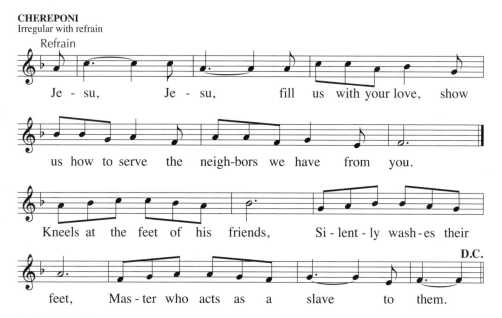

Refrain

Je - su, Je - su, fill us with your love, show
us how to serve the neigh-bors we have from you.
Kneels at the feet of his friends, Si - lent - ly wash-es their
feet, Mas - ter who acts as a slave to them.

D.C.

Text: Tom Colvin, 1969
Tune: Ghana folk song; arr. Tom Colvin, 1969, © 1969, Hope Publishing Co.

Chal #600

Icelandic

For the sake of glimpsing a broader picture than current practice provides, it should be noted that Iceland had a hymn-singing tradition that was never picked up by English-speaking groups and was eventually dropped in Iceland. It consisted of

> An elaborate paraphrasing of hymn tunes. . . the melodies were often sung in *Tvisöngur*—a kind of two-part organum in slow tempo which combined parallel fifths and contrary motion with unisons, octaves, and thirds. This popular tradition was retained in some localities until the beginning of the present [twentieth] century."[16]

Kristín Jóhannesdóttir and Sigurdur K. Sigurdsson, musician and pastor from Iceland studying for a year at Luther Seminary, showed me some of this music, which they say is still sometimes used.[17] It not only includes part singing, but, unlike the other repertoires we have seen, gravitates to the lydian mode. It even includes what is usually considered to be theoretical, the locrian mode, built on a diminished triad. None of this, maybe because it is so unusual in highlighting the tonal instability of the augmented fourth or diminished fifth, has passed into our practice.

Irish

SLANE is an Irish folk tune named for the hill where St. Patrick is reputed to have defied the king by lighting the new fire at the Easter Vigil. In spite of its wide range of an octave and a fourth, it engages congregations quite heartily. It was published in Patrick W. Joyce's *Old Irish Folk Music and Songs* (London, 1909) and joined to the Irish hymn "Be Thou My Vision" in both the Irish *Church Hymnal* (Dublin, 1919) and *The Church Hymnary* (London, 1927). A slightly different version from the one given below, with pickups, can be found in *The Hymnal 1982* at #482.

SLANE
10 10 9 10

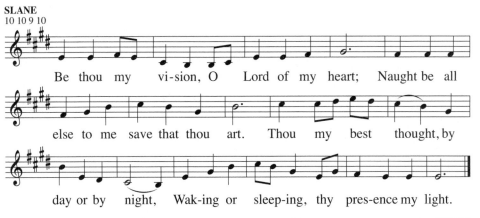

Text: Ancient Irish, *Rob tu mo bhoile, a Comdi cride;* tr. Mary Elizabeth Byrne, *Erin, Vol. II,* 1905   HWB #545
Tune: Irish melody, *Old Irish Folk Music and Songs,* 1909, © Oxford University Press

Vaughan Williams was responsible for the version of we have of ST. COLUMBA, first paired with Henry Baker's "The King of Love My Shepherd Is" in *The English Hymnal* of 1906. George Petrie (1789–1866) included it among the Irish melodies he collected, and Charles Stanford published them in his *Complete Collection of Irish Music as noted by George Petrie* (London, 1902–1905). Another form of the melody was given in *The Church Hymnal* of the Church of Ireland (Dublin, 1874). This is an arch-like tune in which the triplets stimulate interest and help drive to the peak on the high tonic.

ST. COLUMBA
8 7 8 7

Text: Henry Williams Baker, 1868   VU #273
Tune: ancient Irish melody, arr. Charles V. Stanford, 1906

Japanese

SAKURA, a traditional Japanese melody, is another example of an Asian melody. The six pitches, two linked three-note minor motives a fifth apart, are duplicates of one another (a whole step followed by a half step)—one on B with C-sharp and D, and one on E with F-sharp and G. The following problems have to be negotiated by Western ears: 1) in the fourth measure what feels like an augmented fourth from C-sharp to G, though the C-sharp may be regarded as ornamental since it rides back through B; 2) instead of another augmented fourth, a perfect fourth in measure 6 from F-sharp to C-sharp that rides through a third and a second rather than a second and a third as before; 3) the leap of a seventh to begin the phrases at measures 7 and 11; and 4) the augmented fourth between the last two measures. Western congregations have to bracket their aural expetations and approach this music with new ears that require a non-Western pitch memory, which does not immediately perceive melodic lines functionally on a Western harmonic palette. This is quite possible and enlightening, but it requires time and effort. As for all congregational song, there are no quick fixes.

SAKURA
Irregular

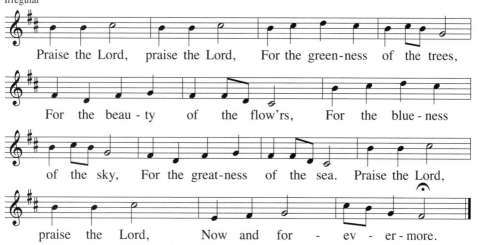

Text: Nobuaki Hanaoka, 1980, *Hymns from the Four Winds*, 1983, © 1980, Nobuaki Hanaoka
Tune: Traditional Japanese melody, tr. © 1983, assigned to Abingdon Press HWB #52

TOKYO is considerably more accessible to Western congregations, though not exactly a folk tune. It was composed in 1958 by Isao Koizumi (b. 1907) in a Chinese mode used in Japanese court music. Though pentatonic, it has the structure of a Western tune. Koizumi was born in Osaka, Japan, studied economics there and also played the organ in Tokyo where he became minister of music at the United States Far East Air Force Chapel Center. He was the music editor of *The Hymnal* (1954) for the United Church of Christ in Japan. Here is TOKYO with I-to Loh's phonetic transliteration of the Japanese, which gives an insight into the sound of this music.

TOKYO
7 5 7 5 D

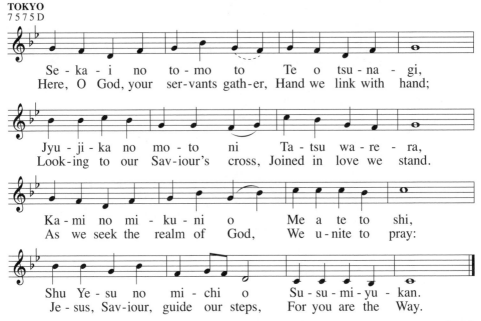

Se - ka - i   no   to - mo   to   Te   o   tsu - na - gi,
Here, O God, your   ser-vants gath-er, Hand we   link with   hand;

Jyu - ji - ka   no   mo - to   ni   Ta - tsu   wa - re - ra,
Look-ing to   our   Sav-iour's   cross, Joined in   love we   stand.

Ka - mi   no   mi - ku - ni   o   Me   a   te   to   shi,
As   we seek the   realm of   God,   We   u - nite to   pray:

Shu Ye - su   no   mi - chi   o   Su - su - mi - yu - kan.
Je - sus, Sav-iour, guide our steps,   For you are the   Way.

Text: Tokuo Yamaguchi 1958; tr. and para. Everett M. Stowe, 1958, alt. 1972, © Estate of Tokuo Yamaguchi,
   phonetic transcription from Japanese by I-to Loh, 1988, © The United Methodist Publishing House
Tune: Isao Koizumi, 1958   VU #362

Native American

Joseph R. Renville (1778–1846) was a Roman Catholic priest from St. Paul, Minnesota. His father was a French-Canadian trader, his mother from the Dakota people. He translated the Bible into Dakota and wrote Dakota hymns, like the one given below, adapting the native tune now called LACQUIPARLE ("Lac qui Parle"—"lake that speaks"—the name of Renville's mission on the Mississippi) to it. The text and tune (also called DAKOTA INDIAN CHANT) were first published in the *Dakota Odowan* (1879). The tune is structured in a congregational ABA shape.

LACQUIPARLE
9 6 9 9 9 6

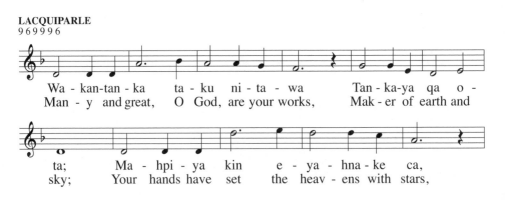

Wa - kan-tan - ka   ta - ku   ni - ta - wa   Tan - ka-ya   qa   o -
Man - y   and great,   O   God, are your works,   Mak - er   of earth and

ta;   Ma - hpi - ya   kin   e - ya - hna - ke   ca,
sky;   Your   hands have   set   the   heav - ens with   stars,

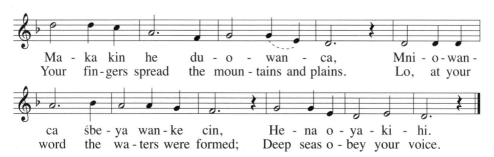

Ma - ka kin he   du - o - wan - ca,   Mni - o - wan -
Your fin-gers spread   the moun - tains and plains.   Lo,   at your

ca   śbe - ya wan - ke   cin,   He - na o - ya - ki - hi.
word   the wa - ters were formed;   Deep seas o - bey your voice.

Text: Dakota Hymn, Joseph R. Renville, 1842, par. by R. Philip Frazier, 1929; alt.   NC #3
Tune: Native American melody (Dakota), adapt. by Joseph R. Renville, 1842

Polish

W ŻŁOBIE LEŻY is a Polish tune that derives from the rhythm of the Mazurka, a Polish country dance in the region of Warsaw. Its origins and date are not known, like the text "Infant Holy" that is linked with it. It first surfaced in English hymnody in 1877[18] and was modified rhythmically. Since English does not have a poetic rhythm comparable to the Polish one, W ŻŁOBIE LEŻY has often been printed in English dress with the two eighth notes at the beginning of phrases interpreted as pickups and a four-part harmonic arrangement that places a new chord on every note, which necessitates a slow tempo.[19] The result is a nineteenth-century Western European choral setting, but the native rhythm of the piece is more hardy and folk-like. In the native context the tempo is faster, eighths begin on the first beat, and strong accents follow on the second or third beat of the measure as in a dance with the click of heels. Whereas the seventeenth and eighteenth centuries flattened out rhythmic chorales into isometric sameness, the late nineteenth century mind-set and the way English accents fall tempt us to run tunes like W ŻŁOBIE LEŻY through a sentimental filter that takes out their bite. (The last two measures are sometimes repeated.)

W ŻŁOBIE LEŻY

4 4 7 4 4 7 4 4 4 4 7

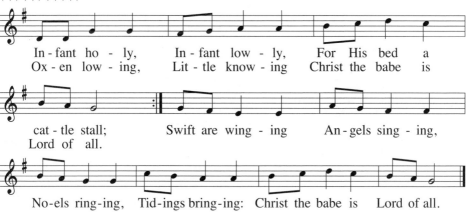

In - fant ho - ly,   In - fant low - ly,   For His bed   a
Ox - en low - ing,   Lit - tle know - ing   Christ the babe   is

cat - tle stall;   Swift are wing - ing   An - gels sing - ing,
Lord of all.

No-els ring-ing, Tid-ings bring-ing: Christ the babe is   Lord of all.

Text: Polish carol; tr. para. Edith M. G. Reed, 1925   Pres #37
Tune: Polish carol

Scottish

The Scottish tune tradition is imbedded in the metrical psalm tunes from the Reformation, but several well-known Scottish tunes entered the stream in the nineteenth century. BUNESSAN was first printed in Lachlan MacBean's *Songs and Hymns of the Gael*—sometimes given as *Songs and Hymns of the Scottish Highlands* (Edinburgh, 1888). There it was paired with "Christ in the Manger" by Mary MacDonald who was born near Bunessan on the Isle of Mull in Scotland. This delightful melody spans a little more than an octave and repeats the same rhythm with two juxtapositions—1) triads versus conjunct motion and 2) right-side up and upside down versions of both in the quarter notes. It is often referred to as an Irish folk tune, but it takes its name from the Scottish place of MacDonald's birth.

BUNESSAN
5 5 5 3 D

Child in the man - ger, In - fant of Mar - y; Out - cast and stran - ger, Lord of all; Child who in - her - its All our trans - gres - sions, All our de - mer - its On Him fall.

Text: Mary MacDonald, 1789-1872; tr. Lachlan Macbean, 1853-1931   Bap #105
Tune: Gaelic melody

BROTHER JAMES' AIR and CRIMOND are two other Scottish tunes. The text often paired with BROTHER JAMES' AIR is from the mid-seventeenth century Scottish Psalter tradition, but the tune comes from a nineteenth-century composer. Though not really a folk tune, it often passes for one and deserves to be considered here. It was written by James Leith Macbeth Bain (ca.1840–1925), a mystic poet and healer who sang to his patients and worked in the slums of Liverpool. This tune is attractive, but its high tonic ending taxes congregations, especially after several repetitions.

BROTHER JAMES' AIR
8 6 8 6 8 6

The Lord's my shep - herd; I'll not want. He
In pas - tures green; he lead - eth me The

makes me down to lie He lead-eth me, he
qui - et wa - ters by.

lead - eth me The qui - et wa - ters by.

Text: *Psalter*, Edinburgh, 1650
Tune: J. L. Macbeth Bain, c. 1840-1925, adapt.

LBW #451

CRIMOND, named for the village of Crimond in northeastern Scotland, is less taxing, but equally engaging. In a relatively slow three beats to the bar, it quietly roams just beyond fifth to fifth around the tonic, stopping away from home at midstream on the high dominant. Like CRIMOND, it is not really a folk tune, having been written either by David Grant (1833–1893), a tobacco dealer and precentor from Aberdeen, or by Jessie Seymour Irvine (1836–1887), the daughter of a minister at the church in Crimond.[20] It first appeared in the *Northern Psalter* (1872) with the hymn "Thou Art the Way, the Truth, the Life." It became popular when it was paired with Psalm 23 (from the seventeenth-century Scottish Psalter) in mid-twentieth century Sunday radio broadcasts by the Glasgow Orpheus Choir and when it was sung at the wedding of Princess Elizabeth in 1947. *The School Hymn Book of the Methodist Church* (London, 1950) printed the text and tune together.

CRIMOND
8 6 8 6

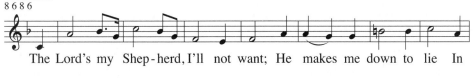

The Lord's my Shep - herd, I'll not want; He makes me down to lie In

pas - tures green; He lead - eth me, the qui - et wa - ters by.

Text: *Scottish Psalter*, 1650
Tune: Jessie Seymour Irvine, 1872

VU #747

John Bell (b. 1949) is a skillful song leader, composer, and Presbyterian minister. He is part of the Scottish Iona Community, a source of renewal in the twentieth-century church.[21] The Community and its leaders like John Bell have mined not only Scottish folk music, but folk music from around the world, as indicated above with the tune CHEREPONI. The following tune, THAINAKY, was composed by John Bell. It is not really a folk tune, but it bears the marks of folk influence as a setting for a text about the Holy Spirit, of whom the wild goose may be an ancient Celtic symbol.[22] In a minor key, with a couple Scotch snaps, its slightly asymmetrical end cleverly (and happily) allows congregations to breathe before successive stanzas.

THAINAKY
11 11 11 11

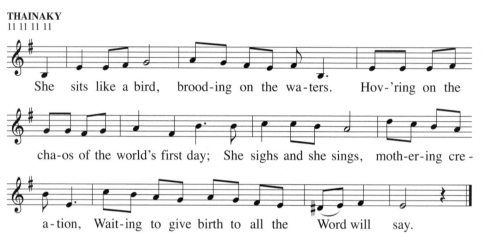

Text & Tune: John Bell, 1988
© 1988, Iona Community, admin. GIA Publications, Inc.

Chal #255

Sicilian

What we call SICILIAN MARINER'S HYMN (also known in various versions as SICILIAN MARINERS and O SANCTISSIMA and O DU FRÖLICHE[23]) has unknown sources. It is first found in *The European Magazine and London Review* 22 (November 1792): 385–386, where it had the Latin text "O Sanctissima," which stimulated the heading, "The Sicilian Mariner's Hymn to the Virgin."[24] Byron Underwood quotes reports that it was sung in unison by Sicilian seamen on board ship at sunset and by gondoliers in Venice.[25] Though the Sicilian seamen may well have sung it in unison, it is a tune easily harmonized in thirds, like STILLE NACHT and SCHÖNSTER HERR JESU.

346

SICILIAN MARINER'S HYMN
878787

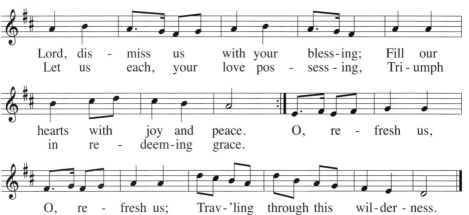

Lord, dis - miss us with your bless-ing; Fill our
Let us each, your love pos - sess-ing, Tri - umph

hearts with joy and peace. O, re - fresh us,
in re - deem-ing grace.

O, re - fresh us; Trav-'ling through this wil-der - ness.

Text: John Fawcett, 1773
Tune: Sicilian melody, 18th c.
                                 Mor #559

Silesian

SCHÖNSTER HERR JESU also goes by the names ST. ELIZABETH or CRUSADER'S HYMN.

SCHÖNSTER HERR JESU
557558

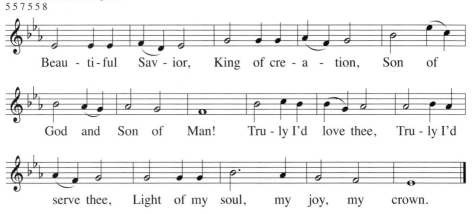

Beau - ti - ful Sav - ior, King of cre - a - tion, Son of

God and Son of Man! Tru - ly I'd love thee, Tru - ly I'd

serve thee, Light of my soul, my joy, my crown.

Text: *Gesangbuch*, Münster, 1677; tr. Joseph A. Seiss, 1823-1904
Tune: Silesian folk tune, 1842
                                 LBW #518

Let us first clarify the names. The text "Schönster Herr Jesu" comes from Münster, Westphalia, from a Jesuit manuscript of 1662. It was printed in the Catholic *Münsterisch Gesangbuch* (Münster) in 1677. The tune called SCHÖNSTER HERR JESU, which went with it there, is #384 in *The Hymnal 1982*.[26] ST. ELIZABETH at #383 in *The Hymnal 1982* is the same as what is called SCHÖNSTER HERR JESU at #518 of the *Lutheran Book of Worship* (given here), though the translations of the hymn differ. The first one ("Fairest Lord Jesus") is an anonymous version of the Jesuit text, the second one by Joseph Seiss ("Beautiful Savior"). Franz Liszt used this melody in *The Legend of St. Elizabeth* (1862) for the Crusaders' March, which is how "CRUSADER'S HYMN" and "ST. ELIZABETH" got attached to it, but it has no connection with the Crusades. It was transcribed by August Heinrich Hoffmann von Fallersleben (1798-1874) who collected folk songs from Silesia— an area in central Europe, now mostly in Poland around the city of Wroclaw— and heard it sung by haymakers in 1839. He published it in 1842 in *Schlesische Volkslieder* (Leipzig) with the text "Schönster Herr Jesu."[27] Stulken thinks it has "roots in older melodies" and notes the similarity with Christian Ernst Graaf's tune from 1766, which Mozart used for a set of variations (K. 24).[28] As Brink and Polman suggest, "the tune consists primarily of a few melodic sequences and their variations,"[29] skillfully assembled "as a melody harmonized in parallel thirds, in a style similar to SILENT NIGHT"[30] [STILLE NACHT], but with a more congregational orientation because of the ongoing rhythmic motion and the absence of the slide. (The same is true for SICILIAN MARINER'S HYMN.)

South African

THUMA MINA comes from Durban, Natal, South Africa, and was first published in *Freedom Is Coming: Songs of Protest and Praise from South Africa* (Fort Lauderdale, 1984). The text moved from Zulu and Xhosa to Swedish to Gracia Grindal's translation in English. This South African call-response piece is new for the English-speaking Anglo-European churches. Though not as much as CHEREPONI, THUMA MINA has, nonetheless, piqued considerable ecumenical interest. It is congregational, so long as the distinctions between "Leader" and "All" are maintained. If everybody tries to sing the leader's part, it becomes meaningless and falls apart. Like the music of Taizé, time will tell whether it and other pieces like it will take root.

THUMA MINA
Irregular

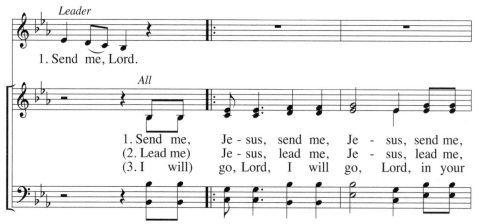

Other verses may be improvised.

Text & Tune: Trad. South African
© 1984, Walton Music Corporation   VU #572

Swedish

Since 1873 TRYGGARE KAN INGEN VARA has been linked with Lina Sandell's text "Children of the Heavenly Father," though Sandell originally used another melody.

TRYGGARE KAN INGEN VARA
8 8 8 8

Text: Lina Sandell, 1832-1903, tr. Ernst W. Olson, 1870-1958, © 1925, 1953, Board of Publication, Lutheran Church in America   Cov #87
Tune: Swedish melody, 1874

Marilyn Stulken[31] details the obscure origins of this tune, which may be a Swedish folk song with German antecedents. She concludes by suggesting the melody may have its origins in the eighteenth century. Wherever and whenever it comes from, the tune as we have it ably fits a congregational idiom. The second phrase is a tonal sequence of the first, a second higher. Together these prepare the upward major sixth that begins the third phrase, which in this context has a folk-like character as it turns around by repeating the downward third from the end of the first phrase followed by its inversion twice in the last phrase. This tightly woven unit fits within the frame of an octave and a minor second, and its regular mazurka-like rhythm is readily accessible to congregations. The mazurka rhythm makes one wonder if it, too, like W ŻŁOBIE LEŻY, has had its accents displaced.

349

O STORE GUD seems to be a Swedish folk melody whose provenance is unknown. It can be found in a hymnal called *Sionsharpan* from 1890.[32] It appeared there with three beats to a measure, like this.

O STORE GUD
11 10 11 10 with refrain

Text: Carl Gustav Boberg
Tune: Swedish folk melody

Sionsharpan, 1890

At some point the rhythm was changed to four beats to a measure, as hymnals print it today, sometimes using the name HOW GREAT THOU ART.[33]

HOW GREAT THOU ART
Irregular with refrain

art, how great Thou art! Then sings my soul, my Sav-ior God, to Thee, How great Thou art, how great Thou art!

Author's original words are "works" and "mighty."

Text: Stuart K. Hine   Meth #77
Tune: Stuart K. Hine
© 1953: Assigned to Manna Music, Inc., renewed 1981

The tune with three beats to a bar is a gentle melody, which moves with a folk-like congregational quality, even though the refrain expands the range to an octave and a fourth and has some wide leaps. The high E-flat near the end is a short note, approached by leap and folded into the curve of the final cadence, hard to elongate without doing violence to the melody. The version with four beats to a bar slows to a non-congregational choral piece or operatic solo aria, with built-in sustained notes at phrase ends and the high E-flat near the end structured melodically by conjunct motion as a temptation for soloists to hold as long as possible. (Soloists love to transpose the melody up as high as they can drive that note and add a fermata, which some hymnals include.) Paul Richardson's comment in the chapter on metrical psalm tunes is especially ad rem here. "When we begin to have long notes between short phrases, we lose the momentum of the rhythmic breath and of the textual thought. This creates not merely a caesura, but a stop." In the four-beat version of this tune, there is a stop in the refrain at every half tied to an eighth, which leads to the temptation to hold the high E-flat at the end. These stops influence the stanzas and give them a propensity to stop at every dotted half note. At each of these points, the momentum has to be regained, only to be immediately lost all over again. Both text and tune turn into a series of separate fragments. When you add to this the intense controversy this hymn spawns[34] and the hostility that its politically correct support generates, it becomes clear that the tune as we know it has lost whatever its folk-like origins may be.

Taiwanese

TOA-SIA is a Taiwanese pentatonic melody. Unlike the Chinese one given above, it projects for Western ears a minor rather than a major tonality. Like the Chinese one, it utilizes big leaps, a similarly wide range of an octave and a fourth, and a pentatonic frame deployed quite differently from white spirituals or a medieval tune like NUN BITTEN WIR. Here it is with an accompaniment that I-to Loh fashioned in hopes of not getting in the way of the tune.

TOA-SIA
7 7 7 7

God cre - at - ed heaven and earth, All things per - fect

brought to birth; God's great power made

dark and light, Earth re-volv-ing day and night.

Text: Trad. Taiwanese hymn; tr. by Boris and Clare Anderson, © 1983, Boris and Clare Anderson　　　　Meth #151
Tune: Trad. Taiwanese melody; harm. by I-to Loh, © 1983, The United Methodist Publishing House

---

1　VU #241, cited here, gives only three stanzas, but *Songs of the People* gives five, where the climax of "For Jesus Is Lord" comes in the fifth.

2　The best source for Asian materials is I-to Loh (General Ed.), *Sound the Bamboo: CCA Hymnal 2000* (Quezon City: R. R. Yan Printing Press, 2000).

3　For more details on Valerius and this collection see William S. Smith, "Let's Hear it for Valerius!", *The Hymn* 54:4 (October 2003): 8–17.

4　Alan Luff, "O Jesus, Crowned with All Renown," Glover, H82C, 3A, 563.

5　EH #574.

6　See, for example, NC #51, for the rhythm as in EH.

7　At EH, #15.

8　As in Cov #124.

9　Armin Haeussler, *The Story of Our Hymns*, 336–338.

10   Stulken, HCLBW, 434.

11   Percy Dearmer, R. Vaughan Williams, Martin Shaw, eds., *The Oxford Book of Carols* (London: Oxford University Press, 1964, first published 1928), 306–307.

12   For the complete Christmas text see Hugh Keyte and Andrew Parrott, *The New Oxford Book of Carols*, 614–617.

13   Ibid., 618.

14   Jeffrey Wasson, "Now the Green Blade Riseth," Glover, H82C, 3A, 412.

15   Hugh Keyte and Andrew Parrott, *The New Oxford Book of Carols*, 638.

16   Shirley McCreedy, "Scandinavian Hymnody, Iceland," Stulken HCLBW, 42–43.

17   On September 13, 2004.

18   Young, CUMH, 275.

19   An example is the setting in *The Hymnbook* (Richmond, 1955), #164. Presbyterians changed the bar line but kept the thick harmonization in Pres #37. LBW #44 has the eighths as pick-ups, but a sparser harmonization.

20   For the dispute about who wrote it, see Robin Leaver, "The Lord My God My Shepherd Is," Glover, H82C, 3B, 1217–1218. Routley, MCH, 85B, seems to think Irvine wrote it and Grant harmonized it.

21   For the ringing cry of the Iona Community's founder, see George F. Macleod, *Only One Way Left: Church Prospect* (Glasgow: The Iona Community, 1956).

22   See Hawn, *Gather Into One*, 190, FN 2.

23   HWB gives the version from *The European Magazine* with dotted notes as O SANCTISSIMA (#209) and a bar form version with even eighths as SICILIAN MARINERS (#621). Wor3 #712 calls the tune O DU FRÖLICHE with the text "O Sanctissima."

24   For the text with a copy of the music, see Nicholas Temperley, "Lord, Dismiss Us with Thy Blessing," Glover, H82C, 641. The Latin text with two stanzas can be found at Wor3 #712.

25   Byron E. Underwood, "The Earliest Source of 'The Sicilian Mariners' Hymn,'" *The Hymn* 27:3 (July 1976): 77.

26   Also given in Zahn, MDEK, #3975.

27   Haeussler, *The Story of Our Hymns*, 234, gives a reproduction of the page.

28   Stulken, HCLBW, 532.

29   Brink/Polman, PsHH, 627.

30   Fyock, HCHWB, 86.

31   Stulken, HCLBW, 496–497.

32   *Sionsharpan* (Chicago: The Mission Friend's Publishing Company, 1890), #12.

33   The hymnal companions and Bryon Underwood, "How Great Thou Art," *The Hymn* 24:4 (October 1973): 106 give a 3/4 arrangement for voice, guitar, and piano by Adolf Edgren from 1891 as the earliest appearance of the tune with the source "*Sanningsvittnet.*" Underwood spells it "*Sanningswittnet* [The Witness for Truth]" and says this was the "organ of the Home Missionary Society of the Evangelical Lutheran Church in Sweden," No. 16 (April 16, 1891), of which the author of the text, Carl Boberg, was editor. J. Irving Erickson, *Twice-Born Hymns* (Chicago: Covenant Press, 1976), 61, says "the arrangements in our Swedish hymnals were in three beats." Bryon Underwood, "How Great Thou Art" (continued from October 1973 issue), *The Hymn* 25:1 (January 1974): 5 cites an 1894 edition of *Sionsharpan* with the melody in four-part harmony, still with three beats to the bar, contrary to the companions which locate the 4/4 version in 1894. Underwood assumes the *Sionsharpan* version of the melody, which is not exactly the same as Edgren's, is dependent on Edgren's arrangement, apparently without realizing a music edition of *Sionsharpan* in 1890, included it before the version by Edgren. Underwood, (January 1974): 5 says the change to 4/4 comes from a Naga choir arrangement, but does not give its date.

34   See, for example, Young, CUMH, 409.

XIV. Twentieth-century Tunes

1. The First Half of the Twentieth Century

Ralph Vaughan Williams

Early in the twentieth century, English hymn tune composition clustered around Ralph Vaughan Williams (1872–1958), a rare first-rate composer who understood and supported congregational song. No other composer of his stature lavished such effort on hymn tunes. He was the musical editor for a remarkable hymnal, mined folk song for its hymnic possibilities, and wrote and arranged tunes in which congregations have delighted.[1] The hymnal was *The English Hymnal* (London, 1906), which has been mentioned in these pages before. In the "Preface" he expressed his concern to rescue hymnody from the pretentiousness into which it had fallen and to get behind the popular tyranny of the moment to the more durable core of the genuinely popular in the sense of what belongs to the folk over time. He argued, therefore, against "the miasma of the languishing and sentimental hymn tunes which so often disfigure our services," and rightly saw this as "a moral rather than a musical issue."[2] He sought what was genuinely congregational, realized it was unison melody that congregations could sing and, therefore, chose "fine melody rather than the exploitation of the trained choir,"[3] kept the pitch low enough for the congregation, and looked to "familiar melodies" that "have stood the test of time."[4] He realized there were "already many hundreds of fine tunes in existence"[5] from many countries and periods,[6] more than could be included "in any one collection."[7]

The English Hymnal, as might be expected, pulled together as many fine melodies as one book could encompass (as well as ones Vaughan Williams regarded as not so fine, but in breadth of spirit did not omit), to which some new ones were added. The additions included two folk songs that have since traveled widely (KINGSFOLD and FOREST GREEN) and four tunes he wrote (DOWN AMPNEY, RANDOLPH, SALVE FESTA DIES, and SINE NOMINE, all listed as "Anonymous" in 1906), three of which are still generally in use.[8] He wrote KING'S WESTON later for *Songs of Praise* (London, 1925). The folk songs were given in the last chapter. The newly composed ones we take up here.

DOWN AMPNEY, named for Vaughan Williams' birthplace, was ingeniously fitted to Bianca da Siena's fervent text. Austin Lovelace observes how "its quietly rising and falling pattern fits both the unusual meter (66.11.D) and the introspective nature of the text," then quotes Routley's atypical compliment that "it is perhaps the most beautiful hymn-tune composed since the *Old Hundredth*."[9]

DOWN AMPNEY

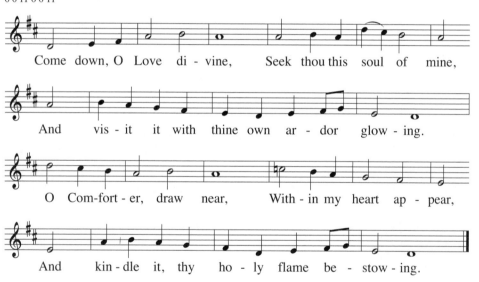

Text: Bianco da Siena, ca. 1367, *Laudi Spirituali del Bianco da Siena*, 1851; tr. Richard F. Littledale, *People's Hymnal*, 1867, alt.   HWB #501
Tune: Ralph Vaughan Williams, *The English Hymnal*, 1906, © Oxford University Press

SALVE FESTA DIES was written for Fortunatus' text that comes from a sixth-century Easter Vigil. The breadth of the refrain is Vaughan Williams at his congregational best. The verses are really choral in conception because they require a different matching of text and music from stanza to stanza. As long as the full assembly joins at the refrain and a smaller group sings the verses, as the structure implies, this tune works very well. If the congregation joins on the verses, trouble is near.

SALVE FESTA DIES
7 9 7 7 with refrain

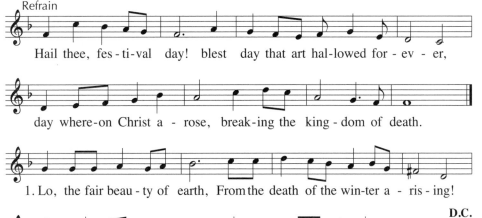

Hail thee, fes-ti-val day! blest day that art hal-lowed for-ev-er,

day where-on Christ a - rose, break-ing the king-dom of death.

1. Lo, the fair beau-ty of earth, From the death of the win-ter a - ris-ing!

D.C.

Ev - 'ry good gift of the year   Now with its Mas-ter re-turns:

2. He who was nailed to the cross Is Lord and the rul - er of na-ture;

D.C.

All things cre - a - ted on earth   Sing to the glo - ry of God:

Text: Venantius Honorius Fortunatus, 540?-600?; tr. *The English Hymnal*, 1906, alt.   H82 #175
Tune: Ralph Vaughan Williams, 1872-1958

SINE NOMINE, though quite popular and often regarded as one of the finest tunes of the twentieth century, is nonetheless a congregational miscalculation—just like the verses of SALVE FESTA DIES when they are used for the full assembly—because the placement of syllables differs from stanza to stanza. The hymn appears to work because the tune is so strong that it carries the words along, even though they turn into a muddle no matter how skillful the leadership. *Christian Worship* has solved the problem by lining up words and music in a responsible congregational hymnic discipline so that they are the same from stanza to stanza. There are those who may object to how some accents fall in such an arrangement, but that problem is minuscule in comparison to the chaos caused by words that fall in different places or just get omitted by congregational singers when the discipline of hymnody is not observed.

SINE NOMINE
10 10 10 with alleluias

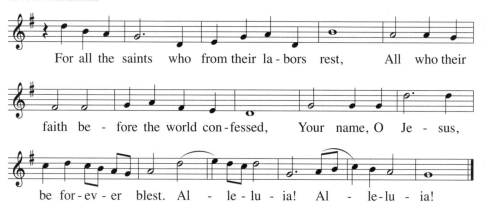

Text: William W. How, 1823-1897, abr., alt.
Tune: Ralph Vaughan Williams, 1872-1958

CW #551

Vaughan Williams composed KING'S WESTON for Caroline Noel's text. It is a strong tune built on the motive in the first measure. The motive's first two notes expand from a second to a third at the seventh measure. Both the original and the expansion are turned around and upside down (the original modified, the expansion an exact inversion) in the last phrase, which itself is an expansion of the former two-measure phrases into a longer summarizing sweep of four measures.

KING'S WESTON
6 5 6 5 D

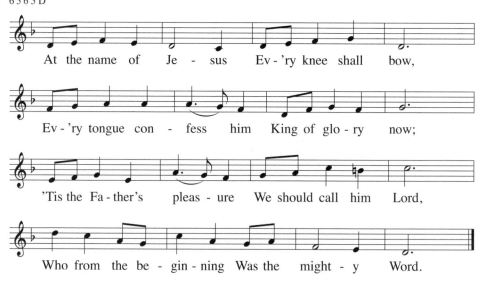

Text: Caroline M. Noel, 1870, alt.
Tune: Ralph Vaughan Williams, 1925, © Oxford University Press

PsH #467

Charles V. Stanford

Charles V. Stanford (1852–1924) composed ENGELBERG for the 1904 edition of *Hymns Ancient and Modern*, to go with "For All the Saints." Though it is a strong and bold tune, it was largely replaced two years later by the tune his student Vaughan Williams wrote, SINE NOMINE, which in its breadth is quite similar. In *The Hymnal 1940* ENGELBERG was paired with "All Praise to Thee, for Thou, O King, Divine," but it found a more lasting home after 1972 when, at John Wilson's request, Fred Pratt Green wrote "When in Our Music God Is Glorified" to go with it. It has also been used with John Geyer's "We Know That Christ Is Raised." Stanford was a prodigious and energetic composer and conductor who, along with his other work, already as an undergraduate became organist at Trinity College, Cambridge. He studied, traveled widely, and had no use for the hackneyed or trite. His most lasting influence was as a demanding teacher of composition. In this tune, as is characteristic also of Vaughan Williams' tunes, the pulse is so strong that the long notes at phrase ends never sit down, but are always propelled onward with enough space for breath.

ENGELBERG

10 10 10 with alleluia

Text: Fred Pratt Green, 1903-2000, © 1972, Hope Publishing Co.   Wor3 #549
Tune: Charles V. Stanford, 1852-1924

Sydney Nicholson

Sydney Nicholson (1875–1947), who named Purcell's tune WESTMINSTER ABBEY, was himself the organist at the Abbey from 1919 to 1927, when he resigned to found and direct what became the Royal School of Church Music. From 1913 until his death he was successively editor, proprietor, and chairman of *Hymns Ancient and Modern*. He wrote CRUCIFER for the 1916 Supplement to that book, for the words given with it here.

CRUCIFER
10 10 with refrain

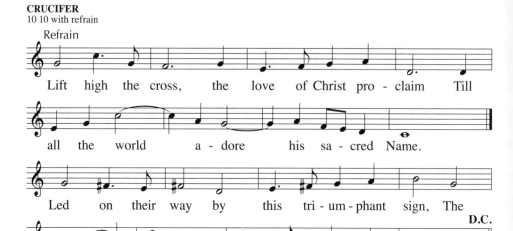

Refrain

Lift high the cross, the love of Christ pro - claim Till all the world a - dore his sa - cred Name. Led on their way by this tri - um - phant sign, The hosts of God in con - quering ranks com - bine.

D.C.

Text: George William Kitchin, 1827-1912; alt. Michael Robert Newbolt, 1874-1956
Tune: Sydney Hugo Nicholson, 1875-1947
Text & Tune by permission of Hymns Ancient & Modern, Ltd.

H82 #473

John Ireland

As noted in Chapter VIII, "My Song Is Love Unknown" was tied to the nineteenth-century Welsh tune RHOSYMEDRE. In the twentieth century, an English tune, LOVE UNKNOWN, was written for the same text at the request of Geoffrey Shaw for *The Public School Hymnal* (London, 1919). Its composer, a sensitive and introverted person named John Ireland (1879–1962), was highly regarded in his lifetime. His study with Stanford, skill as a song writer, and experience as organist and choirmaster (at St. Luke's, Chelsea) probably combined to make this tune possible. It first stretches out in two broad and undulating statements to reach the dominant, and then it unwinds in sequence with the surprise of a C-natural and shorter phrase groups on its way back to the tonic.

LOVE UNKNOWN
6 6 6 6 4 4 4 4

My song is love un - known, My Sav-ior's love for me, Love to the love-less shown That they might love - ly be. O who am I That for my sake My Lord should take Frail flesh and die?

Text: Samuel Crossman, 1664, alt.
Tune: John Ireland, 1918, © John Ireland Trust

Mor #482

Cyril Taylor

SHELDONIAN by Cyril Taylor (1907–1991) has a structure somewhat similar to LOVE UNKNOWN, even with the C-natural, and relates to this gentler stream of twentieth-century tunes.[10] Taylor's tune ABBOT'S LEIGH is better known[11] and relates to the bolder sweep of the SINE NOMINE type. It was written in 1941 when Taylor, a musician and Anglican priest, was working as assistant to the head of Religious Broadcasting for the British Broadcasting Corporation (BBC) and was first used for "Glorious Things of Thee Are Spoken." It served "as an alternative to AUSTRIA, which had been co-opted by the Nazis for "Deutschland, Deutschland über alles." ABBOT'S LEIGH has the distinction, therefore, of being the first hymn tune to be widely introduced and popularized via radio."[12]

There are those who tell me their congregations always sing an E for the C three notes from the end. That has not been my experience, but it points to how congregations make modifications that fit their instincts. In this case, though the low C is implied by its strong use earlier, the longing for a concluding repetition of the fourth from A to E at measure 5 may also be at work here. (The minor seventh is prepared by the earlier reiteration of B-flat.)

ABBOT'S LEIGH
8 7 8 7 D

God is here! As we your peo-ple Meet to
May we find in ful - ler meas-ure What it

of - fer praise and prayer, Here, as in the
is in Christ we share.

world a - round us, All our var - ied skills and

arts Wait the com - ing of the Spir - it

In - to o - pen minds and hearts.

Chal #280

Martin and Geoffrey Shaw

Martin Shaw (1875–1958) and his brother Geoffrey (1879–1943) wrote a few tunes we use,[13] the most potent of which is Martin's PURPOSE.[14] The most familiar is an arrangement of a seventeenth-century English folk song called ROYAL OAK that Martin adapted well to Cecil Frances Alexander's text in *Song Time* (London, 1915), edited by him and Percy Dearmer. This tune ought to pose problems with its upward and downward sixths and then a seventh near the end, but congregations sing it with ease.

ROYAL OAK
7 6 7 6 with refrain

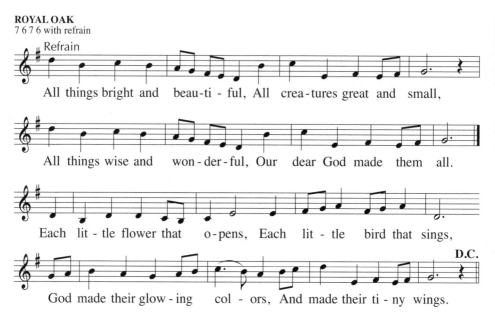

Text: Cecil F. Alexander, 1848; alt.
Tune: English melody, adapt. Martin Shaw, 1915

NC #31

Walter Greatorex

Walter Greatorex (1877-1949)—who, so far as I can tell, is not related to Henry W. Greatorex for whom the nineteenth-century tune GREATOREX is sometimes named—was an Anglican musician who served as director of Gresham's School, Norfolk, England. Benjamin Britten was a student there. Greatorex's tune WOODLANDS was first published in the *Public School Hymnbook* (London, 1919) and named for one of the school houses at Gresham's School. In 1969 the editors of *100 Hymns for Today* chose it for Timothy Dudley-Smith's best-known hymn, his metrical version of the *Magnificat*. That happy linkage has been widely supported. The tune begins with the surge of an upward fourth, which matches well the proclamatory character of the text. That motive is repeated a third lower three phrases later. Part of an upward scale provides contrast in the second phrase. It is expanded across a seventh in the last phrase. Because the outer limits of the scale prepare it, the downward leap of a seventh works well.

WOODLANDS
10 10 10 10

Tell out, my soul, the great-ness of the Lord! Un-num-bered

bless-ings give my spir - it voice; Ten-der to me the prom-ise

of his word; In God my Sav-ior shall my heart re - joice.

Text: *Magnificat anima mea;* Timothy Dudley-Smith, b.1926, © 1962, Hope Publishing Co.   Wor3 #534
Tune: Walter Greatorex, 1877-1949, © Oxford University Press

2. The Second Half of the Twentieth Century

In the last half of the twentieth century a "hymn explosion" was associated with a host of writers like Carl Daw, Timothy Dudley-Smith, Sylvia Dunstan, Martin Franzmann, Fred Pratt Green, Fred Kaan, Thomas Troeger, Jaroslav Vajda, and Brian Wren. Many of their texts and translations have entered the ecumenical stream of hymn singing by local congregations. A number of tunes were also written, not as many as the texts, but a goodly number. Fewer of these have found wide circulation.

Late twentieth century individualism has made it difficult for composers to write congregational music, but the problem is deeper than that. Impressionism in the late nineteenth century and the more jagged compositional "isms" that followed it[15] were attempts to step around the thick nineteenth-century Romantic harmonic palette in order to relate with honesty to the horror of the twentieth century. They could also relate to twentieth-century joy, but the twentieth century was one of the most brutal and destructive periods in human history. Its art and music, like all honest art and music from every period, have reflected the brutality and destruction "in what could be described as one of the most violent and aggressive upheavals in artistic thought in the history of Western music."[16] The problem for hymn tune composition is that congregations cannot sing the jagged complexity of much twentieth-century music. Theologically they are also compelled to sing not only the horror, but the grace of God that goes with them into it.

Twentieth-century hymn tunes do not seem radical, therefore, in light of the isms of twentieth-century musical composition. None is atonal. This is because hymn tunes are folk music, and, as Béla Bartok discovered in his research about folk music, "folk tunes are always tonal."[17] By this he also meant modal— that is, they gravitate to a tonal or modal center. They also cannot employ the kind of multi-metric complexity only print can communicate. They do not have to be regular, as the tyranny of the bar line can suggest, but they do have to be aural rather than visual and structured so that people without musical training can remember them in their ears. In short, they cannot employ dissonant cacophony and disintegrative musical lines used to express the priestly cries from the culture or the prophetic judgments from God, because congregations cannot sing such things. For such jagged musical syntax, which surely has its place, choral and instrumental forces—which can handle what the congregation cannot—have to take up their responsibility.

In the second half of the twentieth century, composers of hymn tunes wrote quite traditional melodies, but also experimented with congregational possibilities, which employed the period's musical syntax. Here are some examples of both kinds, organized alphabetically by composer.

Jan Bender

Jan Bender (1909–1994) wrote WITTENBERG NEW for Martin Franzmann's text, "O God, O Lord of Heaven and Earth," a potent doxology about the grace of Christ in the poisoned twentieth-century air of "our reluctant breath." The tune fits this bold text with a rugged drive propelled by fourths and running headlong before it repeats. At first glance one expects bar form, but the tune is actually AA' or, more precisely, A broken into ab and A' into ac. Bender was a Lutheran church musician from the Netherlands who studied with Hugo Distler (1908–1942) in Lübeck and came to United States to teach.

WITTENBERG NEW
LMD

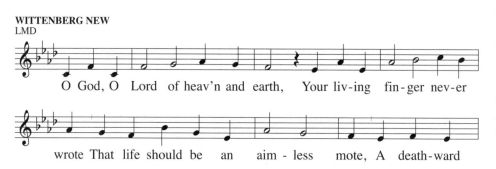

O God, O Lord of heav'n and earth, Your liv-ing fin-ger nev-er wrote That life should be an aim-less mote, A death-ward

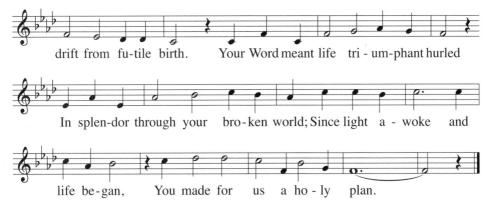

drift from fu-tile birth.   Your Word meant life   tri - um-phant hurled

In splen-dor through your   bro-ken world; Since light   a - woke   and

life be-gan,   You made for   us   a ho - ly   plan.

Text: Martin H. Franzmann, 1907-1976, alt.   LBW #396
Tune: Jan O. Bender, 1909-1994
© 1967, The Lutheran Council in the U.S.A.

Jacques Berthier and Taizé

In 1940 Roger Schultz left his native Switzerland and went to the little town of Taizé, France, to offer hospitality to those who needed it, among them refugees and Jews. His sister Genevieve came to help, but the two of them were forced to leave in 1942. In 1944, when he was able to return, a few brothers joined him. On Easter 1949, as a group of Protestant (Reformed) monks, they committed themselves to celibacy, sharing, and simplicity. Today over a hundred Protestant and Catholic brothers are part of this worshiping community of renewal between divided Christians that cares for the poor and needy.

Each week during the summer thousands of people from many countries, speaking many languages, come to Taizé as a place for worship, devotional retreat, and commitment to the needs of the world. Latin has often been chosen as both the least and the most common language (almost nobody knows it, but almost everybody recognizes something of it), and musical pieces have been fashioned for worship in rounds or short antiphon-like structures that can be learned easily and repeated over and over in a meditative fashion.

Jacques Berthier (1923–1994), a student of Joseph Gelineau's work and organist at St. Ignace Jesuit Church in Paris, composed many of these pieces, but he did it in a communal way that submerged his individual personality. For example, Robert Batastini went to Taizé in 1983 to work on an American edition of this music. Brother Roger asked him if he had additional texts to suggest. Batastini thought there was a need for "easily memorized music that communicants can sing as they approach the table" at communion.[18] Batastini prepared an English text with meter and rhythms, and Berthier then wrote the music. Here it is, as BERTHIER.

BERTHIER
Irregular

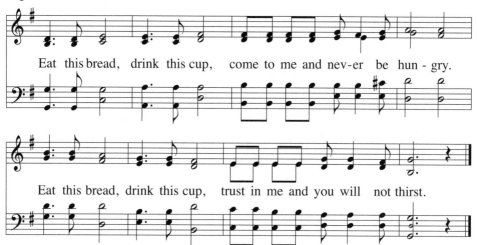

Eat this bread, drink this cup, come to me and nev-er be hun - gry.

Eat this bread, drink this cup, trust in me and you will not thirst.

Text: Robert Batastini and the Taizé Community, 1982
Tune: Jacques Berthier, 1982
© 1984, Les Presses de Taizé, France, admin. by GIA Publications, Inc.   Meth #628

This is a kind of music that stands at the edges of our study. BERTHIER is not a strophic hymn tune. It is rather an antiphon or ostinato, repeated between choral or solo statements of contrasting music. Other ostinatos from Taizé stand alone without any choral or solo material between their repetitions, like JESUS, REMEMBER ME to which, however, numerous descants can be added.

JESUS, REMEMBER ME
PM

Je - sus, re - mem - ber me when you come in - to your king-dom.

Je - sus, re - mem - ber me when you come in - to your king-dom.

Text: Luke 23:42
Tune: Jacques Berthier, 1978
© 1978, 1980, 1981, Les Presses de Taizé, admin. by GIA Publications, Inc.   PsH #217

Here is UBI CARITAS, structured in this setting with the melody in the tenor and the soprano singing a descant.

UBI CARITAS
Irregular

* Translation: Where charity and love are found, God is there.

Text: *Ubi caritas et amor*, 9th c.
Tune: Jacques Berthier, © 1979, Les Presses de Taizé, admin. by GIA Publications, Inc.

HWB #452

Or, a unison line might be used sung in canon, as in GLORIA CANON.

GLORIA CANON
Irregular

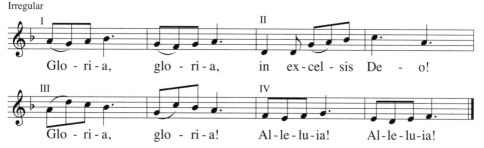

Text: Based on Luke 2:14, Jacques Berthier, 1923-1994, Taizé Community
Tune: Jacques Berthier, 1923-1994, Taizé Community
© 1978, 1980, 1981, Les Presses de Taizé, admin. by GIA Publications, Inc.

Cov #163

How durable Berthier's music for Taizé will be is anybody's guess. It has moved into our hymnals, however, and is used widely. Musically, it is quite accessible because it avoids both an overly thick Romantic musical syntax and an overly complex twentieth-century one. Liturgically, since it can be memorized easily by almost anyone, whether in parts or in unison, it does not require a hymnal after several repetitions and can serve worshipers in ways a more linear stanzaic hymn cannot, as in going to and from the table at communion. It cannot substitute for the more linear hymn, as in a hymn that might be connected with a sermon and requires more heft, but it serves a very important meditative and ritual purpose that the church has sometimes unfortunately forgotten.

Lee Hastings Bristol

DICKINSON COLLEGE is one of the twentieth-century hymn tunes garnered from a choral piece. It was composed by Lee Hastings Bristol (1923–1979) in 1962 for "Lord of All Being Throned Afar," adapted by him as a hymn tune, and published in *More Hymns and Spiritual Songs* (1971). It represents the twentieth century's push out of regular duple or triple meter, in this case into the regular alternation of twos and threes. Bristol was an organist who graduated from Hamilton College in Clinton, New York; studied in London and Geneva; had a successful career as a businessman at Bristol-Meyers; became president of Westminster Choir College in Princeton, New Jersey; was made a fellow of the Hymn Society in America (now called The Hymn Society in the United States and Canada); and received honorary doctorates from numerous schools. Dickinson College in Carlisle, Pennsylvania, for which the tune is named, is one of those schools.

DICKINSON COLLEGE
LM

Text: Fred Pratt Green, 1969, © 1971, Hope Publishing Co.   Meth #589
Tune: Lee Hastings Bristol, Jr., 1962, © 1962, Theodore Presser Co.

V. Earle Copes

V. Earle Copes (b. 1921) wrote KINGDOM in 1960 for the National Conference of Methodist Youth, to go with the text, "For the Bread Which You Have Broken." It is sometimes called "FOR THE BREAD," therefore, but its name "KINGDOM" comes from the last line of the text. It was included in the Methodist *Book of Hymns* (Nashville, 1964). Copes is a Methodist pastor and musician who has held several teaching and editing positions. KINGDOM is a deceptively simple, yet profoundly congregational tune, without any twentieth-century musical snares. It is patterned rhythmically after OMNI DIE, which is also used for Benson's text.[19] OMNI DIE comes from the *Gross Catolisch Gesangbuch* (Nuremberg, 1631) and may have folk origins.

KINGDOM
8 7 8 7

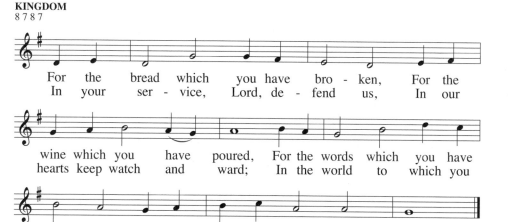

For the bread which you have bro - ken,   For the
In your ser - vice, Lord, de - fend us,   In our

wine which you have poured,   For the words which you have
hearts keep watch and ward;   In the world to which you

spo - ken,   Now we give you thanks,   O   Lord.
send us,   Let your king - dom come,   O   Lord.

Text: Louis F. Benson, 1924, *Hymns, Original and Translated*, 1925, alt.
Tune: V. Earle Copes, 1959, *The Methodist Hymnal*, 1964, Copyright © 1959, Abingdon Press

HWB #477

Peter Cutts

Peter Cutts (b. 1937), an English Congregational church musician and teacher who recently retired from teaching at Andover Newton Seminary in Massachusetts, wrote the tune BRIDEGROOM at Erik's Routley's piano in England for a Coventry Cathedral hymnal that was planned but never finished. The tune was conceived for the text "As the Bridegroom to His Chosen" and was published in *100 Hymns for Today* (London, 1969). It has happily migrated to Carl Daw's "Like the Murmur of the Dove's Song." Like Copes' KINGDOM, it is both simple and congregational. Its hemiola at the third and fourth bars from the end is a happy surprise, which sings naturally.

BRIDEGROOM
87876

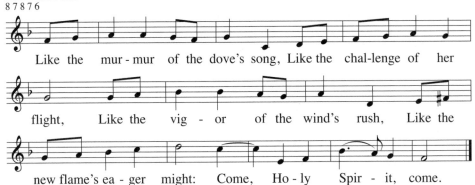

Like the mur-mur of the dove's song, Like the chal-lenge of her

flight, Like the vig - or of the wind's rush, Like the

new flame's ea - ger might: Come, Ho - ly Spir - it, come.

Text: Carl P. Daw, Jr., b.1944, © 1982, Hope Publishing Co.
Tune: Peter Cutts, b.1937, © 1969, Hope Publishing Co.

Cov #280

Cutts' SHILLINGFORD is considerably more adventuresome. It responds to the tonal ambiguity of the twentieth century and to the "otherworldly" mountain peak of the text about the Transfiguration, for which he wrote it. (Peter Cutts wrote the tune soon after Brian Wren wrote the text in 1962.[20]) Though abnormal fare for most worshiping assemblies, it is not as hard as the printed page makes it appear, because it consists only of seconds, thirds, and one perfect fourth at measure 5. The fourth goes to a D-flat, which is prepared by the earlier D-flat at measure 3. The biggest problem is negotiating the slight differences between the first and third phrases and between the second and fourth phrases. A congregation that likes a challenge, led by an able choir, cantor, organist, pianist, or instrumental ensemble, can learn this tune relatively easily, even with the whole tone scale at the end.[21] It challenges the notion that there has to be a tonal or modal center, at least in the classic Western sense, though Cutts skillfully disguises that matter by beginning and ending on an A-flat major chord.

SHILLINGFORD
7 8 7 8 with alleluia

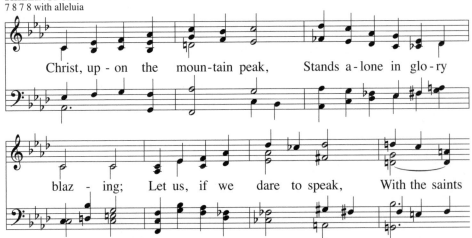

Christ, up - on the moun-tain peak, Stands a - lone in glo - ry

blaz - ing; Let us, if we dare to speak, With the saints

and an - gels praise him: Al - le - lu - ia!

Text: Brian Wren, 1962
Tune: Peter Cutts, 1962
© 1977, Hope Publishing Co.

Meth #260

Richard Dirksen

As SHILLINGFORD represents twentieth-century tonal ambiguity, so INNISFREE FARM represents the twentieth century's irregular metric configurations. It was written by Richard Dirksen (1921–2003) in 1983, when he was Organist and Choirmaster of the Cathedral of Sts. Peter and Paul (the "Washington Cathedral") in Washington, DC, for the text given with it below. Dirksen named it for the studio of Rowan Le Compte, the stained glass artist who designed the rose window of the Cathedral.[22]

Though congregations normally need a tonal or modal center, with SHILLINGFORD the exception that proves the rule, they can more easily handle communally constructed mixed metric schemes if given the chance. This tune explores such a possibility. It moves along with a quiet yet sure stride in which twos and threes alternate irregularly, unlike their regular alternation in DICKINSON COLLEGE.

INNISFREE FARM

11 11 11 5

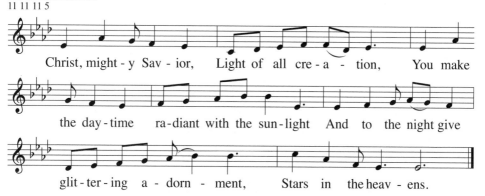

Christ, might - y Sav - ior, Light of all cre - a - tion, You make the day - time ra-diant with the sun-light And to the night give glit - ter - ing a - dorn - ment, Stars in the heav - ens.

Text: Mozarabic, 10th cent.; tr. Alan G. McDougall, 1895-1964; rev. Anne K. LeCroy, b.1930, © 1982, Anne LeCroy
Tune: Richard Wayne Dirksen, b. 1921, © 1982, Richard W. Dirksen

H82 #34

The Standing Commission on Church Music of the Episcopal Church, worried about congregational applicability, asked Dirksen for a more regular metric version in addition to the irregular one. He responded by turning INNISFREE FARM into DECATUR PLACE, named for the home of Paul Callaway, Dirksen's predecessor at the Washington Cathedral.[23] This altered version works, but the graceful wings of the original are clipped when they are boxed in like this.

DECATUR PLACE
11 11 11 5

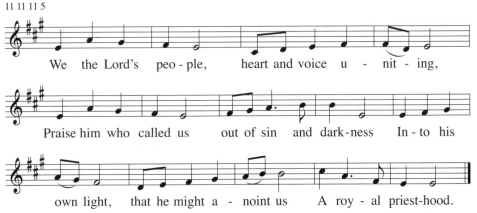

We the Lord's peo-ple, heart and voice u-nit-ing,
Praise him who called us out of sin and dark-ness In-to his
own light, that he might a-noint us A roy-al priest-hood.

Text: John E. Bowers, b.1923, alt.   H82 #51
Tune: Richard Wayne Dirksen, b.1921, © 1984, Richard W. Dirksen

VINEYARD HAVEN is a more festive tune by Dirksen, with a Vaughan Williams-like sweep. Raymond Glover calls it "modal" and "folklike,"[24] but it is tonally somewhat ambiguous. Within a C-minor frame, it plays with both a flatted second degree (phrygian) and a sharped sixth (dorian).

VINEYARD HAVEN
SM with refrain

Re-joice, ye pure in heart! Re-joice, give thanks, and sing!
Your glo-rious ban-ner wave on high, The cross of Christ your King.
Ho-san-na, ho-san-na! Re-joice, give thanks, and sing.

Text: Edward Hayes Plumptre, 1821-1891   H82 #557
Tune: Richard Wayne Dirksen, b.1921
© 1974, Harold Flammer, Inc.

Hugo Distler

DISTLER (also TRUMPETS) has a subversive history. Hugo Distler (1908–1942) was forced to write a tune for "Deutschland und Deutschösterreich" that celebrated the Nazi takeover of Austria. He was not in sympathy with the Nazis and their diabolical schemes and was already in trouble with them before he left Lübeck. When he came to Berlin in 1940 to teach and direct, Nazi youth disrupted his rehearsals. Worried about being drafted, in despair he committed suicide. The tune he wrote is hardly in a Nazi conquering style and can be seen as a veiled protest, not unlike Dmitri Shostakovitch's (1906–1976) work in Soviet Russia.

Jan Bender, one of Distler's students, remembered Distler's tune. When he was on the faculty at Concordia Seminary in St. Louis in the summer of 1970, he asked his faculty colleague Martin Franzmann to write a hymn for it. In obedience to the Servant King and his cross, Franzmann wrote an unveiled protest. Time will tell whether this tune, with its rhythmic challenges and octave leap at the end, will endure; but I have heard congregations sing it with a fervor that matches its spirit.

DISTLER
7 6 7 6 D

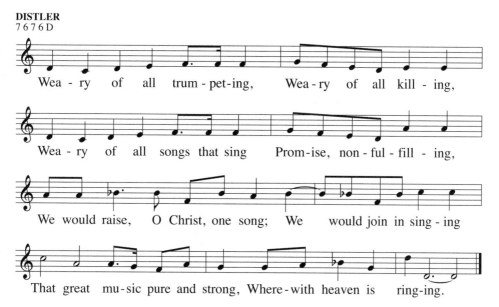

Wea - ry of all trum - pet-ing, Wea - ry of all kill - ing,
Wea - ry of all songs that sing Prom-ise, non - ful - fill - ing,
We would raise, O Christ, one song; We would join in sing - ing
That great mu - sic pure and strong, Where - with heaven is ring-ing.

Text: Martin H. Franzmann, 1907-1976, alt. Inter-Lutheran Commission on Worship
Tune: Hugo Distler, 1908-1942, © 1972, Chantry Music Press, Inc.

H82 #572

Harold Friedell

Harold Friedell (1905–1958) was a church organist and teacher in New York City—St. Bartholomew's Episcopal the last of the churches he served before he died unexpectedly of a heart attack. His tune UNION SEMINARY is named for the School of Sacred Music at Union Seminary where Friedell taught composition. An attractive congregational tune that represents the twentieth century's Romantic tendencies, it began as part of an anthem. Friedell wrote the tune in 1957 for Percy Dearmer's text. Jet E. Turner, a Union graduate, extracted it as a hymn tune, and it was first published like that in *Handbook for Christian Worship* (1970).

UNION SEMINARY
8 7 8 7 4 4 7

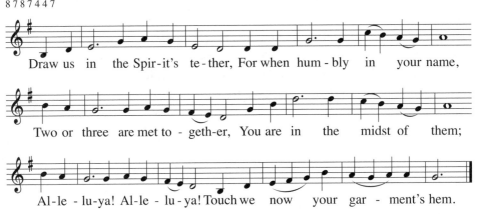

Draw us in the Spir-it's te-ther, For when hum-bly in your name,
Two or three are met to-geth-er, You are in the midst of them;
Al-le - lu-ya! Al-le - lu-ya! Touch we now your gar - ment's hem.

Text: Percy Dearmer, 1931, alt., © Oxford University Press
Tune: Harold Friedell, 1957; adapt. Jet Turner, 1967, © 1957, renewed H.W. Gray Co., all rights reserved;
   used by permission of Warner Brothers Publications

Chal #392

Marty Haugen

Marty Haugen (b. 1950), a graduate of Luther College in Decorah, Iowa, and the St. Paul School of Divinity, St. Paul, Minnesota, is an able congregational tunesmith. He has composed many settings of the Ordinary of the Mass and Morning and Evening Prayer, which are widely sung by Roman Catholic, Lutheran, and other congregations. HEALER is one of his hymn tunes. It illustrates a characteristic of the period that he employs often—a running, broken bass line of fifths, octaves, and tenths, used to support a unison congregational line. The harmonization is a three-part texture, sometimes moving to four parts or two when there are parallel octaves. The augmented fifth in the melody, which is outlined in the sequence at measures 3 through 4 of the stanzas, works because the sequence actually begins a measure earlier and is encompassed by a B minor context. The F-natural turns into a clever coloration that keeps the sequence's major third intact.

HEALER (HAUGEN)
Irregular

Healer of our ev-'ry ill, light of each to-mor-row,
give us peace be-yond our fear, and hope be-yond our sor-row.
You who know our fears and sad-ness, grace us with your
peace and glad-ness. Spir-it of all com-fort, fill our hearts.

Text & Tune: Marty Haugen, 1987, © 1991, GIA Publications, Inc.

VU #619

Hal Hopson

MERLE'S TUNE was composed by Hal Hopson (b. 1933) for Michael Perry's metrical version of the *Benedictus* and published in *The Upper Room Worshipbook* (Nashville, 1985). Hopson is a graduate of Baylor University and Southern Methodist University, where he earned the master of music degree. He has held church music positions in schools and congregations, including Westminster Choir College, and has composed and arranged extensively. This tune uses a major sixth well to set up an initial arc, repeated and turned into an answer in the second phrase. The third phrase moves easily to a minor seventh that has been prepared by the major sixth and the earlier reach to C-natural, and the last phrase comes home by repeating the second phrase.

MERLE'S TUNE
7 6 7 6 D

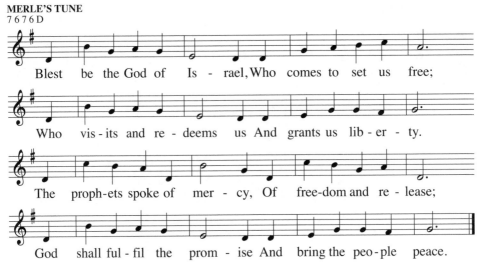

Blest be the God of Is - rael, Who comes to set us free;

Who vis - its and re - deems us And grants us lib - er - ty.

The proph-ets spoke of mer - cy, Of free-dom and re - lease;

God shall ful - fil the prom - ise And bring the peo-ple peace.

Text: Michael A. Perry, 1973, © Hope Publishing Co.
Tune: Hal H. Hopson, 1983, © Hope Publishing Co.

VU p. 901

David Johnson

David Johnson (1922–1987) held several church and collegiate musical posts, among them chairman of the music department at St. Olaf College in Northfield, Minnesota. In 1964, to celebrate the ninetieth anniversary of St. Olaf, Herbert Brokering wrote "Earth and All Stars."[25] Johnson composed the tune of the same name, and the two were published together in *Twelve Folksongs and Spirituals* (Minneapolis, 1968). Here is an example of a sturdy unison twentieth-century tune, which other composers have harmonized (among them Jan Bender and Dale Grotenhuis).

EARTH AND ALL STARS
4 5 7 4 5 7 with refrain

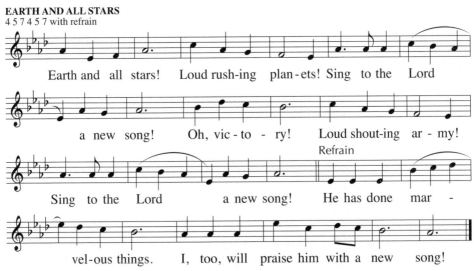

Earth and all stars! Loud rush-ing plan-ets! Sing to the Lord

a new song! Oh, vic - to - ry! Loud shout-ing ar - my!

Refrain

Sing to the Lord a new song! He has done mar -

vel-ous things. I, too, will praise him with a new song!

Text: Herbert F. Brokering, b.1926, abr.
Tune: David N. Johnson, 1922-1987
© 1968, Augsburg Fortress

CW #247

376

Jane Marshall

Jane Marshall (b. 1924) is a graduate of Southern Methodist University in Dallas, Texas, where in 1974 she returned to teach. She served several churches as organist and choir director, among them North Haven United Methodist Church, Dallas, for whom she composed this text and tune to celebrate its twenty-fifth anniversary. They were first published in the United Methodist Church's *Supplement to the Book of Hymns* (Nashville, 1982). Marshall's musical skill and care are evident here. The second half of the melody begins like the first half, but reverses direction upward at the third measure to a climax on D two measures later, after which it returns to the end of the first half, but this time home to the tonic chord rather than away from home to the dominant.

ANNIVERSARY SONG
11 11 11 11

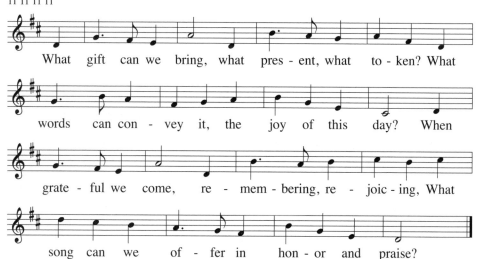

What gift can we bring, what pres - ent, what to - ken? What words can con - vey it, the joy of this day? When grate - ful we come, re - mem - ber - ing, re - joic - ing, What song can we of - fer in hon - or and praise?

Text & Tune: Jane Marshall, 1980, © 1982, Hope Publishing Co.   NC #370

Richard Proulx

Richard Proulx (b. 1937) is a prolific composer. Much of his work is for the church. He was born in St. Paul, Minnesota, where he served as the musician for the Church of the Holy Childhood. He moved to Seattle, Washington, as organist and choirmaster at St. Thomas Episcopal Church, then to a similar post in Chicago at Holy Name Cathedral, and then as composer in residence at the Cathedral of the Madeleine in Salt Lake City, Utah. He has studied widely—at MacPhail College in Minneapolis, Minnesota; the University of Minnesota; the Columbus Boychoir School in Princeton, New Jersey; St. John's University in Collegeville, Minnesota; the Royal School of Church Music in Croydon,

England; and with the Canadian composer Gerald Bales. His tune CASTLEWOOD is named for a street in Chicago and was written for David Mowbray's text. It first appeared in *Worship Third Edition*. Its gentle congregational curves are skillfully crafted. The opening three-note motive is turned upside down at measure 6, but it runs itself out by duplicating the end of the first phrase. Measures 1–5 are balanced by measures 6–10 with a non-symmetrical three-bar measure, the second an answer to the first. Measures 11–13 pursue the balance of the first three bars of the previous two sets. Then the initial motive is given in the upside-down version in the expected three-beat measure, and the final phrase runs itself out right-side up, with three bars like the beginning rather than the expected two bars of measures 4–5. The result is a slightly asymmetrical and uneven seventeen rather than a symmetrical and even sixteen measures. (That is not an arbitrary matter. Counting measures is counting time and symmetry or its absence.) Proulx has fashioned a twentieth-century tune for an unusual meter[26] and managed to make it congregational.

CASTLEWOOD
8 5 8 5 8 4 3

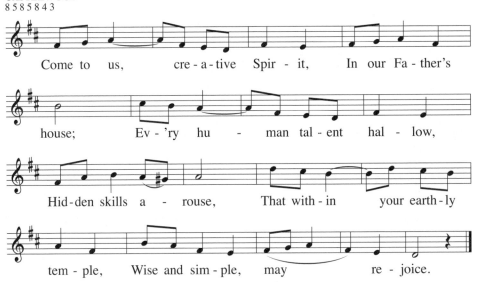

Erik Routley

Erik Routley (1917–1982) enters the narrative at this point as a tune writer. SHARPTHORNE (a place in Sussex, England) was his second attempt at a melody for Albert Bayly's paraphrase of Micah 6:6–8. The first was called TYES CROSS,[27] given in *Rejoice O People* (Swanland, 1950). The second, SHARPTHORNE, appeared in *100 Hymns for Today* (London, 1969). Routley called it "a paraphrase of the old one in the minor mode."[28] It sets the text boldly with a twentieth-century melodic verve and a congregational construction. The first measure of the second phrase repeats the opening measure but moves up a minor sixth rather than a perfect fourth. That takes us away from home to the dominant at the end of the phrase. From there, we make our way to the high tonic, drop an octave, and conclude on the dominant, which Routley cleverly harmonizes with a dominant chord until the last stanza when it becomes part of the tonic chord with a Picardy Third.

SHARPTHORNE
6 6 6 6 3 3 6

1. What does the Lord re - quire For praise and of - fer - ing?
4. How shall our life ful - fill God's law so hard and high?

What sac - ri - fice, de - sire, Or trib - ute bid you bring? Do
Let Christ en - dure our will With grace to for - ti - fy. Then

just - ly, Love mer - cy, Walk hum - bly with your
just - ly, In mer - cy, We'll

God.   hum - bly walk with God.

Text: Albert F. Bayly, 1901-1984, © 1948, Albert F. Bayly, admin. Oxford University Press
Tune: Erik Routley, 1917-1982, © 1969, Hope Publishing Co.   Cov #718

AUGUSTINE was published in *Hymns for Church and School* (London, 1964), for George Herbert's text. Its antiphon is structured for unison singing in B-flat minor, with big organ chords. The stanzas, in traditional four part harmony, move from B-flat major to D major, which turns into F major, which turns into a dominant as it sets up the repeat of the antiphon in B-flat minor. This tune can be sung by congregations in unison, but its mix of two textures is perilously close to a choral conception.

AUGUSTINE
6 6 6 6 with refrain

Text: George Herbert, 1593-1633
Tune: Erik Routley, 1917-1982, © 1976, Hinshaw Music, Inc.

H82 #402

Carl Schalk

In NOW, Carl Schalk (b. 1929) treats fourths in a gentler and more flowing fashion than Bender does in WITTENBERG NEW, stacking them in an upward cascade that leads in the last lines to resolution in a falling third and a ride of seconds. Then he denies the resolution by ending on G, the fifth of the dominant chord, which was the pitch for the pastor's opening Trinitarian salutation to the congregation, intended to follow immediately.[29]

Carl Schalk is one of the late twentieth and early twenty-first centuries' foremost church musicians, composers, and authors, an American who stands in the German Lutheran stream. He wrote this melody for Jaroslav Vajda's unrhymed text, "Now the Silence." The two appeared together in 1969 in the *Worship Supplement* to *The Lutheran Hymnal*.

NOW
Irregular

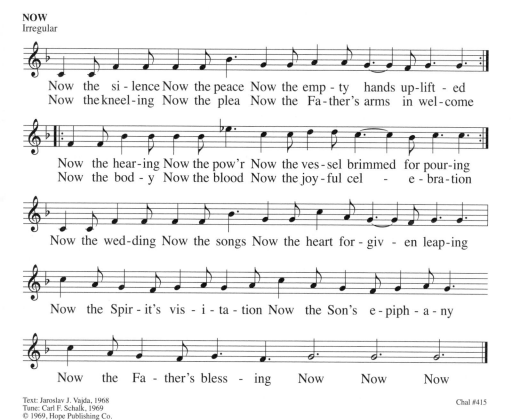

Text: Jaroslav J. Vajda, 1968
Tune: Carl F. Schalk, 1969
© 1969, Hope Publishing Co.

Chal #415

Schalk has written many well-crafted congregational tunes. In the fourteen hymnals we consulted, twelve of them are used thirty-five times, NOW by far the most often. Whether that proportion will hold up or another of Schalk's tunes will turn out to be most durable is anybody's guess. Here is

ROEDER—the maiden name of Schalk's wife, one of his more recent tunes for another of Vajda's unrhymed texts. Text and tune were published together in 1987 in the *Hymnal Supplement II* and sung at the Hymn Society meeting that year in Fort Worth, Texas. Since then many congregations have warmly embraced them. Though quite simple, the tune nonetheless appears in its short life span to bear repetition very well.[30]

ROEDER
5 4 6 7 7

Text: Jaroslav J. Vajda, 1983, © 1983, Jaroslav Vajda
Tune: Carl F. Schalk, 1983, © 1983, GIA Publications, Inc.

VU #229

FORTUNATUS NEW is one of Schalk's more vigorous tunes, though it reflects what Schalk calls the "subdued joy of the Lenten season in its simple, yet sturdy melody."[31] It was written for the text by Fortunatus and first appeared in *Spirit* (St. Louis, 1967).

FORTUNATUS NEW
878787

Sing, my tongue, the   glo-rious bat-tle; Sing the end-ing of the fray.

Now a-bove the cross, the tro-phy, Sound the loud tri-um-phant lay;

Tell how Christ, the world's re-deem-er, As a vic-tim won the day.

Text: Venantius Honorius Fortunatus, 530-609; tr. John M. Neale, 1818-1866, alt.   LBW #118
Tune: Carl F. Schalk, b.1929, © 1967, Concordia Publishing House

Natalie Sleeth

PROMISE (next page) is another well-constructed unison congregational tune with a running bass line, used in this case as a pedal point in the first two phrases. Where the tune moves to the dominant from measures 3 through 6, Sleeth keeps the tonic going in the bass. At the fifth phrase she lets the bass line go with the melody to the subdominant and the relative minor before moving back home to the tonic.

Natalie Sleeth (1930–1992) was a graduate of Wellesley College with a degree in music theory. Her study with Lloyd Pfautsch at Southern Methodist University led to the publication of her choral pieces. PROMISE began in 1985 as an anthem for the Pasadena Community Church, St. Petersburg, Florida, and first appeared as a hymn in 1989 in *The United Methodist Hymnal*.

PROMISE
8 7 8 7 D

In the bulb there is a flow-er; In the seed, an ap-ple tree; In co-
coons, a hid-den prom-ise: But-ter-flies will soon be free! In the
cold and snow of win-ter There's a spring that waits to be, Un-re-
vealed un-til its sea-son, Some-thing God a-lone can see.

Text & Tune: Natalie Sleeth, 1986
© 1986, Hope Publishing Co.

Meth #707

Alfred M. Smith

SURSUM CORDA is now used with a wide variety of texts, but it was composed for "Lift Up Your Hearts," named for the Latin of that text, and submitted anonymously to the committee that prepared *The Hymnal 1940*. "Lift Up Your Hearts" by Henry Montagu Butler has fallen out of use, but the tune remains, linked in *The Hymnal 1982* with another Eucharistic text (given below). Here is one more deceptively simple congregational melody, this one in the shape ABCA. Its composer, Alfred M. Smith (1879–1971), was an Episcopal priest who served churches in Philadelphia and Los Angeles and was a member of the Episcopal City Mission of Philadelphia for many years. He wrote settings of the Eucharist and hymn tunes.

SURSUM CORDA
10 10 10 10

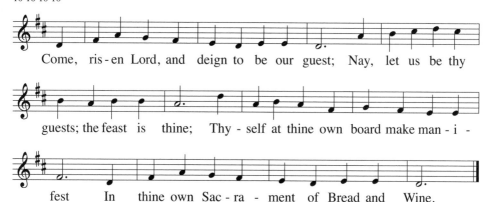

Come, ris - en Lord, and deign to be our guest; Nay, let us be thy guests; the feast is thine; Thy - self at thine own board make man - i - fest In thine own Sac - ra - ment of Bread and Wine.

Text: George Wallace Briggs, 1875-1959, alt.
Tune: Alfred Morton Smith, 1879-1971, © 1941, Mrs. Alfred M. Smith

H82 #306

Heinz Werner Zimmermann

In LITTLE FLOCK, Heinz Werner Zimmermann (b. 1930) explores jazz and the Scotch snap (the sixteenth followed by the dotted eighth). A syncopated melody rides above a pizzicato string bass line with a text about no fear and good cheer that is stimulated by Luke 12:32.

LITTLE FLOCK
6 6 7 6 6

Have no fear, lit-tle flock; Have no fear, lit - tle flock, For the Fa-ther has cho-sen To give you the King-dom; Have no fear, lit-tle flock!

Text: Luke 12:32
Tune: Heinz Werner Zimmermann, b.1930, © CPH Publishing

LBW #476

Zimmermann, a German composer and teacher, in a similar way wrote a syncopated line of quarter and eighth notes to ride above a harmonic underlay of half notes in LAUDATE PUERI.

LAUDATE PUERI
Irregular

Text: Marjorie Jillson, 1970
Tune: Heinz Werner Zimmermann, 1970
© 1973, CPH Publishing

Pres #225

Both of these melodies fit into and call out for the twentieth-century harmonic envelopes in which they were conceived, but they also stand on their own in unison, not unlike the sixteenth-century chorales that stand behind them.

---

1   His arrangements stimulated others in the twentieth century, as in Carlton R. Young's harmonization and arrangement of CHARLESTOWN, Meth #433.

2   R. Vaughan Williams, "Preface, The Music," *The English Hymnal with Tunes* (London: Oxford University Press, 1933, first edition, 1906), ix.

3   Ibid., viii.

4   Ibid.

5   Ibid.

6   Ibid., xiii.

7   Ibid., viii.

8   RANDOLPH is the least used of this group, but it can be found in CW #328, HWB #430, Meth # 673, Pres #540, PsH #316, and VU #423.

9   Gealy, Lovelace, et al., *Companion to the Hymnal*, 137.

10 For the tune, see NC #266, LBW #160, Meth #537.

11 In the fourteen hymnals we consulted six of his tunes are used 37 times, but 25 of the occurrences are of ABBOTT'S LEIGH.

12 Carl Daw, correspondence, May 28, 2004.

13 Sixteen occurrences of five tunes appear in the fourteen hymnals we consulted.

14 Cov #692, H82 #594, HWB # 638, and Wor3 #s 362 and 507, unfortunately dogged by syllabic changes from stanza to stanza.

15 Chase, *Dies Irae*, 307, summarizes these in a single paragraph.

16 Chase, *Dies Irae*, 307.

17 Elliott Schwartz and Barney Childs, eds., *Contemporary Composers on Contemporary Music* (New York: Holt, Rinehart and Winston, 1967), 77.

18 Young, CUMH, 324.

19 H82 #341.

20 Brian Wren, *Faith Looking Forward* (Carol Stream: Hope Publishing Co., 1983), Notes, #17.

21 The D-flat four notes from the end in the pew edition of H82 #130 is wrong.

22 Raymond Glover, "Christ, Mighty Savior, Light of All Creation," Glover, H82C, 3A, 66.

23 Raymond Glover, "We the Lord's People, Heart and Voice Uniting," Glover, H82C, 3A, 93.

24 Raymond Glover, "Rejoice, Ye Pure in Heart," Glover, HC82, 3B, 1031.

25 Another tune of the same name was composed by Jan Bender (Wor #517).

26 The Wor3 "Metrical Index of Tunes" lists it under the heading "One of a Kind."

27 For TYES CROSS, see Robin Leaver, "What Does the Lord Require," Glover, H82, 3B, 1114.

28 Robin Leaver, "What Does the Lord Require," Glover, H82, 3B, 1114.

29   On November 24, 2003, I asked Carl Schalk: "Was NOW structured to end on the dominant with a melody G to fit into the Pastor's Trinitarian salutation on that pitch in *The Lutheran Hymnal* (Saint Louis: Concordia Publishing House, 1941), 5," though no pitch is given there? He responded as follows. "Jerry Vajda asked me early on when I was assigned to attempt to write a tune for the 'Now' text that he had one musical request: That the tune end on "G" so that it would give the pastor the pitch for the beginning of the service as you have described it. Just how often or in what circumstances pastors actually chanted the liturgy to enable his idea to be practical I don't know. Perhaps the Slovaks chanted the liturgy more than most (?). In the 50s when I first went 'out into the field' it was the older pastors who chanted more than those who were coming out of the seminaries at that time (with a few exceptions)."

30   I had not intended to include this tune, but at the Montreat Conference in 2004 several people told me it was their congregations' favorite hymn, which corroborated other comments I had heard. Then, quite independent of these testimonials, Austin Lovelace (correspondence, August 28, 2004) encouraged me to add it because he thinks it "is one of the best things [Schalk] and Vajda ever did."

31   CWH, 149.

PERSPECTIVE

T hree sets of comments will help to provide perspective on the ground we have covered: an overview related to our divisions, a recurring temptation offset by a remarkable resilience, and what hymn tunes represent.

1. OVERVIEW

In some ways the hymnody of nineteenth-century England reflects English civil religion.[1] This was balanced, however, by the Oxford-Cambridge movement's concerns for the church and its integrity, both before and beyond nineteenth-century England, as well as by the breadth of *Hymns Ancient and Modern*, which undercut civil religion. White gospel hymnody in the United States did not have such internal balance or resistance and provoked a rift that has still not been healed. To understand this, a long and tragic trajectory of the Western church has to be understood. It goes something like this.

- The church's conflicts during the first millennium led to the Iconoclastic Controversy. It lasted for over a century, from about 725 until 842. Though mainly visual,[2] it negatively affected hymnody as well.[3] It was the last straw and led in 1054 to a split between the Eastern and Western portions of the church, after which the two groups were officially divorced from one another and each other's resources.

- In principle and partly in practice the people continued to sing in both bodies, but choirs at times choked their singing. The despotism of choirs that Bishop Gore referred to has not only been a nineteenth-century English temptation.

• At the Reformation, Lutherans and Calvinists sought to recover the people's singing with vigor, but after the Reformation Protestants found themselves cut off not only from the Eastern Orthodox, but from Western Roman Catholics as well. This development denied some fundamental themes and intentions of the sixteenth century Reformers and eventually undermined the congregation's song wherever the bones of the church's historic forms of worship were cut away.

• In the sixteenth century Zwinglians, Anabaptists, and English Baptists argued against any singing at all in worship. Ulrich Zwingli (1484–1531)[4] and Anabaptists[5] who agreed with him could find no biblical warrant for any music at worship, and English Baptists were nervous about "set forms."[6] All of these groups—already by the end of the sixteenth century for Zwinglians and Anabaptists, and after Benjamin Keach (1640–1704)[7] for the English Baptists—eventually embraced congregational singing, but they imparted an underlying sectarian mindset to Protestants and pushed them further away from catholic roots and resources.

• Pietism in Europe, the Wesleyan movement in England, and a broad swath of churches that highlighted the importance of feelings had the effect of denying catholic roots. Lutheran Pietists never officially broke from their Lutheran moorings, but did break away from the catholic liturgical emphasis on Word and Sacraments along with the chorale and its music that Lutherans espoused. Wesleyans, called Methodists, actually broke off—or were forced out (the blame for breaks is not one-sided in any of these cases)—from the Anglicans against the Wesleys' wishes, producing a similar isolation. Pietism is often associated solely with the "heart religion" of Moravians, Lutherans, and Methodists; but it was more ubiquitous than that.[8] It extended to Presbyterians, Baptists, Congregationalists, and other Reformed churches. It had Roman Catholic parallels stretching from Cornelius Jansen (1585–1638) to seventeenth-century Sacred Heart devotion among Jesuits to private devotions at the Mass, which substituted for and neglected its communal character. The effect of these movements was to narrow musical styles. In the process, congregational singing, though sometimes initially stimulated, was ultimately choked by ingrown tendencies that lacked catholic ballast and choral help. By the twentieth century, wealthier congregations in any of these streams where feelings had became paramount, even though congregational singing may have been in their roots, paradoxically paid choirs to sing for them.

Throughout this history, there was a tension between a sectarian and a catholic spirit. Both "Protestants" and "Catholics" have had sectarian capacities and temptations. The distinctions are not always easy to delineate and can be parsed sociologically, theologically, and liturgically. One sectarian signal is to what extent a group breaks away from the church's historic forms. Aidan

Kavanagh's comment gets to the heart of things quickly: "Schisms breed where Ordo is ignored or tampered with, even by the well-meaning."[9] The church's song disappears with the schism, even when momentarily it may appear otherwise.

Whatever may be said about sectarian or catholic motifs, the debate normally centered around what God was understood to be doing. This was true even when those who espoused "heart religion" or sanctification were accused of emphasizing human will at the expense of God's action. Many issues, however, related in part to the American frontier and rural and urban revivalism, were bubbling up. They popped to the surface in the nineteenth century when Finney introduced techniques. If human techniques could be devised to convert people, the frame of reference was altered and questions like these were unleashed:

- Do you need God at all?
- Is there a God?[10]
- Do you need the church?
- Does "God" have anything to do with the "church"?
- Do you need Word and sacraments?
- Does "God" have anything to do with them?
- Does the anxious bench turn into a sacrament and dislodge the Eucharist?[11]
- Do you need catechisms?
- Is there any reason to teach the faith of the church?
- Is there such a thing as the faith of the church, or is faith only an individual matter that suddenly appears out of nowhere under the white heat of emotional fire generated by human effort?
- What is weekly worship? Is it necessary?
- Is a singular revival experience sufficient?
- Can you make a decision for God, or does human sin preclude such a choice?
- What is sin?
- Is Christianity about the individual, the communal "body" of Christ, or both?
- What are Christian implications for ethics in relation to the society, not just to the individual who is being "saved"?

Questions of this sort led to confessional, sacramental, and "catholic" concerns. They had not been neglected by the sixteenth-century reformers, but the church's divisions permitted both Protestants and Roman Catholics to ignore them, allowing prejudice and suspicion between the two groups to increase. The nineteenth-century currents, in spite of the prejudice, nevertheless caused some Protestants to revisit the Reformation and its catholic heritage, even though doing so was often as unpopular in the United States as it was in England. Other Protestants—Unitarians, for example—did not raise catholic concerns and were not especially friendly toward Roman Catholics, but they were not enamored by revivalism either. Roman Catholics revisited their roots.

Hymnic consequences to the nineteenth century developments often avoided the questions. After Finney, the next logical step was to identify with the culture in such a way that music became one of the techniques to convert people. Ideas about sanctification and heart religion were modified to support this position. The notion that music was about sentimental feelings was easily allied with the modifications, so that music became a central converting technique. A series of threads came together, and gospel hymnody developed. It tied into the feelings of the culture and its civil religion with what H. Wiley Hitchcock calls "a kind of religious pop art almost irresistible in its visceral appeal; at its worst, an embarrassingly trivial sacred counterpart of the sentimental 'songs of hearth and home' of the same era."[12] Or, as William Reynolds says, Sunday school hymns—which is where gospel hymnody started—were "designed for immediate appeal."[13]

Donald Hustad isolated a central problem. He suggested a chief pitfall of traditional evangelism was canonizing "evangelism's pattern and style, the preaching and music . . . as the norm for regular church worship."[14] His point was that "normal church life needs a pattern of worship that is less specialized and more complete."[15] (Though I realize there are vast differences between them, it is nonetheless interesting to note that the comment of Donald Hustad, a Baptist associated with Billy Graham's crusades, has affinities with the one about Ordo and schism made by Aidan Kavanagh, a Roman Catholic Benedictine monk.) Normal church life needs a more catholic hymnody to go with it. If the church had not been splitting itself into pieces for two millennia and had been able to integrate the worship and hymnody of normal church life with the evangelical concerns and gospel hymns of specialized revivals, the rift we still live with may have been avoided.[16] The long history of divisions and Finney's New Measures' techniques made this impossible, however.

Some thought that Christianity was about more than visceral, immediate appeal and the embarrassingly trivial; that hymn tunes and music in the church should not be a thin syntactical technique of conversion; and that such a syntax should not be a normative vehicle for Christian worship. They looked to their historic resources. Lutherans embarked on confessional and liturgical renewal. They sought to recover the rhythmic chorale, sometimes by an actual recovery and sometimes as a symbol. Some Anglicans (Episcopalians) in the United States paralleled their English Oxford-Cambridge cousins. E. H. Johnson edited a hymnal for Baptists called *Sursum Corda* (Philadelphia, 1898), which avoided gospel hymns.[17] *The Hymnal* of the Presbyterian Church USA (1895), edited by Louis F. Benson, the foremost hymnologist of his time, affirmed the congregation's hymn singing with a broad swath of resources that eschewed gospel hymnody. Other denominational hymnals followed suit well into the twentieth century. Folk song provided a renewing source. The Mercersburg movement in the German Reformed Church, with its fecund ecumenical insights, spawned hymnic and musical implications, but did not run them out.[18]

In the nineteenth century Protestants and Roman Catholics, though engaged in activity and research that would prove to be common, were largely separated. The Protestants were split between a *Hymns Ancient and Modern* or a Mason mentality on the one hand and a gospel hymnody mentality on the other. Roman Catholics were at work in Solesmes and the Caecilian movement and could ignore Protestant motifs. After the Second Vatican Council, from 1963 to 1965, however, this split between Protestants and Roman Catholics became increasingly difficult to maintain. Many portions of the church took the opportunity to overcome long-standing divisions. Pursuing ecumenical hymns and tunes was one way to get at this.

At the same time, due to a misreading of the Second Vatican Council and its concerns about inculturation, the heritage of Finney's techniques, faulty ecclesiological presuppositions, and an increasingly consumptive culture of marketing, other parts of the church (divisions now appeared within denominational groupings, not between them) abandoned the church's legacy of hymns and their tunes. Roman Catholics wrote reams of composed "folk music," initially attractive, but with little staying power.[19] Among Protestants this music morphed into praise choruses, which are sometimes called "teeny hymns." Their repetitive form (short fragments of psalms repeated at length) makes it seem that they could be used similarly to Taizé's music or comparable African pieces, and it is certainly possible that in the future a few of them could pass into the church's repertoire—similar to what we have seen before. At the moment, however, they are conceived as throwaway entertainment meant to attract, in a musical syntax for praise teams to sing and play with amplification. As in the culture's venues where there are loud dance bands, some people may sing along now and then or even occasionally join in more or less vigorously. This is not congregational music, however, which is why it stands outside our congregational purview. Its amplification alone—not unlike overly loud organ playing it replaces—discourages congregational singing, and it does not have traction across an ecumenical spectrum of congregations who actually sing.

Where we are headed, as in the past, will only become apparent after we have been there. All of our pre-modern, modern, and post-modern rhetoric with its predictions, no matter how helpful, will be trumped by history itself and by the hand of God. If history is any indication, a recurring temptation and a remarkable resilience will be apparent.

2. A RECURRING TEMPTATION AND A REMARKABLE RESILIENCE

A theme keeps recurring in a study of this kind. It is the continual temptation to take the song of the people of God away from them. This may take the form of:

- Medieval priests and choirs who shut out the congregation;
- Musical developments emphasizing the organ, other instruments, choirs, or compositions at the expense of the congregation;[20]
- Anti-congregational tunes;
- Collapse from within, as in lining out;
- Tempos taken too slowly;
- Tempos taken too fast;
- Participatory congregational music at worship turned into concerts and entertainment;
- Tunes in the service of feelings;
- Decibel levels from organs or amplified instruments and voices that hide and destroy the congregation's singing;
- Musicians who lead in such a way that congregations cannot breathe;
- Carpeted rooms that absorb sound and make singing impossible;
- Congregations who sit so as to isolate themselves from one another, making both physical and musical contact difficult;
- Barrel organs or more modern versions of "canned" music, which silence the church by denying its incarnational integrity;
- Or any other snare you might imagine or uncover in the church's history and practice.

Whatever the case, the result is the same: the people are silenced.

The remarkably resilient thing is that there always seem to have been and still seem to be congregations that sing in spite of all the forces that would silence them. Some congregations sing no matter how divided they are. They sometimes manage to sing even when clergy and musicians do horrible things to them. Across time and space, they sort out what they can and cannot sing no matter who tries to convince them otherwise or who tries to seduce them with the latest fad. There are also clergy and musicians who care—clergy who support the singing of their people; organists whose musical playing invites congregations to sing; conductors, choirs, and musical ensembles who know their role, back away from microphones, and musically encourage the congregation's singing. The remarkably resilient thing is this: that in spite of all the snares twenty centuries have produced, congregations still sing.

The persistence of congregational singing, just like the presence of the church itself, points to God's grace. Apart from God's grace, there are no guarantees. The most a study like this can do is to help us make good choices based on what the church has learned. It can help us isolate what tunes seem to work best for congregational song, make it most healthy, and deserve to be sung and used as models.

Ultimately, however, a study like this suggests continual vigilance by the church's leaders on behalf of the people and their song. If it has contributed to that vigilance, it will have done a good thing.

3. HYMN TUNES

A hymn tune is not much in the world's view of things. It is not a large symphony or an oratorio. It is not even a short choral piece. It holds little attraction in the world. It consists of a few phrases, several lines of notes that serve the church's need to sing. Appearances can be deceiving, however. Jesus had something to say about greatness being defined by small tasks of servanthood.[21]

Hymn tunes are a strong symbol of the priesthood of all believers, in spite of, or maybe because of, their insignificance. They are not the only musical symbol of the people's being that grows out of their baptism. That symbol includes congregational settings of the Ordinary and canticles in prose, psalm tones, antiphons, and prayer responses. Hymn tunes are part of this cluster. They are a musical symbol of the priesthood of all believers not only individually, but also collectively and in combination with all the other seemingly insignificant pieces of the congregation's song. They form an ecumenical melodic mosaic of the people's musical office across the width and breadth of the church. They stand in judgment on a church that is blinded by the commodification of its mission and message, by quick fixes, programs, platforms, movements, marketing, and the Pandora's box of needs—all of which constitute a vanishing mist of temptation into the culture's seductive madness. Hymn tunes remind us that there are no quick fixes, no decibel levels or choirs, organs, bands, or praise teams that can substitute for the song of the body of the baptized itself. There is only the sanity of the body of Christ that does its work note by note, phrase by phrase, hymn tune by hymn tune, piece by piece, person by person, from the inside out community by community in communion with the whole church catholic past and present—singing its remarkable heritage of hymns and tunes around Word, font, and table.

Hymn tunes are weak little things that in their powerful weakness stand in judgment on the church when it forgets its being, its song, those called to sing, and those the singers are called to serve. Hymn tunes are weak little things that in their powerful weakness enable the church to sing the faith.

1   James F. White, *The Cambridge Movement* (Cambridge: Cambridge University Press, 1962), 31, for example, points to Neale's "persistent nationalism."

2   The visual elements and gesture are not the topics of this book, but they are important to worship and, though often ignored or treated with disdain by Protestants and neglected of late by Roman Catholics, nonetheless live in a close relationship to music. See Peter Jeffrey, "A Chant Historian Reads *Liturgiam Authenticam* 4: Human and Angelic Tongues," *Worship* 78:4 (July 2004): 330–341.

3   The development of hymnody in the East in the early church, unlike the West, exceeded psalmody. Kenneth Levy cites over 60,000 incipits in Follieri's six-volume survey, notes other unpublished thousands, and suggests ten of thousands "must have disappeared" in the Iconoclastic controversies (Kenneth Levy, "Byzantine rite, music of the," NGDM, 3, 557).

4   See Westermeyer, *Te Deum*, 149–153.

5   Ibid., 173–178.

6   Ibid., 182–185.

7   Ibid., 188–190.

8   See Westermeyer, *Te Deum*, 226.

9   Aidan Kavanagh, "Time Capsule: On Order," GIA *Quarterly* 15:3 (Spring 2004): 20.

10 A Finneyite position leads logically to Ludwig Feuerbach's notion that God is simply a human projection. It is not far from there to a Marxist stance that religion is the opiate of the people controlled by the state. Christianity, now turned into a religion and one without God, is shorn of its prophetic power and becomes a civil religious exercise.

11 See John Witvliet, *Worship Seeking Understanding* (Grand Rapids: Baker Academic, 2003), 193–194.

12 H. Wiley Hitchcock, "Introduction," *Gospel Hymns Nos. 1 to 6 Complete*, n.p.

13 William J. Reynolds, "Baptist Hymnody in America," *Handbook to The Baptist Hymnal* (Nashville: Church Street Press, 1992), 43.

14 Donald P. Hustad, *Jubilate! Church Music in the Evangelical Tradition* (Carol Stream: Hope Publishing, Company, 1981), 143.

15 Donald P. Hustad, *Jubilate II: Church Music in Worship and Renewal* (Carol Stream: Hope Publishing Company, 1993), 243.

16 One possible way to see collaboration rather than dispute might be to understand the nineteenth-century revivalist impulse as not related to worship so much as to the church's oratorio tradition, which stretches back through Madan and Lock Hospital to free-standing oratorios and medieval mystery plays.

17 Paul A. Richardson, "The Resources: American Baptist Hymnals," *Handbook to The Baptist Hymnal*, 71, calls Johnson the leading figure in the "cultivated tradition," a term he borrows from Wiley Hitchcock, who sets it against the "vernacular tradition." The "cultivated" versus "vernacular" typology is another way to get at this period, though, as Richardson notes, the distinctions are often muddied by mixes.

18 See Paul Westermeyer, "What Shall We Sing in a Foreign Land? Theology and Cultic Song in the German Reformed and Lutheran Churches of Pennsylvania, 1830–1900," PhD Dissertation (Chicago: The University of Chicago, 1978).

19 For a thumbnail sketch of immediate reactions to Vatican II, see Donald Boccardi, *The History of American Catholic Hymnals Since Vatican II* (Chicago: GIA Publications, Inc., 2001), 24–26. For twentieth-century Roman Catholic documents and analysis, see Michael Joncas, *From Sacred Song to Ritual Music: Twentieth-Century Understandings of Roman Catholic Worship Music* (Collegeville: The Liturgical Press, 1997).

20 It needs to be clear that choirs and organs are not by definition negative, as Marilyn Stulken pointedly reminded me (correspondence, June 17, 2004) by saying, "It has never been my experience [for nearly 50 years] that organ and choirs silenced a congregation." Many church musicians, like Stulken, respect the people and their singing, as well as choirs, organs, and other instruments. They are among the church's heroes. Unfortunately their presence has not denied or stopped the presence of the anti-heroic tendencies.

21 See, for example, Mark 10:43–44.

APPENDIX. A TUNE OF THE DAY PROPOSAL

T he church repeatedly learns that in its finitude it cannot sing everything and that not everything is worth learning, especially considering the span of our life, which is shorter than yesterday when it is past, or like grass that has withered in the evening.[1] Living in God's dwelling place, however, gives us a song to sing, and in the shortness of our breath we might as well sing what is worth the time and effort. So the church has set up cycles that keep what is worth singing in play. Such cycles may be superficially generated by high-handed attempts of authoritarian figures to control, but this sets in motion a legalism the church rejects. The real reasons for such cycles are more substantive. Without them and the consensus they seek to express, the church is more controlled by high-handed authorities, usually narrowly local and short-sighted ones with private agendas on whom there are no checks and balances. Further, without such cycles the church has no memory bank and succumbs to communal amnesia. Cycles of hymns are fundamentally about remembering the whole story by means of the church year, which serves as a discipline and check on our individual authoritarianism and private agendas. Cycles of hymns, therefore, have to start with the hymns, that is, the texts. Since this is a study of tunes, however, the central concern here is about tunes for the texts, tunes that are worth committing to the memory bank and singing year after year. Texts are critical, so they will not be forgotten as we proceed, but this cycle focuses on tunes.

What follows is a list of tunes and their texts from which congregations can construct a yearly sequence. By leaning on past cycles, ones currently in use, and the resources that suggest them,[2] this set of tunes and their texts is conceived for days and seasons across one year, not for specific lessons across three years. The three-year lectionary is a good idea, and there are fine resources that suggest hymns for it.[3] This proposal does not mean to rule them out, but trying to tie hymn tunes to a three-year cycle generally means the possibility of singing a given tune only once every three years. That is too long for the memory bank to survive, so what follows gives suggestions for constructing a one-year sequence. It is valuable not only for the memory bank, but for the contextual themes that hymns and the church's music supply, into which lessons and preaching do their more specific work.

The concern here is for one relatively weighty hymn and tune of the day, which is connected to the day's and the season's themes. Newer tunes are not omitted, and—because this is constructed with the fourteen hymnals we analyzed in mind—some choices of tunes will not be considered the finest ones by everybody. Where possible, however, tunes that have had the most traction over time have been chosen.

Those churches interested in a sequence of this kind will likely find these tunes and their texts most useful in connection with the readings and the sermon. Some churches will choose to use them differently, some will not be interested in such a sequence at all, some will find this list helps them organize what they are already doing unconsciously and less than systematically, and some will find it sets their imaginations to work—possibly stimulating ecumenical groups to do it better. (Those not interested could simply regard this list as providing a worthy set of texts and tunes to cover the Christian message and story, however they are employed.) For those who are interested, I assume the presence and use of a wide range of other hymns and tunes that serve different roles, for entrance and sending rites, for example, or for singing around the table as people come and go to communion where less linear heft is appropriate, or in teaching quite apart from worship. I do not want to suggest what these other hymns and tunes might be. They need to be selected with more local considerations in mind, in a less systematic but still possibly a sequential way, that keeps them in play but allows them to come and go more easily than the hymn of the day. There is, of course, a whole other set of hymns and tunes for daily prayer, some of which will and some of which will not overlap with this set.[4]

I assume the tunes selected from this list will fit into a bigger congregational scheme of things, with three parts: 1) a broad memory bank of many genres, with maybe 100 to 300 hymns and tunes or so in it (maybe fewer tunes than texts), to which additions and subtractions are constantly being made in a living flow; 2) two to five or so settings of the Eucharist and a couple settings of Morning and Evening Prayer, plus unnumbered short psalm tones and antiphons that can easily be learned and led by choirs or cantors at the moment; 3) choirs, organists, and other instrumentalists who lead the congregation, alternate with it, and—according to local capacities—provide the more complex musical pieces that require rehearsals. Different traditions will construe this congregational context in different ways (and some congregations will see it as an ideal to be sought if not a present reality), but what is proposed here should not be understood apart from it.

Another concern is for a modest common ecumenical memory bank. As I indicated in the first chapter, there is a remarkable consensus among various parts of the church that includes common ecumenical shapes and forms for worship. The Church Year is among these shapes. As I also indicated, who does and who does not attend to this common life is not a given. Denominational labels do not tell you much, because congregations in denominations that historically have followed the Church Year and Hymn of the Day cycles may reject them, just as congregations in denominations that have historically rejected them may now eagerly embrace them. This proposal is for those from whatever tradition who hunger for a cycle like this. In recent years I have received requests asking for just this sort of thing—which is why it is included here.

The tunes that are present in all fourteen of the hymnals we surveyed may or may not fit a cycle like this, partially because they may work better in other ways (ADESTE FIDELES as an entrance hymn, for example), and partially because they are the ones that will likely remain in play without any conscious effort. Many of them are included in this Appendix, but not all. Some tunes are included that are not discussed in this book, which, as promised, does not pretend to cite every tune available. Metrical psalms are generally avoided on the premise that they or their prose versions will be used between readings.

The list below includes over 275 tunes and gives multiple possibilities from which churches can construct their own yearly sequences. It can be adapted by all the churches who use the fourteen hymnals we surveyed because, with only a few exceptions (the exceptions are there because I tried not to force inappropriate choices), the suggestions give at least one tune and text in each of the fourteen hymnals for every Sunday and festival of the Church Year. They also attempt to accommodate sequences already in use. That is why so many alternatives and repetitions are present. As the list indicates, though we share a lot, we also diverge a lot. An ecumenical list has to be longer than one might hope, and has to include some tunes not in the foremost rank, partly because we have chosen so many different tunes for the same texts. Those in traditions that find some pairings of texts and tunes incongruous should use another of the suggestions. Individual congregations will have to adapt this list thoughtfully to fit their traditions and common life. It would probably be best to choose one hymn and tune for each day in a balanced cycle, then to stick with it for the sake of a cross-generational memory bank. Of course, the hymns and tunes listed here could and should also be used at other times and for other occasions as well, and obviously some modifications could and should be made year by year. Just as with other disciplines, legalism is not helpful. But the absence of legalism should not undo the discipline.

The calendar of Sundays and special days, with their readings, are from the Revised Common Lectionary.[5] Adaptations will have to be made where there are denominational or local variations.

A TUNE OF THE DAY SEQUENCE

Season of Advent

1	WACHET AUF	"Wake, Awake" ["Wake, O Wake," "Sleepers, Wake!", "Keep Awake"]
	O HEILAND, REISS DIE HIMMEL AUF	"O Savior, Rend the Heavens Wide"
	HYFRYDOL or STUTTGART	"Come, Thou Long Expected Jesus"
2	FREU DICH SEHR (GENEVAN 42)	"Comfort, Comfort"
	WINCHESTER NEW	"On Jordan's Banks"
	FOREST GREEN	"Blessed Be the God of Israel" (Daw or Quinn)
	MERLE'S TUNE or THORNBURY	"Blessed Be the God of Israel" (Perry)
3	VENI REDEMPTOR GENTIUM or NUN KOMM, DER HEIDEN HEILAND	"Redeemer [Savior] of the Nations, Come"
	MERTON or FREUEN WIR UNS ALL IN EIN	"Hark! A Thrilling Voice Is Sounding"
	CONDITOR ALME	"Creator of the Stars of Night" ["O Loving Founder of the Stars"]
	BEREDEN VÄG FÖR HERRAN	"Prepare the Royal Highway" ["Prepare the Way, O Zion"]

4   VENI, EMMANUEL   "O Come, O Come, Emmanuel"

Season of Christmas

Nativity of the Lord (Christmas Day)

DIVINUM MYSTERIUM   "Of the Father's Love [or "Parent's Heart" or "Of Eternal Love] Begotten"

Christmas 1

ES IST EIN ROS   "Lo, How a Rose E'er Blooming" ["Lo, How a Rose Is Growing," "Behold a Branch Is Growing"]

VOM HIMMEL HOCH   "From Heaven Above"

GO TELL IT   "Go, Tell It on the Mountain"

CHRISTE REDEMPTOR OMNIUM or GONFALON ROYAL   "O Savior of Our Fallen Race"

New Year's Day

ST. ANNE   "O [Our] God, Our Help in Ages Past"

ROK NOVY or SIXTH NIGHT   "Greet Now [Now Greet] the Swiftly Changing Year"

Christmas 2

TEMPUS ADEST FLORIDUM   "Gentle Mary Laid Her Child"

LOBT GOTT, IHR CHRISTEN   "Let All Together Praise Our God"

PUER NOBIS NASCITUR   "Unto Us a Boy Is Born"

ST. LOUIS or FOREST GREEN   "O Little Town of Bethlehem"

KOMT, VERWONDERT	"Come and Stand Amazed, You People"
RAQUEL	"Sing of Mary, Pure and Lowly"

Season of Epiphany

Epiphany

WIE SCHÖN LEUCHTET	"O Morning Star" ["How Brightly Beams," "How Lovely Shines," "How Bright Appears"]
GREENSLEEVES	"What Child Is This"

1 (Baptism of the Lord)

CHRIST, UNSER HERR	"To Jordan Came the Christ, Our Lord"
RENDEZ À DIEU	"When John Baptized by Jordan's River"
COMPLAINER or DE EERSTEN ZUN DE LAATSTEN or KING'S LYNN	"When Jesus Came to Jordan" or "What Was Your Vow and Vision"
WINCHESTER NEW or PUER NOBIS NASCITUR	"On Jordan's Bank the Baptist's Cry" or "The Baptist Shouts on Jordan's Shore" or "To Jordan's River Came Our Lord" or "When Jesus Comes to Be Baptized"
GENEVAN 130	"Lord, When You Came to Jordan"
SALZBURG (77.77D)	"Sing of God Made Manifest"
CAITHNESS or ST. BERNARD	"Christ, When for Us You Were Baptized"
THIS ENDRIS NYGHT	"'I Come,' the Great Redeemer Cries"

2

HERR CHRIST, DER EINIG GOTTES SOHN	"The Only Son from Heaven"
SALZBURG (77.77D)	"Songs of Thankfulness and Praise" or "Sing of God Made Manifest"

404

KINGSFOLD	"O Sing a Song of Bethlehem"
ERHALT UNS, HERR	"When Christ's Appearing Was Made Known"
PUER NOBIS NASCITUR	"What Star Is This"
RATISBON	"Christ, Whose Glory Fills the Skies"

3 FREUT EUCH, IHR
    LIEBEN or
SHEFFIELD or
FARMER or
ES FLOG EIN KLEINS
    WALDVÖGELEIN or
ELLACOMBE or
CRÜGER   "Hail to the Lord's Anointed" or
    "Hail to God's Own Anointed" or
    "We Hail You God's Anointed"

FESTAL SONG	"Arise, Your Light Has Come"
LAUDATE DOMINUM	"The Kingdom of God"

AZMON or
DUNDEE   "The People Who in Darkness Walked"

ABBOT'S LEIGH or
ROWTHORN   "Lord, You Give the Great Commission"

4 DONNE SECOURS or
VICAR or
SO I SEND YOU or
ANCIENT OF DAYS   "Hope of the World"

WOJTKIEWIECZ   "Rise, Shine, You People"

SHARPTHORNE or
MICAH or
BISHOP TUCKER   "What Does the Lord Require"

O WALY WALY (GIFT
    OF LOVE)   "Though I May Speak with Bravest Fire"

5 DEO GRACIAS or
PUER NOBIS NASCITUR   "Oh, Love, How Deep"

ACCLAMATIONS	"This Is the Threefold Truth"
NETTLETON	"God, We Praise You"
FOUNDATION	"How Firm a Foundation"
LIGHT or BLOMSTERTID	"Sometimes a Light Surprises"

6   (except when the Last Sunday after Epiphany)

JESU, MEINE FREUDE or GUD SKAL ALTING MAGE	"Jesus, Priceless Treasure" ["Jesus, All My Gladness"]
GENEVAN 107 (OLD 107TH) or MOZART or ST. MICHAEL'S or ST. MATTHEW	"Your Hand[s], O Lord, in Days of Old" ["Thine Arm, O Lord, in Days of Old"]
PICARDY (in part, as a Response)	The Beatitudes ("Blessed Are the Poor in Spirit")
AZMON or DUNDEE	"The People Who in Darkness Walked"

7   (except when the last Sunday after Epiphany)

IN BABILONE or LORD, REVIVE US	"Son of God, Eternal Savior"
WESTMINSTER ABBEY or EDEN CHURCH or REGENT SQUARE or UNSER HERRSCHER	"Christ Is made the Sure Foundation"
KIRKEN DEN ER ET GAMMELT HUS	"Built on a [the] Rock"
NATIVITY	"Christ Is the King and He Shall Reign"
WITTENBERG NEW	"O God, O Lord of Heaven and Earth"

8   (except when the Last
     Sunday after Epiphany)

LOBT GOTT DEN HERREN, IHR or MIT FREUDEN ZART	"Sing Praise to God" ["All Praise to God"]
SINE NOMINE or ENGELBERG	"All Praise to Thee"
IN DICH HAB ICH GEHOFFET	"In You, O Lord, I Put My Trust"

9   Transfiguration
     (Epiphany 4 for churches that
     do not observe the last
     Sunday after Epiphany
     with Transfiguration)

DEO GRACIAS or WAREHAM	"Oh, Wondrous Type" ["O Wondrous Sight"]
PICARDY	"Transform Us"
MOUNTAIN PEAK or MOWSLEY or TRANSFIGURATION or SHILLINGFORD	"Jesus on the Mountain Peak" ["Christ Upon the Mountain Peak"]
SWABIA	"'Tis Good ["How Good"] Lord, to Be Here!"

Season of Lent

Ash Wednesday

AUS TIEFER NOT (DE PROFUNDIS)	"Out of the Depths ["From Depths of Woe," "From Deepest Woe"] I Cry to You"
GENEVAN 130	"Out of the Depths I Cry, Lord"
DEPTHS	"Out of the Depths"
ST. BRIDE	"Out of the Depths I Call"

| MACPHERSON'S FAREWELL | "Up from the Depths I Cry to God" |

| ST. FLAVIAN or CAITHNESS | "Lord, Who throughout These Forty Days" ["O Lord, throughout These Forty Days"] |

| HEINLEIN (AUS DER TIEFE RUFE ICH) | "Forty Days and Forty Nights" |

| ERHALT UNS, HERR | "Again We Keep This Solemn Fast" |

1 EIN FESTE BURG — "A Mighty Fortress"

PICARDY — "Once When Jesus Christ Was Hungry"

LONESOME VALLEY — "Jesus Walked This Lonesome Valley"

DEO GRACIAS or
PUER NOBIS
    NASCITUR or
DEUS TUORUM MILITUM — "O Love, How Deep" [O Love, How Vast"]

2 HERZLICH LIEB — "Lord, Thee [You] I Love with All My Heart"

ST. CRISPIN or
DIE HELLE SONN
    LEUCHT or
ROCKINGHAM — "God Loved the World"

LEONI (YIGDAL) — "The God of Abraham Praise"

FOUNDATION or
    ST. DENIO — "How Firm a Foundation"

3 LLANGLOFFAN or
KING'S LYNN or
PIKE or
ST. THEODULPH — "O God of Earth and Altar" or "O God of Every Nation"

WONDROUS LOVE — "What Wondrous Love Is This"

ES WOLLE GOTT UNS
    GNÄDIG SEIN — "May God Bestow on Us His Grace"

	CWM RHONDDA	"Guide Me, O Thou Great Jehovah" ["Guide Me, O My Great Redeemer," "Guide Me Ever, Great Redeemer"]
4	RHOSYMEDRE or LOVE UNKNOWN	"My Song Is Love Unknown"
	RESTORATION	"Come, Ye Sinners, Poor and Needy"
	THIRD MODE MELODY or RESTING PLACE or EVAN or KINGSFOLD or VOX DILECTI	"I Heard the Voice of Jesus Say"
	NYGREN or LIFE RESTORED	"A Woman and a Coin"
5	HERZLIEBSTER JESU	"Ah, Holy Jesus" ["O Dearest Jesus"]
	DETROIT	"Forgive Our Sins"
	O WELT ICH MUSS DICH LASSEN or GENEVAN 6 (PSALM 6)	"O Food to Pilgrims Given" [O Bread of Life from Heaven"]
6	Sunday of the Passion or Palm Sunday	
	VEXILLA REGIS	"The Royal Banners Forward Go"
	HERZLICH TUT MICH VERLANGEN	"O Sacred Head"
	AN WASSERFLÜSSEN BABYLON	"A Lamb Goes Uncomplaining Forth"
	BANGOR	"Alone Thou Goest Forth, O Lord"
	THE KING'S MAJESTY	"Ride on! Ride on in Majesty"

Holy Week

Monday

ST. MAGNUS	"The Head That Once Was Crowned with Thorns"
ST. CHRISTOPHER	"Beneath the Cross of Jesus"

Tuesday

OAKLEY	"O Christ, Our King, Creator, Lord"
ELTHAM	"Nature with Open Volume Stands"

Wednesday

BOURBON or ST. CROSS	"It Happened on That Fateful Night"
BANGOR	"Alone Thou Goest Forth, O Lord"

Holy Thursday

ADORO TE DEVOTE	"Thee We Adore, O Hidden Savior" or "God with Hidden Majesty" or "Truth Whom We Adore"
PANGE LINGUA or GRAFTON	"Now, My Tongue, the Mystery Telling" ["Of the Glorious Body Telling"]
CHEREPONI	"Jesu, Jesu, Fill Us with Your Love"
JESUS TOOK A TOWEL	"Jesus Took a Towel"
BOURBON or ST. CROSS	"It Happened on That Fateful Night"
UBI CARITAS (Mode 6)	"Where True Charity and Love Dwell"

Good Friday

PANGE LINGUA or FORTUNATUS NEW	"Sing, My Tongue"

| HERZLICH TUT MICH VERLANGEN | "O Sacred Head" |
| WERE YOU THERE | "Were You There" (at the Easter Vigil if the last stanza is "raised him from the tomb") |

Holy Saturday

| O TRAURIGKEIT | "O Sorrow Deep" |

Season of Easter

Resurrection of the Lord

Easter Vigil

GO DOWN, MOSES	"When Israel Was in Egypt's Land"
ENGELBERG or NATIONAL CITY	"We Know That Christ Is [Was] Raised"
BUNESSAN	"Baptized in Water"
GAUDEAMUS PARITER (AVE VIRGO VIRGINUM) or ST. KEVIN	"Come, You [Ye] Faithful, Raise the Strain"

Easter Day

CHRIST LAG IN TODESBANDEN	"Christ Jesus Lay in Death's Strong Bands"
CHRIST IST ERSTANDEN or SURGIT IN HAEC DIES	"Christ Is Arisen" "Christ the Lord Is Risen Today"
GAUDEAMUS PARITER (AVE VIRGO VIRGINUM) or ST. KEVIN	"Come, You [Ye] Faithful, Raise the Strain"

	SONNE DER GERECHTIGKEIT or SALZBURG	"At the Lamb's High Feast We Sing"
	LANCASHIRE or ELLACOMBE	"The Day of Resurrection"

for the choir:

	VICTIMAE PASCHALI (pm)	"Christians to the Paschal Victim"
2	O FILII ET FILIAE or GELOBT SEI GOTT	"O Sons and Daughters of the King" ["O Sons and Daughters, Let Us Sing"]
3	LASST UNS ERFREUEN	"Now All the Vault of Heaven Resounds"
	DOMHNACH TRIONOIDE	"Daylight Fades"
	VRUECHTEN	"This Joyful Eastertide" or "Because You Live, O Christ"

	GAUDEAMUS PARITER
	    (AVE VIRGO
	    VIRGINUM) or
	ST. KEVIN
		"Come, You [Ye] Faithful, Raise the Strain"

	ASCENSION (MONK) or LLANFAIR	"Hail the Day That Sees Him Rise" or "Jesus Christ Is Risen Today" or "Christ the Lord Is Risen Today"
	RENDEZ À DIEU	"New Songs of Celebration Render"
	VICTORY	"The Strife Is O'er"
4	ST. COLUMBA or DOMINUS REGIT ME	"The King of Love My Shepherd Is"
	CRIMOND	"The Lord's My Shepherd" or "The Lord, My Shepherd, Rules My Life"
	RESIGNATION (CONSOLATION, CMD)	"My Shepherd Will Supply My Need" or "My Shepherd Is the Living God"

5   SONNE DER
        GERECHTIGKEIT or
    SALZBURG   "At the Lamb's High Feast We Sing"

    MIT FREUDEN ZART   "With High Delight"

    O QUANTA QUALIA or
    AMERICAN HYMN   "Blessing and Honor"

    DUKE STREET   "I Know that My Redeemer Lives"

    W ŻŁOBIE LEŻY   "Christ Is Risen"

    CENTRAL   "Cristo Vive" ("Christ Is Risen")

    IN MANUS TUAS   "O God, I Love Thee"

    ST. FULBERT   "I Love Thee, Lord"

    LAUDATE DOMINUM   "O Praise Ye the Lord" ["Sing Praise to the
                                    Lord"] or
                                "Give Praise to the Lord" ["Give Praise to
                                    Our God"]

6   TRURO   "Christ Is Alive"

    DOWN AMPNEY   "Come Down [Forth], O Love Divine"

    NUN FREUT EUCH   "Dear Christians, One and All, Rejoice"

    SHADES MOUNTAIN   "There in God's Garden"

    SLANE   "Be Thou My Vision"

Ascension (Fortieth day, Sixth Thursday of Easter)

    LASST UNS ERFREUEN or
    JAM LUCIS ORTO
        SIDERE or
    DEO GRACIAS   "A Hymn of Glory Let Us Sing" ["Sing
                                    We Triumphant Hymns of Praise"]

    BRYN CALFARIA   "Look, O Look, the Sight Is Glorious" ["Look,
                                    You [Ye] Saints! The Sight Is
                                    Glorious"] or "Lord, Enthroned in
                                    Heavenly Splendor"

DARWALL'S 148TH (DARWALL) or GOPSAL or LAUS REGIS	"Rejoice, the Lord Is King" ["Rejoice, Give Thanks and Sing"]
IN BABILONE	"Hail, Thou Once Despised Jesus"
CORONATION or MILES LANE	"All Hail the Power of Jesus' Name"
DIADEMATA	"Crown Him with Many Crowns"

7

HYFRYDOL or ALLELUIA or LOWELL	"Alleluia! Sing to Jesus" or "Alleluia! Gracious Jesus"

DEO GRACIAS or
PUER NOBIS
    NASCITUR or
DEUS TUORUM
    MILITUM
	"O Love, How Deep, How Broad" ["O Love, How Vast"]

JESU, MEINE FREUDE or GUD SKAL ALTING MAGE	"Jesus, Priceless Treasure" ["Jesus, All My Gladness"]

Pentecost

VENI CREATOR SPIRITUS	"Veni Creator Spiritus" or "Come, Holy Ghost" or "Come, Holy Spirit" or "Come, O Creator Spirit" or "O Holy Spirit"
KOMM, HEILIGER GEIST, HERRE GOTT	"Come, Holy Ghost, God and Lord"
KOMM, GOTT SCHÖPFER	"Creator Spirit, Heavenly Dove" ["O Holy Spirit, By Whose Breath," "Come, Holy Ghost, Creator Blest," "Come, Holy Ghost, Our Souls Inspire"]
DICKINSON COLLEGE	"Creator Spirit, Come"

DONATA	"Spirit of God, Unleashed on Earth"
SUNRISE for the choir: VENI SANCTE SPIRITUS	"Spirit, Working in Creation" "Holy Spirit, Lord Divine" ["Come, Thou Holy Spirit Bright"]

Season after Pentecost

Trinity Sunday (First Sunday after Pentecost)

GROSSER GOTT	"Holy God, We Praise Your [Thy] Name"
NICAEA	"Holy, Holy, Holy"
MOSCOW	"Thou, Whose Almighty Word" ["God, Whose Almighty Word"] or "Come, Thou Almighty King"

Sunday between May 24 and 28 (Proper 3)

LOBT GOTT DEN HERREN, IHR or MIT FREUDEN ZART	"Sing Praise to God " ["All Praise to God"]

Sunday between May 29 and June 4 (Proper 4)

SOLID ROCK (THE SOLID ROCK) or MELITA or MAGDALEN	"My Hope Is Built on Nothing Less"
BEACH SPRING or BLAENHAFREN or PLEADING SAVIOR or IN BABILONE or EBENEZER (TON-Y-BOTEL)	"Lord, Whose Love in [through] Humble Service"
EBENEZER (TON-Y- BOTEL)	"Thy Strong Word Didst [Did] Cleave the Darkness"
NUN BITTEN WIR	"To God the Holy Spirit Let Us Pray" ["We Now Implore God the Holy Ghost"]
MICHAEL	"All My Hope on God Is Founded" [All My Hope Is Firmly Grounded"] or "God, Our Help and Constant Refuge"

415

FOUNDATION or
LYONS   "How Firm a Foundation"

Sunday between June 5 and 11 (Proper 5)

AZMON   "O for a Thousand Tongues to Sing"

GENEVAN 107
   (OLD 107TH) or
MOZART or
ST. MICHAEL'S or
ST. MATTHEW   "Your Hand[s], O Lord, in Days of Old"
                       ["Thine Arm, O Lord, in Days of Old"]

GERONTIUS or
NEWMAN   "Praise to the Holiest in the Height"

LEONI (YIGDAL)   "The God of Abraham Praise"

Sunday between June 12 and 18 (Proper 6)

LOBE DEN HERREN   "Praise to the Lord, the Almighty" ["Praise Ye
                       the Lord," "Sing Praise to God"]

HANOVER or
LYONS   "O Worship the King"

OLD HUNDREDTH
   (OLD 100TH,
   GENEVAN 134TH)   "All People That on Earth Do Dwell"

Sunday between June 19 and 25 (Proper 7)

FOUNDATION or
LYONS   "How Firm a Foundation"

WESTMINSTER ABBEY or
EDEN CHURCH or
REGENT SQUARE or
UNSER HERRSCHER   "Christ Is Made the Sure Foundation"

SLANE   "Be Thou My Vision" or
                "Christ Be My Leader" or
                "Lord of All Hopefulness"

Sunday between June 26 and July 2 (Proper 8)

WER NUR DEN LIEBEN GOTT LÄSST WALTEN	"If Thou But Suffer God to Guide Thee" ["If You But Trust in God to Guide You," "If You Will Only Let God Guide You," "If You Will Trust in God to Guide You,"]
DISTRESS or ERHALT UNS HERR or CANONBURY or KENTRIDGE or TALLIS' CANON	"O Christ, the Healer, We Have Come"
CHARTERHOUSE or WELWYN	"O Jesus Christ, May Grateful Hymns Be Rising"
WESTMINSTER ABBEY or EDEN CHURCH or REGENT SQUARE or UNSER HERRSCHER	"Christ Is Made the Sure Foundation"

Sunday between July 3 and 9 (Proper 9)

THIRD MODE MELODY or RESTING PLACE or EVAN or KINSFOLD or VOX DILECTI	"I Heard the Voice of Jesus Say"
LAUDA ANIMA (BENEDIC ANIMA, PRAISE MY SOUL)	"Praise, My Soul, the King [God] of Heaven"
BANGOR or LONDON NEW or DUNDEE	"God Moves in a Mysterious Way" ["O God, in a Mysterious Way"]
FOUNDATION or LYONS	"How Firm a Foundation"

Sunday between July 10 and 16 (Proper 10)

ST. FLAVIAN or
DUNDEE or
CALL STREET or
WALDEN   "Almighty God, Your Word Is Cast"

LLANGLOFFAN or
KING'S LYNN or
PIKE or
ST. THEODULPH   "O God of Earth and Altar" or
                                "O God of Every Nation"

TWENTY-FOURTH or
ST. PETER or
CHESHIRE or
LAND OF REST   "Where Charity and Love Prevail"

ST. THOMAS (Williams) "Let Justice Flow like Streams"

CHRISTPRAISE or
MARION   "O Praise the Gracious Power"

HERZLICH LIEB   "Lord, Thee [You] I Love with All My Heart"

NUN DANKET
    ALLE GOTT   "Now Thank We All Our God"

Sunday between July 17 and 23 (Proper 11)

KING'S WESTON or
WYE VALLEY   "At the Name of Jesus"

AR HYD Y NOS or
EAST ACKLAM   "For the Fruit of All [His] Creation"

O WELT, ICH MUSS
    DICH LASSEN or
GENEVAN 6 (PSALM 6)   "O Food to Pilgrims Given" ["O Bread of Life
                                from Heaven"]

O QUANTA QUALIA   "O What Their Joy and Their Glory Must Be"

Sunday between July 24 and 30 (Proper 12)

CWM RHONDDA or
RHUDDLAN or
REGENT SQUARE   "God of Grace and God of Glory"

IN BABILONE	"There's a Wideness in God's Mercy" ("Lives Would Be All Sunshine" repaired as in H82)
O WELT, ICH MUSS DICH LASSEN or GENEVAN 6 (PSALM 6)	"O Food to Pilgrims Given" ["O Bread of Life from Heaven"]
TWENTY-FOURTH or ST. PETER or CHESHIRE or LAND OF REST	"Where Charity and Love Prevail"
LONDON NEW or DUNDEE	"God Moves in a Mysterious Way" ["O God, in a Mysterious Way"]

Sunday between July 31 and August 6 (Proper 13)

AURELIA	"The Church's One Foundation" or "O Christ, the Great Foundation"
O WELT, ICH MUSS DICH LASSEN	"O Food to Pilgrims Given" [O Bread of Life from Heaven"]
RENDEZ À DIEU	"Father, We Thank Thee" ["Father, We Thank You, for You Planted"]

Sunday between August 7 and 13 (Proper 14)

MELITA	"Eternal Father, Strong to Save" or "Almighty Father, Strong to Save"
OMNI DIE	"For the Faithful Who Have Answered"
HOW CAN I KEEP FROM SINGING	"My Life Flows On in Endless Song"
REPTON	"He Comes to Us as One Unknown"
AUCH JETZT MACHT GOTT	"How Shall They Hear the Word of God"
DURROW	"Speak Forth Your Word, O Father"
LITTLE FLOCK	"Have No Fear, Little Flock"

DONNE SECOURS or
VICAR or
SO I SEND YOU or
ANCIENT OF DAYS   "Hope of the World"

HERZLICH TUT MICH
   VERLANGEN
   (PASSION CHORALE) "Commit Thou All That Grieves Thee"

Sunday between August 14 and 20 (Proper 15)

ENGELBERG or
FREDERICKTOWN   "When in Our Music God Is Glorified"

Sunday between August 21 and 27 (Proper 16)

AUSTRIA (AUSTRIAN
   HYMN) or
RUSTINGTON or
ABBOT'S LEIGH   "Glorious Things of Thee [You] Are Spoken"
                                ["Glories of Your Name Are Spoken"] or
                "God, We Praise You" (Te Deum)

TOULON   "The Voice of God Goes Out Through All the
                World"

MICHAEL   "All My Hope on God Is Founded" [All My
                Hope Is Firmly Grounded"] or
                "God, Our Help and Constant Refuge"

WER NUR DEN LIEBEN
   GOTT LÄSST
   WALTEN   "If Thou But Suffer God to Guide Thee" ["If You
                But Trust in God to Guide You," "If You
                Will Only Let God Guide You," "If You
                Will Trust in God to Guide You,"]

WESTMINSTER ABBEY or
EDEN CHURCH or
REGENT SQUARE or
UNSER HERRSCHER   "Christ Is Made the Sure Foundation"

Sunday between August 28 and September 3 (Proper 17)

CRUCIFER   "Lift High the Cross"

SONG 1   "Eternal Ruler of the Ceaseless Round"

Sunday between September 4 and 10 (Proper 18)

BOURBON or
BRESLAU or
DISTRESS or
GERMANY or
KEDRON or
NUN LASST UNS DEN
    LEIB BEGRABEN or
O JESU, MI DULCISSIME or
QUEBEC (HESPERUS)   "Take Up Your Cross"

AUF, AUF, MEIN HERZ   "Awake, My Heart with Gladness"

MACHS MIT MIR, GOTT   "Come, Follow Me"

GENEVAN 107
    (OLD 107TH) or
MOZART or
ST. MICHAEL'S or
ST. MATTHEW   "Your Hand[s], O Lord, in Days of Old"
                             ["Thine Arm, O Lord, in Days of Old"]

Sunday between September 11 and 17 (Proper 19)

IN DIR IST FREUDE   "In Thee [You] Is Gladness ["Lord of All
                                   Gladness]

DETROIT   "Forgive Our Sins As We Forgive"

NYGREN or
LIFE RESTORED   "A Woman and a Coin"

PASSION CHORALE
    (HERZLICH TUT
    MICH VERLANGEN)   "Our [My] Father, We [I] Have Wandered" ["O
                                God, How We Have Wandered"]

ELTHAM   "Nature with Open Volume Stands"

Sunday between September 18 and 24 (Proper 20)

SLANE   "Be Thou My Vision" or
                        "Christ Be My Leader" or
                        "Lord of All Hopefulness"

GROSSER GOTT   "Holy God, We Praise Your [Thy] Name"

LAUDA ANIMA (BENEDIC
    ANIMA, PRAISE
    MY SOUL)   "Praise, My Soul, the King [God] of Heaven"

Sunday between September 25 and October 1 (Proper 21)

ST. DENIO   "Immortal, Invisible, God Only Wise"

DOWN AMPNEY   "Come Down [Forth], O Love Divine"

ST. THOMAS (WILLIAMS)   "O Bless the Lord, My Soul!"

Sunday between October 2 and 8 (Proper 22)

NUN DANKET
    ALLE GOTT   "Now Thank We All Our God"

ST. DENIO   "Immortal, Invisible"

ROUEN (ISTE
    CONFESSOR)   "Only-Begotten, Word of God Eternal"

Sunday between October 9 and 15 (Proper 23)

OLD HUNDREDTH
   (OLD 100TH,
   GENEVAN 134TH)   "All People That on Earth Do Dwell"

GOTT SEI GELOBET   "O Lord, We Praise You, Bless You and Adore
                     You" ["You, Lord, We Praise"]

JESU, MEINE FREUDE or
GUD SKAL ALTING MAGE   "Jesus, Priceless Treasure" ["Jesus, All My
                     Gladness"]

Sunday between October 16 and 22 (Proper 24)

RUSTINGTON or
BEACH SPRING or
NETTLETON or
HYFRYDOL or
AUSTRIAN HYMN   "God, Whose Giving Knows No Ending"

HANOVER or
LYONS   "O Worship the King"

INTERCESSOR or
LE CÉNACLE   "By Gracious Powers"

RHUDDLAN or
KOMM, O KOMM, DU
  GEIST DES LEBENS "Judge Eternal, Throned in Splendor"

Sunday between October 23 and 29 (Proper 25)

ITALIAN HYMN   "Come, Thou [Now,] Almighty King" or
          "God, Whose Almighty Word" ["Thou,
            Whose Almighty Word"]

Sunday between October 30 and November 5 (Proper 26)

HYFRYDOL or
BEECHER   "Love Divine, All Loves Excelling" or
          "Alleluia! Sing to Jesus"

Sunday between November 6 and 12 (Proper 27)

MARION or
VINEYARD HAVEN   "Rejoice, O Pilgrim Throng" ["Rejoice, Ye
           [You] Pure in Heart"]

DARWALL'S 148TH
  (DARWALL) or
GOPSAL or
LAUS REGIS   "Rejoice, the Lord Is King" ["Rejoice, Give
           Thanks and Sing"]

RENDEZ À DIEU   "Father, We Thank Thee Who Hast Planted"

ST. STEPHEN or
MORNING SONG
  (CONSOLATION) "The King Shall Come When Morning Dawns"

Sunday between November 13 and 19 (Proper 28)

HELMSLEY or
ST. THOMAS (87.87.87,
  HOLYWOOD) or
REGENT SQUARE or
UNSER HERRSCHER "Lo, He Comes with Clouds Descending"

ES IST GEWISSLICH "The Day Is Surely Drawing Near"

ST. MICHAEL or BELLWOODS	"O Day of God, Draw Near"
ABBOT'S LEIGH	"Lord of Light"
MORNING SONG (CONSOLATION)	"O Holy City, Seen of John"
OLD 107TH or YORK	"The Lord Will Come and Not Be Slow"
ERHALT UNS, HERR	"Lord, Keep Us Steadfast in Your Word"
GOTTES SOHN IST KOMMEN	"Once He Came in Blessing"
DISTLER	"Weary of All Trumpeting"

Reign of Christ or Christ the King, last Sunday after Pentecost (Proper 29)

KING'S WESTON or WYE VALLEY	"At the Name of Jesus"
DUKE STREET	"Jesus Shall Reign"

Special Days

February 2 – Presentation of the Lord

KUORTANE (NYLAND)	"O Lord, Now Let Your Servant"
MORNING SONG	"My Master, See, the Time Has Come"
LAND OF REST	"Lord, Bid Your Servant"
NUNC DIMITTIS	"Now May Your Servant, Lord"
SONG 1	"Lord God, You Now Have Set Your Servant Free"
OLD 120TH or PRESENTATION	"Hail to the Lord Who Comes"
WESTMINSTER ABBEY or LINDSBORG	"In His Temple Now Behold Him"
CANONBURY (first and last phrases)	Song of Simeon

424

March 25 – Annunciation of the Lord

GABRIEL'S MESSAGE   "The Angel Gabriel from Heaven Came"

VENI REDEMPTOR
     GENTIUM or
NUN KOMM, DER
     HEIDEN HEILAND   "Redeemer [Savior] of the Nations, Come"

ANNUNCIATION   "To a Maid Whose Name Was Mary"

May 31 – Visitation of Mary to Elizabeth

KINGSFOLD   "My Soul Proclaims Your Greatness, Lord"

MAGNIFICAT   "My Soul Gives Glory to the Lord"

MORNING SONG   "My Soul Gives Glory to My God"

WALNUT   "My Soul Proclaims with Wonder"

WOODLANDS or
BIRMINGHAM   "Tell Out, My Soul"

ANGELUS   "My Soul Now Magnifies the Lord"

September 14 – Holy Cross

PANGE LINGUA or
FORTUNATUS NEW   "Sing My Tongue"

CRUCIFER   "Lift High the Cross"

November 1 – All Saints

SINE NOMINE   "For All the Saints"

Fourth Thursday of November (U.S.), Second Monday of October (Canada) – Thanksgiving Day

NUN DANKET   "Now Thank We All Our God"

ST. GEORGE'S WINDSOR   "Come, You [Ye, O] Thankful People, Come"

KREMSER   "We Praise You, O God" or
     "We Gather Together"

AR HYD Y NOS or
EAST ACKLAM   "For the Fruit[s] of All [This] Creation"

1   See Psalm 90.
2   For example, the various seasonal, topical, scriptural indices and layouts in the hymnals; Gary Baumler and Kermit Moldenhauer, ed., *Christian Worship Manual* (Milwaukee: Northwestern Publishing House, 1993), 528–536; the various tables in the *Book of Common Worship* (Louisville: Westminster/John Knox Press, 1993); *The Episcopal Musician's Handbook* (Milwaukee: The Living Church Foundation, for various years); Marion J. Hatchett, *A Liturgical Index to the Hymnal 1982* (New York: The Church Hymnal Corporation, 1986); *The Hymnal of the Protestant Episcopal Church in the United States of America 1940* (New York: The Church Pension Fund, 1943), 804–806; *Indexes for Worship Planning, Revised Common Lectionary, Lutheran Book of Worship, With One Voice* (Minneapolis: Augsburg Fortress, 1996); *The Revised Common Lectionary* (Nashville: Abingdon Press, 1992), which is an ecumenical starting point; Carl Schalk, ed., *Key Words in Church Music* (St. Louis: Concordia Publishing House, 1978), 164–165; LBW, 929–931; *Living Liturgy* (Collegeville: The Liturgical Press, for various years); NC, 912–918; *Sundays and Seasons* (Minneapolis: Augsburg Fortress, for various years); VU, 998–1012; and Wor3 #1205.
3   An excellent one is *Hymns for the Gospels* (Chicago: GIA Publications, Inc., 2001).
4   For such a list see Hatchett, *A Liturgical Index to the Hymnal 198*, 9–175.
5   *The Revised Common Lectionary*, 21–24.

BIBLIOGRAPHY

Print

Adams, Susan L., Colbert S. Cartwright, and Daniel B. Merrick. *Chalice Hymnal Worship Leader's Companion*. St. Louis: Chalice Press, 1998.

African American Heritage Hymnal. Chicago: GIA Publications, 2001.

Ameln, Konrad. *The Roots of German Hymnody of the Reformation Era*. St. Louis: Concordia Publishing House, 1964.

Anderson, E. Byron, and Bruce T. Morrill, eds. *Liturgy and the Moral Self: Humanity at Full Stretch Before God, Essays in Honor of Don E. Saliers*. Collegeville: Liturgical Press, 1998.

Apel, Willi. *Gregorian Chant*. Bloomington: Indiana University Press, 1958.

Aufdemberge, C. T. *Christian Worship: Handbook*. Milwaukee: Northwestern Publishing House, 1997.

Augustine. *Confessions*.

Baumler, Gary, and Kermit Moldenhauer, eds. *Christian Worship: Manual*. Milwaukee: Northwestern Publishing House, 1993.

Bäumker, Wilhelm. *Das katholische deutsche Kirchenlied in seinen Singweisen von den frühesten Zeiten bis gegen Ende des siebzehnten Jahrhunderts*, 4 vols. Hildesheim: Georg Olms Verlagsbuchhandlung, 1962. First published 1883–1911 by Herder.

Baptist Hymnal. Nashville: Convention Press, 1975.

The Baptist Hymnal. Nashville: Convention Press, 1991.

Benson, Louis F. *The English Hymn: Its Development and Use in Worship*. Richmond: John Knox Press, 1962. Reprinted from the 1915 edition.

Bighley, Mark S. *The Lutheran Chorales in the Organ Works of J. S. Bach*. St. Louis: Concordia Publishing House, 1986.

Blackley, R. John. "Rhythmic Interpretation of Chant." In *The Hymnal 1982 Companion* 1, 238–252. New York: Church Hymnal Corporation, 1990.

Blankenburg, Walter. "The Music of the Bohemian Brethren." Translated by Hans Heinsheimer. In *Protestant Church Music: A History*, edited by Blume, et al., 593–607. New York: W. W. Norton & Company, 1974.

Blume, Friedrich, et al. *Protestant Church Music: A History*. New York: W. W. Norton & Company, 1974.

———. "The Period of the Reformation." Translated by F. Ellsworth Peterson. In *Protestant Church Music: A History*, edited by Blume, et al., revised by Ludwig Finscher. (New York: W. W. Norton & Company, 1974): 3-123.

Boccardi, Donald. *The History of American Catholic Hymnals Since Vatican II*. Chicago: GIA Publications, 2001.

Bonhoeffer, Dietrich. *Life Together* in *Dietrich Bonhoeffer's Works Volume 5*. Minneapolis: Fortress Press, 1996.

Book of Common Worship. Louisville: Westminster/John Knox Press, 1993.

The Book of Hymns: Official Hymnal of the United Methodist Church. Nashville: The United Methodist Publishing House, 1964.

Brink, Emily R. "The Genevan Psalter." In *Psalter Hymnal Handbook*, edited by Emily R. Brink and Bert Polman, 28–39. Grand Rapids: CRC Publications, 1998.

Brink, Emily R., and Bert Polman, eds. *Psalter Hymnal Companion*. Grand Rapids: CRC Publications, 1998.

Calvin, John. *Commentary on the Book of Psalms*. Grand Rapids: Wm. B. Eerdmans Publishing Company, 1949.

———. *Institutes of the Christian Religion*. Edited by John T. McNeill. Philadelphia: Westminster Press, 1960.

Chalice Hymnal. St. Louis: Chalice Press, 1995.

Chase, Robert. *Dies Irae: A Guide to Requiem Music*. Lanham: The Scarecrow Press, 2003.

Christian Worship: A Lutheran Hymnal. Milwaukee: Northwestern Publishing House, 1993.

A Collection of Tunes, Set to MUSIC, As they are commonly SUNG at the FOUNDERY. London: A. Pearson, 1742. Reprinted in 1981 by Bryan F. Spinney.

Congregational Song: Proposals for Renewal. Minneapolis: Augsburg Fortress, 2001.

The Covenant Hymnal: A Worshipbook. Chicago: Covenant Publications, 1996.

Davisson, A. *Kentucky Harmony*. 1816. A facsimile of the first edition with an introduction by Irving Lowens. Minneapolis: Augsburg Publishing House, 1976.

Dearmer, Percy, R. Vaughan Williams, and Martin Shaw, eds. *The Oxford Book of Carols*. London: Oxford University Press, 1964. First published in 1928.

Diehl, Katharine Smith. *Hymns and Tunes – An Index*. New York: Scarecrow, 1966.

Dix, Gregory. *The Shape of the Liturgy*. London: Dacre Press, 1960. First published in 1945.

The Encyclopedia of the Lutheran Church. 3 vols. Edited by Julius Bodensieck. Minneapolis: Augsburg Publishing House, 1965.

The English Hymnal with Tunes. London: Oxford University Press, 1906.

Erickson, J. Irving. *Twice-Born Hymns.* Chicago: Covenant Press, 1976.

Eskew, Harry. "Shape-Note Hymnody in the Shenandoah Valley, 1816–1860." Ph.D. dissertation, Tulane University, 1966.

Eskew, Harry, and Hugh T. McElrath. *Sing with Understanding: An Introduction to Christian Hymnology,* 2nd ed. Nashville: Church Street Press, 1995. First published in 1980.

Eskew, Harry, David W. Music, and Paul A. Richardson. *Singing Baptists: Studies in Baptist Hymnody in America.* Nashville: Church Street Press, 1994.

Evangelisches Gesangbuch für Rheinland und Westfalen. Dortmund: W. Crüwell, 1901.

Falconer, Keith A. "The Development of Plainchant to the Counter Reformation." In *The Hymnal 1982 Companion* 1, 160–176. New York: Church Hymnal Corporation, 1990.

Faulkner, Quentin. *Wiser Than Despair: The Evolution of Ideas in the Relationship of Music and the Christian Church.* Westport: Greenwood Press, 1996.

Foley, Edward. *From Age to Age: How Christians Celebrated the Eucharist.* Chicago: Liturgy Training Publications, 1991.

———, ed. *Worship Music: A Concise Dictionary.* Collegeville: Liturgical Press, 2000.

Forman, Kristen L., ed. *The New Century Hymnal Companion: A Guide to the Hymns.* Cleveland: Pilgrim Press, 1998.

Frost, Maurice. *English & Scottish Psalm & Hymn Tunes, c. 1543–1677.* London: S.P.C.K., 1953.

———. *Historical Companion to Hymns Ancient and Modern.* London: William Clowes & Sons, 1962.

Fyock, Joan A., comp. *Hymnal Companion Prepared by Churches in the Believers Tradition.* Elgin: Brethren Press, 1996.

Gajard, Dom Joseph. *The Solesmes Method.* Translated by R. Cecile Gabain. Collegeville: The Liturgical Press, 1960.

Gealy, Fred D., Austin Lovelace, Carlton R. Young, and Emery Stevens Bucke, eds. *Companion to the Hymnal: A Handbook to the 1964 Methodist Hymnal.* Nashville: Abingdon, 1970.

Glover, Raymond F., ed. *The Hymnal 1982 Companion,* 4 vols. New York: The Church Hymnal Corporation, 1990, 1994.

Graham, Fred Kimball. *"With One Heart and One Voice": A Core Repertory of Hymn Tunes Published for Use in the Methodist Episcopal Church in the United States, 1808–1878 (Drew University Studies in Liturgy, No.12).* Lanham: The Scarecrow Press, 2004.

Greene, Richard Leighton. *The Early English Carols.* Oxford: Clarendon Press, 1977.

Grew, Eva Mary. "Martin Luther and Music." In *Music and Letters* XIX, 67–78. 1938.

Grime, Paul, and Joseph Herl. *Hymnal Supplement 98.* St. Louis: Commission on Worship, Lutheran Church—Missouri Synod, 1998.

Haeussler, Armin. *The Story of Our Hymns: The Handbook to the Hymnal of the Evangelical and Reformed Church.* St. Louis: Eden Publishing House, 1952.

Handbook to The Baptist Hymnal. Nashville: Church Street Press, 1992.

Hatchett, Marion J. *A Liturgical Index to the Hymnal 1982.* New York: Church Hymnal Corporation, 1986.

Hawn, C. Michael. *Gather into One: Praying and Singing Globally.* Grand Rapids: William B. Eerdmans, 2003.

Higginson, J. Vincent. *Handbook for American Catholic Hymnals.* Hymn Society of America, 1976.

Hildebrandt, Franz, Oliver A. Beckerlegge, and James Dale, eds. *The Works of John Wesley, Volume 7, A Collection of Hymns for the Use of the People Called Methodists.* Oxford: Clarendon Press, 1983.

Hiley, David. *Western Plainchant: A Handbook.* Oxford: Clarendon Press, 1995.

Hustad, Donald P. *Dictionary-Handbook to Hymns for the Living Church.* Carol Stream: Hope Publishing Company, 1978.

———. *Jubilate! Church Music in the Evangelical Tradition.* Carol Stream: Hope Publishing Company, 1981.

———. *Jubilate II: Church Music in Worship and Renewal.* Carol Stream: Hope Publishing Company, 1993.

The Hymnal as Authorized and Approved for Use by the General Convention of the Episcopal Church . . . MCMXVI. New York: Church Pension Fund, 1933.

The Hymnbook. Richmond: Presbyterian Church in the United States / Presbyterian Church in the United States of America / United Presbyterian Church of North America, Reformed Church in America, 1955.

Hymnal: A Worship Book Prepared by Churches in the Believers Church Tradition. Elgin: Brethren Press; Newton: Faith and Life Press; Scottdale: Mennonite Publishing House, 1992.

The Hymnal Containing Complete Orders of Worship Authorized by the General Synod of the Evangelical and Reformed Church. Saint Louis: Eden Publishing House, 1941.

The Hymnal of the Protestant Episcopal Church in the United States of America 1940. New York: Church Pension Fund, 1940.

The Hymnal 1940 Companion. New York: Church Pension Fund, 1949.

The Hymnal 1982 according to the Use of The Episcopal Church. New York: Church Hymnal Corporation, 1985.

Hymnal Supplement. Chicago: GIA Publications, 1991.

Indexes for Worship Planning, Revised Common Lectionary, Lutheran Book of Worship, With One Voice. Minneapolis: Augsburg Fortress, 1996.

Irwin, M. Eleanor. "PHOS HILARON: The Metamorphoses of a Greek Christian Hymn." *The Hymn* 40, no. 2 (April 1989): 7–12.

Jackson, George Pullen. *White Spirituals in the Southern Uplands: The Story of the Fasola Folk, Their Songs, Sings, and "Buckwheat Notes."* New York: Dover Publications, 1965. First published in 1933.

Jenson, Robert W. *Systematic Theology, Volume 1, The Triune God.* Oxford: Oxford University Press, 1997.

Joncas, Michael. *From Sacred Song to Ritual Music: Twentieth-Century Understandings of Roman Catholic Worship Music.* Collegeville: Liturgical Press, 1997.

Jungmann, Josef A. *The Mass: An Historical, Theological, and Pastoral Survey.* Translated by Julian Fernandez. Edited by Mary Ellen Evans. Collegeville: Liturgical Press, 1976.

Julian, John. *A Dictionary of Hymnology.* New York: Dover Publications, 1957. Reprint of 2nd edition, 1907.

Keyte, Hugh, and Andrew Parrot, eds. *The New Oxford Book of Carols.* Oxford: Oxford University Press, 1992.

Krentz, Michael Edgar. "The Use of Sequences in German Lutheran Churches During the Sixteenth Century." Doctoral Research Project. Evanston: Northwestern University, 1981.

Kyriale. New York: J Fischer & Bro., 1927.

Kirchenbuch für Evangelisch-Lutherische Gemeinden. Philadelphia: General Council Publication Board, 1906.

Landes, W. Daniel, and Mark G. Putnam. *The Electronic Encyclopedia of Hymnology.* Nashville: Putnam Graphics and Media Design, 2000.

Leaver, Robin A. *Goostly Psalmes and Spirituall Songes: English and Dutch Metrical Psalms from Coverdale to Utenhove, 1535–1566.* Oxford: Clarendon Press, 1991.

The Liber Usualis. New York: Desclee Company, 1959.

Liederkranz für Sonntag-Schulen und Jugen-Vereine. St. Louis: Eden Publishing House, 1898.

Little, Patrick. "Two Hymn Tunes by Sir John Goss." *Hymn Society of Great Britain and Ireland Bulletin* 235 17, no. 2 (April 2003): 44–51.

Lovelace, Austin. *The Anatomy of Hymnody.* Chicago: GIA Publications, 1965.

Loewen, Alice, Harold Moyer, and Mary Oyer. *Exploring the Mennonite Hymnal: Handbook.* Newton: Faith and Life Press, 1983.

Luff, Alan. *Welsh Hymns and Their Tunes.* Carol Stream: Hope Publishing Company, 1990.

———. "Joseph Parry." *Hymn Society of Great Britain and Ireland Bulletin* 235 17, no. 2 (April 2003): 41–43.

Lutheran Book of Worship. Minneapolis: Augsburg Publishing House, 1978.

The Lutheran Hymnal. Saint Louis: Concordia Publishing House, 1941.

Lutheran Worship, Prepared by The Commission on Worship of The Lutheran Church – Missouri Synod. St. Louis: Concordia Publishing House, 1982.

Luther's Works. 55 vols. Philadelphia: Fortress Press, 1957–1986.

MacDougall, Hamilton C. *Early New England Psalmody: An Historical Appreciation, 1620–1820.* Brattleboro: Stephen Daye Press, 1949.

Marrocco, W. Thomas, Harold and Gleason. *Music in America: An Anthology from the Landing of the Pilgrims to the Close of the Civil War, 1620–1865.* New York: W. W. Norton & Company, 1964.

McKay, David P., and Richard Crawford. *William Billings of Boston: Eighteenth-Century Composer.* Princeton: Princeton University Press, 1975.

McCutchan, Robert Guy. *Hymn Tune Names: Their Sources and Significance.* New York: Abingdon Press, 1957.

McKim, LindaJo H. *The Presbyterian Hymnal Companion.* Louisville: Westminster/John Knox Press, 1993.

McKinnon, James W. "Ambrose," *The New Grove Dictionary of Music and Musicians* (London: MacMillan Publishers Limited, 1980), 1, 313-314.

———. "The Meaning of the Patristic Polemic Against Musical Instruments," *Current Musicology* I (1965): 69–82.

———. *Music in Early Christian Literature.* Cambridge: Cambridge University Press, 1987.

Mouw, Richard J., and Mark A. Noll. *Wonderful Words of Life: Hymns in American Protestant History and Theology.* Grand Rapids: William B. Eerdmans Publishing Company, 2004.

Moravian Book of Worship. Bethlehem: Moravian Church in America, 1995.

Morosan, Vladimir. *Choral Performance in Pre-Revolutionary Russia*. Madison: Musica Russica, 1994. First published in 1984.

Murray, James R. *Dainty Songs for Little Lads and Lasses*. Cincinnati: John Church Co., 1887.

Music, David W., ed. Hymnology: *A Collection of Source Readings*. Lanham: Scarecrow Press, 1996.

———. *Instruments in Church: A Collection of Source Documents*. Lanham: Scarecrow Press, 1998.

The New Century Hymnal. Cleveland: Pilgrim Press, 1995.

The New Grove Dictionary of American Music. Edited by H. Wiley Hitchcock and Stanley Sadie. London: Macmillan Press Limited, 1986.

The New Grove Dictionary of Music & Musicians. Edited by Stanley Sadie. London: Macmillan Publishers Limited, 1980.

Nichols, James Hastings. *Corporate Worship in the Reformed Tradition*. Philadelphia: Westminster Press, 1968.

Niebuhr, H. Richard. *Christ and Culture*. New York: Harper & Row, 1951.

Oettinger, Rebecca Wagner. *Music as Propaganda in the German Reformation*. Aldershot: Ashgate, 2001.

Ogasapian, John. *English Cathedral Music in New York City: Edward Hodges of Trinity Church*. Richmond: Organ Historical Society, 1994.

Patrick, Millar. *Four Centuries of Scottish Psalmody*. London: Oxford University Press, 1949.

———. *The Story of the Church's Song*. Revised by James Rawlings Snydor. Richmond: John Knox Press, 1962.

Pemberton, Carol A. *Lowell Mason: His Life and Work*. Ann Arbor: UMI Research Press, 1985.

Perry, David W. *Hymns and Tunes Indexed*. Croydon: Hymn Society of Great Britain and Ireland, 1980.

Peters, Erskine, ed. *Lyrics of the Afro-American Spiritual*. Westport: Greenwood Press, 1993.

Pidoux, Pierre. *Le Psautier Huguenot, I, Les Mélodies; II, Documents et Bibliographie*. Kassel: Édition Baerenreiter Bâle, 1962.

Pfatteicher, Philip H., and Carlos Messerli. *Manual on the Liturgy, Lutheran Book of Worship*. Minneapolis: Augsburg Publishing House, 1979.

Pilgrim Hymnal. Boston: Pilgrim Press, 1958.

Pocknee, Cyril E. *The French Diocesan Hymns and Their Melodies*. London: The Faith Press, 1954.

Polack, W. G. *The Handbook to the Lutheran Hymnal*. Saint Louis: Concordia Publishing House, 1958.

Pratt, Waldo Selden. *The Music of the French Psalter of 1562: A Historical Survey and Analysis, with the Music in Modern Notation*. New York: Columbia University Press, 1939.

The Presbyterian Hymnal. Louisville: Westminster/John Knox Press, 1990.

Psalter Hymnal. Grand Rapids: CRC Publications, 1987.

Quasten, Johannes. *Music and Worship in Pagan & Christian Antiquity*. Washington: National Association of Pastoral Musicians, 1973.

Rainbow, Bernarr. *The Choral Revival in the Anglican Church (1839–1872)*. London: Barrie & Jenkins, 1970.

Rasmussen, Jane. *Musical Taste as a Religious Question in Nineteenth-Century America*. Lewiston: The Edwin Mellon Press, 1986.

Reese, Gustave. *Music in the Middle Ages*. New York: W. W. Norton & Company, 1940.

Renewing Worship Songbook: New Hymns and Songs for Provisional Use. Minneapolis: Evangelical Lutheran Church in America, 2003.

The Revised Common Lectionary. Nashville: Abingdon Press, 1993.

Reynolds, William J. *Companion to the Baptist Hymnal*. Nashville: Broadman Press, 1976.

———. *Hymns of Our Faith*. Nashville: Broadman Press, 1964.

Reynolds, William, Milburn Price, and David Music. *A Survey of Christian Hymnody*. 4th ed. Carol Stream: Hope Publishing Company, 1999. First published in 1963.

Ronander, Albert C., and Ethel K. Porter. *Guide to the Pilgrim Hymnal*. Philadelphia: United Church Press, 1966.

Routley, Erik. *Christian Hymns Observed: When in Our Music God Is Glorified*. Princeton: Prestige Publications, 1982.

———. *The Church and Music: An Enquiry into the History, the Nature, and the Scope of Christian Judgment on Music*. London: Gerald Duckworth & Co., 1950.

———. *Church Music and the Christian Faith*. Carol Stream: Agape, 1978.

———. *English Hymns and Their Tunes: A Survey*. London: Hymn Society of Great Britain & Ireland, 1981.

———. *An English-Speaking Hymnal Guide*. Chicago: GIA Publications, 1979.

———. *The Music of Christian Hymnody: A Study of the Development of the Hymn Tune since the Reformation, with Special Reference to English Protestantism*. London: Independent Press Limited, 1957.

———. *The Music of Christian Hymns*. Chicago: GIA Publications, 1981.

———. *The Musical Wesleys*. London: Herbert Jenkins, 1961.

————. A Panorama of Christian Hymnody. Chicago: GIA Publications, 1979: revised and expanded 2005.

Sankey, Ira, James McGranahan, George C. Stebbins, and Philip B. Bliss. Gospel Hymns Nos. 1 to 6 Complete. New York: Da Capo Press, 1972. Unabridged reproduction of the "Excelsior Edition," 1895.

Schalk, Carl. Music in Early Lutheranism: Shaping the Tradition (1524–1672). St. Louis: Concordia, 2001.

————, and Carl Halter, eds. A Handbook of Church Music. St. Louis: Concordia Publishing House, 1978.

————. Key Words in Church Music. St. Louis: Concordia Publishing House, 1978.

————. Luther on Music: Paradigms of Praise. St. Louis: Concordia Publishing House, 1988.

Schuler, Richard J. "The Congregation: Its Possibilities and Limitations in Singing." In Cum Angelis Canere, 313–331. St. Paul: Catholic Church Music Associates, 1990.

Schwartz, Elliott, and Barney Childs, eds. Contemporary Composers on Contemporary Music. New York: Holt, Rinehart and Winston, 1967.

Schweitzer, Albert. J. S. Bach. Boston: Bruce Humphries Publishers, 1962. First published in French in 1905, 2 vols.

Seaman, William A., ed. Companion to the Hymnal of the Service Book and Hymnal. Minneapolis: Commission on the Liturgy and Hymnal, 1976.

Singenberger, Johann. Orgelbuch zu J. Mohr's "Caecilia." Regensburg, Rome & New York: Friedrich Pustet, 1899.

Sionsharpan. Chicago: Mission Friend's Publishing Company, 1890.

Skeris, Robert A., ed. Cum Angelis Canere. St. Paul: Catholic Church Music Associates, 1990.

The Scottish Psalter 1929: Metrical Version and Scriptural Paraphrases, With Tunes. London: Oxford University Press, 1930.

Service Book and Hymnal Authorized by the Lutheran Churches cooperating in The Commission on the Liturgy and Hymnal. Minneapolis: Augsburg Publishing House, 1958.

Southern, Eileen. The Music of Black Americans: A History. New York: W. W. Norton & Company, 1983.

Spener, Philip Jacob. Pia Desideria. Translated by Theodore G. Tappert. Philadelphia: Fortress Press, 1964.

Stanislaw, Richard, and Donald P. Hustad. Companion to the Worshiping Church: A Hymnal. Carol Stream: Hope Publishing Company, 1993.

Stephan, John. The "Adeste Fideles": A Study on Its Origin and Development. South Devon: "PUBLICATIONS," Buckfast Abbey, 1947.

Stevens, John, ed. "Medieval Carols." Musica Britannica: A National Collection of Music IV. 2nd ed. Stainer & Bell, 1970.

Stulken, Marilyn Kay. Hymnal Companion to the Lutheran Book of Worship. Philadelphia: Fortress Press, 1981.

————. With One Voice Reference Companion. Minneapolis: Augsburg Fortress, 2000.

————, and Catherine Salika. Hymnal Companion to Worship—Third Edition. Chicago: GIA Publications, 1998.

Temperley, Nicholas, ed. The Hymn Tune Index: A Census of English-Language Hymn Tunes in Printed Sources from 1535 to 1820. 4 vols. New York: Oxford University Press, 1998.

————. The Music of the English Parish Church. Cambridge: Cambridge University Press, 1979.

Terry, Richard R. Calvin's First Psalter [1539]. London: Ernest Benn Limited, 1932.

The 389 Chorales of Johann Sebastian Bach with English Texts by Henry S. Drinker. Association of American Choruses, Choral Series No. 1, n.d.

The United Methodist Hymnal: Book of United Methodist Worship. Nashville: The United Methodist Publishing House, 1989.

This Far by Faith: An African American Resource for Worship. Minneapolis: Augsburg Fortress, 1999.

Thompson, Bard. Liturgies of the Western Church. Cleveland: Meridian Books, 1961.

Thompson, J. Michael. "Sequence," In Worship Music: A Concise Dictionary, 278. Collegeville: Liturgical Press, 2000.

Vajda, Jaroslav. Now the Joyful Celebration. St. Louis: Morning Star, 1987.

Voices United: The Hymn and Worship Book of the United Church of Canada. Etobicoke: United Church Publishing House, 1996.

Walker, William. The Southern Harmony and Musical Companion. Edited by Glenn C. Wilcox. Lexington: University of Kentucky Press, 1987. Reproduction of the fourth printing of the 1854 edition.

Walter, Thomas. The Grounds and Rules of Music Explained: Or, An Introduction to the Art of Singing by Note, Fitted to the Meanest Capacities. Boston: Benjamin Mecom, 1760. First edition published in 1721.

Ward, Andrew. Dark Midnight When I Rise: The Story of the Fisk Jubilee Singers, How Black Music Changed America and the World. New York: Amistad, 2000.

Ward, Tom R. "The Office Hymn." In The Hymnal 1982 Companion 1, 269–281. New York: Church Hymnal Corporation, 1990.

Wasson, D. DeWitt, comp. *Hymntune Index and Related Hymn Materials.* 3 vols. Lanham: Scarecrow Press, 1998.

Watson, J. R. *The English Hymn: A Critical and Historical Study.* Oxford: Clarendon Press, 1997.

Westermeyer, Paul. *Te Deum: The Church and Music.* Minneapolis: Fortress Press, 1998.

———. *The Church Musician.* 2nd ed. Minneapolis: Augsburg Fortress, 1997.

———. "Liturgical Music: Soli Deo Gloria." In *Liturgy and the Moral Self: Humanity at Full Stretch Before God, Essays in Honor of Don E. Saliers,* 193–206. Edited by E. Byron Anderson and Bruce T. Morrill. Collegeville: Liturgical Press, 1998.

———. "Te Deum Laudamus: Church Music, the People's Office—Part 1: Past: Participation or Audience." *Cross Accent* 10, no. 1 (Spring 2002): 30–36.

———. "What Shall We Sing in a Foreign Land? Theology and Cultic Song in the German Reformed and Lutheran Churches of Pennsylvania, 1830–1900." PhD diss. Chicago: University of Chicago, 1978.

White, B. F., and E. J. King. *The Sacred Harp.* Includes "The Story of The Sacred Harp" by George Pullen Jackson. Nashville: Broadman Press, 1968. Facsimile of the 3rd edition, 1859.

White, James F. *The Cambridge Movement: The Ecclesiologists and the Gothic Revival.* Cambridge: Cambridge University Press, 1962.

White, James F., ed. *John Wesley's Sunday Service of the Methodists in North America.* Bristol, 1784. Reprinted by the United Methodist Publishing House, 1984.

Wilson, John. "John Darwall and the 148th Metre." *The Hymn Society of Great Britain & Ireland Occasional Paper.* Second Series no. 5, April 2002.

Witvliet, John. *Worship Seeking Understanding: Windows into Christian Practice.* Grand Rapids: Baker Academic, 2003.

Worship Third Edition: A Hymnal and Service Book for Roman Catholics. Chicago: GIA Publications, 1986.

Wren, Brian. *Faith Looking Forward.* Carol Stream: Hope Publishing Company, 1983.

Young, Carlton R. *Companion to the United Methodist Hymnal.* Nashville: Abingdon Press, 1993.

Zager, Daniel. "Popular Music and Music for the Church." *Lutheran Forum* 36, no. 3 (Fall 2002): 20–27.

Zahn, Johannes. *Die Melodien der deutschen evangelischen Kirchenlieder.* 6 vols. Gütersloh: C. Bertelsmann, 1889, 1890, 1891, 1892, and 1893.

Discography

Luther's Works on CD-ROM. 55 vols. Fortress Press and Concordia Publishing House, Libronix Digital Library System, 2002.

McCreesh, Paul, with the Gabrieli Consort and Players. *Bach Epiphany Mass c. 1740.* (P) 1988. Original sound recording made by Deutsche Grammophon. Archiv 457 631-2.

———. *Praetorius Christmette, Lutheran Mass for Christmas Morning as It Might Have Been Celebrated around 1620.* (P) 1994. Original sound recording made by Deutsche Grammophon. Archiv 439 931-2.

———. *Schütz Christmas Vespers as It Might Have Been Celebrated at the Court of Dresden c. 1664.* (P) 1999. Original sound recording made by Deutsche Grammophon. Archiv 289 463 046-2.

Messerli, Carlos, and Carl Schalk, et al., eds. *Celebrating the Musical Heritage of the Lutheran Church.* Thrivent Financial for Lutherans, n.d.

Routley, Erik. *Christian Hymns: An Introduction to Their Story.* 6 cassettes with pamphlet. Princeton: Prestige Publications. 1980.

SAVAE (San Antonio Vocal Arts Ensemble). *Ancient Echoes.* Original sound recording made by World Library Publications. ISBN-1-58549-164-1.

Simon, Paul. "American Tune." *There Goes Rhymin' Simon.* (P) 1973. Original sound recording made by Warner Bros. Records. 9 25589-2.

Sutton, Bret, and Pete Hartman, Pete. *Primitive Baptist Hymns of the Blue Ridge.* (P) 1982. Original sound recording made by University of North Carolina Press. 0-8078-4083-1.

Titon, Jeff Todd, and Kenneth M. George. *Powerhouse for God.* (P) 1982. Original sound recording made by University of North Carolina Press. 0-8078-4084-X.

ACKNOWLEDGMENTS

This section lists all material under copyright in this book. It is organized by hymn tune name. If a text is under copyright, it is included in parentheses under the tune name with which it is paired. (To locate a particular text, consult the Hymn Index to find the page on which it appears; this page will also include the tune name. Page numbers for hymn tunes can be found in the Tune Index.) These credits represent the most accurate information available at the time of printing. The copyright credits that appear with the hymns and tunes throughout the narrative are not necessarily the most current because the information is intentionally cited as it appears in the source hymnals. Every effort has been made to contact the copyright holders. GIA Publications, Inc. regrets any omissions or errors.

ABBOT'S LEIGH Tune © 1942, ren. 1970 and Text ("God is here!") © 1979 Hope Publishing Co., Carol Stream, IL 60188. All rights reserved. Used by permission.

ADORO DEVOTE Text ("Humbly I adore thee, verity unseen") © 1940 The Church Pension Fund.

ALLEIN GOTT IN DER HÖH Text ("All glory be to God on high") © 1978 *Lutheran Book of Worship* (admin. Augsburg Fortress).

ANNIVERSARY SONG Tune and Text ("What gift can we bring, what present, what token?") © 1982 Hope Publishing Co., Carol Stream, IL 60188. All rights reserved. Used by permission.

ASH GROVE Text ("Let all things now living") © 1939 E.C. Schirmer Music Co.

AUGUSTINE Tune © 1976 Hinshaw Music, Inc.

AUS TIEFER NOT Text ("Out of the depths I cry to you") © 1978 *Lutheran Book of Worship* (admin. Augsburg Fortress).

AVE HIERARCHIA Text ("Once he came in blessing") © 1978 *Lutheran Book of Worship* (admin. Augsburg Fortress).

BEACH SPRING Text ("Lord, whose love in humble service") © Oxford University Press. Used by permission. All rights reserved. Photocopying this copyright material is illegal.

BEREDEN VÄG FÖR HERRAN Text ("Prepare the royal highway") © 1978 *Lutheran Book of Worship* (admin. Augsburg Fortress).

BERTHIER Tune and Text ("Eat this bread, drink this cup") © 1984 Les Presses de Taizé (France), admin. GIA Publications, Inc.

BRIDEGROOM Tune © 1969 and Text ("Like the murmur of the dove's song") © 1982 Hope Publishing Co., Carol Stream, IL 60188. All rights reserved. Used by permission.

CAITHNESS Text ("Christ, when for us you were baptized") © 1982 The Church Pension Fund.

CANTAD AL SEÑOR Text ("Cantad al Senor/Oh, sing to our God") © Gerhard Cartford.

CASTLEWOOD Tune © 1986, 1989 GIA Publications, Inc. Text ("Come to us, creative Spirit") © Stainer & Bell Publications (admin. Hope Publishing Co., Carol Stream, IL 60188). All rights reserved. Used by permission.

CENTRAL Tune and Spanish Text ("Cristo vive, fuera el llanto") © 1962 Metho Press, Ltd. Translation ("Christ is risen, Christ is living") © 1974 Hope Publishing Co., Carol Stream, IL 60188. All rights reserved. Used by permission.

CHEREPONI Tune and Text ("Jesu, Jesu") © 1969 Hope Publishing Co., Carol Stream, IL 60188. All rights reserved. Used by permission.

CHESHIRE Text ("Where charity and love prevail") Copyright © 1960, World Library Publications. 3825 N. Willow Rd., Schiller Park, IL 60176. www.wlpmusic.com All rights reserved. Used by permission.

CHRIST IST ERSTANDEN Text ("Christ is arisen") © Concordia Publishing House.

CHRISTE SANCTORUM Text ("Father, we praise thee") from *The English Hymnal* © Oxford University Press 1906. Used by permission. All rights reserved. Photocopying this copyright material is illegal.

COLERAINE Text ("I seek my refuge in you, LORD") © 1987 CRC Publications.

CONDITOR ALME SIDERUM Text ("Creator of the stars of night") © 1940 The Church Pension Fund.

CRUCIFER Tune and Text ("Lift high the cross") © 1974 Hymns Ancient & Modern, Ltd. (admin. Hope Publishing Co., Carol Stream, IL 60188). All rights reserved. Used by permission.

CULROSS Text ("God, you have given us power to sound") © Oxford University Press. Used by permission. All rights reserved. Photocopying this copyright material is illegal.

DAS NEUGEBORNE KINDELEIN Text ("Great God, Your love has called us here") © 1977 Hope Publishing Co., Carol Stream, IL 60188. All rights reserved. Used by permission.

DECATUR PLACE Tune © 1984 Washington National Cathedral Music. Text ("We the Lord's people") © Rev. Canon John E. Bowers.

DEN SIGNEDE DAG Text ("O day full of grace") © 1978 *Lutheran Book of Worship* (admin. Augsburg Fortress).

DEO GRACIAS Tune © 1947 Mercury Music Corp. (admin. Theodore Presser Co.).

DETROIT Text ("Forgive our sins as we forgive") from *English Praise* © Oxford University Press 1969. Used by permission. All rights reserved. Photocopying this copyright material is illegal.

DEUS TUORUM MILITUM Text ("Whom shall I send?") © 1971 Hope Publishing Co., Carol Stream, IL 60188. All rights reserved. Used by permission.

DICKINSON COLLEGE Tune © 1962 Theodore Presser Co. Text ("The church of Christ, in ev'ry age") © 1971 Hope Publishing Co., Carol Stream, IL 60188. All rights reserved. Used by permission.

DISTLER Tune and Text ("Weary of all trumpeting") © 1972 Chantry Music Press (admin. Augsburg Fortress).

DOVE OF PEACE Text ("I come with joy, a child of God") © 1977 Hope Publishing Co., Carol Stream, IL 60188. All rights reserved. Used by permission.

DOWN AMPNEY Tune from *The English Hymnal* © Oxford University Press 1906. Used by permission. All rights reserved. Photocopying this copyright material is illegal.

EARTH AND ALL STARS Tune and Text ("Earth and all stars! Loud rushing planets!") © 1968 Augsburg Publishing House (admin. Augsburg Fortress).

EBENEZER Text ("Thy strong word didst cleave the darkness") © 1969 Concordia Publishing House.

EIN' FESTE BURG Text ("A mighty fortress is our God") © 1978 *Lutheran Book of Worship* (admin. Augsburg Fortress).

ENGELBERG Text ("When in our music God is glorified") © 1972 Hope Publishing Co., Carol Stream, IL 60188. All rights reserved. Used by permission.

FAITHFULNESS Tune and Text ("Great is thy faithfulness") © 1923, ren. 1951 Hope Publishing Co., Carol Stream, IL 60188. All rights reserved. Used by permission.

FORTUNATUS NEW Tune © 1967 Concordia Publishing House.

GAUDEAMUS PARITER Text ("Faithful Christians, one and all") © 1989 Jaroslav J. Vajda (admin. Concordia Publishing House).

GENEVAN 12 Text ("Help, LORD, for those who love your truth have vanished") © 1987 CRC Publications.

GENEVAN 25 Text ("LORD, to you my soul is lifted") © 1987 CRC Publications.

GENEVAN 42 Text ("As a deer in want of water") © 1987 CRC Publications.

GENEVAN 47 Text ("Nations, clap your hands") © 1987 CRC Publications.

GENEVAN 65 Text ("Praise is Your right, O God, in Zion") © 1987 CRC Publications.

GENEVAN 68 Text ("Let God arise and by his might") © 1987 CRC Publications.

GENEVAN 77 Text ("I cried out to God to help me") © 1987 CRC Publications.

GENEVAN 98 Text ("Sing, sing a new song to the LORD God") © 1987 CRC Publications.

GENEVAN 101 Text ("I praise your justice, LORD") © 1987 CRC Publications.

GENEVAN 103 Text ("Come, praise the LORD, my soul") © 1987 CRC Publications.

GENEVAN 107 Text ("Thanks be to God our Savior") © 1987 CRC Publications.

GENEVAN 124 Text ("If God the LORD were not our constant help") © 1987 CRC Publications.

GENEVAN 130 Text ("Out of the depths I cry, LORD") © 1987 CRC Publications.

GENEVAN 134 (OLD HUNDREDTH) Text ("You servants of the LORD our God") © 1987 CRC Publications.

GENEVAN 138 Text ("With all my heart I thank you, LORD") © 1987 CRC Publications.

GLORIA CANON Tune and Text ("Gloria, gloria, in excelsis Deo!") © 1978, 1980, 1981 Les Presses de Taizé (France), admin. GIA Publications, Inc.

GO, TELL IT Text ("Go, tell it on the mountain") © 1940 Edith M. Work.

GOTT SEI DANK Text ("Spread, oh, spread, almighty Word") © 1978 *Lutheran Book of Worship* (admin. Augsburg Fortress).

GOTT SEI GELOBET UND GEBENEDEIET Text ("O Lord, we praise you") © 1941 Concordia Publishing House.

HEALER (HAUGEN) Tune and Text ("Healer of our ev'ry ill") © 1991 GIA Publications, Inc.

HOW GREAT THOU ART Tune and Text ("O Lord my God!") Copyright © 1953 S. K. Hine. Assigned to Manna Music, Inc., 35255 Brooten Road, Pacific City, OR 97135. Renewed 1981 by Manna Music, Inc. All Rights Reserved. Used by Permission. (ASCAP).

INNISFREE FARM Tune © 1982 Washington National Cathedral Music. Text Translation ("Christ, mighty Savior") © 1982 The United Methodist Publishing House (admin. by The Copyright Company c/o The Copyright Company, Nashville, TN) All Rights Reserved. International Copyright Secured. Used By Permission.

ISTE CONFESSOR Text ("This is the feast day of the Lord's true witness") © Peter J. Scagnelli.

JERUSALEM Text ("O day of peace") © 1982 Hope Publishing Co., Carol Stream, IL 60188. All rights reserved. Used by permission.

JESAIA, DEM PROPHETEN Text ("Isaiah in a vision did of old") © 1978 *Lutheran Book of Worship* (admin. Augsburg Fortress).

JESUS, REMEMBER ME Tune and Text ("Jesus, remember me") © 1978, 1980, 1981 Les Presses de Taizé (France), admin. GIA Publications, Inc.

KEDRON Text ("God marked a line and told the sea") from *Borrowed Light* © 1994 Oxford University Press, Inc. Used by permission. All rights reserved. Photocopying this copyright material is illegal.

KING'S WESTON Tune from *Songs of Praise*, Enlarged Edition © Oxford University Press 1931. Used by permission. All rights reserved. Photocopying this copyright material is illegal.

KINGSFOLD Tune from *The English Hymnal* © Oxford University Press 1906. Used by permission. All rights reserved. Photocopying this copyright material is illegal. Text ("And have the bright immensities") © Morehouse Group.

KIRKEN DEN ER ET GAMMELT HUS Text ("Built on a rock the Church shall stand") © 1958 *Service Book & Hymnal* (admin. Augsburg Fortress).

KOMM, HEILIGER GEIST, HERRE GOTT Text ("Come, Holy Ghost, God and Lord") © 1941 Concordia Publishing House.

KUORTANE Text ("O Lord, now let your servant") © Board of Publication, Lutheran Church in America (admin. Augsburg Fortress).

KYRIE, GOTT VATER Text ("Kyrie! God, Father in heav'n above") © Concordia Publishing House.

LASST UNS ERFREUEN Text ("A hymn of glory let us sing") © 1978 *Lutheran Book of Worship* (admin. Augsburg Fortress).

LAUDATE PUERI Tune and Text ("Praise the Lord!") © 1973 Concordia Publishing House.

LAUDES DOMINI Text ("When morning gilds the skies") © 1992 The Pilgrim Press/United Church Press; word alt. © 1992 The Pilgrim Press.

LEWIS-TOWN Text ("O Son of God, in Galilee") © Lutheran Church in America (admin. Augsburg Fortress).

LITTLE FLOCK Tune and Text ("Have no fear, little flock") © Concordia Publishing House.

LOBE DEN HERREN Text ("Praise to the Lord, the Almighty") © 2000 Augsburg Fortress.

LOBT GOTT, IHR CHRISTEN Text ("Let all together praise our God") © 1969 Concordia Publishing House.

LOST IN THE NIGHT Text ("Lost in the night do the people yet languish") © Augsburg Publishing House (admin. Augsburg Fortress).

LOVE UNKNOWN Tune © John Ireland Charitable Trust.

MACHT HOCH DIE TÜR Text ("Fling wide the door") © 1978 *Lutheran Book of Worship* (admin. Augsburg Fortress).

MAN-CHIANG-HUNG Tune and Text ("Fount of love, our Savior God") © 1977 Chinese Christian Literature Council, Ltd.

MCKEE Tune © 1940 Estate of Henry T. Burleigh.

MERLE'S TUNE Tune and Text ("Blest be the God Israel") © Hope Publishing Co., Carol Stream, IL 60188. All rights reserved. Used by permission.

NOEL NOUVELET Text ("Sing we now of Christmas") © 1966 Augsburg Publishing House (admin. Augsburg Fortress).

NOORMARKKU Text ("Your kingdom come, O Father") © 1970 Lutheran World Federation.

NOW Tune and Text ("Now the silence Now the peace") © 1969 Hope Publishing Co., Carol Stream, IL 60188. All rights reserved. Used by permission.

NUNC ANGELORUM Text ("The glorious angels came today") © 1969 Concordia Publishing House.

NYT YLÖS, SIELUNI Text ("Arise, my soul, arise!") © 1958 *Service Book & Hymnal* (admin. Augsburg Fortress).

O DASS ICH TAUSEND ZUNGEN HÄTTE (KÖNIG) Text ("Oh, that I had a thousand voices") © 1941 Concordia Publishing House.

O HEILAND, REISS DIE HIMMEL, AUF Text ("O Savior, rend the heavens wide") © 1969 Concordia Publishing House.

O WALY, WALY Text ("When love is found") © 1983 Hope Publishing Co., Carol Stream, IL 60188. All rights reserved. Used by permission.

O WELT, ICH MUSS DICH LASSEN Text ("Now rest beneath night's shadow") © 1941 Concordia Publishing House.

PANGE LINGUA Text ("Sing, my tongue, the glorious battle") © 1982 The Church Pension Fund.

PRECIOUS LORD Tune and Text ("Precious Lord, take my hand") © 1938 Hill & Range Songs, Inc./Unichappell Music, Inc./Warner Brothers Publishing.

PROMISE Tune and Text ("In the bulb there is a flower") © 1986 Hope Publishing Co., Carol Stream, IL 60188. All rights reserved. Used by permission.

QUEM PASTORES Text ("Quem pastores laudavere"). Adaptation ("Angel voices, richly blending") © 1969 James Quinn, S.J., Selah Publishing Co., Inc., North American agent. www.selahpub.com.

REPTON Text ("How clear is our vocation, Lord") © 1982 Hope Publishing Co., Carol Stream, IL 60188. All rights reserved. Used by permission.

RESONET IN LAUDIBUS Refrain Text ("Long ago and far away") © 1958 Augsburg Fortress. Verse Translation © 1928 Oxford University Press.

ROEDER Tune © 1983 GIA Publications, Inc. Text ("God of the sparrow") © 1983 Jaroslav J. Vajda (admin. Concordia Publishing House)

RUSTINGTON Text ("God, whose giving knows no ending") © 1961 The Hymn Society of America (admin. Hope Publishing Co., Carol Stream, IL 60188). All rights reserved. Used by permission.

SAKURA Transcription © 1983 Abingdon Press (admin. by The Copyright Company, Nashville, TN) All Rights Reserved. International Copyright Secured. Used By Permission. Text ("Praise the Lord, praise the Lord, for the greenness of the trees") © 1980 Nobuaki Hanaoka.

SCHMÜCKE DICH Text ("Soul, adorn yourself with gladness") © 1978 *Lutheran Book of Worship* (admin. Augsburg Fortress).

SHARPTHORNE Tune © 1969 Hope Publishing Co., Carol Stream, IL 60188. All rights reserved. Used by permission. Text ("What does the Lord require for praise and offering?") © Oxford University Press. Used by permission. All rights reserved. Photocopying this copyright material is illegal.

SHILLINGFORD Tune and Text ("Christ, upon the mountain peak") © 1977 Hope Publishing Co., Carol Stream, IL 60188. All rights reserved. Used by permission.

SO NIMM DENN MEINE HÄNDE Text ("Lord, take my hand and lead me") © 1978 *Lutheran Book of Worship* (admin. Augsburg Fortress).

ST. MICHAEL Text ("O day of God, draw nigh") © Emmanuel College.

ST. THOMAS (HOLYWOOD) Text ("Tantum ergo"). Translation ("Come adore this wondrous presence") © James Quinn, S.J., Selah Publishing Co., Inc., North American agent. www.selahpub.com.

ST. THOMAS (WILLIAMS) Text ("Break out, O Church of God") © 1990 Broadman Press (SESAC). All rights reserved.

SURSUM CORDA Tune © 1941 Mrs. Alfred M. Smith (Doris Wright Smith). Text ("Come, risen Lord, and deign to be our guest") from *Songs of Praise*, Enlarged Edition © Oxford University Press 1931. Used by permission. All rights reserved. Photocopying this copyright material is illegal.

THAINAKY Tune and Text ("She sits like a bird, brooding on the waters") © 1988 Iona Community, admin. GIA Publications, Inc.

THUMA MINA Tune and Text ("Send me, Lord") © 1984 Walton Music Corporation.

TOA-SIA Harmonization © 1983 The United Methodist Publishing House (admin. by The Copyright Company c/o The Copyright Company, Nashville, TN) All Rights Reserved. International Copyright Secured. Used By Permission. Text ("God created heaven and earth") © 1983 Boris & Clare Anderson.

TOKYO Tune © Jasrac House. Text ("Sekai no tomo to Te o tsunagi") © Estate of Tokuo Yamaguchi. Phonetic Transcription ("Here, O Lord, your servants gather") © 1989 The United Methodist Publishing House (admin. by The Copyright Company c/o The Copyright Company, Nashville, TN) All Rights Reserved. International Copyright Secured. Used By Permission.

TRURO Text ("Christ is alive!") © 1975 Hope Publishing Co., Carol Stream, IL 60188. All rights reserved. Used by permission.

TRYGGARE KAN INGEN VARA Text ("Children of the heav'nly Father") © 1925, 1953 Board of Publication, Lutheran Church in America (admin. Augsburg Fortress).

UBI CARITAS Tune © 1979 Les Presses de Taizé (France), admin. GIA Publications, Inc.

UNION SEMINARY Tune © 1957 H. W. Gray Co., Warner Brothers Publishing. Text ("Draw us in the Spirit's tether") from *Songs of Praise*, Enlarged Edition © Oxford University Press 1931. Used by permission. All rights reserved. Photocopying this copyright material is illegal.

VENI REDEMPTOR GENTIUM Text ("Redeemer of the nations, come") © 1982 The Rev. Dr. Charles P. Price Fund.

VEXILLA REGIS Tune © Schola Antiqua.

VINEYARD HAVEN Tune Copyright © 1974 (Renewed) Harold Flammer Music, a div. of Shawnee Press, Inc. International Copyright Secured. All Rights Reserved. Reprinted by Permission of Shawnee Press, Inc.

VOM HIMMEL HOCH Text ("From heav'n above to earth I come") © 1978 *Lutheran Book of Worship* (admin. Augsburg Fortress).

WACHET AUF Text ("Wake, awake, for night is flying") © 1999 Concordia Publishing House.

WAREHAM Text ("The church of Christ, in ev'ry age") © 1971 Hope Publishing Co., Carol Stream, IL 60188. All rights reserved. Used by permission.

WIE SCHÖN LEUCHTET Text ("O Morning Star, how fair and bright!") © 1978 *Lutheran Book of Worship* (admin. Augsburg Fortress).

WIR GLAUBEN ALL Text ("We all believe in one true God") © 1941 Concordia Publishing House.

WITTENBERG NEW Tune and Text ("O God, O Lord of heav'n and earth") © 1967 The Lutheran Council in the U.S.A. (admin. Augsburg Fortress).

WOODLANDS Tune © Oxford University Press. Used by permission. All rights reserved. Photocopying this copyright material is illegal. Text ("Tell out, my soul, the greatness of the Lord") © 1962 Hope Publishing Co., Carol Stream, IL 60188. All rights reserved. Used by permission.

WUNDERBARER KÖNIG Text ("God is truly present") © 2001 *Congregational Song* (admin. Augsburg Fortress).

HYMN INDEX

Tune Index

Tunes that are common to 9 – 13 hymnals are marked with a single asterisk (*).
Tunes common to all 14 hymnals are marked with two asterisks (**).

113TH PSALM TUNE (see GENEVAN 68)
A SOLIS ORTUS 65
ABBOT'S LEIGH* 361, 405, 420, 424
ABERYSTWYTH* 217-218
ACCLAMATIONS 406
ADESTE FIDELES** 193-194, 210, 401
ADORO DEVOTE 223
ADORO TE DEVOTE (ADORO DEVOTE) 410
AGINCOURT HYMN* (see DEO GRACIAS)
AJALON (see PETRA)
ALL SAINTS NEW 316
ALLEIN GOTT IN DER HÖH* 53, 62
ALLELUIA 414
AMAZING GRACE** (NEW BRITAIN) 278
AMERICA* (NATIONAL ANTHEM) 178
AMERICAN HYMN 413
AMSTERDAM 168, 186
AMSTERDAM TUNE (see AMSTERDAM)
AN WASSERFLÜSSEN BABYLON 409
ANCIENT OF DAYS 405, 420
ANGELUS 425
ANNIVERSARY SONG 377
ANNUNCIATION 425
ANTIOCH** 297-298
AR HYD Y NOS* 211-212, 418, 425
ASCENSION 412
ASH GROVE* 212-213
ASSURANCE* (BLESSED ASSURANCE)
    306-307
AUCH JETZT MACHT GOTT 419
AUF, AUF MEIN HERZ 175, 421
AUGHTON* (see HE LEADETH ME)
AUGUSTINE 380
AURELIA** 229-231, 234, 252, 419
AUS DER TIEFE RUFE ICH (see HEINLEIN)
AUS TIEFER NOT* (DE PROFUNDIS) 60, 95,
    407
AUSTRIA* (AUSTRIAN HYMN) 151, 361, 420
AUSTRIAN HYMN* (AUSTRIA) 422
AVE HIERARCHIA 124
AVE MARIA KLARER** (see ELLACOMBE)
AVE VIRGO VIRGINUM (see GAUDEAMUS
    PARITER)
AVON* (see MARTYRDOM)
AWAY IN A MANGER 319
AZMON** 301, 405-406, 416

BALM IN GILEAD* 281-282, 285

BANGOR 409-410, 417
BEACH SPRING* 272-273, 415, 422
BEATITUDO 251
BEECHER* 316-317, 423
BELLEVUE* (see FOUNDATION)
BELLWOODS 424
BENEDIC ANIMA* (see PRAISE MY SOUL)
BENEVENTO 195
BEREDEN VÄG FÖR HERRAN 64, 402
BERTHIER 365-366
BETHEL 214
BIRMINGHAM 425
BISHOP TUCKER 405
BLAENHAFREN 415
BLESSED ASSURANCE* (see ASSURANCE)
BLOMSTERTID 406
BOURBON 410, 421
BREAD OF LIFE* (SHERWIN) 318-319
BREAK BREAD* 283, 287, 289
BREAK BREAD TOGETHER* (see BREAK
    BREAD)
BRESLAU 421
BRETHREN (see FOUNDATION)
BRIDEGROOM* 369-370
BRISTOL 112
BROMSWICK TUNE (see HANOVER)
BROTHER JAMES' AIR* 344-345
BRYN CALFARIA* 216-217, 413
BUNESSAN* 344, 411

CAITHNESS 110-112, 141, 404, 408
CAITHNESS TUNE (see CAITHNESS)
CALL STREET 418
CANON (see TALLIS' CANON)
CANON TUNE (see TALLIS' CANON)
CANONBURY* 315, 417, 424
CANTAD AL SEÑOR 326-327
CANTERBURY (see SONG 13)
CAROL* 314-315
CASTLEWOOD 378
CATON (see ROCKINGHAM)
CENTRAL 325-326, 413
CHARTERHOUSE 417
CHEREPONI* 338-339, 346, 348, 410
CHESHIRE 109, 112, 418-419
CHINA* (see JESUS LOVES ME)
CHRIST IST ERSTANDEN 29, 37-38, 72, 411
CHRIST LAG IN TODESBANDEN* 29, 73, 411

GENERAL INDEX